THIRD EDITION

MARKETING PUBLIC HEALTH

STRATEGIES TO PROMOTE SOCIAL CHANGE

Elissa A. Resnick, MPH
Institute for Health Research and Policy
University of Illinois, Chicago
Chicago, IL

Michael Siegel, MD, MPH
Department of Community Health Sciences
Boston University School of Public Health
Boston, MA

World Headquarters
Jones & Bartlett Learning
5 Wall Street
Burlington, MA 01803
978-443-5000
info@jblearning.com
www.jblearning.com

Jones & Bartlett Learning books and products are available through most bookstores and online booksellers. To contact Jones & Bartlett Learning directly, call 800-832-0034, fax 978-443-8000, or visit our website, www.jblearning.com.

Production Credits

Publisher: Michael Brown
Editorial Assistant: Kayla Dos Santos
Editorial Assistant: Chloe Falivene
Production Manager: Tracey McCrea
Senior Marketing Manager: Sophie Fleck Teague
Manufacturing and Inventory Control Supervisor: Amy Bacus
Composition: diacriTech

Cover Design: Michael O'Donnell
Cover Images: Berries: © Lee Prince/ShutterStock, Inc.; Walking: © lidian/ShutterStock, Inc.; No Smoking: © L. Watcharapol/ShutterStock, Inc.; Cell phone: © Marquis/ShutterStock, Inc.
Printing and Binding: Edwards Brothers Malloy
Cover Printing: Edwards Brothers Malloy

To order this product, use ISBN: 978-1-4496-8385-6

Library of Congress Cataloging-in-Publication Data
Resnick, Elissa.
  Marketing public health : strategies to promote social change / Elissa Resnick, Michael Siegel.
    — 3rd ed.
      p. cm.
  Rev. ed. of: Marketing public health / Michael Siegel, Lynne Doner Lotenberg. 2nd ed. c2007.
  Includes bibliographical references and index.
  ISBN 978-1-4496-4523-6 (pbk.)
  1. Public health—Marketing. I. Siegel, Michael, M.D. II. Siegel, Michael, M.D. Marketing public health. III. Title.
  RA427.S53 2013
  362.1068'8—dc23
                          2012011500
6048
Printed in the United States of America
16 15 14 13 12   10 9 8 7 6 5 4 3 2 1

DEDICATION

To Mom, Dad, and my husband, Dan, for their never-ending love and encouragement, and to Stuart Shifron, who was with me every step of the way.

E.R.

To my wife, Rebecca, for her love, patience, and support, and to Sammy and Miriam, for bringing joy to all the days.

M.S.

TABLE OF CONTENTS

FOREWORD

In the 19th and 20th centuries, the most important improvements in the public's health may have come from innovations in plumbing and general sanitation, and in inoculation against disease. These environmental changes may have had more impact than the curative work of doctors. Many other successes in public health have contributed to increasing the life span of the average American by about 30 years over the past century. We can see some of these successes, for example, through decreases in infant mortality, the management of AIDS, the increasing use of seat belts, and the decrease in smoking rates from about 50% of the adult population in 1970 to about 20% today.

But all is not positive. The state of the public's health is not as good as it could be. Although some changes have led to longer and healthier lives, others have led to a diminution of health. Labor-saving devices, leisure products, and easily accessible, good-tasting, unhealthy food have led to a new class of health issues. For example, about 65% of the U.S. population now is overweight or obese.

Clearly, there is a relationship between positive and negative developments in public health. As one set of problems was conquered, leading to a longer and potentially healthier life, new issues arose that threatened the previous gains.

We can attribute the successes to a variety of public health practices in law enforcement, message campaigns, and environmental changes. Although social marketing has had some impact in each of these three strategic categories, it has been underused as a way to manage behavior. It is possible that future environmental breakthroughs may come from social marketing, wherein strategies can be developed, for example, to make it easier for people to eat well and include more physical activity in their lives.

Marketers generally believe that almost everybody does almost everything out of immediate self-interest. Many public health message campaigns tell people what they should be doing to achieve long-term good health, when these people are merely seeking a nice appearance, less hassle in their lives, or a quick sugar fix to pick them up in the afternoon. This has led to disconnects whereby people tend to know what they should be doing to improve their health and are motivated to do so but aren't following through. For example, although 78% of adults believe obesity is a serious problem, only 38% consume the proper level of produce; whereas 58% want to lose weight, only 27% are seriously trying to do so. Perhaps we need a better understanding of self-interest.

Social marketing offers a planning tool based on the use of marketing research to define targets, specific desired behavioral outcomes, an increase in benefits that reinforce self-interest, and a way to decrease the barriers that inhibit behavior. Commercial marketers are adamant about focusing on behavior, on setting specific goals, and on measuring results. These foci can offer potentially major contributions to public health practice, which often neglects each of these. Marketing works as a result of listening carefully to what consumers say, yet all too often public health efforts are paternalistic in telling consumers what they ought to do, rather than first listening to what people want for themselves.

The marketing model can work well in combination with the epidemiologic model of public health. Although epidemiologic research is well suited to defining health problems and broad classes of affected people, marketing research provides insights on how the environment needs to be changed so behavior can follow. Whereas epidemiologic research gives insight to a top-down model of soliciting behavior, marketing research gives insight to a bottom-up participative perspective.

The current definition of marketing is based on creating, communicating, and delivering value to the target while developing long-term relationships: *creating* deals with the development of desired benefits, *delivering* pertains to the reduction of the barriers that keep people from behaving correctly, and *communicating* involves informing and persuading in the interests of motivating behavior.

So we have three important questions before us: (1) Why are people behaving poorly with respect to their own health? (2) Why has the field of public health not had more consistent successes? (3) What can we do about these problems? *Marketing Public Health: Strategies to Promote Social Change, Third Edition* tries to answer these questions by considering both the pitfalls currently existing in public health practice and the potential for moving forward using social marketing. This combination of analyzing pitfalls and recommending practice gives *Marketing Public Health* its strength.

A disconnect of health practice concerns preventive care versus curative care. In the United States, a vast amount of money is spent on curing, whereas a vastly greater impact is made through preventive practice. Perhaps this is because curative medicine shows immediate response at a visible individual level, whereas the impact of preventive medicine is much more difficult to observe. *Marketing Public Health* tries to show how marketing can be used to move the field of public health forward, in addition to showing how to use marketing to remedy specific public health problems.

To solve public health problems, there needs to be a proper understanding of the issues that led to today's problems before strategic solutions can be proposed. *Marketing Public Health* begins with a cogent layout of the underlying issues before moving on to a discussion of strategic and tactical contributions from social marketing. Without having a clear understanding of the state of the government and its health policies, the potential solutions have less context and less value. Readers will benefit from the careful exposition of current public health practice (as put forth in the first half of the text) as a base for understanding the strategic and tactical practice of social marketing (as described in the second half).

Michael L. Rothschild
University of Wisconsin

ACKNOWLEDGMENTS

This book draws on the work of scholars and practitioners in a range of disciplines. Their inspiration, ideas, and experiences were invaluable to us. We especially thank those who allowed us to share some of their work through examples and case studies included in this volume.

Our editor at Jones & Bartlett Learning, Mike Brown, was the driving force behind both the first and second edition of this book. Elana Premack Sandler brought this edition up to date through her expertise in social media and public health, which led to her contribution of Chapter 13. The staff of Health Unlimited and Health Unlimited Rwanda, particularly the contributing authors for Chapter 14—Narcisse Kalisa, Prudence Uwabakurikiza, Samuel Kyagambiddwa, Jeannette Wijnants, and Stephen Collens—were kind enough to take time from their vital health promotion work to share their experiences for the benefit of our readers.

Finally, we are indebted to the many family members who put up with our distractions and mumblings during the year we spent preparing this third edition.

INTRODUCTION

In 2010, President Obama signed the Affordable Care Act into law in an effort to reform the U.S. health insurance system. Although the law includes funds dedicated to amending unhealthy behaviors (e.g., smoking cessation programs and the First Lady's "Let's Move" campaign to combat obesity), the main goals are to decrease costs of and improve access to health care for Americans (HealthCare.gov, 2012). Debates both leading up to and after the bill signing focused on these access issues and dominated the mass media and the public agendas. As a result, the impression left on the American public was that access to health care was of singular importance when it comes to improved health outcomes.

Although health care access is important, one must question the impact that doctors' office visits can have on health. According to a 2009 study, the average U.S. adult primary care visit lasts 20.8 minutes (Chen, Farwell, & Jha, 2009). Compared with the time spent making decisions about eating, smoking, and exercising, 20.8 minutes may be insignificant. Yet these other factors, along with dozens more, received far less attention than the Affordable Care Act. The push to pass this bill focused the sole attention of policymakers, the media, and the public on medical care and diverted it away from major causes of illness and death. Given that the leading causes of death are increasingly attributable to chronic diseases and lifestyle factors, one could argue that public health resources would have been better spent on increasing access to healthy foods or opportunities for physical activity. However, it is difficult for these interventions to make it onto the mass media, political, and public agendas as long as the focus on medical care remains strong.

As a result, the essential connection between behavioral and social factors and the public's health has been effectively obscured in the minds of the public and policymakers. With public health political capital being spent on improving access to care, policymakers may be less likely to promote legislation that mitigates lifestyle factors (e.g., improving school nutrition, increasing opportunities for physical activity). Meanwhile, the public may be less likely to view their own behaviors as affecting their health, because the media implies that increased access to medical care is all that is needed to treat illnesses. This situation illustrates the interrelated nature of the mass media, political, and public agendas as well as the need for public health practitioners to take a more active role in shaping these agendas.

Public health programs must now compete vigorously for public attention and resources. Even within the category of public health funding, practitioners must convince policymakers and the public that emerging threats (such as the swine flu outbreak of 2009) require supplemental funding and not simply a shift in funding from critical existing programs to the threat of the month. Strengthening the public health infrastructure so that it can respond to any threat has been overlooked for far too long.

The current social, political, and environmental climate is growing more and more hostile toward public health. Consequently, the public health community faces unprecedented threats to its funding, its ability to respond appropriately and effectively to existing and imminent crises, and its very existence at the national, state, and local levels. It is no longer enough for public health professionals to work to protect the health of the public. Public health practitioners must work to protect the survival of public health as an institution.

This threat to the survival of the public health profession comes at the same time as these changes in the social, political, and economic environments also present a direct threat to the public's health itself. Unhealthy lifestyles, behaviors, and deteriorating social and environmental conditions threaten the public's health. As the chief causes of death in the United States have gradually shifted from communicable illnesses to chronic diseases, lifestyle and behavioral risk factors, as well as social and environmental conditions, have become the key determinants of the public's health. In contrast to its successes in controlling infectious diseases, the public health movement has been ineffective in controlling the emerging chronic disease epidemic. Programs intended to change individual behaviors and lifestyles have often been ineffective, and public health professionals have not fully accepted the role of advocating for changes in social conditions and social policies. As a result, the public health community is equipped neither to confront existing public health crises nor to prevent new ones.

Despite these threats, tools are available to help the public health profession save itself and enable it to confront existing and emerging public health crises. There are public health initiatives that have successfully changed societal behaviors, improved social conditions, reformed social policies, and retained and even increased funding for public health programs and departments.

The common feature of many of these initiatives is public health practitioners' strategic use of marketing principles to promote social change. Understanding and applying marketing principles is essential for public health practitioners to confront the imposing challenges successfully— challenges both to the public's health and to the survival of the public health profession. However, public health practitioners are not typically trained in the principles of marketing.

Marketing Public Health: Strategies to Promote Social Change, Third Edition, is designed to help public health practitioners understand basic marketing principles and strategically apply these principles in planning, implementing, and evaluating public health initiatives. We hope this book will provide public health practitioners at all levels of government and in the private sector with a valuable tool to create and deliver more effective initiatives to change individual behavior, improve social and economic conditions, advance social policies, and compete successfully for public attention and resources.

We argue that the key to creating and running effective public health programs is to abandon the traditional practice of deciding what policymakers or the public ought to want and then trying to sell it to them in the absence of significant demand. Instead, public health practitioners must first learn the needs and wants of their target audience (policymakers or the public) and package the desired behavior (a change in individual health behavior or the adoption of public health programs and policies) so the target audience recognizes that it will meet those needs and wants. This requires practitioners to understand the audience's motivation, opportunity, and ability to engage in the desired behavior and to create product offerings that increase opportunities to engage in the behavior, increase skills, and/or increase motivation. Often, this means addressing the social, economic, and policy environments. Successful product offerings provide compelling benefits, increase convenience or access, and, when necessary, reduce barriers. Rather than appealing exclusively to the benefits of improved health, public health practitioners must learn to identify benefits that are salient and compelling to the target audience and then create and deliver product offerings that provide these benefits. Compelling benefits often are tangible, immediate, and/or connected to powerful and influential core values: freedom, independence, autonomy, control, fairness, democracy, and free enterprise.

In this third edition, not only have we brought the material up to date, we have also tried to make it come alive in a more meaningful way for current public health students and practitioners. Examples from areas of newer public health interest over the past few years are included throughout. A new case study from the field of suicide prevention through social media illustrates the principles and strategies discussed in the book in a way that makes it immediately apparent to readers how the material can be used in modern, real-life public health marketing efforts. In addition, a case study from the field of international health makes this edition relevant to the global practice of public health.

This edition has been influenced both by changes in the marketing environment and by the latest thinking among marketing and social marketing researchers and practitioners. Discussion of current emphases, such as building relationships with audiences rather than managing individual transactions, using the power of branding, ensuring that audience self-interest is considered and addressed, and using social media, have been incorporated into the book in both its narrative and its case studies and examples.

The book is organized into six sections. Section I serves as a call to action and begins by describing threats to the public's health and establishing that changing individual behavior, social and economic conditions, and social policy are important to confront the chronic disease epidemic successfully (Chapter 1). Chapter 2 describes the threats to the survival of public health as an institution.

Section II discusses the challenges that public health professionals face as they work to effect change and ways to overcome these challenges. Chapter 3 illustrates the difficulties in promoting social changes, and Chapter 4 describes the challenges in promoting public health as an institution. This section ends with Chapter 5, which presents key marketing concepts and discusses how they apply to individual behavior and policy changes.

Section III is divided into three chapters, each of which details steps public health professionals should take as they plan marketing efforts. Chapter 6 presents a strategic planning process. Chapter 7 describes how some commonly used formative research techniques can be used to support the strategic planning process. Finally, Chapter 8 discusses how to frame and deliver messages about the proposed behavior or policy so they appeal to the most salient core values, thereby increasing the likelihood that they will result in social change.

Section IV covers the process of developing and implementing the tactics, or components, involved in an initiative. Chapter 9 discusses the use of formative research findings to develop messages that are relevant, compelling, and actionable for the target audience. Subsequently, Chapter 10 provides guidance on developing and assessing mass media and other promotional activities and materials.

Section V discusses tracking, evaluating, and refining social change efforts. First, Chapter 11 introduces process evaluation techniques to help planners track and monitor the implementation of marketing efforts. The chapter also discusses how to use the information to make improvements. Chapter 12 then discusses issues in assessing the outcomes of marketing-based efforts using traditional approaches to summative evaluation and presents some techniques for assessing outcomes and using the results to make program refinements.

Section VI presents two case studies. In Chapter 13, guest contributor Elana Premack Sandler examines the use of social media to address lesbian, gay, bisexual, and transgender suicide. In Chapter 14, guest contributors Narcisse Kalisa, Prudence Uwabakurikiza, Samuel Kyagambiddwa, Jeannette Wijnants, and Stephen Collens illustrate the innovative use of marketing principles to promote healthier sexual behaviors among women in Rwanda. Both cases demonstrate how the principles outlined in the text can be used to improve public health.

Although marketing principles have been applied to some efforts to change health-related behaviors for many years, the integration of marketing principles into day-to-day public health practice is a relatively new concept, and one that has not yet been fully developed. These principles can provide powerful tools for influencing all the factors that contribute to social change: the individual, the environment, and social policy.

This book attempts to describe how marketing principles might become part of public health practice and how it can be used to develop and implement more effective public health initiatives. If our ideas stimulate further thought, research, and, most importantly, experimentation among public health practitioners, we will have achieved our goal. It is our hope that the efforts that come from practitioners who read this book will provide far more answers to the difficult questions we pose here than does the book itself. In the final analysis, the experience of public health practitioners will teach us to develop and implement more effective programs to promote social change and improve the quality of life today and tomorrow.

References

Chen, L.N., Farwell, W. R., & Jha, A.K. (2009). Primary care visit duration and quality: Does good care take longer? *Archives of Internal Medicine, 169*(20), 1866–1872.

HealthCare.gov. (2012). Introducing MyCare. Retrieved April 25, 2012, from http://www.healthcare.gov/index.html

A Call to Action

To confront the chronic disease epidemic that threatens to dominate human health in the 21st century, public health practice must begin to focus on far more than providing basic medical care. To establish a favorable environment for human well-being, public health practitioners must concentrate on effecting social change by helping to modify individual behaviors and lifestyles, to improve social and economic conditions, and to reform social policies.

This section serves as a call to action by demonstrating that the most critical threats to both the public's health and public health as an institution can be addressed only with profound social changes.

CHAPTER

1

Emerging Threats to the Public's Health: Need for Social Change

An epidemic of chronic disease threatens the public's health. Fueling this epidemic are unhealthy lifestyles and behaviors, deteriorating social conditions, and an increasingly hazardous environment, coupled with a crisis in access to quality health care. The emerging chronic disease epidemic poses both a threat to the public's health and a challenge to public health practice. Public health practice must focus on far more than the provision of medical care. It must, first and foremost, dedicate its efforts to modifying individual lifestyle and behavior, to improving social and economic conditions, and to reforming social policy to establish an environment that fosters optimal human health. In other words, the business of public health must focus on creating social change.

The United States is experiencing an epidemic unlike any in its history. Chronic disease is now responsible for 7 of every 10 deaths in the country each year—1.7 million deaths in all (Kung et al., 2008). The impact extends beyond mortality rates: approximately one-fourth of people with chronic conditions have one or more limitations on their daily activities (Anderson, 2004); 100 million Americans—more than one-third of the U.S. population—experience disability or severe limitation of their daily activities due to chronic disease. Chronic disease afflicts more than 120 million Americans and is projected to affect up to 134 million by the year 2020. By then, the costs associated with the epidemic will approach $1 trillion per year.

Unlike previous epidemics, the historic proportions associated with chronic disease today are not reported as front-page news, efforts to confront the issues are not among the priority program activities of most local health departments, and policymakers allocate precious few resources

3

to eliminating the epidemic or even to slowing its spread. Improving sanitation and hygiene will do little to stem the tide. Even the medical profession is nearly powerless against it.

The primary and most urgent challenge to public health today is to find a way to halt the epidemic of chronic disease that threatens to dominate the population in the 21st century. Chronic diseases—heart disease, cancer, stroke, injuries, chronic obstructive lung disease, diabetes, and liver disease—are the chief causes of death among Americans in the 21st century (**Figure 1-1**).

By far, the leading causes of death in the United States are heart disease and cancer, which accounted for 25% and 23% of all deaths, respectively, in 2007 (National Center for Health Statistics [NCHS], 2011). Injuries, including motor vehicle accidents, suicides, homicides, falls, and drownings, accounted for an additional 156,000 deaths annually (6.4% of all deaths) and were the leading causes of death among persons aged 15 to 24 years in 2007 (NCHS, 2011). Violence, in particular, is an alarming part of the chronic disease epidemic. Homicide alone is the leading cause of death among Blacks aged 15 to 24 and is the second leading cause of death among all persons in this age group (NCHS, 2011; Rosenberg, Powell, & Hammond, 1997; Satcher, 1996). Annually, cerebrovascular diseases (stroke) and chronic lower respiratory tract diseases cause an additional 135,000 and 127,000 deaths, respectively (10.9% of all deaths; NCHS, 2011).

Chronic diseases also cause a substantial amount of disability and suffering among Americans. Approximately 100 million people in the

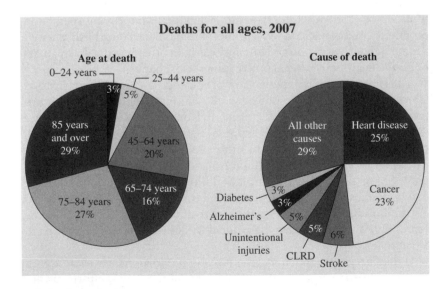

Figure 1-1 Causes of Death—United States, 2007

Source: National Center for Health Statistics. (2011). *Health, United States, 2010: With Special Feature on Death and Dying*, p. 33. Hyattsville, MD.

United States have one or more chronic medical conditions, such as heart disease, stroke, cancer, arthritis, diabetes, lung disease, osteoporosis, multiple sclerosis, and mental retardation; about 40% of this population has more than one chronic condition (Hoffman, Rice, & Sung, 1996). The direct medical costs associated with chronic diseases accounted for about 76% of all direct medical expenditures in the nation (Hoffman et al., 1996). Furthermore, chronic diseases resulted in 11.6% of all individuals, and 32.6% of those ages 65 years and over, having limitation of activity (i.e., limitation of their ability to perform activities usual for their age group) in 2006 (NCHS, 2009).

Despite advances in medical knowledge and treatment, little progress has been made in stemming the epidemic. Although stroke mortality rates declined by 71% and heart disease mortality rates declined by 61% from 1970 to 2007 (NCHS, 2011), only about one-third of the decline in mortality was due to a reduction in the incidence of cardiovascular disease (Sytkowski, Kannel, & D'Agostino, 1990), and the burden of disease morbidity is expected to increase, especially among the elderly (Bonneux et al., 1994). Although fewer people are dying of their disease, nearly the same proportion has cardiovascular disease and suffers from their chronic conditions (Bonneux et al., 1994; Centers for Disease Control and Prevention [CDC], 1993). Between 1997–1998 and 2008–2009, the percent of persons reporting a diagnosis of heart disease or a heart condition decreased by one-half of a percent (from 12.0% to 11.5%), whereas the percentage of persons reporting a diagnosis of stroke increased from 2.3% to 2.7% (NCHS, 2011).

Thus, the overall health status among the American population seems to be worsening, not improving. Between 1993 and 2001, the adjusted proportion of adults who self-rated their health status as being poor increased from 3.3% to 4.1% (Zahran et al., 2005). The proportion of adults who reported more than 13 days of activity limitation due to ill health increased from 5.3% to 5.9%. Also, the adjusted proportion who reported more than 13 unhealthy days due to poor physical health increased from 9.3% to 10.2% (Zahran et al., 2005).

Overall cancer death rates have remained essentially unchanged for the past 50 years (NCHS, 2011). There has been a modest decline in mortality from colorectal cancer, stomach cancer, uterine cancer, and liver cancer, but these changes have been more than offset by the striking increase in lung cancer mortality (American Cancer Society, 1994; NCHS, 2011). Although lung cancer death rates among men peaked in the early 1990s, rates are still increasing among women (NCHS, 2011).

The overall rate of suicide in the United States has decreased slightly since 1950. However, among U.S. teenagers the suicide rate has more than doubled (NCHS, 2011). In this same time period, the overall homicide rate has increased slightly, whereas the homicide rate among teenagers has nearly tripled, mostly due to the widespread availability of firearms (NCHS, 2011; Satcher, 1996).

The incidence of diabetes among adults more than tripled from 1980 through 2009 (CDC, 2011). The burden of this disease falls largely on minority populations: Data from 2005–2008 show that 10.9% of adults over age 20 years have either physician-diagnosed or undiagnosed diabetes. This percentage falls to 9.2% among non-Hispanic Whites and increases to 16.9% among Mexicans and 19.9% among Blacks (NCHS, 2011). Rates of diabetes also increase as poverty increases (NCHS, 2011). Diabetes is merely one example of the increased burden of disease among minority and underserved populations. Ischemic heart disease death rates, which were higher among Whites than Blacks in 1980, have declined in both groups but more rapidly among Whites, so that rates are now higher among Blacks than Whites (NCHS, 2011).

The disparity in overall mortality between higher and lower socioeconomic groups continues to increase in the United States (Pappas et al., 1993). Between 1960 and 1986, overall mortality declined in all socioeconomic groups, but declines were significantly greater among persons with higher income and higher levels of education (Pappas et al., 1993). In communities that are particularly poor, death rates among Blacks have changed little since 1960 (Jenkins et al., 1977; McCord & Freeman, 1990; Pappas et al., 1993).

A striking disparity between higher and lower socioeconomic groups is evident not only in mortality but in morbidity as well. Although only 9.5% of non-poor individuals (those with incomes at least 200% of the poverty level) reported limitation of activity due to chronic disease in 2006, 22.1% of poor individuals (below the poverty threshold) reported limitation of activity, compared with 8.7% of those above 200% of the poverty level (NCHS, 2009). Although only 4.3% of individuals at or above 400% of the poverty level reported fair or poor health in 2009 (compared with good or excellent health), 21.8% of poor persons did (NCHS, 2011).

The contrast in health status between higher and lower socioeconomic class groups is itself a component of the chronic disease epidemic. Several studies have shown that the persistence of social class differences in health status is a stronger determinant of overall poor health than the level of poverty and disadvantage in a community (Henig, 1997; Kennedy, Kawachi, & Prothrow-Stith, 1995; Marmot, Bobak, & Smith, 1995; McCord & Freeman, 1990; Navarro, 1997; Townsend & Davidson, 1982; Wilkinson, 1990, 1992, 1997). Johns Hopkins University professor Vincente Navarro (1997, p. 335) pointed out the following:

A poor person in Harlem, New York City, is likely to have worse health status than a middle-class person in Bangladesh (one of the poorest countries in the world), even though the former has, in absolute terms, more resources (monetary resources and goods and services) than the latter. Still, to be poor in Harlem is far more difficult (because of the social and psychological distance from the rest of society) than to be middle class in Bangladesh. It is not class structure but class relations that affect the levels of health of our populations.

The chronic disease epidemic must be viewed with no less urgency and concern than traditional infectious disease "epidemics" that have plagued society for centuries. As Dr. David Satcher, former director of the CDC, noted, chronic disease (violence, in particular) "can erode the well-being of neighborhoods and destroy communities with the same deadly impact as the outbreak of a fatal disease" (Satcher, 1996, p. 1707). And an editorial in *American Journal of Public Health* asserted, "We should be as much concerned about the thousands of people who are homeless in American cities and the thousands of children in residentially unstable families as we are when there is an epidemic of an infectious disease affecting a few hundred people, and we should respond with the same urgency" (Breakey, 1997, p. 153).

Recognizing the factors fueling the chronic disease epidemic is necessary to understand why medical and traditional public health efforts have been virtually powerless in confronting chronic disease. These factors are (1) unhealthy lifestyles and behaviors, (2) deteriorating social and economic conditions, and (3) a crisis in access to quality health care.

■ UNHEALTHY LIFESTYLES AND BEHAVIORS

A large body of medical and public health literature documents the role of individual behavior in disease, especially chronic disease. A series of large, population-based, cohort studies identified behavioral risk factors for a variety of chronic diseases, most notably heart disease, stroke, and cancer (Slater & Carlton, 1985). The Harvard Report on Cancer Prevention concluded that two-thirds of cancer deaths alone could be prevented by changes in individual behavior (Colditz et al., 1996).

Researchers from the CDC estimated that of the 2.4 million annual deaths in the United States, more than 400,000 could be prevented by eliminating tobacco use, approximately 365,000 could be prevented through improved diet and physical activity, another 85,000 could be prevented by eliminating excess alcohol consumption, and an additional 20,000 could be prevented by eliminating unsafe sexual practices (Mokdad et al., 2004, 2005). Other behavior-related, preventable causes of death include workplace, home, recreational, and roadway injuries; firearms-related injuries; high blood pressure and high cholesterol levels (which are related to diet and physical activity); illicit drug use; and breast and cervical cancer (where early screening could impact prognosis; CDC, 1995; Mokdad et al., 2004; U.S. Department of Health and

Human Services [USDHHS], 1995). In total, about 1.1 million American lives, or nearly one-half of all deaths, could be saved each year by changes in individual health-related behaviors.

■ DETERIORATING SOCIAL AND ECONOMIC CONDITIONS

Poverty

The single best predictor of a person's health status is his or her socioeconomic status (Adler et al., 1997; Antonovsky, 1967; Gregorio, Walsh, & Paturzo, 1997; Hemingway et al., 1997; Kaplan & Lynch, 1997; Kawachi et al., 1997; Kitagawa & Hauser, 1973; Lynch, Kaplan, & Shema, 1997; Marmot et al., 1995; McDonough et al., 1997; Moss, 1997; Pappas et al., 1993; Patrick & Wickizer, 1995; Power et al., 1997; Satcher, 1996; Susser, Watson, & Hopper, 1985; Syme & Berkman, 1976; Yeracaris & Kim, 1978). Age-adjusted death rates for White males in 1986 ranged from 2.4 per thousand among men with an income greater than $25,000 to 16.0 per thousand among those with an income below $9,000 (Pappas et al., 1993). A similar pattern held for White females (1.6 vs. 6.5 per thousand, respectively), Black males (3.6 vs. 19.5 per thousand, respectively), and Black females (2.3 vs. 7.6 per thousand, respectively).

Even after controlling for differences in unhealthy behaviors and lifestyles (e.g., smoking, alcohol use, drug use) and for access to health care, poverty remains a strong, independent predictor of poor health (Haan, Kaplan, & Camacho, 1987; Lantz et al., 1998). Controlling for baseline health status, race, income, employment status, access to medical care, health insurance coverage, smoking, alcohol consumption, physical activity, body mass index, and several other factors, persons living in poverty-stricken areas still have about a two to three times higher mortality rate than those who do not (Haan et al., 1987; Lantz et al., 1998). As Henig (1997) concluded, "the very fact of being poor is itself an independent risk factor for getting sick" (p. 103).

Poverty is a particularly strong risk factor for disease and death among children. Children who grow up in poverty are eight times more likely to die from homicide, five times more likely to have a physical or mental disability, five times more likely to be subject to child abuse, three times more likely to die in childhood, and twice as likely to be killed in an accident (Children's Defense Fund, 1994). Lisbeth Schorr (1989) summarized the problem succinctly: "Poverty is the greatest risk factor of all. Family poverty is relentlessly correlated with high rates of school-age childbearing, school failure, and violent crime—and with all their antecedents. Low income is an important risk factor in itself, and so is relative poverty—having significantly less income than the norm, especially in a society that places a high value on economic success" (p. xxii).

Efforts to improve the public's health must therefore address the problem of poverty. Not only is poverty a social and economic problem, but it is also a fundamental threat to public health.

Despite the importance of poverty as a public health problem and in spite of the so-called war on poverty during the Great Society reforms of the 1960s and President Lyndon Johnson's expressed national "commitment to eradicate poverty," poverty remains nearly as widespread as it was during the late 1960s and has become more prevalent in recent years (Bok, 1996; NCHS, 2011). The proportion of the population living below the official poverty line dropped from 22.4% in 1959 to 11.2% in 1974; however, it has increased overall since then, reaching 15.1% in 1993, the highest rate of poverty in the United States since the mid-1960s (Bok, 1996; NCHS, 1997). Although the proportion of persons living below the poverty level declined during the 1990s, it increased from 11.3% to 14.3% between 2000 and 2009 (NCHS, 2011; U.S. Bureau of the Census [Census], 2010a). Thus, the rate of poverty in the United States in 2002 was actually higher than it was 35 years earlier, in 1974. The proportion of people living in extreme poverty (income less than half the official poverty line) also has increased, rising from 30% of those below the poverty line in 1975 to 40% in the late 1980s (Bok, 1996) and reaching 45% in the 2000 U.S. Census (Census, 2000b).

Not only have rates of abject poverty increased, but the mean family income for the lowest 40% income segment in the country has declined since 1972 (Bok, 1996). Family income for the highest 40% income segment during the same period has increased, widening the gap in income disparity between the middle and upper class and the poor. Mean family income among the lowest 20% income segment decreased from $10,769 in 1972 (in constant 1992 dollars) to $9,708 in 1992 and among the second lowest 20% income segment from $23,725 to $23,337 (Bok, 1996). At the same time, mean family income among the highest 20% income segment increased from $82,534 to $99,252 and among the second highest 20% income segment from $47,588 to $53,365.

Hunger

The health consequences of hunger go beyond medical conditions associated with nutritional deficiencies and include inability to concentrate in school, feelings of worthlessness, and other psychological problems (Meyers et al., 1989; Pollitt, Gersovitz, & Garginlo, 1978; Rose & Oliveira, 1997; Sidel, 1997). Thus, hunger can significantly affect a person's physical and mental well-being. Estimates suggest that at least 4 million children under age 12 in the United States experience hunger daily and an additional 9.6 million may experience hunger at some point during the year (Sidel, 1997; Wehler et al., 1995). In 2009, 14.7% of U.S. households were food insecure (having limited or uncertain availability of nutritionally adequate, safe, or acceptable foods) at some time during the year, the highest rate of food insecurity since national surveys began in 1995 (U.S. Department of Agriculture, 2011).

Educational Attainment

Education is one of the most important determinants of health status. Age-adjusted death rates for White males in 1986 ranged from 2.8 per thousand among those with at least 4 years of college to 7.6 per thousand among those without a high school diploma (Pappas et al., 1993). Similarly, death rates for these educational groups ranged from 1.8 to 3.4 per thousand among White females, 6.0 to 13.4 per thousand among Black males, and 2.2 to 6.2 per thousand among Black females.

Education is strongly related to unhealthy behaviors. For example, educational attainment is one of the best predictors of smoking status. In 1994, adult smoking prevalence ranged from 12.3% among adults with 16 or more years of education to 38.2% among those with only 9 to 11 years of education (CDC, 1996). In 2009, age-adjusted adult smoking prevalence was 28.9% among those aged 25 years and over with no high school diploma but only 9.0% among those with a college degree (NCHS, 2011). Independent of its relation to behavior, education influences a person's ability to access and understand health information. For example, people who are illiterate will not be helped by written educational materials produced by public health practitioners.

The United States has made little progress in improving the educational attainment of its population during the past two decades. The overall proportion of adults ages 25 and older with a high school diploma (or equivalency) increased from 75.2% in 1990 to 81.1% in 2000 to 87.1% in 2010 (Census, 1990, 2000a, 2010b). Perhaps of even more concern, the Department of Education estimates that about 35% of 18-year-olds in the nation are functionally illiterate (Harris, 1996; U.S. Department of Education, 1994). In 1992, more than one-fifth of all adults in the United States (representing more than 38 million individuals) scored in the lowest level of literacy measured in the National Adult Literacy Survey (U.S. Department of Education, 2002).

Housing

The lack of adequate and stable housing is associated with a number of chronic and severe health problems. Homelessness is associated with tuberculosis, trauma, depression and other mental illnesses, alcoholism, drug abuse, sexually transmitted diseases, and poor nutrition (Breakey, 1997; Breakey & Fischer, 1995; Dellon, 1995; Greene, Ennett, & Ringwalt, 1997; Robertson, Zlotnick, & Westerfelt, 1997). The lifetime prevalence of homelessness (the percentage of persons who report having been homeless at some time in their lives) in the United States is about 7.4%, and the 5-year prevalence of homelessness is 3.1% (Breakey, 1997; Link et al., 1994). In any given year, nearly 1% of the population experiences homelessness, as do 6.3% of people living in poverty (Burt & Aron, 2000). Although accurate estimates of trends in homelessness are not available, no evidence exists that the extent of homelessness is decreasing (Breakey, 1997) and available evidence suggests that the number of homeless persons has markedly increased over the past two decades (Urban Institute, 2002).

Even among those who do have housing, the quality of housing conditions is a significant concern. In 1991, 6.7% of all housing units had a leaking roof, 5.1% had open cracks in the ceiling or walls, and 5.0% had unusable toilets (Bok, 1996). The percentage of families eligible for federal assistance through public housing, subsidized housing, and rent supplements who receive such aid is only 30% (Bok, 1996). Although the federal government provides about $90 million in housing subsidies each year, $70 million of it is in the form of tax deductions for homeowners (Bok, 1996). For families not receiving subsidies or living in public housing, 77% pay more than half their income for rent (Bok, 1996).

The health consequences of poor-quality housing can be substantial. A study published in the *New England Journal of Medicine* found that exposure to cockroach debris may be the leading cause of asthma among inner-city children (Rosenstreich et al., 1997). Children who were exposed to higher levels of cockroach allergen not only had higher rates of hospitalization for asthma but also had more symptoms of wheezing, more physician visits, and more days of school absence than other asthmatic children. The high exposure to cockroaches in the inner city may explain both the high prevalence of asthma in the inner city and the increase in the incidence of asthma among inner-city children over the past 30 years (Platts-Mills & Carter, 1997).

Another example of important health consequences caused by poor housing is lead poisoning among children. Peeling lead-paint chips in older housing is still the chief cause of lead poisoning. Children living in houses built before 1946 are at greatest risk. From 1991 to 1994, about 16% of poor children living in such housing had elevated blood lead levels, putting them at risk for significant neurological and psychological impairment, including decreased school performance and IQ (CDC, 1997).

Unemployment

Unemployment is recognized as a major predictor of morbidity and mortality in the population. Catalano (1991) showed that for every 1% increase in unemployment during the 1980s, there was a 5% increase in mortality from heart disease and stroke and a 6% increase in homicide deaths. Economic strains associated with unemployment pose especially large health risks to disadvantaged people (Smith, 1987).

Overall unemployment rates in the United States fell slightly during the latter part of the 20th century, decreasing from 8.5% in 1975 to 4.9% in 1997 (U.S. Department of Labor, 1997). Unemployment rates remained relatively stable and were still at 5.8% in 2008 but increased to 9.3% in 2009 (U.S. Department of Labor, 2010). This rate, however, does not affect all demographics equally: The 2009 unemployment rates were 14.8% for African Americans, 12.1% for Hispanics, 8.5% for Whites, and 7.3% for Asians (U.S. Department of Labor, 2010).

Environmental Hazards

Exposure to environmental toxins is associated with a wide range of chronic health problems. Among the environmental hazards that cause the greatest disease burden are secondhand smoke (53,000 deaths per year; Glantz & Parmley, 1991; Wells, 1988), indoor radon (7,000 to 30,000 deaths per year; National Research Council, 1998; U.S. Environmental Protection Agency, 1992), and arsenic in drinking water (about 4,700 deaths per year; A.H. Smith et al., 1992). The CDC estimated that approximately 17% of all deaths in the United States could be prevented by reducing exposure to environmental hazards (CDC, 1995; USDHHS, 1995).

Despite improvements in environmental quality for the advantaged segment of the population, disadvantaged segments of the population still suffer from the adverse health effects of an unhealthy environment. A classic example of the disproportionate burden of environmental risk on the disadvantaged is the problem of childhood lead poisoning. Although the problem has been recognized for decades, the lead content in paint and gasoline has been regulated for many years, and the federal and state governments have spent millions of dollars on lead abatement programs, lead poisoning is still a significant health problem for poor, inner-city children (CDC, 1997). From 1991 to 1994, more than 16% of low-income children who lived in houses built before 1946 had elevated blood lead levels, compared with 4.1% and 0.9% of middle- and high-income children, respectively (CDC, 1997).

A report by the Pew Environmental Health Commission at Johns Hopkins University reported that the ability of public health professionals to prevent health problems due to environmental hazards is being severely impaired by the nation's lack of adequate surveillance of environmental factors contributing to human disease. The panel's chairman, former Senator Lowell Weicker Jr., noted that an epidemic of environmentally caused diseases should be addressed with no less urgency and no less comprehensiveness than infectious disease threats that affect far fewer people: "We responded quickly to the threat of West Nile virus, tracking and monitoring every report of infected birds and people, but 20 years into the asthma epidemic, this country is still unable to track where and when attacks occur and what environmental links may trigger them" (Reuters Health, 2000).

Crime and Violence

In 1984, former Surgeon General C. Everett Koop declared violence to be an epidemic and a public health problem: "Violence is as much a public health issue for me and my successors in this country as smallpox, tuberculosis, and syphilis were for my predecessors in the last two centuries" (Henig, 1997, p. 110). In 1988, CDC researchers Mercy and Houk called for a similar approach to the problem of violence: "The time has come for us to address this problem in the manner in which we have addressed and dealt successfully with other threats to the public health" (p. 1284). CDC director David Satcher said, "If you look at the major cause of death today it's not smallpox or polio or even infectious diseases. Violence is the leading cause of lost life in this country today. If it's not a public health problem, why are all those people dying from it?" (Applebome, 1993, p. A7).

The disadvantaged communities in the United States have been ravaged by violence. After a decrease in the rate of firearm-related deaths from 1970 to 2000, rates have remained stable at 10.2 deaths per 100,000 people (NCHS, 2011). Furthermore, homicide remains the second leading cause of death among young people, ages 15 to 24, and the homicide death rate remains six times higher among African American males than among the general population (NCHS, 2011). There are more than 200 million guns in private ownership throughout the United States and 5.5 million new ones introduced each year, of which 100,000 are carried by children to school each day (Bok, 1996). The link between the availability of firearms and the increasing homicide rate is "every bit as strong as the studies that linked cigarettes to lung cancer" (Taubes, 1992, p. 215). In addition, child abuse rates have increased from 10 per thousand children in 1976 to 45 per thousand in 1992; some of this increase may be attributable to increased reporting of abuse, but at least a portion is due to a real increase in incidence (Bok, 1996).

In 2009, there were 1.3 million violent crimes in the United States, including more than 15,000 murders, 88,000 cases of forcible rape, and 806,000 cases of aggravated assault (U.S. Department of Justice, 2009). Despite a 5.2% decline in the rate of violent crime between 2005 and 2009, there is still one murder every 34 minutes, one forcible rape every 6 minutes, and one aggravated assault every 39 seconds in this country (U.S. Department of Justice, 2009).

Social Support

The availability of a social support network—family, friends, and community programs to which an individual can turn for help, advice, reassurance, and consolation—is a strong determinant of health status (Berkman, 1984; Berkman & Breslow, 1983; Berkman & Syme, 1979; Broadhead et al., 1983; Cassel, 1976; Corin, 1995; Patrick & Wickizer, 1995;

Pilisuk & Minkler, 1985; Schorr, 1989). Even after controlling for most other known determinants of health—socioeconomic status, access to health care, and individual behaviors and lifestyle factors—the absence of social support remains a strong, independent predictor of disease (Berkman & Syme, 1979). As Schorr (1989) argued, "Formal social supports protect people from an amazing variety of pathological states, including destructive family functioning, low birthweight, depression, arthritis, tuberculosis, and even premature death" (p. 155).

The focus on what policymakers have termed "welfare reform" has taken a devastating toll on the availability and quality of social support networks in American communities. By reducing the level of government provision of basic needs—food, housing, transportation, child care, and health care—welfare "reform" has forced traditional social support networks, such as community support programs, to abandon their supportive tasks and instead scramble to find ways to meet the basic needs of their clients (Pilisuk & Minkler, 1985). As Pilisuk and Minkler (1985) argue, the primary value of welfare benefits is that it allows alternative support systems (families, friends, and community programs) to provide exactly the kind of support needed to keep people healthy.

"Family and community effectiveness in the provision of social support depends heavily on the broader economic and social environment. To build and maintain strong supportive ties, we must provide those programs, services, and policies on a societal level, which can help meet basic human needs. For it is only within this broader context of system-level support and commitment to people of all ages and places that social support on the individual and community levels can fulfill its potential" (Pilisuk & Minkler, 1985, p. 11).

The real threat that welfare reform poses to the public's health is that it renders ineffective the systems of social support in the family and community that are so closely tied to health status (Broadhead et al., 1983; Cassel, 1976; Cobb, 1976; Cohen & Syme, 1985; Pilisuk & Minkler, 1985). By forcing social support networks to concentrate on filling gaps in the basic needs of the poor rather than on providing a true social support system for those in distress, welfare reform as it is currently crafted makes it increasingly more difficult to achieve within communities the social conditions in which people can be healthy. Lisbeth Schorr (1989) summarized the problem:

> For those living in persistent and concentrated poverty, it is reformed services and institutions that will furnish the essential footholds for the climb out of poverty. Yet in the legislative, academic, and political forums where antipoverty strategies and welfare reform are debated, the spotlight is only on short-term measures to reduce the numbers now on welfare, now unable to work productively.

The shocking deficiencies in the health, welfare, and education of poor children, the long-term investments that could help the vulnerable children of today to become the productive and contributing adults of tomorrow, are rarely on the agenda. . . . Children and families have needs that cannot be met by economic measures alone, and that cannot be met by individual families alone. (pp. xxiii, xxiv)

■ A CRISIS IN ACCESS TO QUALITY HEALTH CARE

Inadequate access to health care services is associated with increased burdens of economic hardship, poor health, and increased mortality (Blendon et al., 1994; Donelan et al., 1997; Franks, Clancy, & Gold, 1993; Henry J. Kaiser Family Foundation, 1994; Lurie et al., 1984; Lurie et al., 1986; Weissman & Epstein, 1994). The CDC estimated that about 11% of all deaths could be prevented by improving the population's access to quality medical treatment (CDC, 1995; USDHHS, 1995). In spite of the widespread recognition of this problem and the rhetoric about the importance of ensuring all citizens access to health care, the proportion of uninsured Americans increased from 13.6% in 1970 to 15.4% in 1995 (Bok, 1996; NCHS, 1997). Approximately 18% of the population—more than 46 million people—lack health insurance (NCHS, 2011). As of 2009, 8.5% of all children (under age 19) lacked any health insurance coverage (NCHS, 2011). Lack of insurance tends to be a problem of the poor. Although only 5.8% of non-poor individuals (incomes at or above 400% of the poverty level) lacked health insurance coverage in 2009, 30.4% of individuals below the poverty level had no health insurance coverage (NCHS, 2009).

The problem of access to quality health care among the poor is not limited to lack of insurance. Several studies have shown that disadvantaged populations tend to receive inferior health care, regardless of whether they have health insurance (Burstin, Lipsitz, & Brennan, 1992; Dalen & Santiago, 1991; Diehr et al., 1991; Goldberg et al., 1992; Kahn et al., 1994; Kasiske et al., 1991; Wenneker & Epstein, 1989; Yergan et al., 1987). For example, even among those who are insured by Medicaid, access to high-quality health care is limited. Several studies have shown that Medicaid patients are less likely to receive preventive care and that their physical health fares worse under Medicaid-managed care than under fee-for-service care (Ware et al., 1996). Ware and associates (1996) found that during a 4-year follow-up period, poor patients treated under Medicaid-managed care suffered greater declines in physical health status than those treated under traditional, fee-for-service Medicaid. Even without managed care, Medicaid patients have less access to continuing care and preventive care than patients who are privately insured (Davidson et al., 1994; Kerr & Siu, 1993).

Similarly, poor elderly patients who are enrolled in Medicare managed care may be less likely to have access to the intensive rehabilitation and support services that are necessary to keep them self-sufficient and avoid institutionalization. Retchin and associates (1997) found that compared with fee-for-service Medicare patients, Medicare managed care patients who suffer a stroke are more likely to be discharged to nursing homes and less likely to be placed in rehabilitative settings or discharged to home. Access to home health care and outcomes under Medicare managed care have also been shown to be worse than under traditional, fee-for-service Medicare (Experton et al., 1997; Shaugnessy, Schlenker, & Hittle, 1994). Ware and colleagues (1996) reported that elderly patients in health maintenance organizations had more significant declines in physical health compared with those who remained in fee-for-service settings over a 4-year follow-up period.

There is hope, however, that the problem of inadequate access to health care may be lessened with the Affordable Care Act, which was signed into law in March 2010. Although the effects of this law remain to be seen, the aims include expanding coverage to those denied health insurance due to preexisting conditions, increasing the number of people covered by Medicaid, and encouraging more businesses to provide insurance by offering tax credits (USDHHS, 2010).

■ IMPLICATIONS OF THE CHRONIC DISEASE EPIDEMIC FOR PUBLIC HEALTH PRACTICE

During the 19th and early 20th centuries, when the chief causes of preventable death were infectious diseases spread by contaminated water and food, the focus of public health practice was building a societal infrastructure for proper sanitation and hygiene and for the delivery of vaccines and treatments to the population. The chronic disease epidemic of the early 21st century, however, is largely related to individual lifestyle and behavior, deteriorating economic and social conditions, and the failure of social policy to address problems such as affordable and accessible health care of high quality for all Americans. Thus, public health practice must now focus on modifying individual lifestyle and behavior, improving social and economic conditions, and reforming social policy.

To start, at least 1.1 million American lives, or nearly one-half of all deaths, could be saved each year by changes in individual health-related behaviors (**Figure 1-2**; Mokdad et al., 2004, 2005). Although public health practice clearly has to focus on modifying individual lifestyle and behavior, it is important to note that personal behavior does not take place in a vacuum. Rather, it takes place in the context of a historical, cultural, and political environment and in communities with varying economic and social conditions. To change individual behavior, one cannot ignore

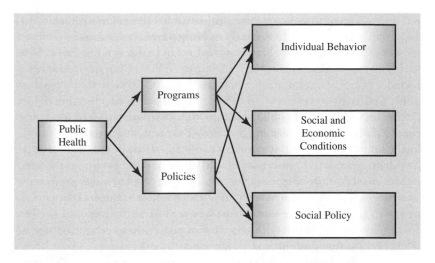

Figure 1-2 An Overview of the Functions of Public Health: Creating Social Change

the conditions and environment in which that behavior takes place. In fact, some argue that focusing on the economic and social conditions that give rise to unhealthy behaviors is essential to changing those behaviors. Because behavior is a product of the social conditions and social norms of the community in which a person lives (Tesh, 1994), "discussing changes in lifestyles without first discussing the changes in the social conditions which give rise to them, without recognizing that the lifestyle is derivative, is misleading" (Berliner, 1977, p. 119).

Social and economic factors not only influence health behaviors and individual lifestyle but also are themselves independently related to health status. Several decades of research have demonstrated that lower social class, social deprivation, and lack of social support are among the most important determinants of health (Antonovsky, 1967; Berkman, 1984; Bright, 1967; Cassel, 1976; Conrad, 1994; Frey, 1982; Haan et al., 1987; Kitagawa & Hauser, 1973; Marmot, 1982; Morris, 1979, 1982; Rose & Marmot, 1981; Salonen, 1982; Stockwell, 1961; Syme & Berkman, 1976; Yeracaris & Kim, 1978). Moreover, the strong association between these socioeconomic factors and health is not entirely explained by differences in individual lifestyle and health behaviors between members of higher and lower social class groups (Haan et al., 1987; Lantz et al., 1998; Rose & Marmot, 1981; Salonen, 1982; Slater & Carlton, 1985; Slater, Lorimor, & Lairson, 1985; Wiley & Camacho, 1980). Link and Phelan (1996) proposed a novel view of the relationship between socioeconomic status and disease, asserting that socioeconomic status must be viewed as a "fundamental cause" of disease.

Lantz et al., writing in the *Journal of the American Medical Association*, noted that "Although reducing the prevalence of health risk behaviors in low-income populations is an important public health goal, socioeconomic differences in mortality are due to a wider array of factors and, therefore, would persist even with improved health behaviors among the disadvantaged" (1998, p. 1703). "We must look to a broader range of explanatory risk factors, including structural elements of inequality in our society" (p. 1708). The Institute of Medicine report (1988) on the future of public health, noting the importance of social and economic factors as determinants of health status, suggested that public health must take a much wider view of disease than in the past: "Public health programs, to be effective, should move beyond programs targeted on the immediate problem, such as teen pregnancy, to health promotion and prevention by dealing with underlying factors in the social environment. To deal with these factors, the scope of public health will need to encompass relationships with other social programs in education, social services, housing, and income maintenance" (p. 113).

The late Sol Levine noted that social factors "mean not only poverty but also social class, family, community, gender, ethnicity, racism, political economy, and culture. We have to learn how these interact with health, how, for example, culture, political economy, and racism may affect the community and family environment, which, in turn, may influence people's health. We have to look not only at individual characteristics but at the features of the society as well" (Henig, 1997, p. 102).

Because social and economic conditions are themselves a product of social policy, public health practice must also focus on changing social policy. Poverty is not a consequence of individual frailty, lack of responsibility, and lack of motivation, as some have argued. Rather, it is the product of social and economic conditions created and maintained by the historical, political, and cultural environment in which society has developed (Zaidi, 1988). Social policy contributes, at least in part, to the environment that determines social and economic conditions in the community. The availability of adequate food, housing, and jobs; the quality of the physical environment; access to medical services; the extent of social support in the community; and the amount of economic, employment, and educational opportunity are all influenced strongly by social policies. Former Harvard University president Derek Bok (1996) argued that "current levels of poverty are not immutable but are the result of policy choices, choices that seem at odds with the stated desire of most Americans to do more for the deserving poor" (p. 35).

For example, government assistance for single mothers with no earned income is only 27% of the median family income in the United States, compared with 38% in France, 47% in Germany, 60% in Britain, and 64% in Sweden (Bok, 1996). The rate of poverty among single mothers in the United States is more than twice the rate in each of the other countries (Bok, 1996). Quite simply, social policy has a direct and understandable effect on social conditions.

To confront threats to the public's health effectively, the three major functions of public health must be (1) modifying individual behavior and lifestyle, (2) improving social and economic conditions, and (3) reforming social policies. All represent fundamental aspects of social change. Ultimately, then, public health is in the business of creating or facilitating social change (Figure 1-2).

It should be noted that although chronic diseases have replaced infectious diseases as the chief causes of death in the United States, the nation has experienced a reemergence of infectious diseases, primarily due to acquired immunodeficiency syndrome (AIDS). Although the death rate from AIDS decreased from 16.2 in 1995 to 3.7 in 2007, its incidence has remained relatively stable during the past 18 years, with 41,000 reported cases in 1990 and 37,000 diagnoses in 2008 (NCHS, 1997, 2011). With the rise of AIDS has come increased risk for other infectious diseases, such as drug-resistant tuberculosis. In addition, influenza and pneumonia caused more than 52,000 deaths in 2007 (NCHS, 2011). The threat of emerging infectious diseases also remains a critical public health concern because of the potential for a worldwide avian flu epidemic (Parry, 2005) and because of already established threats, such as West Nile virus (Gorsche & Tilley, 2005) and severe acute respiratory syndrome, or SARS (Lu et al., 2005).

Infectious diseases, like chronic diseases, are strongly related to individual lifestyles and behaviors, social and economic conditions, and social policy. Infection with the human immunodeficiency virus (HIV), for example, is commonly precipitated by intravenous drug use. The spread of tuberculosis infection, especially multi–drug-resistant strains, is promoted by crowded and unsanitary living conditions. And the failure of society to develop rational policies to control the spread of HIV infection—such as needle exchange programs—that have been shown to be among the most highly effective interventions available has contributed to the AIDS epidemic (Lurie & Drucker, 1997).

■ CONCLUSION

The major implication of the chronic disease and emerging infectious disease epidemics for public health policy and practice is that public health must focus on far more than the provision of medical care. It must, first and foremost, focus on modifying individual lifestyle and behavior, improving social and economic conditions, and reforming social policy that contributes to an environment in which it is difficult for people to be healthy. Ultimately, then, public health is in the business of creating or facilitating social change.

The three-pronged attack that is necessary to control the epidemic of chronic disease and emerging infectious diseases in the United

States—modifying individual lifestyle and behavior, improving social and economic conditions, and reforming social policy—is not one that public health practitioners have traditionally been well equipped to conduct. And it has not been one at which public health has been particularly successful. Chapter 2 explores the threats to the survival of public health as an institution and why the task of marketing public health programs and policies is necessary for public health practitioners to effect change.

References

Adler, N.E., Boyce, W.T., Chesney, M.A. Folkman, S., & Syme, S.L. (1997). Socioeconomic inequalities in health: No easy solution. In P.R. Lee & C.L. Estes (Eds.), *The nation's health* (5th ed., pp. 18–31). Sudbury, MA: Jones and Bartlett.

American Cancer Society. (1994). *Cancer facts & figures—1994.* New York, NY: Author.

Anderson, G. (2004). *Chronic conditions: Making the case for ongoing care.* Baltimore, MD: Johns Hopkins University.

Antonovsky, A. (1967). Social class, life expectancy, and overall mortality. *Milbank Memorial Fund Quarterly, 45,* 31–73.

Applebome, P. (1993, September 26). CDC's new chief worries as much about bullets as about bacteria. *The New York Times,* p. A7.

Berkman, L.F. (1984). Assessing the physical health effects of social networks and social support. *Annual Reviews of Public Health, 5,* 413–432.

Berkman, L.F., & Breslow, L. (Eds.). (1983). *Health and ways of living: The Alameda County Study.* New York, NY: Oxford University Press.

Berkman, L.F., & Syme, S.L. (1979). Social networks, host resistance, and mortality: A nine-year follow-up study of Alameda County residents. *American Journal of Epidemiology, 109,* 186–204.

Berliner, H. (1977). Emerging ideologies in medicine. *Review of Radical Political Economics, 9,* 116–124.

Blendon, R.J., Donelan, K., Hill, C.A., Carter, W., Beatrice, D., & Altman, D. (1994). Paying medical bills in the United States: Why health insurance isn't enough. *Journal of the American Medical Association, 271,* 949–951.

Bok, D. (1996). *The state of the nation.* Cambridge, MA: Harvard University Press.

Bonneux, L., Barendregt, J.J., Meeter, K., Bonsel, G.J., & van der Maas, P.J. (1994). Estimating clinical morbidity due to ischemic heart disease on congestive heart failure: The future rise of heart failure. *American Journal of Public Health, 84,* 20–28.

Breakey, W.R. (1997). Editorial: It's time for the public health community to declare war on homelessness. *American Journal of Public Health, 87,* 153–155.

Breakey, W.R., & Fischer, P.J. (1995). Mental illness and the continuum of residential stability. *Social Psychiatry and Psychiatric Epidemiology, 30,* 147–151.

Bright, M. (1967). A follow-up study of the Commission on Cultural Illness Morbidity Survey in Baltimore, II. Race and sex differences in mortality. *Journal of Chronic Diseases, 20,* 717–729.

Broadhead, W.E., Kaplan, B.H., James, S.A., Wagner, E.H., Shoenbach, V.J., Grimson, R., . . . Gehlbach, S.H. (1983). The epidemiological evidence for a relationship between social support and health. *American Journal of Epidemiology, 117,* 521–537.

Burstin, H.R., Lipsitz, S.R., & Brennan, T.A. (1992). Socioeconomic status and risk for substandard medical care. *Journal of the American Medical Association, 268,* 2383–2387.

Burt, M., & Aron, L. (2000). *America's homeless II: Populations and services.* Washington, DC: The Urban Institute.

Cassel, J. (1976). The contribution of the social environment to host resistance. *American Journal of Epidemiology, 104,* 107–123.

Catalano, R. (1991). The health effects of economic insecurity. *American Journal of Public Health, 81,* 1148–1152.

Centers for Disease Control and Prevention. (1993). *Cardiovascular disease surveillance: Ischemic heart disease, 1980–1989.* Atlanta, GA: Centers for Disease Control and Prevention, National Center for Chronic Disease Prevention and Health Promotion, Division of Chronic Disease Control and Community Intervention.

Centers for Disease Control and Prevention. (1995). *1994: Ten leading causes of death in the United States.* Atlanta, GA: Centers for Disease Control, National Center for Injury Prevention and Control.

Centers for Disease Control and Prevention. (1996). Cigarette smoking among adults—United States, 1994. *Morbidity and Mortality Weekly Report, 45,* 588–590.

Centers for Disease Control and Prevention. (1997). Update: Blood lead levels— United States, 1991–1994. *Morbidity and Mortality Weekly Report, 46,* 141–146.

Centers for Disease Control and Prevention. (2011). Diabetes data & trends. Retrieved March 21, 2012, from http://www.cdc.gov/diabetes/statistics/incidence/fig1.htm

Children's Defense Fund. (1994). *Wasting America's future.* Washington, DC: Author.

Cobb, S. (1976). Social support as a moderator of life stress. *Journal of Psychosomatic Medicine, 38,* 300–314.

Cohen, S., & Syme, S.L. (Eds.). (1985). *Social support and health.* New York, NY: Academic Press.

Colditz, G.A., DeJong, D., Hunter, D.J., Trichopoulos, D., & Willett, W.C. (1996). Harvard report on cancer prevention, vol. 1: Causes of human cancer. *Cancer Causes and Control, 7*(Suppl. 1), S3–S59.

Conrad, P. (1994). Wellness in the workplace: Potentials and pitfalls of worksite health promotion. In H.D. Schwartz (Ed.), *Dominant issues in medical sociology* (3rd ed., pp. 556–567). New York, NY: McGraw-Hill.

Corin, E. (1995). The cultural frame: Context and meaning in the construction on health. In B.C. Amick III, S. Levine, A.R. Tarlov, & D.C. Walsh (Eds.), *Society and health* (pp. 272–304). New York, NY: Oxford University Press.

Dalen, J.E., & Santiago, J. (1991). Insuring the uninsured is not enough. *Archives of Internal Medicine, 151,* 860–862.

Davidson, A.E., Klein, D.E., Settipane, G.A., & Alario, A.J. (1994). Access to care among children visiting the emergency room with acute exacerbations of asthma. *Annals of Allergy, 72,* 469–473.

Dellon, E.S. (1995). The health status of the Providence-area homeless population. *Rhode Island Medicine, 10,* 989–999.

Diehr, P.K., Richardson, W.C., Shortell, S.M., & LoGerfo, J.P. (1991). Increased access to medical care. *Medical Care, 10,* 989–999.

Donelan, K., Blendon, R.J., Hill, C.A., Hoffman, C., Rowland, D., Frankel, M., & Altman D. (1997). Whatever happened to the health insurance crises in the United States? Voices from a national survey. In P.R. Lee & C.L. Estes (Eds.), *The nation's health* (5th ed., pp. 283–291). Sudbury, MA: Jones and Bartlett.

Experton, B., Li, Z., Branch, L.G., Ozminkowski, R.J., & Mellon-Lacey, D.M. (1997). Impact of payor-provider type on health care use and expenditures among the frail elderly. *American Journal of Public Health, 87,* 210–216.

Franks, P., Clancy, C.M., & Gold, M.R. (1993). Health insurance and mortality: Evidence from a national cohort. *Journal of the American Medical Association, 270,* 737–741.

Frey, R.S. (1982). The socioeconomic distribution of mortality rates in Des Moines, Iowa. *Public Health Reports, 97,* 545–549.

Glantz, S.A., & Parmley, W.W. (1991). Passive smoking and heart disease: Epidemiology, physiology, and biochemistry. *Circulation, 83,* 1–12.

Goldberg, K.C., Hartz, A.J., Jacobsen, S.J., Krakauer, H., & Rimm, A.A. (1992). Racial and community factors influencing coronary artery bypass graft surgery rates for all 1986 Medicare patients. *Journal of the American Medical Association, 267,* 1473–1477.

Gorsche, R., & Tilley, P. (2005). The rash of West Nile virus infection. *Canadian Medical Association Journal, 172,* 1440.

Greene, J.M., Ennett, S.T., & Ringwalt, C.L. (1997). Substance use among runaway and homeless youth in three national samples. *American Journal of Public Health, 87,* 229–235.

Gregorio, D.I., Walsh, S.J., & Paturzo, D. (1997). The effects of occupation-based social position on mortality in a large American cohort. *American Journal of Public Health, 87,* 1472–1475.

Haan, M., Kaplan, G.A., & Camacho, T. (1987). Poverty and health: Prospective evidence from the Alameda County Study. *American Journal of Epidemiology, 125,* 989–998.

Harris, I.B. (1996). *Children in jeopardy: Can we break the cycle of poverty?* New Haven, CT: Yale University Press.

Hemingway, H., Nicholson, A., Stafford, M., Roberts, R., & Marmot, M. (1997). The impact of socioeconomic status on health functioning as assessed by the SF-36 questionnaire: The Whitehall II Study. *American Journal of Public Health, 87,* 1484–1490.

Henig, R.M. (1997). *The people's health: A memoir of public health and its evolution at Harvard.* Washington, DC: Joseph Henry Press.

Henry J. Kaiser Family Foundation. (1994). *Project LEAN idea kit for state and community programs to reduce dietary fat.* Menlo Park, CA: Author.

Hoffman, C., Rice, D., & Sung, H.Y. (1996). Persons with chronic conditions: Their prevalence and costs. *Journal of the American Medical Association, 276*, 1473–1479.

Institute of Medicine, Committee for the Study of the Future of Public Health. (1988). *The future of public health*. Washington, DC: National Academies Press.

Jenkins, C.D., Tuthill, R.W., Tannenbaum, S.I., & Kirby, C.R. (1977). Zones of excess mortality in Massachusetts. *New England Journal of Medicine, 296*, 1354–1356.

Kahn, K.L., Pearson, M.L., Harrison, E.R., Desmond, K.A., Rogers, W.H., Rubenstein, L.V., . . . Keeler, E.B. (1994). Health care for Black and poor hospitalized Medicare patients. *Journal of the American Medical Association, 271*, 1169–1174.

Kaplan, G.A., & Lynch, J.W. (1997). Editorial: Whither studies on the socioeconomic foundations of population health? *American Journal of Public Health, 87*, 1409–1411.

Kasiske, B.L., Neylan, J.F., Riggio, R.R., Danovitch, G.M., Kahana, L., Alexander, S.R., & White, M.G. (1991). The effect of race on access and outcome in transplantation. *New England Journal of Medicine, 324*, 302–307.

Kawachi, I., Kennedy, B.P., Lochner, K., & Prothrow-Stith, D. (1997). Social capital, income inequality, and mortality. *American Journal of Public Health, 87*, 1491–1498.

Kennedy, B., Kawachi, I., & Prothrow-Stith, D. (1995). Income distribution and mortality: Cross-sectional ecological study of the Robin Hood Index in the United States. *British Medical Journal, 312*, 1004–1007.

Kerr, E.A., & Siu, A.L. (1993). Follow-up after hospital discharge: Does insurance make a difference? *Journal of Health Care for the Poor & Underserved, 4*, 133–142.

Kitagawa, E.M., & Hauser, P.M. (1973). *Differential mortality in the United States: A study in socioeconomic epidemiology*. Cambridge, MA: Harvard University Press.

Kung, H.C., Hoyert, D.L., Xu, J.Q., & Murphy, S.L. (2008). Deaths: Final data for 2005. Retrieved March 21, 2012, from http://www.cdc.gov/nchs/data/nvsr/nvsr56/nvsr56_10.pdf

Lantz, P.M., House, J.S., Lepkowski, J.M., Williams, D.R., Mero, R.P., & Chen, J. (1998). Socioeconomic factors, health behaviors, and mortality: Results from a nationally representative prospective study of US adults. *Journal of the American Medical Association, 297*, 1703–1708.

Link, B.G., & Phelan, J.C. (1996). Review: Why are some people healthy and others not? The determinants of health of populations. *American Journal of Public Health, 86*, 598–599.

Link, B.C., Susser, E., Stueve, A., Phelan, J., Moore, R.E., & Struening, E. (1994). Lifetime and five-year prevalence of homelessness in the United States. *American Journal of Public Health, 84*, 1907–1912.

Lu, S.N., Jiang D.D., Liu, J.W., Lin, M.C., Chen, C.L., Su, I.J., & Chen, S.S. (2005). Outbreak of severe acute respiratory syndrome in southern Taiwan, 2003. *American Journal of Tropical Medicine & Hygiene, 73*, 423–427.

Lurie, N., Ward, N.B., Shapiro, M.F., & Brook, R.H. (1984). Termination from Medi-Cal: Does it affect health? *New England Journal of Medicine, 311*, 480–484.

Lurie, N., Ward, N.B., Shapiro, M.F., Gallego, C., Vaghaiwalla, R., & Brook, R.H. (1986). Termination of medical benefits: A follow-up study one year later. *New England Journal of Medicine, 314,* 1266–1268.

Lurie, P., & Drucker, E. (1997). An opportunity lost: HIV infections associated with lack of a national needle-exchange programme in the USA. *The Lancet, 349,* 604–608.

Lynch, J.W., Kaplan, G.A., & Shema, S.J. (1997). Cumulative impact of sustained economic hardship on physical, cognitive, psychological, and social functioning. *New England Journal of Medicine, 337,* 1889–1895.

Marmot, M., Bobak, M., & Smith, G.D. (1995). Explanations for social inequalities in health. In B.C. Amick III, S. Levine, A.R. Tarlov, & D.C. Walsh (Eds.), *Society and health* (pp. 172–210). New York, NY: Oxford University Press.

Marmot, M.G. (1982). Socioeconomic and cultural factors in ischemic heart disease. *Advances in Cardiology, 29,* 68–76.

McCord, C., & Freeman, H.P. (1990). Excess mortality in Harlem. *New England Journal of Medicine, 332,* 173–178.

McDonough, P., Duncan, G.J., William, D., & House, J. (1997). Income dynamics and adult mortality in the United States, 1972 through 1898. *American Journal of Public Health, 87,* 1476–1483.

Mercy, J.A., & Houk, V.N. (1988). Firearm injuries: A call for science. *New England Journal of Medicine, 319,* 1283–1285.

Meyers, A.F., Sampson, A.E., Weitzman, M., Rogers, B.L., & Kayne, H. (1989). School Breakfast Program and school performance. *American Journal of Diseases of Children, 143,* 1234–1239.

Mokdad, A.H., Marks, J.S., Stroup D.F., & Gerberding, J.L. (2004). Actual causes of death in the United States, 2000. *Journal of the American Medical Association, 291,* 1238–1245.

Mokdad, A.H., Marks, J.S., Stroup D.F., & Gerberding, J.L. (2005). Correction: Actual causes of death in the United States, 2000. *Journal of the American Medical Association, 293,* 293–294.

Morris, J.N. (1979). Social inequalities undiminished. *The Lancet, 1,* 87–90.

Morris, J.N. (1982). Epidemiology and prevention. *Milbank Memorial Fund Quarterly, Health and Society, 60,* 1–16.

Moss, N. (1997). Editorial: The body politic and the power of socioeconomic status. *American Journal of Public Health, 87,* 1411–1413.

National Center for Health Statistics. (1997). *Health, United States, 1996–97, and injury chartbook* (DHHS Publication No. PHS 97–1232). Hyattsville, MD: U.S. Department of Health and Human Services, Centers for Disease Control and Prevention.

National Center for Health Statistics. (2009). *Health, United States, 2008: With chartbook.* Hyattsville, MD: U.S. Department of Health and Human Services, Centers for Disease Control and Prevention.

National Center for Health Statistics. (2011). *Health, United States, 2010: With special feature on death and dying.* Hyattsville, MD: U.S. Department of Health and Human Services, Centers for Disease Control and Prevention.

National Research Council. (1998). *Health effects of exposure to radon: BEIR VI.* Washington, DC: National Academy of Sciences, National Research Council, Committee on the Biological Effects of Ionizing Radiation (BEIR VI), Committee on Health Risks of Exposure to Radon.

Navarro, V. (1997). Topics for our times: The "Black Report" of Spain—The Commission of Social Inequalities in Health. *American Journal of Public Health, 87,* 334–335.

Pappas, G., Queen, S., Hadden, W., & Fisher, G. (1993). The increasing disparity in mortality between socioeconomic groups in the United States, 1960 and 1986. *New England Journal of Medicine, 329,* 103–109.

Parry, J. (2005). WHO launches "plan of war" to tackle avian flu. *British Medical Journal, 331,* 70.

Patrick, D.L., & Wickizer, T.M. (1995). Community and health. In B.C. Amick III, S. Levine, A.R. Tarlov, & D.C. Walsh (Eds.), *Society and health* (pp. 46–92). New York, NY: Oxford University Press.

Pilisuk, M., & Minkler, M. (1985, Winter). Social support: Economic and political considerations. *Social Policy, 15*(3), 6–11.

Platts-Mills, T.A.E., & Carter, M.C. (1997). Asthma and indoor exposure to allergens. *New England Journal of Medicine, 336,* 1382–1384.

Pollitt, E., Gersovitz, M., & Garginlo, M. (1978). Educational benefits of the United States school feeding program: A critical review of the literature. *American Journal of Public Health, 68,* 477–481.

Power, C., Hertzman, C., Matthews, S., & Manor, O. (1997). Social differences in health: Life cycle effects between ages 23 and 33 in the 1958 British birth cohort. *American Journal of Public Health, 87,* 1499–1503.

Retchin, S.M., Brown, R.S., Yeh, S.J., Chu, D., & Moreno, L. (1997). Outcomes of stroke patients in Medicare fee for service and managed care. *Journal of the American Medical Association, 278,* 119–124.

Reuters Health. (2000, September 7). *Nation faces an environmental health gap.* New York, NY: Author.

Robertson, M.J., Zlotnick, C., & Westerfelt, A. (1997). Drug use disorders and treatment contact among homeless adults in Alameda County. *American Journal of Public Health, 87,* 221–228.

Rose, D., & Oliveira, V. (1997). Nutrient intakes of individuals from food-insufficient households in the United States. *American Journal of Public Health, 87,* 1956–1961.

Rose, G., & Marmot, M.G. (1981). Social class and coronary heart disease. *British Heart Journal, 45,* 13–19.

Rosenberg, M.L., Powell, K.E., & Hammond, R. (1997). Applying science to violence prevention. *Journal of the American Medical Association, 277,* 1641–1642.

Rosenstreich, D.L., Eggleston, P., Kattan, M., Baker, D., Slavin, R.G., Gergen, P., . . . Malveaux, F. (1997). The role of cockroach allergy and exposure to cockroach allergen in causing morbidity among inner-city children with asthma. *New England Journal of Medicine, 336,* 1356–1363.

Salonen, J.T. (1982). Socioeconomic status and risk of cancer, cerebral stroke, and death due to coronary heart disease and any disease: A longitudinal study in eastern Finland. *Journal of Epidemiology and Community Health, 36,* 294–297.

Satcher, D. (1996). CDC's first 50 years: Lessons learned and relearned. *American Journal of Public Health, 86,* 1705–1708.

Schorr, L.B. (1989). *Within our reach: Breaking the cycle of disadvantage.* New York, NY: Anchor Books.

Shaugnessy, P., Schlenker, R.E., & Hittle, D.F. (1994). Home health care outcomes under capitated and fee-for-service payment. *Health Care Financing Review, 16*, 187–222.

Sidel, V.W. (1997). Annotation: The public health impact of hunger. *American Journal of Public Health, 87*, 1921–1922.

Slater, C., & Carlton, B. (1985). Behavior, lifestyle, and socioeconomic variables as determinants of health status: Implications for health policy development. *American Journal of Preventive Medicine, 14*, 372–378.

Slater, C.H., Lorimor, R.J., & Lairson, D.R. (1985). The independent contributions of socioeconomic status and health practices to health status. *Preventive Medicine, 14*, 372–378.

Smith, A.H., Hopenhayn-Rich, C., Bates, M.N., Goeden, H.M., Hert-Picciotto, I., Duggan, M.H., . . . Smith, M.T. (1992). Cancer risks from arsenic in drinking water. *Environmental Health Perspectives, 97*, 259–267.

Smith, R. (1987). *Unemployment and health*. London, England: Oxford University Press.

Stockwell, E.G. (1961). Socioeconomic status and mortality in the United States. *Public Health Reports, 76*, 1081–1086.

Susser, M., Watson, W., & Hopper, K. (1985). *Sociology in medicine* (3rd ed.). Oxford, England: Oxford University Press.

Syme, S.L., & Berkman, L.F. (1976). Social class, susceptibility and sickness. *American Journal of Epidemiology, 104*, 1–8.

Sytkowski, P.A., Kannel, W.B., & D'Agostino, R.B. (1990). Changes in risk factors and the decline in mortality from cardiovascular disease: The Framingham Heart Study. *New England Journal of Medicine, 332*, 1635–1641.

Taubes, G. (1992). Violence epidemiologists test the hazards of gun ownership. *Science, 258*, 215.

Tesh, S.N. (1994). Hidden arguments: Political ideology and disease prevention policy. In H.D. Schwartz (Ed.), *Dominant issues in medical sociology* (3rd ed., pp. 519–529). New York, NY: McGraw-Hill.

Townsend, P., & Davidson, N. (1982). *Inequalities in health: The Black Report*. Hamondsworth, England: Penguin.

Urban Institute. (2002). *Preventing homelessness: Meeting the challenge*. Retrieved March 21, 2012, from http://www.urban.org/url.cfm?ID=900475

U.S. Bureau of the Census. (1990). 1990 Census of population and housing. Table P57. Educational attainment, persons 25 years and over. 1990 Summary Tape File 3 (STF 3). Washington, DC: Author. Retrieved March 21, 2012, from http://www.census.gov/main/www/cen1990.html

U.S. Bureau of the Census. (2000a). Census 2000. Table P37. Sex by educational attainment for the population 25 years and over. Census 2000 Summary File 3 (SF 3). Washington, DC: Author. Retrieved March 21, 2012, from http://www.census.gov/main/www/cen2000.html

U.S. Bureau of the Census. (2000b). Census 2000. Table P88. Ratio of income in 1999 to poverty level. Census 2000 Summary File 3 (SF 3). Washington, DC: Author. Retrieved March 21, 2012, from http://www.census.gov/main/www/cen2000.html

U.S. Bureau of the Census. (2010a). Educational attainment in the United States: 2010. Detailed tables. Table 1. Washington, DC: Author. Retrieved March 21, 2012, from http://2010.census.gov/2010census/data/

U.S. Bureau of the Census. (2010b). Current population survey: Annual social and economic (ASEC) supplement survey, 2010. Washington, DC: Author. Retrieved March 21, 2012, from http://www.census.gov/hhes/www/poverty/data/incpovhlth/2010/index.html

U.S. Department of Agriculture. (2011). *Food security in the United States.* Retrieved March 21, 2012, from http://www.ers.usda.gov/Briefing/foodsecurity/

U.S. Department of Education. (1994, April). *The reading report card. 1971–88.* Washington, DC: U.S. Department of Education, National Center for Education Statistics, National Assessment of Educational Progress.

U.S. Department of Education. (2002, April). *Adult literacy in America: A first look at the findings of the National Adult Literacy Survey.* Retrieved March 21, 2012, from http://nces.ed.gov/pubs93/93275.pdf

U.S. Department of Health and Human Services. (1995). *Healthy people 2000: Midcourse review and 1995 revisions.* Washington, DC: U.S. Department of Health and Human Services, Public Health Service.

U.S. Department of Health and Human Services. (2010). *Full text of the affordable care act.* Washington, DC: Author. Retrieved March 21, 2012, from http://www.healthcare.gov

U.S. Department of Justice. (2009). *Crime in the United States 2009: Uniform crime reports.* Retrieved March 21, 2012, from http://www2.fbi.gov/ucr/cius2009/offenses/violent_crime/index.html

U.S. Department of Labor. (1997). *Employment and earnings.* Washington, DC: U.S. Department of Labor, Bureau of Labor Statistics.

U.S. Department of Labor. (2010). *Labor force characteristics by race and ethnicity, 2009.* Washington, DC: U. S. Department of Labor, Bureau of Labor Statistics.

U.S. Environmental Protection Agency. (1992). *A citizen's guide to radon* (2nd ed.). Washington, DC: Author.

Ware, J.E., Jr., Bayliss, M.S., Rogers, W.H., Kosinski, M., & Tarlov, A.R. (1996). Differences in 4-year health outcomes for elderly and poor, chronically ill patients treated in HMO and fee-for-service systems. Results from the Medical Outcomes Study. *Journal of the American Medical Association, 276,* 1039–1047.

Wehler, C.A., Scott, R.I., Anderson, J.J., Summer, L., & Parker, L. (1995). *Community childhood hunger identification project: A survey of childhood hunger in the United States.* Washington, DC: Food Research and Action Center.

Weissman, J.S., & Epstein, A.M. (1994). *Falling through the safety net: The impact of insurance on access to care.* Baltimore, MD: Johns Hopkins University Press.

Wells, A.J. (1988). An estimate of adult mortality in the United States from passive smoking. *Environment International, 14,* 249–265.

Wenneker, M.B., & Epstein, A.M. (1989). Racial inequalities in the use of procedures for patients with ischemic heart disease in Massachusetts. *Journal of the American Medical Association, 261,* 253–257.

Wiley, J.A., & Camacho, T.C. (1980). Life-style and future health: Evidence from the Alameda County Study. *Preventive Medicine, 9,* 1–21.

Wilkinson, R.G. (1990). Income distribution and mortality: A "natural" experiment. *Sociology of Health and illness, 12,* 391–412.

Wilkinson, R.G. (1992). Income distribution and life expectancy. *British Medical Journal, 304,* 163–168.

Wilkinson, R.G. (1997). Comment: Income, inequality, and social cohesion. *American Journal of Public Health, 87,* 1504–1506.

Yeracaris, C.A., & Kim, J.H. (1978). Socioeconomic differentials in selected causes of death. *American Journal of Public Health, 68,* 432–451.

Yergan, J., Flood, A.N., LoGerfo, J.P., & Diehr, P. (1987). Relationship between patient race and the intensity of hospital services. *Medical Care, 25,* 592–603.

Zahran, H.S., Kobau, R., Moriarty, D.G., Zack, M.M., Holt, J., & Donehoo, R. (2005). Health-related quality of life-surveillance—United States, 1993–2002. *MMWR Surveillance Summaries, 54*(SS-4), 1–36.

Zaidi, S.A. (1988). Poverty and disease: Need for structural change. *Social Science and Medicine, 27,* 119–127.

2

Emerging Threats to the Survival of Public Health

The survival of public health as a societal institution is threatened by emerging changes in the health care delivery system, the economy, the political climate, the public sentiment regarding public health and government in general, and the public health community itself. First, a misunderstanding of the relative importance of individual medical treatment compared with population-based prevention programs has led to a health system in which individual treatment rather than societal prevention is the dominant focus. This misunderstanding has fostered the illusion that health care reform is the solution to the nation's public health crises and that integration of public health into managed care represents an important area of focus for public health. As a consequence, public health practitioners have been sidetracked from their mission as agents for social change. Also, political and economic forces directly threaten funding for public health departments and their policies and programs. These factors include budget cuts, a misplaced emphasis on bioterrorism preparedness, the increasing influence of special interest groups, and the increasing antiregulatory sentiment in the nation. The greatest threat to the survival of the public's health, however, comes from within the public health movement itself. The public health community has lost a unified vision of its fundamental role and mission. To overcome these threats, the public health movement must rediscover a strong, unifying model with a common vision, mission, and values to which the public and policymakers can relate. It is not enough to promote the health of its constituents: The public health movement must now promote its own survival.

Unfortunately, the attention of the public health practitioner cannot be focused entirely on improving the health of the public, because the public's health is only one thing the public health practitioner must save. Emerging changes in the health care delivery system, the economy, the political climate, public sentiment regarding government, and changes in the public health community itself now threaten the very survival of public health as a societal institution. In addition to promoting the health of constituents, public health must now find a way to promote its own survival.

The survival of public health as a societal institution is threatened because of the adverse consequences of three major factors: (1) the persistent emphasis on individual rather than societal health and on treatment rather than prevention, (2) economic and political factors that directly threaten public health funding, and (3) the loss, among public health practitioners, of a unified vision of the role and mission of public health.

■ MISUNDERSTANDING OF THE IMPORTANCE OF MEDICAL TREATMENT COMPARED WITH POPULATION-BASED PREVENTION

Despite the widely held perception that recent advances in medical treatment have resulted in a dramatic decline in mortality, there is substantial evidence that the observed decline in mortality in the developed world during the 18th to 20th centuries was attributable largely to public health and not medical interventions (Evans, Barer, & Marmor, 1994; Lee & Estes, 1997; Levine, Feldman, & Elison, 1983; Turnock, 1997). The most extensive research into this hypothesis was conducted by Thomas McKeown, a physician and historical demographer who, over the course of more than 20 years, developed a convincing analysis of the reasons for mortality declines observed in England and Wales during the past three centuries (McKeown, 1971, 1976, 1978; McKeown, Record, & Turner, 1975).

McKeown concluded that declines in mortality observed during the 18th century were due to environmental changes, such as purification of water, efficient sewage disposal, and improved food, hygiene, and nutrition (McKeown, 1978). During the 19th century, McKeown argued, the declines in mortality were due only to a reduction in infectious diseases; chronic disease rates remained stable (McKeown et al., 1975). According to McKeown and colleagues, the three major factors that contributed to the decline were (1) rising standards of living, (2) improved hygiene, and (3) improved nutrition (McKeown et al., 1975). Although the smallpox vaccination campaign was effective, McKeown attributed only 5% of the decline in mortality in the latter half of the 19th century to immunization. McKeown argued that declines in infectious disease rates account for about 75% of the mortality reductions observed during the 20th century (through 1971; McKeown et al., 1975). Although immunization played a limited role, the dominant factors in the control of infectious disease were improved nutrition and hygiene (McKeown et al., 1975).

In research on the reasons for the dramatic decline in mortality in the United States during the 20th century, John and Sonja McKinlay

(1977, 1994) found that no more than 4% of the observed decline was due to medical treatment for infectious diseases. This conclusion is supported by the work of Rene Dubos (1959) and others (Cassel, 1976; Kass, 1971; Leavitt & Numbers, 1994; Lee & Estes, 1997; Magill, 1955; Powles, 1973; Weinstein, 1974). The U.S. Public Health Service (1995) estimated that of the 30 years added to life expectancy since 1900, only 5 years are due to improvements in clinical medicine, whereas 25 years are attributable to population-based, public health programs. McKinlay and McKinlay (1994) also demonstrated that the steep decline in mortality between 1900 and 1950 slowed during the 1950s and leveled off during the 1960s. This was the precise period in which medical care expenditures skyrocketed. Increased spending for medical care does not necessarily translate into reduced mortality (Hingson et al., 1981; Kim & Moody, 1992).

The work of McKeown, McKinlay and McKinlay, and others helped to reveal a shift in the 20th century in the type of diseases most responsible for mortality. The shift—known as the epidemiologic transition—was from infectious diseases to chronic diseases as the dominant cause of death in developed countries (Omran, 1971). Whereas infectious diseases accounted for 40% of total mortality in the United States in 1900, they accounted for only 6% of mortality in 1973 (McKinlay & McKinlay, 1994). The proportion of total mortality attributable to chronic diseases (including injuries) increased form 20% to 67% during the same period.

The U.S. Department of Health and Human Services (USDHHS) estimated that approximately 75% of all premature deaths in the nation are preventable (Centers for Disease Control and Prevention [CDC], 1995; USDHHS, 1995). Of these, about 63% could have been avoided by changes in individual behavior and another 23% by changes in social and environmental conditions. Only 15% of these deaths were deemed preventable through improved access to medical care.

As McKinlay and McKinlay (1994) pointed out, the policy implications of the hypothesis that public health measures, not medical treatment, are the dominant reason for improvements in the health of the population are profound. If this perspective is accurate, then the critical strategy to achieve meaningful health reform is not the better provision of more organized, higher quality, lower cost medical services but the societal commitment to social change. Preventing disease and illness requires changing the conditions in which people live, improving the quality of the environment, and reforming public policy. As Tesh argued, "it appears that social and political events that affect the standard of living, rather than microorganisms, are the salient determinants of health and disease" (1994, p. 520). Nevertheless, the current view of disease prevention continues to rely on germ theory and lifestyle theory as the explanation for illness. The most prominent public health programs aim to control infectious disease and change individual behavior. "Changing the physical environment is, from this perspective, a third choice, and to attack poverty as a way to reduce disease becomes a last resort" (Tesh, 1994, p. 521).

The observed shift in causes of mortality from infectious to chronic diseases has similar implications for the improvement of the public's health. Because chronic disease is largely related to individual and societal behavior, social conditions, and social policy, public health must inherently be committed to social change. Medical care is certainly important, and recent evidence (Ford et al., 2007) suggests that some of the modern medical interventions for atherosclerotic heart disease may explain declines in heart disease mortality during the past five decades. However, the most substantial gains in human health will be achieved only through public health—that is, the societal institution whose mission is the promotion of social change.

Even if the ultimate aim of prevention programs is to change individual behavior, the physical, social, and political environment in which people live must be the primary level of intervention. Because behavior is a product of the social conditions and social norms of the community in which a person lives (Tesh, 1994), discussing lifestyle changes without discussing the social conditions that give rise to them is misleading (Berliner, 1977). Public health practitioners cannot ignore the decades of research demonstrating that lower social class, social deprivation, and lack of social support are among the most important determinants of health (Conrad, 1987; Morris, 1982; Syme & Berkman, 1976). Substantial and sustained improvement in public health will require, first and foremost, social change.

The challenge to public health is presented clearly in a 1994 article by David Mechanic, who wrote, "The determinants of health risks are far too complex and forceful to succumb to ordinary efforts to inform the public and change its practices. Effective health promotion requires a deeper scrutiny of the structure of communities and the routine activities of everyday life, as well as stronger interventions than those characteristic of much that goes on. Current efforts still function largely at the margins" (Mechanic, 1994, p. 569).

An additional reason that prevention rather than treatment of illness must form the core of a national public health strategy is that advances in medical treatment tend to disproportionately benefit the socioeconomically advantaged and, consequently, increase the disparity in health status between rich and poor Americans. Dutton (1994) argued that the gap between health status of higher and lower socioeconomic classes is only partly due to differences in access to medical care:

But much of the gap undoubtedly stems from a variety of nonmedical factors, including a hazardous environment, unsafe and unrewarding work, poor nutrition, lack of social support, and, perhaps most important of all, the psychological and emotional stress of being poor and feeling powerless to do anything about it. . . . To be efficient as well as effective, health care must remedy not only the consequences of poverty, but must aid in efforts to change the underlying circumstances that perpetuate it. This is the most fundamental form of disease prevention, and perhaps ultimately the only truly effective one. (p. 479)

Foege, Amler, and White (1985) also emphasized the importance of disease prevention in closing the gap in health disparity between rich and poor.

The government's spending priorities, however, do not reflect the importance of preventive public health measures compared with the limited effect of medical treatment on the health status of the population (CDC, 1997; Eilbert et al., 1996; Eilbert et al., 1997; McGinnis, 1997; Public Health Foundation, 1994). In 2008, national health care expenditures totaled $2.24 trillion, or approximately $7,700 per person (National Center for Health Statistics [NCHS], 2011). In the same year, total public health expenditures were estimated to be $69.4 billion, only 3% of all national health care expenditures (NCHS, 2011). This means the nation spends about $32 for medical treatment for each $1 spent on the primary prevention of disease. And these figures include individual medical services provided by public health agencies; the actual investment in preventive, population-based public health programs is substantially lower.

Although health care spending continues to skyrocket, funding for preventive public health measures is barely keeping pace with inflation. The U.S. Public Health Service (1995) estimated that although total U.S. health expenditures increased by more than 210% between 1981 and 1993, the proportion of these expenditures used for population-based public health measures declined by 25%. Between 1999 and 2002, the proportion of total national health expenditures devoted to public health programs declined from 3.6% to 3.0% (NCHS, 2011).

The societal focus on individual-level treatment rather than population-based prevention interventions is reflected not only by the nation's spending priorities but by the issues that dominate the national health agenda. Perhaps the two best examples of this are the inappropriate attention given to health care reform and to integration of public health into managed care as potential solutions to the nation's public health crisis. It is a widespread fallacy that health care reform can solve many of the nation's public health problems. An equal inaccuracy holds that managed care organizations present a great opportunity for public health advancement. Each of these fallacies represents a direct threat to public health practice in this country because they are sidetracking the public, policymakers, and, most importantly, public health practitioners from the vital need to focus on social change as the vehicle to achieve societal improvement in health.

■ ILLUSION OF HEALTH CARE REFORM AS A SOLUTION TO THE PUBLIC HEALTH CRISIS

The health care reform debate in the United States is dominated by arguments over health care delivery and reimbursement methods for medical care, not by arguments about how to deliver adequate, population-based prevention programs and policies to the American people. Therefore, the debate is hardly pertinent when determining how to improve the public's health. "In spite of the evidence pointing to deficiencies in health-supporting milieus, resulting in damage that had to be remedied by health care, by the 1990s the health policy debate—in the United States and other countries—had moved to an almost exclusively economic argument about health care services, as though these considerations alone were pertinent to better health" (Milio, 1995, p. 98). Addressing the implications of the health care reform discussion, Miller (1995) suggested the following: "The most disturbing conclusion is that current proposals are about financing, not about health care. . . . Consequently, health 'reform' is mainly about money and somewhat less about the organization of health services, and is not about broad, preventive measures that would reduce illness and injury and improve health functioning" (p. 356).

This country's failure to consider the real health care crisis and its inappropriate focus on one small aspect of the problem as the solution to the whole problem could spell doom for public health. If public and legislative debate continues to dwell on reforming the method of reimbursing physicians and hospitals, rather than on the method for ensuring the societal conditions in which people can be healthy, then the field of public health will be lost amid the complexities and conflicts of public debate.

■ ILLUSION OF MANAGED CARE AS AN OPPORTUNITY FOR PUBLIC HEALTH

Since the emergence of managed care, the field of public health has become preoccupied with it and its implications for the public's health. Managed care has dominated the agendas of major public health conferences, scientific journals, and policy debates. The emphasis on managed care's implications for the public's health is appropriate, given the research indicating the adverse consequences of managed care on medical services and outcomes, especially for the poor, the disadvantaged, the elderly, and the chronically ill (Anders, 1996; Bickman, 1996; Brown et al., 1993; Clement et al., 1994; Experton et al., 1997; Miller & Luft, 1994; Retchin & Brown, 1991; Retchin et al., 1997; Retchin & Preston, 1991; Shaughnessy, Schlenker, & Hittle, 1994; Ware et al., 1996; Webster & Feinglass, 1997; Wickizer, Lessler, & Travis, 1996).

However, some public health practitioners have suggested that managed care presents tremendous opportunities for the advancement of public health goals. Although efforts to integrate some aspects of public health into managed care systems certainly are important, they cannot and should not substitute for the basic effort to strengthen and preserve public health's independent role and independent infrastructure. The practitioner should not mistakenly believe managed care can be changed in a way that will allow public health to be practiced correctly. Why? Because public health and managed care are fundamentally different in their overall mission, their underlying values, and their primary goals and incentives.

Overall Mission

Managed care is simply a system of sick care delivery. But the delivery of sick care is only a small subset of public health practice. As the Institute of Medicine (1988) defined it, the mission of public health is to fulfill "society's interest in assuring conditions in which people can be healthy" (p. 7). Access to quality health care certainly is necessary to ensure conditions in which people can be healthy, but it takes more than medical care to ensure that people are truly healthy.

Creating conditions in which people can be healthy requires social change: improving the communities' infrastructure, restructuring the physical and social environments to promote healthy behaviors, and establishing social norms that support, rather than undermine, healthy behaviors. Ensuring that people are truly healthy requires the elimination of social, economic, and political barriers to an individual's ability to achieve fulfillment in his or her personal development, education, occupation, and family well-being. None of these requirements can be achieved solely through a health care system, even under ideal conditions. The best managed care could ensure only the public's access to quality health care, not the quality of the public's health.

As Keck (1992) explained, there is a basic philosophical difference in the fundamental questions that managed care and public health seek to answer. Although managed care asks "how do we pay for services?", public health asks "how do we maintain and restore health?" (p. 1208).

Underlying Values

The underlying values of managed care are inconsistent with those of public health. Public health is based on the principle of social justice: the assertion that society has an inherent interest in ensuring a basic level of well-being for all people, regardless of their age, race, income, social status, or health status. Managed care, especially when practiced in a for-profit environment, tends toward social injustice. Although the system works well for people who are healthy, it is relatively unfair to the sickest and poorest individuals, who are generally those who need the most intensive intervention. The system of market justice, on which managed care is based, tends to produce inequalities in social, economic, and health status.

Managed care plans step back from the individual patient and allocate resources among their patient pools. The role of public health, however, is to step back even farther and allocate public health resources among the entire population. Because of the disparities in health status, risk factors, and social and environmental conditions between different population subgroups, this means spending large amounts of money for people who are living in poverty, in the inner city, and in disadvantaged communities. This public health reality is incompatible with the mission of managed care: to reduce and control health care costs. Under managed care, people living in poverty cannot possibly receive the intensive intervention that is required.

The USDHHS (2010), in its *Healthy People 2020* goals for the nation, called for public health efforts to eliminate health disparities between advantaged and disadvantaged population groups. However, the managed care system tends to increase the disparity in health status between low- and high-income groups. Because managed care was developed to reduce health care spending and the groups that require the most expensive health care are the poor, the elderly, the disabled, and the chronically, terminally, and mentally ill, it is these groups that tend to face a disproportionate burden of the reduction in health care spending.

Primary Goals and Incentives

The bottom line for managed care organizations is controlling medical costs for their overall patient pool, not providing the services that are in the best interests of individual patients. This is a basic, practical dilemma that cannot be overcome in a for-profit, managed care environment. Dr. Jerome Kassirer (1995b), former editor of the *New England Journal of Medicine*, noted in a 1995 editorial that "although many see this as an abstract dilemma, I believe that increasingly the struggle will be more concrete and stark: physicians will be forced to choose between the best interests of their patients and their own economic survival" (p. 50). The best interests of the public's health cannot be served under a system in which quarterly earnings and shareholder value are critical concerns.

The conflict between the need to control costs and maintain corporate profit and the goal of improving the public's health is illustrated by the way in which health maintenance organizations (HMOs) use the cost savings generated by their practices. In 1994, publicly traded HMOs spent only about 75% of their patients' premiums on direct patient care (Anders, 1996). The remainder was used for executive salaries, marketing, administrative costs, retained earnings, stockholder payouts, and acquisition of other HMOs. In for-profit HMOs, the health of the public is not, and will not ever be, the chief concern. Government and nonprofit health agencies and organizations are unique in having improvement of public health as their primary charge.

Managed care and public health also conflict in terms of their inherent incentives to offer expensive prevention initiatives. Attempts to encourage HMOs to enhance and expand prevention programs have generally been unsuccessful; HMOs do not appear to be interested in long-term benefits to their patients because those patients remain in a specific health plan for only a few years. Denying treatment (i.e., not expanding prevention programs) is the most effective way to increase short-term profits (Mallozzi, 1996). In contrast, prevention initiatives offer public health agencies and organizations the most effective strategies to achieve their goals of improving the societal conditions that affect health.

As long as HMOs are accountable primarily to their shareholders rather than to their patients, their providers, and their communities as a whole, the best interests of the public's health cannot be served. Investors generally want to see a return on their investments in a relatively short time period. For this reason, for-profit HMOs will always weigh short-term gains more heavily than intensive and costly preventive interventions whose payoff is in the distant future. For example, paying for intensive psychotherapy for youths with severe emotional problems might destroy an HMO's profit margin in the short term; the fact that this early intervention may prevent severe psychopathology many years in the future is of little interest to most investors. These types of interventions, however, are essential to promote public health effectively.

The public health view is long term; social change takes many years, sometimes even decades. Programs must be administered repeatedly, consistently, and over a long period of time before the necessary changes in social conditions, norms, behavior, and policy can take place. The quarterly report framework that managed care uses for program evaluation and decision making is inappropriate for practicing public health.

Why an Emphasis on Managed Care Is Dangerous for Public Health

Because public health and managed care differ fundamentally in almost every basic premise, it is unrealistic to believe that major public health achievements can be attained through the managed care system. Managed care is simply a method for the delivery and reimbursement of sick care; it cannot ever be a societal effort to create and facilitate social change. Managed care represents a threat to the survival of public health precisely because practitioners believe they can integrate public health initiatives into the managed care system. The institution that is charged with marketing social change—public health—must remain independent of managed care and must retain its focus on its fundamental mission.

Although there is pressure for public health agencies to become involved in efforts to add a more preventive focus to managed care, public health practitioners must not become so sidetracked by managed care that they lose sight of the real area in which the health of the population depends: stimulating social change for the population, not simply improving health care for the individual. To survive, public health must find, claim, and maintain its place as a societal institution outside the managed care system. Only external to this system of health care delivery can the mission of public health be accomplished. And by sidetracking public health practitioners from the real issue at hand—the need to create and facilitate social change—the present preoccupation with finding ways to realize some marginal benefits from convincing managed care corporations to incorporate some public health programs is threatening to erode the practice of public health.

■ POLITICAL AND ECONOMIC FACTORS THAT DIRECTLY THREATEN PUBLIC HEALTH FUNDING

Budget Crises

Although funding cuts for public health programs have plagued government agencies for at least two decades, unprecedented measures to reduce or eliminate many of the critical public health functions of government have emerged due to federal and state budget crises during recent years. Funding for statewide tobacco control programs provides an excellent illustration of this dangerous trend. Despite tremendous success in reducing cigarette smoking as well as public exposure to secondhand smoke (Siegel, 2002), funding for a state tobacco prevention program in Massachusetts was cut by 95%, from a high of approximately $54 million per year to just $2.5 million in fiscal year 2004 (Campaign for Tobacco-Free Kids, 2005b). In spite of unprecedented declines in youth smoking attributable to an aggressive antismoking media campaign in Florida (Bauer et al., 2000; Siegel, 2002), the Florida legislature and governor cut funding for the program in every year since 1998 (the program's inception) and essentially eliminated the program in 2003 (Campaign for Tobacco-Free Kids, 2005b). In Minnesota, a successful youth-directed smoking prevention marketing campaign was eliminated completely in 2003, accompanied by an 81% cut in overall state tobacco control program funding (Campaign for Tobacco-Free Kids, 2005b). The elimination of the Target Market program in Minnesota was demonstrated to have resulted in a significant increase in youth susceptibility to cigarette smoking (CDC, 2004).

In November 1998, the signing of a multistate settlement between Attorneys General in 46 states and the major tobacco companies resulted in the availability of $246 billion to these states over 25 years, sufficient to fund smoking prevention programs in every state. However, largely due to state budget crises, as of fiscal year 2006, only four states were using this money to fund tobacco prevention programs at the minimum level recommended by the CDC (Campaign for Tobacco-Free Kids, 2005a). Overall, states were allocating only 2.6% of their tobacco revenue in fiscal year 2006 to tobacco prevention and cessation programs (Campaign for Tobacco-Free Kids, 2005a).

Overall, state spending for public health has been an equally dismal failure, especially in light of the infusion of $1.8 billion of federal money into state public health preparedness after the bioterrorism fears instilled by the September 11, 2001, tragedy and subsequent anthrax attacks (Trust for America's Health, 2003). Despite this infusion of federal funding, nearly two-thirds of states cut funds to public health programs from fiscal year 2002 to 2003 (Trust for America's Health, 2003). During 2003, states reportedly faced a collective budget deficit of $66.6 billion; this may help explain why only 18 states were able to maintain their funding of public health services from 2002 to 2003 (Trust for America's Health, 2003).

These decreases in public health funding call into question both the ability of states to fight the chronic disease epidemic and their ability to prepare for bioterrorism, emerging infectious diseases, or other public health emergencies. A review of the preparedness of state health departments after the receipt of $1.8 billion of federal funds (Trust for America's Health, 2003) revealed that states were not only ill-prepared for a public health emergency but for routine disease prevention activities as well:

> Many state health departments are losing resources, and, therefore, capacity. Yet health departments are being called upon to expand their traditional scope to include preventing and preparing for bioterrorism, as well as responding to emerging infectious diseases, such as West Nile virus. The technical capabilities of many state and local health departments are being stretched to the point that emergency response and disease prevention services are in jeopardy. Although the states have received $1.8 billion in federal preparedness funds, many have cut their own spending on public health services. Consequently, there is evidence that the impact of the federal funds to help states has been diluted. (p. 13)

It is clear that a substantial number of states have used the availability of increased federal funding for public health as an excuse to cut their own funding for public health and divert that money to meet other budget needs, resulting in a net decrease, not increase, in overall public health funding. To make matters worse, much of the existing funding has been earmarked for the newly needed programs in bioterrorism and emergency preparedness, meaning that basic chronic disease prevention programs are being sacrificed.

New and Perceived Public Health Threats: Bioterrorism and Emerging Infectious Diseases

The threat of bioterrorism and emerging infectious diseases has certainly increased attention to public health preparedness. However, there has also been a negative impact of this shift in focus: namely, some degree of decreased attention to existing chronic disease threats. As discussed above, despite the federal infusion of $1.8 billion into state public health funding in fiscal years 2002 and 2003 in response to bioterrorism threats, nearly two-thirds of states cut overall funding for public health programs. With much of the money earmarked for bioterrorism and other aspects of public health preparedness, funding for existing public health threats— largely, chronic diseases—has actually declined.

According to the Trust for America's Health (2003), the focus on bioterrorism, especially on a possible smallpox terrorist threat, diverted resources away from other critical public health services:

> Achieving a battle-ready public health defense at the federal, state and local levels will take many years of sustained commitment, fund- ing and oversight, especially because over the past two decades, the nation's public health infrastructure has greatly deteriorated. Initially, Congress, HHS and CDC narrowly focused the federal preparedness investment on bioterrorism concerns. Last year's controversial small- pox vaccination initiative, which pulled valuable time, resources and staffing away from other critical public health functions, illustrates the pitfalls of over-emphasizing a single threat (p. 27).

A number of researchers have written that bioterrorism preparedness itself has wasted public health resources without benefit and has diverted funding from essential public health needs (Cohen, Gould, & Sidel, 2004; Dowling & Lipton, 2005; Sidel, Cohen, & Gould, 2005). Although many predicted that bioterrorism funding would strengthen public health infrastructure by bringing funding not only for bioterrorism but also for other functions of public health, this has not come to fruition. Instead, bio- terrorism preparedness has shifted priorities and weakened the public health infrastructure and its ability to deal with real and existing threats (Cohen et al., 2004). In fact, Cohen et al. (2004) go so far as to suggest that bioterror- ism preparedness has been a disaster for public health, squandering public health resources and diverting them away from real public health needs.

Cohen et al. (2004) concluded that "Massive campaigns focusing on 'bioterrorism preparedness' have had adverse health consequences and have resulted in the diversion of essential public health personnel, facilities, and other resources from urgent, real public health needs" (p. 1667). "In short, bioterrorism preparedness programs have been a disaster for public health. Instead of leading to more resources for dealing with natural disease as had been promised, there are now fewer such resources. Worse, in response to bioterrorism preparedness, public health institutions and procedures are being reorganized along a military or police model that subverts the relationships between public health providers and the communities they serve" (p. 1669). Thus, not only has the perceived need for bioterrorism preparedness diverted public health resources, it has also adversely affected the organization of the public health infrastructure and the relationship between public health institutions and the communities they are supposed to serve.

Cohen et al. (2004) concluded with a clear message on the dangers of the current focus on bioterrorism preparedness for public health: "In light of the daily toll of thousands of deaths from illnesses and accidents that could be prevented with even modest increases in public health resources here and around the world, we believe that the huge spending on bio-terrorism preparedness programs constitutes a reversal of any reasonable sense of priorities. . . . These programs represent a catastrophe for American public health, and we hope it is not too late to change this dangerous direction" (p. 1670).

Even with the infusion of funding for bioterrorism and other public health emergency preparedness, a review found that states are woefully unprepared for a public health emergency, especially a potential pandemic flu outbreak (Trust for America's Health, 2003). The overwhelming majority of states, as of 2003, did not have a plan for confronting a pandemic flu outbreak, were not prepared to communicate with health care practitioners and the public about any emerging health threats, and did not have sufficient laboratory facilities.

Decreased spending on state public health programs translates into reduced funding for local programs as well. Local public health programs are already funded at very low levels. Using data derived from a survey of more than 2,000 local health departments throughout the country, CDC estimated that the median per capita expenditure by local health departments in 1995 was just $20, and the mean per capita expenditure was $26 (Gordon et al., 1997). This amounts to just under a dime per day. The Trust for America's Health (2003) report revealed that most of the funding to state health departments for better public health emergency preparedness was not filtering down to the local level. Only 17 states, as of 2003, had allocated at least 50% of their received federal public health capacity-building funds directly to local health departments. Not surprisingly, "a recent U.S. Conference of Mayors report found that in almost half of the states, major cities feel shut out of the state planning process for public health preparedness and claim state priorities do not reflect local concerns" (Trust for America's Health, 2003, p. 11).

Influence of Special Interest Groups

The continued influence of powerful special interest groups, especially at the federal level, threatens many public health programs. An excellent case in point is federal funding for research on firearms-related injuries. In 1995, the National Rifle Association (NRA) lobbied Congress to eliminate all funding for the National Center for Injury Prevention and Control (NCIPC), a $46 million center that serves as the nation's leading agency dedicated to the prevention and control of intentional and unintentional injuries ("Gun Violence Remains," 1996; "House Cuts $2.6m," 1996; Kassirer, 1995a; Kent, 1996). Because gun-related deaths are a significant part of injury mortality, research on firearms control is a central part of the center's mission. The NRA was successful in getting Congress to consider a bill that would have eliminated the NCIPC completely. The bill failed, but 1 year later, the NRA returned with a less ambitious objective: to eliminate funding for the firearms injury research at the center, which amounted to $2.6 million in 1995. In 1996, both the House of Representatives and the Senate approved a $2.6 million cut in the NCIPC budget to eliminate firearms injury research at CDC (HR3755: Health and Human Services FY97 Appropriations Bill). Ultimately, a congressional compromise worked out in the last days of the legislative session restored the $2.6 million to the NCIPC budget but diverted most of it to study traumatic brain injury (Kong, 1997). In addition, a clause in the appropriations bill prohibited any of the NCIPC funds from being used to advocate or promote gun control ("Gun Violence Remains," 1996; Kong, 1997).

Since fiscal year 1997, Congress has included in its appropriations to the CDC language indicating that "none of the funds made available for injury prevention and control at the Centers for Disease Control and Prevention may be used to advocate or promote gun control" (U.S. Senate, 2003, p. 1171). In addition, language added in the fiscal year 2003 appropriations legislation included a detailed and burdensome requirement to ensure that the CDC was not using any funds in any way that could be construed as trying to influence the development of responsible gun control policy (NCIPC, 2005).

These severe and purely politically motivated restrictions on the practice of public health are present in large part thanks to the efforts of the NRA, which is spending approximately $8 million each year to influence legislators to vote against any proposals that would restrict the production, sale, or use of firearms (Burchfield, 2000). Of note, 75% of the 263 House members who voted to cut the NCIPC's funding accepted contributions from the NRA during the prior 3 years and only six recipients of NRA funding voted against the funding cut (Montgomery & Infield, 1996). The NRA's influence was also instrumental in the 1995 House passage of a bill to repeal the ban on assault weapons (HR125: Gun Ban Repeal Act of 1995), which passed 239 to 173 but was not approved by the Senate. The NRA's influence on both bills is highlighted by the fact that 366 of the 421 members who voted on the NCIPC funding cut voted in a consistent manner on the repeal of the assault weapons ban ("How Members of Congress Voted," 1997). Ultimately, the 1994 federal assault weapons ban was allowed to expire in 2004, allowing 19 types of military-style assault weapons back into the hands of civilians. Failure of the effort to renew the assault weapons ban was attributed to a lobbying campaign by the NRA (Associated Press, 2004).

The magnitude of the extent to which special interest lobbying attempts to influence federal policymaking is demonstrated by an examination of the nature and amount of the top federal lobbying spenders. Between 1998 and 2004, Altria Group Inc., parent to Philip Morris—the nation's largest cigarette manufacturer—spent $101.2 million on federal lobbying, making it the second highest spender (Center for Public Integrity, 2005). Eleven of the remaining top 20 lobbying spenders representing manufacturing, defense, electrical, oil, telecommunications, or pharmaceutical interests combined to spend nearly $750 million on federal lobbying during this 7-year period.

Increasing Antiregulatory Sentiment

The practice of public health relies on a sense of public trust in government's ability to protect societal interests and a shared sense that the government has the responsibility to fund and conduct programs to accomplish this. However, recent public opinion polls have documented low levels of public trust in government and public acknowledgment of a central role and responsibility in protecting societal interests.

A 2008 poll by the Pew Research Center for the People & the Press (2008) found that favorable ratings of the federal government dropped to just 37%, having reached a high of 82% in 2001. These ratings are not much better than a decade earlier, when a 1994 poll found that 70% of Americans were dissatisfied with the overall performance of the federal government, 70% believed that government programs were inefficient and wasteful, and 69% believed that the federal government created more problems than it solved (Weisberg, 1996).

Perhaps more threatening than the public's lack of trust in government is the public's disinterest in the responsibility of government to promote the common good. The progressive movement, which launched large-scale government programs to address public health issues and social problems, was based on the assertion "that social evils will not remedy themselves, and that it is wrong to sit by passively and wait for time to take care of them . . . that the people of the country should be stimulated to work energetically to bring about social progress, that the positive powers of government must be used to achieve this end" (Weisberg, 1996, p. 157).

As Weisberg argued in his 1996 book, *In Defense of Government*, the values that underlie government's charge to promote social justice have not disappeared, but they need to be restored to prominence in the public, political, and media agendas: "Building a workable public activism is not a matter of starting from scratch but rather of recovering and renewing lost principles" (p. 158). What needs to be restored, according to Weisberg (1996), is the assertion of "the national government's responsibility for the welfare of the entire polity" (p. 159).

In a 1997 *American Journal of Public Health* editorial, Dr. Fitzhugh Mullan of the journal *Health Affairs* emphasized the same point, but referred specifically to the restoration of the public health movement:

> An acute hazard for the reinvention workers of our movement is that the pendulum of national life is swinging so far in the direction of proprietary and individual interests . . . a tougher and ultimately more central job is to retain public and communitarian principles, no small task when the rhetoric of this 'post-health-care-reform' era, both inside and outside the government, is so strongly oriented to the private sector. Yet it will be the response to this challenge—the stewardship of the public trust despite the siren calls of devolution and privatization—that will render the ultimate commentary on the leadership of federal public health. . . . (p. 24)

■ LOST VISION OF PUBLIC HEALTH

In recent years, the public health community has lost a unified vision of its role and mission (Brown, 1997). The vision of public health as a form of social justice and of the mission of the public health practitioner as advocating for social justice and social change no longer guides the public health movement.

Public health has deep historical roots in what Beauchamp (1976) termed the "egalitarian tradition." Beauchamp proclaimed that "public health should be a way of doing justice, a way of asserting the value and priority of all human life" (p. 8). Turnock (1997) also explained that the underlying philosophy of public health is social justice: "In the case of public health, the goal of extending the potential benefits of the physical and behavioral sciences to all groups in the society, especially when the burden of disease and ill health within that is unequally distributed, is largely based on principles of social justice" (pp. 15–16).

Public health was founded on three basic principles: (1) the principles of social justice, (2) the notion of an inherent public responsibility for social health and welfare, and (3) the responsibility of the public health practitioner to advocate for social justice and collective, societal action.

The first principle—social justice—is based on the view that health is not an individual privilege but a social good that should be equally available to all individuals: "While many forces influenced the development of public health, the historic dream of public health that preventable death and disability ought to be minimized is a dream of social justice" (Beauchamp, 1976, p. 6).

The second principle—public responsibility for social health and welfare—is based on the assertion that government is responsible for achieving and preserving social justice. There is a collective, societal burden to ensure equal health protection and basic standards of living for all people: "Another principle of the public health ethic is that the control of hazards cannot be achieved through voluntary mechanisms but must be undertaken by governmental or non-governmental agencies through planned, organized and collective action that is obligatory or nonvoluntary in nature" (Beauchamp, 1976, p. 8). Burris (1997) explained: "While much of the most important public health work is done in the private sector and the work of the state must take a wide variety of forms beyond direct regulation, 'public health' without the dynamic leadership of government in deploying the nation's wealth against the ills arising from individual choices in the market is a contradiction in terms" (p. 1608).

The third principle—advocacy—is based on the view that the public health practitioner is, first and foremost, an advocate for social change: "Doing public health involves more than merely elaborating a new social ethic, doing public health involves the political process and the challenging of some very important and powerful interests in society. . . . While professional prestige is an important attribute in the modern day public policy process, public health is ultimately better understood as a broad social movement. . . . The political potential of public health goes beyond professionalism; at its very heart is advocacy of an explosive and radical ethic" (Beauchamp, 1976, p. 10).

The idea that public health's role is to promote social change dates back at least 150 years. Public health arose out of the establishment of healthy social conditions as a societal goal and recognition of public institutions as responsible for achieving this social goal (Institute of Medicine, 1988). Public health is not just about studying problems and proposing solutions. It is about organizing the community to support and implement those solutions. And organizing the community requires social and political intervention. As the Institute of Medicine (1988) explained, "the history of public health has been one of identifying health problems, developing knowledge and expertise to solve problems, and rallying political and social support around the solutions" (p. 70).

Public health cannot be separated from the political process. In fact, politics is at the heart of public health. As Dr. Gro Harlem Brundtland, chief of the World Health Organization, stated, "you cannot implement it [public health] without making it a political issue" (Altman, 1998, p. C3).

Rosemary Stevens (1996) outlined these fundamental principles of public health in an *American Journal of Public Health* editorial reviewing the vision of Dr. Henry Sigerist (1891–1957), a medical historian and public health advocate: "For Sigerist, as for many of us who were socialized into public health in the 20th century, health is quite simply a social good. The role of the state is to enhance and protect that good for all members of the population; indeed, in his view, the state has a public duty to do so" (p. 1522). Furthermore, it is the role of the public health practitioner to advocate for the necessary social reforms. For Sigerist, advocacy was a responsibility for the individual as well as for the public health institution. Sigerist "threw his own energy, commitment, and enthusiasm on the side of what he perceived to be social equity and justice" (Fee, 1996, p. 1644).

The principles of social justice, societal responsibility for public health and welfare, and advocacy for social change remain the three pillars of public health today. As expressed in a 1996 American Public Health Association (APHA) policy statement, "long-standing principles of the APHA establish a commitment to the right of all people to attain and maintain good health, through population based public health services and through access to personal health care services. . . . Further, it is the responsibility of society at large, and the public health system in particular, to safeguard the public interest in achieving these objectives" (APHA, 1997, p. 511).

Public health has begun to lose sight of its historical foundation and fundamental principles. No longer united by a common vision of its mission and role, public health has come to be viewed by many in the field more as an elite profession rather than a broad, social movement. In recent years, the "advocacy of an explosive and radical ethic" is all but lost. This, more than anything else, threatens the survival of public health as an institution.

Perhaps the most poignant illustration of the loss of the vision of public health as a broad social movement and its takeover by elite professionalism is the efforts of three national public health organizations—the National Center for Tobacco-Free Kids, the American Cancer Society, and the American Heart Association—to promote a congressionally mediated, "global" settlement to all but a strictly defined subset of past, present, and future lawsuits by citizens, businesses, and public bodies against the tobacco industry (Califano, 1998; "Koop Opposes Immunity in Tobacco Deal," 1997; LoPucki, 1998; McGinley & Harwood, 1997; "The Reynolds Papers," 1998; Schwartz, 1998; Shackelford, 1997; Siegel, 1996, 1997; "Tobacco Talk," 1998; Torry, 1998; Weinstein & Levin, 1997). The process by which the settlement was pursued and promoted violated the core principles of public health, eschewed social justice, and co-opted a broad, social movement, wresting it from the hands of community public health practitioners across the nation and into the hands of a few powerful individuals and organizations (McGinley & Harwood, 1997; Shackelford, 1997; Siegel, 1996, 1997; Weinstein & Levin, 1997). The very organizations that claimed to represent the interests of cancer and heart disease victims were willing to trade away the legal rights of these victims. The leadership of these organizations also remained willing to consider a deal that would grant the tobacco industry immunity for its wrongdoing, even after the grassroots membership of these organizations made it clear they opposed the concept of using the legal rights of American citizens as a bargaining chip.

A more recent example is the effort of the American Legacy Foundation, arguably the nation's most heavily funded antismoking organization, to forge corporate partnerships with conglomerates and companies that are the leading reasons for youth exposure to cigarette advertising in magazines and to portrayals of smoking in movies (Siegel, 2005a), both of which have been shown to be strong factors in smoking initiation (Pucci & Siegel, 1999; Sargent et al., 2005). As of 2005, the American Legacy Foundation maintained corporate partnerships with Time Warner (Siegel, 2005a), whose Warner Brothers movie division is the leading source of youth exposure to smoking in movies (Polansky & Glantz, 2004) and whose Time Inc. magazine division publishes magazines such as *Sports Illustrated, People Weekly, Entertainment Weekly*, and *TIME Magazine*, which collectively exposed more than 4 million adolescents to a total of 219 tobacco advertisements in 2004 (Siegel, 2005a). The American Legacy Foundation also partnered with the Hearst Corporation (Siegel, 2005b), which at the same time bombarded youths with ads for Kool and Camel cigarettes and for Skoal (smokeless tobacco) through its *Cosmopolitan, Esquire*, and *Popular Mechanics* publications and with Condé Nast Publications (Siegel, 2005c), which heavily exposed youths to cigarette ads for Camel and Kool through its *Vogue, Glamour*, and *GQ* magazines.

The American Legacy Foundation went so far as to honor Time Inc. with an award for "reaching millions with an anti-tobacco message" at a $500-per-plate fundraiser, expressing gratification that "a selection of Time Inc.'s magazines . . . do not accept any tobacco product advertising" (Siegel, 2005a). It turns out that only 5 of the more than 125 Time Inc. publications did not accept tobacco advertising and the top 4 Time Inc. magazines alone reached millions of youths with pro-tobacco messages, carrying more than 100 cigarette ads per year (Siegel, 2005a). This represents a troubling example of the loss of the vision of public health as a broad social movement and its takeover by elite professionalism. The efforts of the American Legacy Foundation undermined years of work by public health advocates to attempt to eliminate cigarette advertising in Time Inc. publications, and without their knowledge or consultation.

An article in the *American Journal of Public Health* illustrated another way in which health advocates have compromised public health values. Many health advocacy groups, such as professional medical and nursing associations, the American Heart Association, the American Lung Association, and the American Cancer Society, have hired lobbyists who also represent the tobacco industry (Goldstein & Bearman, 1996).

For example, in 1994, more than 300 health organizations employed one or more tobacco lobbyists (Goldstein & Bearman, 1996).

Perhaps the most egregious example is the appointment of former tobacco industry lobbyist Kim Belshe as director of the California Department of Health Services in 1994. Belshe had been a lobbyist for the tobacco industry and had lobbied against Proposition 99, an initiative to establish a comprehensive, statewide tobacco control program funded by an increase in the state cigarette excise tax. There could hardly be a more inappropriate person to serve as director of a state health department than a former tobacco industry lobbyist who opposed one of the most important public health interventions in the state.

Although some public health organizations have turned to professional lobbyists with dubious associations, many other public health groups have gone so far as to halt all advocacy to prevent the appearance of improper lobbying activity. The widely held perception that education is the only appropriate role for public health agencies and that advocacy is illegal or inappropriate for public health officials has arisen largely because of a widespread misunderstanding of the difference between advocacy and lobbying.

Many public health practitioners are under the impression that advocacy is synonymous with lobbying and therefore is restricted by federal law. Lobbying, however, is a very specific and legally defined term. As defined in the Internal Revenue Service Code, lobbying refers to an attempt to influence the outcome of legislation through communication with a legislator, government official, or the public (26 U.S.C.S. 4911). Generally, a communication is considered lobbying only if it (1) refers to specific legislation and (2) promotes a specific vote on that legislation (National Cancer Institute, 1993). Policy advocacy activities, such as researching, developing, planning, implementing, enforcing, and evaluating public health policy, are not lobbying unless they involve the promotion of a specific vote on specific legislation.

Even when public health practitioners are convinced their activities are legal, they often are scared into inaction by pressure from special interest groups. A prime example is the use of federal funds to advocate for the control of tobacco use. The tobacco industry has used the Freedom of Information Act (FOIA) to intimidate tobacco control practitioners, often scaring them to inaction by forcing them to copy hundreds or even thousands of documents and accusing them of illegal activity (Levin, 1996; Mintz, 1997). For example, the Association for Non-smokers-Minnesota was hit with such a request. A spokesperson for the group explained, "They wanted people such as myself to be intimidated and fearful and confused—and at least to some extent they succeeded. Truly, we did almost nothing in the way of tobacco control for about three months" (Levin, 1996, p. D4). Similar FOIA requests were made to state health departments in California, Massachusetts, Indiana,

Colorado, and Washington (Levin, 1996; Mintz, 1997). According to an article in the journal *Tobacco Control*, the tobacco control section of the California Department of Health Services, which administers Proposition 99, received 59 FOIA requests from 1991 to 1993 (Aguinaga & Glantz, 1995). Although the tobacco industry's statements and actions imply something was wrong with the way tobacco control funds were being used, ethics board reviews cleared all the groups whose activities were challenged (Levin, 1996). Nevertheless, the tobacco industry's objective was accomplished: Many tobacco control groups have been scared into inaction or into a state of reserved action.

■ CONCLUSION

The public health movement is involved in a fight not only to protect the public from the emerging epidemic of chronic disease that threatens to dominate life in the 21st century but also to save itself as a vital and integral part of the societal infrastructure. A continuing societal focus on health care reform as the solution to the nation's public health crisis and on individual medical treatment rather than population-based prevention threatens to obscure the need for public health. The emergence of managed care and the perception, even among public health practitioners, that public health can somehow be integrated into a managed care system threaten to erode the independent role of the public health professional. Budget cuts, the emergence of bioterrorism and infectious disease threats, special interest group influence, and increasing antigovernment sentiment each contribute to unprecedented threats to public health infrastructure and programs. Finally, the failure of public health practitioners to assert their primary role as advocates for social change and the loss of a common vision for public health represent internal, yet critical, threats to the viability of the public health movement.

This is no longer only a fight to protect people's health. It is now a life-and-death struggle for public health as a societal institution.

References

Aguinaga, S., & Glantz, S.A. (1995). The use of public records acts to interfere with tobacco control. *Tobacco Control, 4,* 222–230.

Altman, L.K. (1998, February 3). Next W.H.O. chief will have politics in name of science. *The New York Times,* p. C3.

American Public Health Association. (1997). Policy statements adopted by the governing council of the American Public Health Association, November 20, 1996. *American Journal of Public Health, 87,* 495–518.

Anders, G. (1996). *Health against wealth: HMOs and the breakdown of medical trust.* New York, NY: Houghton Mifflin.

Associated Press. (2004, September 13). Congress lets assault weapons ban expire: Gun dealers say it never worked; many police wanted it, though. Retrieved March 15, 2007, from http://msnbc.msn.com/id/5946127/

Bauer, U.E., Johnson, T.M., Hopkins, R.S., & Brooks, R.G. (2000). Changes in youth cigarette use and intentions following implementation of a tobacco control program: Findings from the Florida Youth Tobacco Survey, 1998–2000. *Journal of the American Medical Association, 284*(6), 723–728.

Beauchamp, D. (1976). Public health as social justice. *Inquiry, 13*, 3–14.

Berliner, H. (1977). Emerging ideologies in medicine. *Review of Radical Political Economics, 9*, 116–124.

Bickman, L. (1996). A continuum of care: More is not always better. *American Psychologist, 51*, 689–701.

Brown, E.R. (1997). Leadership to meet the challenges to the public's health. *American Journal of Public Health, 87*, 554–557.

Brown, R.S., Clement, D.G., Hill, J.W., Retchin, S.M., & Bergeron, J.W. (1993). Do health maintenance organizations work for Medicare? *Health Care Financing Review, 15*, 7–23.

Burchfield, B. (2000, April 5). Statement of Bobby R. Burchfield before the Senate Committee on Rules and Administration. Retrieved March 15, 2007, from http://rules.senate.gov/hearings/2000/0450burchfield.htm

Burris, S. (1997). The invisibility of public health: Population-level measures in a politics of market individualism. *American Journal of Public Health, 87*, 1607–1610.

Califano, J.A., Jr. (1998, January 9). Sellout to big tobacco. *The Washington Post*, p. A21.

Campaign for Tobacco-Free Kids. (2005a). *A broken promise to our children: The 1998 state tobacco settlement seven years later*. Retrieved March 15, 2007, from http://www.tobaccofreekids.org/reports/settlements/2006/full report.pdf

Campaign for Tobacco-Free Kids. (2005b). *The impact of reductions to state tobacco control program funding*. Retrieved March 21, 2012, from http:// tobaccofreekids.org/research/factsheets/pdf/0270.pdf

Cassel, J. (1976). The contribution of the social environment to host resistance. *American Journal of Epidemiology, 104*, 107–123.

Center for Public Integrity. (2005). Top 100 companies and organizations. Retrieved March 15, 2007, from http://www.publicintegrity.org/lobby/top .aspx?act=topcompanies

Centers for Disease Control and Prevention. (1995). *1994: Ten leading causes of death in the United States*. Atlanta, GA: Centers for Disease Control and Prevention, National Center for Injury Prevention and Control.

Centers for Disease Control and Prevention. (1997). Estimated expenditures for essential public health services—Selected states, fiscal year 1995. *Morbidity and Mortality Weekly Report, 46*, 150–152.

Centers for Disease Control and Prevention. (2004). Effect of ending an antitobacco youth campaign on adolescent susceptibility to cigarette smoking—Minnesota, 2002–2003. *Morbidity and Mortality Weekly Report, 53*, 301–304.

Clement, D.G., Retchin, S.M., Brown, R.S., & Steagall, M.H. (1994). Access and outcomes of elderly patients enrolled in managed care. *Journal of the American Medical Association, 271*, 1487–1492.

Cohen, H.W., Gould, R.M., & Sidel, V.W. (2004). The pitfalls of bioterrorism preparedness: The anthrax and smallpox experiences. *American Journal of Public Health, 94,* 1667–1671.

Conrad, P. (1987). The experience of illness: Recent and new directions. *Research in the Sociology of Health Care, 6,* 1–31.

Dowling, K.C., & Lipton, R.I. (2005). Bioterrorism preparedness expenditures may compromise public health. *American Journal of Public Health, 95,* 1672.

Dubos, R. (1959). *Mirage of health.* New York, NY: Harper & Row.

Dutton, D.B. (1994). Social class, health, and illness. In H.D. Schwartz (Ed.), *Dominant issues in medical sociology* (3rd ed., pp. 470–482). New York, NY: McGraw-Hill.

Eilbert, K.W., Barry, M., Bialek, R., & Garufi, M. (1996). *Measuring expenditures for essential public health services.* Washington, DC: Public Health Foundation.

Eilbert, K.W., Barry, M., Bialek, R., Garufi, M., Maiese, D., Gebbie, K., & Fox, C.E. (1997). Public health expenditures: Developing estimates for improved policy making. *Journal of Public Health Management and Practice, 3,* 1–9.

Evans, R.G., Barer, M., & Marmor, T.R. (Eds.). (1994). *Why are some people healthy and others not? The determinants of health of populations.* New York, NY: Aldine DeGruyter.

Experton, B., Li, Z., Branch, L.G., Ozminkowski, R.J., & Mellon-Lacey, D.M. (1997). The impact of payor/provider type on health care use and expenditures among the frail elderly. *American Journal of Public Health, 87,* 210–216.

Fee, E. (1996). The pleasures and perils of prophetic advocacy: Henry E. Sigerist and the politics of medical reform. *American Journal of Public Health, 86,* 1637–1647.

Foege, W.H., Amler R.W., & White, C.C. (1985). Closing the gap: Report of the Carter Center health policy consultation. *Journal of the American Medical Association, 254,* 1355–1358.

Ford, E.S., Ajani, U.A., Croft, J.B., Critchley, J.A., Labarthe, D.R., Kottke, T.E., . . . Capewell, S. (2007). Explaining the decrease in U.S. deaths from coronary disease, 1980–2000. *New England Journal of Medicine, 356,* 2388–2398.

Goldstein, A.O., & Bearman, N.S. (1996). State tobacco lobbyists and organizations in the United States: Crossed lines. *American Journal of Public Health, 86,* 1137–1142.

Gordon, R.L., Gerzoff, R.B., & Richards, T.B. (1997). Determinants of US local health department expenditures, 1992 through 1993. *American Journal of Public Health, 87,* 91–95.

Gun violence remains a public health risk that's still hard to track. (1996, November). In *The nation's health* (p. 24). Washington, DC: American Public Health Association.

Hingson, R., Scotch, N.A., Sorenson, J., & Swazey, J.P. (1981). *In sickness and in health: Social dimensions of medical care.* St. Louis, MO: C.V. Mosby.

House cuts $2.6m for CDC gun study: Critics, including NRA, say injury research based toward firearms control. (1996, July 14). *The Boston Globe,* p. A19.

How members of Congress voted on issues affecting public health. (1997, February). In *The nation's health* (pp. 8–16). Washington, DC: American Public Health Association.

Institute of Medicine, Committee for the Study of the Future of Public Health. (1988). *The future of public health.* Washington, DC: National Academies Press.

Kass, E.H. (1971). Infectious diseases and social change. *Journal of Infectious Diseases, 123,* 110–114.

Kassirer, J.P. (1995a). A partisan assault on science: The threat to the CDC. *New England Journal of Medicine, 333,* 793–794.

Kassirer, J.P. (1995b). Managed care and the morality of the marketplace. *New England Journal of Medicine, 332,* 50–52.

Keck, C.W. (1992). Creating a healthy public. *American Journal of Public Health, 82,* 1206–1209.

Kent, C. (1996, August 5). Fight over federal agency pits medicine vs. NRA: Funding for research on firearms injuries at issue. *American Medical News,* pp. 3, 52.

Kim, K., & Moody, P. (1992). More resources, better health? A cross-national perspective. *Social Science and Medicine, 34,* 837–842.

Kong, D. (1997, September 25). State loses funds to track gun injuries. *The Boston Globe,* p. B2.

Koop opposes immunity on tobacco deal (1997, December 23). *The Los Angeles Times,* p. D12.

Leavitt, J.W., & Numbers, R.L. (1994). Sickness and health in America: The role of public health in the prevention of disease. In H.D. Schwartz (Ed.), *Dominant issues in medical sociology* (3rd ed., pp. 529–537). New York, NY: McGraw-Hill.

Lee, P.R., & Estes, C.L. (Eds). (1997). *The nation's health* (5th ed). Sudbury, MA: Jones and Bartlett.

Levin, M. (1996, April 21). Legal weapon: Tobacco companies, facing increasingly strong opposition, have turned to open-records laws to fight back, inundating state offices with requests for documents. *The Los Angeles Times,* pp. D1, D4.

Levine, S., Feldman, J.J., & Elison, J. (1983). Does medical care do any good? In D. Mechanic (Ed.), *Handbook of health, health care, and the health professions* (pp. 394–404). New York, NY: Free Press.

LoPucki, L.M. (1998, January 20). Some settlement [op-ed column]. *The Washington Post,* p. A15.

Magill, T.P. (1955). The immunologist and the evil spirits. *Journal of Immunology, 74,* 1–8.

Mallozzi, J. (1996, December). Consumer advocacy in Medicare HMOs. *States of Health, 6,* 1–9.

McGinley, L., & Harwood, J. (1997, August 1). Grass-roots activists try to derail tobacco settlement. *The Wall Street Journal,* p. A16.

McGinnis, J.M. (1997). What do we pay for good health? *Journal of Public Health Management and Practice, 3,* viii–ix.

McKeown, T. (1971). A historical appraisal of the medical task. In G. McLachlan & T. McKeown (Eds.), *Medical history and medical care: A symposium of perspectives* (pp. 29–55). New York, NY: Oxford University Press.

McKeown, T. (1976). *The modern rise of population.* New York, NY: Academic Press.

McKeown, T. (1978, April). Determinants of health. *Human Nature, 1,* 60–67.

McKeown, T., Record, R.G., & Turner, R.D. (1975). An interpretation of the decline of mortality in England and Wales during the twentieth century. *Population Studies, 29,* 391–422.

McKinlay, J.B., & McKinlay, S.M. (1977). The questionable contribution of medical measures to the decline of mortality in the United States in the twentieth century. *Milbank Memorial Fund Quarterly, Health and Society, 55*, 405–428.

McKinlay, J.B., & McKinlay, S.M. (1994). Medical measures and the decline of mortality. In P. Conrad & R. Kern (Eds.), *The sociology of health & illness: Critical perspectives* (4th ed., pp. 10–23). New York, NY: St. Martin's Press.

Mechanic, D. (1994). Promoting health. In H.D. Schwartz (Ed.), *Dominant issues in medical sociology* (3rd ed., pp. 569–575). New York, NY: McGraw-Hill.

Milio, N. (1995). Health, health care reform, and the care of health. In M. Blunden & M. Dando (Eds.), *Rethinking public policy-making: Questioning assumptions, challenging beliefs* (pp. 92–107). Thousand Oaks, CA: Sage Publications.

Miller, R.H., & Luft, H.S. (1994). Managed care plan performance since 1980: A literature analysis. *Journal of the American Medical Association, 271*, 1512–1519.

Miller, S.M. (1995). Thinking strategically about society and health. In B.C. Amick III, S. Levine, A.R. Tarlov, & D.C. Walsh (Eds.), *Society and health* (pp. 342–358). New York, NY: Oxford University Press.

Mintz, J. (1997, April 19). 3-year-old U.S. program cuts smoking, draws fire. *The Washington Post*, p. A1.

Montgomery, L., & Infield, T. (1996, July 12). House votes to cut gun studies. The $2.6 million for the CDC was put to political use, critics said the vote was "very important," said the NRA. *Philadelphia Inquirer*, p. A1.

Morris, J.N. (1982), Epidemiology and prevention. *Milbank Memorial Fund Quarterly, Health and Society, 60*, 1–16.

Mullan, F. (1997). Federal public health, semi-reinvented. *American Journal of Public Health, 87*, 21–24.

National Cancer Institute. (1993, March 11). *Restrictions on lobbying and public policy advocacy by government contractors: The ASSIST contract*. Bethesda, MD: U.S. Department of Health and Human Services, National Institutes of Health, National Cancer Institute.

National Center for Health Statistics. (2011). *Health, United States, 2010: With special feature on death and dying*. Hyattsville, MD: U.S. Department of Health and Human Services, Centers for Disease Control and Prevention.

National Center for Injury Prevention and Control. (2005). Letter to grantees: Restriction of funding. Retrieved March 15, 2007, from http://www.cdc.gov/ncipc/res-opps/restrictions.htm

Omran, A.R. (1971). The epidemiologic transition: A theory of the epidemiology of population change. *Milbank Quarterly, 49*, 509–538.

Pew Research Center for the People & the Press. (2008, May 14). The federal government's favorable fall even farther. Retrieved March 21, 2012, from http://pewresearch.org/pubs/836/opinion-federal-government-institutions

Polansky, J.R., & Glantz, S.A. (2004). *First-run smoking presentations in U.S. movies 1999–2003*. Retrieved March 21, 2012, from http://repositories.cdlib.org/ctcre/tcpmus/Movies2004

Powles, J. (1973). On the limitations of modern medicine. *Science, Medicine, and Man, 1*, 1–30.

Public Health Foundation. (1994). *Measuring state expenditures for core public health functions*. Washington, DC: Author.

Pucci, L.G., & Siegel, M. (1999). Exposure to brand-specific cigarette advertising in magazines and its impact on youth smoking. *Preventive Medicine, 29*, 313–320.

Retchin, S.M., & Brown, B. (1991). Elderly patients with congestive heart failure under prepaid care. *American Journal of Medicine, 90*, 236–242.

Retchin, S.M., Brown, R.S., Yeh, S.J., Chu, D., & Moreno, L. (1997). Outcomes of stroke patients in Medicare fee for service and managed care. *Journal of the American Medical Association, 278*, 119–124.

Retchin, S.M., & Preston, J.A. (1991). The effects of cost containment on the care of elderly diabetics. *Archives of Internal Medicine, 151*, 2244–2248.

The Reynolds papers. (1998, January 16). *The Washington Post*, p. A20.

Sargent, J.D., Beach, M.L., Adachi-Mejia, A.M., Gibson, J.J., Titus-Ernstoff, L.T., Carusi, C.P., . . . Dalton, M.A. (2005). Exposure to movie smoking: Its relation to smoking initiation among US adolescents. *Pediatrics, 116*, 1183–1191.

Schwartz, J. (1998, January 22). Anti-tobacco activists may heal rift: Koop works to unite public health groups. *The Washington Post*, p. A10.

Shackelford, L. (1997, December 29). AMA leaders have betrayed doctors to protect big tobacco. *The Louisville Courier-Journal*, p. D2.

Shaughnessy, P., Schlenker, R.E., & Hittle, D.F. (1994). Home health care outcomes under capitated and fee-for-service payment. *Health Care Financing Review, 16*, 187–222.

Sidel, V.W., Cohen, H.W., & Gould, R.M. (2005). Sidel et al. respond. *American Journal of Public Health, 95*, 1672–1673.

Siegel, M. (1996, December 22). Tobacco: The $10 billion dollar debate. *The Washington Post*, p. C7.

Siegel, M. (1997, May 4). What sort of tobacco settlement? *The Washington Post*, p. C7.

Siegel, M. (2002). The effectiveness of state-level tobacco control interventions: A review of program implementation and behavioral outcomes. *Annual Review of Public Health, 23*, 45–71.

Siegel, M. (2005a, March 6). American Legacy Foundation honors top tobacco ad publisher. [Web log post]. Retrieved March 21, 2012, from http://tobacco analysis.blogspot.com/2005/03/american-legacy-foundation-honors-top.html

Siegel, M. (2005b, August 23). Weekly update on leader in tobacco control movement: The Hearst Corporation. [Web log post]. Retrieved March 21, 2012, from http://tobaccoanalysis.blogspot.com/2005/08/weekly-update-on-leader-in-tobacco_23.html

Siegel, M. (2005c, August 30). Weekly update on leader in tobacco control movement: Condé Nast Publications. [Web log post]. Retrieved March 21, 2012, from http://tobaccoanalysis.blogspot.com/2005/08/weekly-update-on-leader-in-tobacco_30.html

Stevens, R. (1996). Editorial: Public health history and advocacy in the money-driven 1990s. *American Journal of Public Health, 86*, 1522–1523.

Syme, S.L., & Berkman, L.F. (1976). Social class susceptibility and sickness. *American Journal of Epidemiology, 104*, 1–8.

Tesh, S.N. (1994). Hidden arguments: Political ideology and disease prevention policy. In H.D. Schwartz (Ed.), *Dominant issues in medical sociology* (3rd ed., pp. 519–529). New York, NY: McGraw-Hill.

Tobacco talk. (1998, January 30). *The Washington Post*, p. A22.

Torry, S. (1998, February 6). Signals change on tobacco deal: White House bends on industry protection. *The Washington Post*, p. A18.

Trust for America's Health. (2003, September). Ready or not? Protecting the public's health in the age of bioterrorism. Retrieved March 15, 2007, from http://healthyamericans.org/state/bioterror/Bioterror.pdf

Turnock, B.J. (1997). *Public health: What it is and how it works*. Gaithersburg, MD: Aspen.

U.S. Department of Health and Human Services. (1995). *Healthy people 2000: Midcourse review and 1995 revisions*. Washington, DC: U.S. Department of Health and Human Services, Public Health Service.

U.S. Department of Health and Human Services. (2010). *Healthy people 2020: The visions, mission, and goals of Healthy People 2020*. Retrieved March 15, 2007, from http://www.healthypeople.gov

U.S. Public Health Service. (1995). *For a healthy nation: Returns on investment in public health*. Washington, DC: Author.

U.S. Senate. (2003). *Congressional record—Senate, January 15, 2003* (p. 1171). Washington, DC: U.S. Senate.

Ware, J.E., Jr., Bayliss, M.S., Rogers, W.H., Kosinski, M., & Tarlov, A.R. (1996). Differences in 4-year health outcomes for elderly and poor, chronically ill patients treated in HMO and fee-for-service systems. Results from the Medical Outcomes Study. *Journal of the American Medical Association, 276*, 1039–1047.

Webster, J.R., & Feinglass, J. (1997). Stroke patients, "managed care," and distributive justice. *Journal of the American Medical Association, 278*, 161–162.

Weinstein, H., & Levin, M. (1997, December 15). Smoking foes split as factions oppose industry immunity. Health: As Congressional battle looms, groups struggle over how to gain passage of proposed $368.5 billion settlement. Fissure may threaten the deal, some say. *The Los Angeles Times*, p. A1.

Weinstein, L. (1974). Infectious disease: Retrospect and reminiscence. *Journal of Infectious Diseases, 129*, 480–492.

Weisberg, J. (1996). *In defense of government: The fall and rise of public trust*. New York, NY: Scribner.

Wickizer, T.M., Lessler, D., & Travis, D.M. (1996). Controlling inpatient psychiatric utilization through managed care. *American Journal of Psychiatry, 153*, 339–345.

SECTION

II

Challenges

Once public health practitioners recognize the elements that threaten both the public's health and public health as an institution, they can begin the task of overcoming those obstacles. They can do so by making changes to both social norms and social policies. However, traditional public health training does not foster the skills needed to make such changes.

This section identifies the challenges practitioners face as they work to market social changes and public health as an institution. The ways that practitioners can use basic marketing principles to confront these challenges effectively are also introduced.

CHAPTER

3

Challenges for Marketing Social Change

The basic public health product is social change, and the fundamental mission of the public health practitioner is to market social change. Unlike most traditional products, however, those public health must market tend to have negative demand, no demand, or unwholesome demand. People do not want the product, do not care about the product, or desire an alternative product whose use is counterproductive to the goal of improving health. In addition, the environment is hostile to public efforts to stimulate demand for social change. This chapter describes the unfavorable state of demand for social change as well as the formidable challenges facing public health practitioners as they market public health.

Public health aims to satisfy the human need for health by facilitating a series of individual and societal exchange processes. These exchanges include the adoption of individual behavior and lifestyle changes and the adoption of societal programs to improve social and economic conditions. Marketing is defined as "human activity directed at satisfying needs and wants through exchange processes" (Kotler, 1976, p. 5). Thus, whether they realize it or not, public health practitioners are in the business of marketing.

Marketing involves an exchange process, which is simply the transfer between two parties of something that has value to each party. The marketer's task is to facilitate exchanges so customers can fulfill their needs and wants. Usually, the marketer benefits from the exchange by obtaining money, whereas the customers benefit by obtaining a good or service that satisfies a need or desire. Public sector and nonprofit marketers may, however, benefit in nonmonetary ways, through the fulfillment of their institutional missions, desires, and goals.

Health is certainly something that people need and want. It, however, is not something that comes without paying a monetary or non-monetary price. To achieve health, people must give up something of value: pleasure, convenience, time, and/or money. For example, to achieve cardiovascular health, a person may have to sacrifice the pleasure associated with smoking, accept the inconvenience of having to read food nutrition labels, devote time to exercise, and pay for physician visits and blood pressure medication.

Similarly, on a societal level, a healthy population simply cannot be created without paying a price. The public must be willing to give up something of value—usually, public resources—to achieve a healthy society. For example, government may have to pay for health care for the uninsured, food and shelter for the poor, and public education programs to teach people the benefits of quitting smoking. Sometimes, the cost to society is not in dollars but in something else of value, such as the desire to interfere as little as possible with the marketplace. To improve societal health, government may have to impose environmental health regulations on corporations, consumer product safety rules on manufacturers, or even professional practice guidelines on physicians.

In any case, achieving health, whether individual or societal, requires an exchange. And the role of the public health practitioner can be viewed as facilitating the individual- and societal-level exchanges necessary to satisfy the human need and desire for health. Public health activity is directed at satisfying the human desire and need for health by promoting or facilitating the exchange of behaviors and lifestyles at the individual level and the exchange of social programs and policies at the societal level. Thus, public health, by its very nature, is in the business of marketing.

Kotler (1976) described three potential alternatives to an exchange: self-production, coercion, and supplication. However, an exchange is necessary for the individual or society at large to obtain its need and desire for health because the alternatives are not readily available. For example, an individual is unable to create health for him- or herself (self-production), cannot forcibly obtain health from others (coercion), and cannot effectively plead for others to provide health to him or her (supplication). However, the individual can obtain health through an exchange. The individual can give up something valued to obtain health. To improve cardiovascular health, he or she may give up cigarettes, start exercising, or reduce fat intake. The individual may trade the freedom of unprotected sex to obtain the promise of freedom from AIDS.

Similarly, society cannot simply create healthy individuals, cannot somehow steal health for its people, and cannot effectively plead with individuals or business to provide for a healthy public. Instead, society can give up something of value—in most cases, fiscal resources—to adopt a public health program that is designed to improve the health of its citizens.

In both examples, something of value must be exchanged for the promise of health. In the first case, the individual forfeits a valued behavior, like smoking, or a valued experience, like the pleasure of unprotected sex, in exchange for the prospect of improved health. In the second case, society exchanges fiscal resources for the prospect of improved population health.

Public health practitioners must promote exchanges to increase the adoption of individual behaviors (or elimination of unhealthy behaviors) and the adoption of programs to improve social and economic conditions. The overall task is to create or facilitate social change. In other words, the primary challenge of the public health practitioner is to market social change.

Social change, then, can be viewed as the product public health is trying to sell. A product is simply "something that is viewed as capable of satisfying a want. . . . Anything capable of rendering a service, that is, satisfying a need, can be called a product" (Kotler, 1976, p. 5). And in the eyes of the public health practitioner, changes in behavior, social conditions, and social policy can help to satisfy the public's desire for health. That is, social change is a product because the public health practitioner views it as something capable of satisfying the individual and societal desire for healthy citizens and healthy communities.

Public health can be considered marketing because it involves a set of core activities directed at satisfying an important need and desire of the public—health—through a variety of individual and societal-level exchanges that take place continually. The product of public health— social change—may not be tangible, but it can be considered a product in a marketing sense because it is perceived by the public health practitioner as capable of satisfying the human desire for health.

■ UNIQUE MARKETING CHALLENGE

The public health practitioner's fundamental task of marketing social change is a unique challenge for three reasons: (1) the unfavorable state of individual and societal demand for social change, (2) the hostile environment in which social change must be marketed, and (3) the limited training of public health practitioners in the skills necessary to market social change.

Unfavorable State of Demand for Social Change

Protecting and promoting the public's health is a unique marketing challenge because of the special nature of the products that public health practitioners are asked to promote. These products fall into a particular niche in the marketing world that, although not exclusive to public health products, poses especially difficult barriers that must be overcome. Specifically, the products of public health—changes in behavior, social conditions, and social policy—tend to be unwanted, considered unimportant, or directly opposed to alternative products that people desire. The public and the policymakers generally do not want

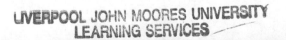

social change, do not care about social change, or are committed to social norms that directly oppose social change. This places public health in the initial stages of the product life cycle and creates a special challenge faced by marketers of traditional products only when they are first being introduced into the marketplace.

Kotler (1976) described eight states of the demand level for a product that require differing marketing tasks. Most traditional consumer products are in one of five of these eight states: full, overfull, faltering, irregular, or latent demand. Products in a state of full demand, where demand is at the desired level, simply require maintenance marketing. Products in a state of overfull demand, where demand is higher than the level at which the marketer is able to supply it, require demarketing: temporarily or permanently discouraging customers from using the product. Products in a state of faltering demand, where demand is less than its former level, require remarketing: altering the product, the target audience, or the marketing effort. Products in a state of irregular demand, where demand is seasonal or fluctuates widely, require synchromarketing: efforts to synchronize the fluctuations in demand and supply. Finally, products in a state of latent demand, where people share a strong need for a product that does not yet exist, require developmental marketing: creating and marketing a product to satisfy the existing demand. In all five cases, there is preexisting demand for the product; the marketer's task is simply to maintain, enhance, reform, or retime marketing efforts or, in the case of latent demand, to create a product to satisfy high levels of existing public demand.

Under these five demand states, it is reasonably possible to achieve significant changes in individual brand choices, product choices, and product use in the market. For example, within 3 years of introducing its Joe Camel marketing campaign in 1986, the youth market share for Camel cigarettes increased from less than 3% to 8%; after an additional 3 years, Camel's youth market share was up to 16% (Pollay et al., 1996; U.S. Department of Health and Human Services, 1994). Within 1 year of introducing a new 64-bit television video game system, Nintendo achieved a commanding 50% share of the market (Jensen, 1997). Within 4 years of an intensified marketing effort, Clorox increased its market share from 29% in 1992 to 40% in 1996 (Neff, 1997). And within 2 years of the initiation of the products in 1995, 17% of users of skin cream were buying Revitalist Plentitude antiaging cream (Zbar, 1997) and nearly 48% of Internet search engine users were using the Excite search engine (Heath, 1997).

In contrast, the public health product—social change—is generally in one of three demand states: negative demand, no demand, or unwholesome demand. Most commonly, public health products are in a state of negative demand, where the public dislikes the product, does not want the product, and is not willing to pay a price to obtain the product, regardless of its promised benefits. For example, people generally have a negative demand for low-fat foods. The public enjoys the taste of high-fat foods and the convenience associated with their availability and easy access and prefers not to sacrifice taste and convenience for the more distant promise of long-term health benefits. The high public demand for fast-food restaurants is a testament to the negative demand for healthy, low-fat diets. On a societal level, the adoption of programs to help people living in poverty by way of income redistribution is in negative demand. Policymakers stringently avoid the adoption of programs that would significantly redistribute income away from the wealthy and toward the poor. Policymakers often are more willing to pay the price of higher crime rates, more drug use, and higher rates of uncompensated medical care than to jeopardize their chances for reelection by increasing taxes on the wealthy and powerful.

Some public health products are in a state of no demand. People are simply uninterested in the product. For example, programs to provide job training for the homeless are not in great demand by policymakers. Officials are not necessarily making a conscious decision to avoid such programs—there simply is not a great deal of political pressure to address the needs of the homeless in the first place.

Other public health products must be marketed in an environment of unwholesome demand. These are products for which there are alternatives, under high demand by the public, considered to be unhealthy and undesirable by public health practitioners. On an individual level, tobacco, alcohol, and drugs are products for which there is unwholesome demand. On a societal level, there is an unwholesome demand among policymakers for "welfare reform" policies that cut social support for individuals without providing adequate job training, child care, and other support services. These programs are undesirable by public health standards because they lead to adverse health outcomes. To reduce tobacco, alcohol, or drug use or to promote the adoption of programs that provide social support for poor individuals, public health practitioners must "demarket" popular alternative behaviors or social programs that run counter to the goals of improving health.

Unlike traditional marketers, then, public health marketers are almost always faced with a market in which there is no demand for their product, negative demand for their product, or an unwholesome demand for an alternative product whose use runs counter to the practitioners' desires and the goals of improving health. All three of public health practitioners' products—changes in lifestyle, changes in social and economic conditions, and changes in social policy—face this problem of an unfavorable state of preexisting demand.

Lifestyle Change
The most striking examples of the unfavorable state of demand for lifestyle change are addictive behaviors. These unhealthy behaviors are, by

definition, highly resistant to change. They represent an extreme example of unwholesome demand: These behaviors severely harm individual health but are highly desired by those who are addicted to them. For example, demand for heroin among heroin addicts is extremely high. Despite the devastating effects of heroin on all aspects of the addict's life, the behavior is sustained at a high rate. Even among addicts who are successfully maintained on methadone for long periods of time, the overall relapse rate among patients who discontinue methadone is at least 50% (Weddington, 1990/1991). Similarly, despite the serious health consequences of smoking and the availability of a wide range of cessation programs ranging from hypnosis to acupuncture, the overall relapse rate for smokers who successfully graduate from cessation programs, even with nicotine replacement therapy, is about 80% (Fiore et al., 1994; Orleans et al., 1994; Silagy et al., 1994).

As a result of the unwholesome demand that exists for addictive behaviors, the public health movement has been relatively unsuccessful in reducing tobacco, alcohol, and illicit drug use. The decline in adult smoking prevalence from 42% in 1965 to 25% in 1990 was a result of 25 years of persistent antismoking messages (Giovino et al., 1995; Susser, 1995). Even so, smoking prevalence among adults has declined only slightly since then, reaching just under 21% in 2009, a decline of only 4% in 19 years (National Center for Health Statistics [NCHS], 2011). Although smoking within the past 30 days among high school seniors has declined from 30% in 1980 to 21% in 2006, rates have only decreased 1% since then (NCHS, 2011). The 40% reduction in alcohol-related traffic fatalities between 1980 and 1994 was the result of an intensive, 15-year public health campaign (Wald, 1996). However, there has been no further progress, with annual alcohol-related traffic deaths remaining at about 17,000 in both 1995 and 2004 (National Highway Traffic Safety Administration, 1997, 2005). And despite the adverse consequences of drug use and the highly publicized "Just Say No" campaigns, rates of marijuana use among high school seniors have increased since 1990; past-month use of marijuana increased from 14.0% in 1990 to 20.6% in 2009 (NCHS, 2011).

Public health interventions also have met with limited success in reducing high blood pressure, high cholesterol levels, and obesity. Several large-scale interventions conducted during the 1970s and 1980s to reduce heart disease risk factors failed to produce substantial differences in mortality rates in treated and comparison communities (Farquhar et al., 1990; Lefebvre et al., 1987; Luepker et al., 1994; Multiple Risk Factor Intervention Trial Research Group, 1982; Schwab & Syme, 1997). More recently, health indicators have revealed little progress in addressing these problems. The proportion of adults with high cholesterol has decreased only slightly, from 17.0% during the period 1999–2002 to 14.6% during the period 2007–2008 (NCHS, 2011). Obesity has actually increased in prevalence, rising from 29.9% in 1999–2002 to 33.7% in 2007–2008 (NCHS, 2011). The proportion of adults with high blood pressure also increased, from 28.9% to 32.6% between these same time periods (NCHS, 2011).

Changes in Social and Economic Conditions

Changing the social and economic infrastructure of society to create conditions that facilitate healthy individual behavior is a reform that tends to be under negative demand or no demand by the public and policymakers. Social and economic conditions are difficult to change, and investing the resources and effort to overcome barriers to change is not a priority for the general public or for most policymakers. Many politicians simply do not care about improving conditions for a segment of the population whose welfare will not affect their reelection chances (no demand). Among other policymakers, there has been a declining interest in providing support and resources to improve social and economic conditions for individuals living in poverty (negative demand).

For example, the maximum level of Aid for Families with Dependent Children benefits for poor families fell by more than 17% between 1970 and 1996, after adjustment for inflation, in all 50 states (Kilborn, 1996). Nonwelfare human service benefits were also reduced sharply. During the period 1994 to 1996 alone, federal subsidies for public housing declined by 11.1%, funding for programs to assist the homeless in finding and retaining housing was reduced by 31.3%, funding for food stamps dropped by 32.2%, emergency assistance to provide shelter for homeless families declined by 44.1%, and federal fuel assistance fell by 49.2% (John W. McCormack Institute of Public Affairs, 1997). Between 1990 and 1996, federal funding for the prevention of homelessness among families fell by 64.0%. There is clearly a negative demand among the public and policymakers for public investment in sincere efforts to improve social and economic conditions. If anything, demand for such an investment in society's social and economic infrastructure is declining.

Changes in Social Policy

The negative demand among the public and policymakers for the social policy reforms needed to create conditions in which people can be healthy is perhaps best illustrated by the 1995 U.S. Food and Drug Administration (FDA) regulations on the sale and promotion of tobacco products (FDA, 1996). The Clinton Administration's willingness, and the FDA's determination, to take on the tobacco industry by regulating tobacco for the first time in history represented the most positive political environment ever for social policy reform in the area of tobacco control. In asserting jurisdiction over tobacco products, the FDA found that nicotine is addictive, that cigarettes are a drug-delivery device, and that tobacco products kill more than 400,000 Americans each year (FDA, 1996). In spite of these findings, the FDA regulations did very little to change social policy regarding tobacco sale, marketing, and use in the nation. Given the magnitude of this public health problem and the finding that cigarettes represented a drug-delivery device not unlike others the FDA regulates, the most appropriate action, at least from a public health perspective, would have been to regulate the safety of the product. This might have taken the form of regulating the production, sale, and marketing of tobacco, for example, making cigarettes and smokeless tobacco a prescription product, requiring a reduction or elimination in the level of nicotine in tobacco products, or eliminating the marketing of these deadly products. Any of these actions would have represented a significant and profound change in social policy regarding tobacco.

However, due to perceived public and political opposition to meaningful social policy reform, the FDA proposed regulations that would confront only the sale and marketing of tobacco to minors (FDA, 1996), which were already either illegal or widely recognized as violating accepted social policy norms. The proposed FDA regulations left the production, sale, and marketing of tobacco essentially intact (FDA, 1996). They merely required enforcement of preexisting laws that restricted the sale of tobacco to minors and placed modest restrictions on forms of tobacco advertising and promotion that appeal to youth. In this way the FDA regulations did not represent a true change in social policy. They simply strengthened the enforcement of the existing policy: that tobacco should not be sold or marketed to persons under the age of 18.

The FDA's failure to provide a rational, public health justification for the decision to regulate tobacco only insofar as it represents an addictive threat to adolescents highlights the intensity of policymakers' resolve not to alter deeply ingrained norms of social policy.

As the FDA example demonstrated, changing social policy is under negative demand: Policymakers are willing to pay a price to avoid tampering with long-standing social policy norms.

A Hostile Public Health Marketing Environment

Few commercial marketers have to compete with high-intensity, well-financed campaigns that aim to reduce demand for their products. There is no industry dedicated to convincing people to avoid eating in restaurants or to stop wearing shoes.

In contrast, public health practitioners often face high-intensity campaigns conducted specifically to counteract their marketing efforts. Marketers of public health products must compete with industries that aim to promote unhealthy behaviors. At the same time that public health practitioners try to convince people not to smoke and not to drink, the tobacco and alcohol industries are spending $15 billion and $2 to $3 billion each year, respectively, for the sole purpose of trying to get people to smoke cigarettes and drink alcohol (Federal Trade Commission, 1999, 2005). At the same time that public health officials are trying to convince

Congress and state legislators that firearms are a leading cause of death among young Americans, the National Rifle Association is spending approximately $8 million each year to influence legislators to vote against any proposals that would restrict the production, sale, or use of firearms (Burchfield, 2000).

In addition to opposition to public health efforts by major industries and lobbying groups, the social environment itself, with its deeply ingrained social norms, often contributes to a hostile environment in which to market social change. For example, despite a vigorous campaign to increase physical activity among the population and despite a high level of public demand for ways to increase physical activity, the social and occupational environments are hostile to this type of change. Workplace schedules generally are not designed to allow for a sufficient period of physical activity during the work day. Public transportation systems and urban planning are not developed well enough to allow large numbers of people to walk or bike to work. Intense marketing of and easy access to beer, fast food, and high-fat products undermine individual attempts to improve diet and reduce weight. In 2009, nearly half of adults met neither the aerobic activity nor the muscle strengthening guidelines, and between 2005 and 2008, nearly 68% reported being overweight (NCHS, 2011).

Limited Capacity of Public Health Practitioners to Market Social Change

The capacity of public health practitioners to market social change is limited by three factors: (1) inadequate emphasis on the advocacy role in public health, (2) limited expertise in advocacy skills among current public health practitioners, and (3) lack of training of public health students and practitioners in advocacy skills.

Inadequate Emphasis on Advocacy in Public Health Practice
The public health practitioner is, first and foremost, an advocate for social change. As Linda Rae Murray, president of the American Public Health Association, stated in an interview, "public health is intimately, inextricably melded with social justice. And social justice is really the frame around which public health needs to function in our country" (2011). The historical roots of the public health movement lie in the efforts of visionaries whose lives were dedicated to advocating for social change. It was the social reforms advocated by these figures that gave public health its source, its mission, its foundation, and its original vision.

The public health movement has lost its appreciation of advocacy as its primary tool and its sense of a common, unifying social mission that can serve as a rallying cry for the movement (Institute of Medicine, 1988; Stevens, 1996). Many public health officials have confused advocacy and lobbying, and in an effort not to violate federal laws that restrict lobbying by government and nonprofit agencies, they have completely renounced any semblance of a role in social advocacy. As the Institute of Medicine (1988) report on the future of public health showed, "although public health professionals have traditionally recognized influences of the physical environment on health status, they have been less adept at recognizing health-related influences in the business, economic, and social environment and in fashioning and advocating strategies to control these factors" (p. 113). The report later concludes that "too frequently, public health professionals view politics as a contaminant rather than as a central attribute of democratic governance" (p. 154).

Public health practitioners need a new job description: one that lists advocacy as the chief role and responsibility of the job and that calls on the public health practitioner to mobilize community support for societal efforts to produce social change. As Turnock (1997) concluded in his book, *Public Health: What It Is and How It Works*, "the public health system, from national to state and local levels, must recognize these circumstances and move beyond capably providing services to aggressively advocating and building constituencies for efforts that target the most important of the traditional health risk factors and that promote social policies that both minimize and equalize risks throughout the population. These represent a new job description for public health in the United States, but one that is both necessary and feasible" (pp. 355–356).

Limited Expertise in Advocacy Among Current Public Health Practitioners

Even among public health agencies that still retain an advocacy role, few individual practitioners have been thoroughly trained in advocacy, and many skills necessary to advocate effectively are incompletely developed. As the Institute of Medicine (1988) noted, "effective public health action for many problems requires organizing the interest groups, not just assessing a problem and determining a line of action based on top-down authority" (p. 122). The Institute of Medicine found, however, that most public health workers have not received formal education in public health itself, much less in other critical areas needed for effective advocacy, including political science, community organizing, and management. Public health workers tend to lack skills that derive from education in these areas, including skills in media advocacy, political activity, community organizing, and coalition building.

Inadequate Training in Advocacy for Public Health Students and Practitioners

A convention of public health practitioners and academicians met in 1992 to develop a set of universal competencies for public health professionals (Sorenson & Bialek, 1992; Turnock, 1997). One of the competencies developed was advocating for public health programs and resources (Sorenson & Bialik, 1992). The Institute of Medicine (1988) recommended a set of political skills and capacities that should be essential components of training for all public health students and practitioners: "public health agencies should be able to mobilize the support of important constituencies, including the general public, to compete successfully for scarce resources, to handle conflict over policy priorities and choices, to establish linkages with other organizations, and to develop a positive public image" (p. 154). These are essentially skills in advocacy.

Dr. Barry Levy, a former American Public Health Association president, wrote of the need for public health leaders as follows:

> [Those who] educate and inform, who facilitate grassroots advocacy to shape public policy. . . . Leaders with a holistic vision of public health, who appreciate the relevance of education, employment and housing to public health, who create horizontal integration of programs and services. . . . Leaders who do not fight to get a seat at the table, but who figuratively are the table—who set the stage, frame the issues, pose the questions and engage a wide range of people and organizations in the issues that affect them and their communities. Leaders who work for social justice. Leaders who empower the disadvantaged. (Levy, 1996, p. 2)

As a discipline, advocacy is rarely taught and is certainly not emphasized in schools of public health. For example, in 1997 and 1998, fewer than one-third of accredited schools of public health in the United States offered a course in public health advocacy, and fewer than half offered a course in media advocacy or mass communication.

■ CONCLUSION

The combination of the unfavorable state of public demand for social change, the hostile environment in which public health practitioners must market social change, and the limited training of public health practitioners in marketing and advocacy makes confronting the emerging threats to the public's health a formidable marketing challenge for the public health practitioner. But the same marketing principles that help explain why social change is so difficult to create can also be used to redefine and reposition the public health product so that it is in demand by the public and by policymakers.

References

Burchfield, B. (2000, April 5). Statement of Bobby R. Burchfield before the Senate Committee on Rules and Administration. Retrieved March 15, 2008, from http://rules.senate.gov/hearings/2000/04500burchfield.htm

Farquhar, J. W., Fortmann, S.P., Flora, J.A., Taylor, D.B., Haskell, W.L., Williams, P.T., . . . Wood, P.D. (1990). Effects of community-wide education on cardiovascular disease risk factors. *Journal of the American Medical Association, 264,* 359–365.

Federal Trade Commission. (1999, September). *Self-regulation in the alcohol industry: A review of industry efforts to avoid promoting alcohol to underage consumers.* Retrieved March 21, 2012, from http://www.ftc.gov/reports/alcohol/alcoholreport.htm

Federal Trade Commission. (2005). *Federal Trade Commission cigarette report for 2003.* Retrieved March 21, 2012, from http://www.ftc.gov/reports/cigarette05/050809cigrpt.pdf

Fiore, M.C., Smith, S.S., Jorenby, D.E., & Baker, T.B. (1994). The effectiveness of the nicotine patch for smoking cessation: A meta-analysis. *Journal of the American Medical Association, 271,* 1940–1947.

Giovino, G.A., Schooley, M.W., Zhu, B., Chrismon, J.H., Tomar, S.L., Peddicord, J.P., . . . Eriksen, M.P. (1995). Surveillance for selected tobacco use behaviors—United States, 1900–1994. *Morbidity and Mortality Weekly Report (CDC Surveillance Summaries), 43*(SS-3), 1–43.

Heath, R.P. (1997, June 30). The marketing 100: Excite. *Advertising Age, 68*(26), p. s10.

Institute of Medicine, Committee for the Study of the Future of Public Health. (1988). *The future of public health.* Washington, DC: National Academies Press.

Jensen, J. (1997, July 14). Nintendo plots fall ad campaign for its 64 system: Branding efforts for software, hardware will share message. *Advertising Age, 68*(28), pp. 3, 36.

John W. McCormack Institute of Public Affairs. (1997, January 10). *Over the edge: Cuts and changes in housing, income support, and homeless assistance programs in Massachusetts.* Boston: University of Massachusetts-Boston, John W. McCormack Institute of Public Affairs.

Kilborn, P.T. (1996, December 6). Welfare all over the map. *The New York Times,* p. 3E.

Kotler, P. (1976). *Marketing management: Analysis, planning, and control* (3rd ed.). Englewood Cliffs, NJ: Prentice-Hall.

Lefebvre, R.C., Lasater, T.M., Carleton, R.A., & Peterson, G. (1987). Theory and delivery of health programming in the community: The Pawtucket Heart Health Program. *Preventive Medicine, 16,* 80–95.

Levy, B.S. (1996, December). Putting the public back in public health. *The Nation's Health,* p. 2.

Luepker, R.V., Murray, D.M., Jacobs, D.R., Mittelmark, M.B., Bracht, N., Carlaw, R., . . . Blackburn, H. (1994). Community education for cardiovascular disease prevention: Risk factor changes in the Minnesota Heart Health Program. *American Journal of Public Health, 84,* 1383–1393.

Multiple Risk Factor Intervention Trial Research Group. (1982). Multiple Risk Factor Intervention Trial: Risk factor changes and mortality results. *Journal of the American Medical Association, 248,* 1465–1477.

Murray, L.R. (2011). Interview with New Public Health. Faces of Public Health: A Q&A with Linda Rae Murray, President of the American Public Health Association. [Web log post]. Retrieved March 21, 2012, from http://blog.rwjf.org/publichealth/2011/05/23/public-health-school-graduationa-qa-with-linda-rae-murray-president-of-the-american-public-health-association/?cid=xtw_pubhealth

National Center for Health Statistics. (2011). *Health, United States, 2010: With special feature on death and dying*. Hyattsville, MD: U.S. Department of Health and Human Services, Centers for Disease Control and Prevention.

National Highway Traffic Safety Administration. (1997). *Alcohol involvement in fatal traffic crashes 1995* (Tech. Rep. DOT HS 808-547). Washington, DC: Author.

National Highway Traffic Safety Administration. (2005). Traffic safety facts: Alcohol-related fatalities in 2004. Retrieved March 15, 2007, from http://www-nrd.nhtsa.dot.gov/pdf/nrd-30/NCSA/RNotes/2005/809904.pdf

Neff, J. (1997, June 30). The marketing 100: Clorox. *Advertising Age, 68*(26), p. 218.

Orleans, C.T., Resch, N., Noll, E., Keintz, M.K., Rimer, B.K., Brown, T.V., & Snedden, T.M. (1994). Use of transdermal nicotine in a state-level prescription plan for the elderly—A first look at "real-world" patch users. *Journal of the American Medical Association, 271*, 601–607.

Pollay, R.W., Siddarth, S., Siegel, M., Haddix, A., Merritt, R.K., Giovino, G.A., & Eriksen, M.P. (1996). The last straw? Cigarette advertising and realized market shares among youths and adults, 1979–1993. *Journal of Marketing, 60*, 1–16.

Schwab, M., & Syme, S.L. (1997). On paradigms, community participation, and the future of public health. *American Journal of Public Health, 87*, 2049–2051.

Silagy, C., Mant, D., Fowler, G., & Lodge, M. (1994). Meta-analysis on efficacy of nicotine replacement therapies in smoking cessation. *The Lancet, 343*, 139–142.

Sorenson, A.A., & Bialek, R.G. (Eds.). (1992). *The public health faculty/agency forum*. Gainesville: University of Florida Press.

Stevens, R. (1996). Editorial: Public health history and advocacy in the money-driven 1990s. *American Journal of Public Health, 86*, 1522–1523.

Susser, M. (1995). Editorial: The tribulations of trials—Interventions in communities. *American Journal of Public Health, 85*, 156–158.

Turnock, B.J. (1997). *Public health: What it is and how it works*. Gaithersburg, MD: Aspen.

U.S. Department of Health and Human Services. (1994). *Preventing tobacco use among young people: A report of the Surgeon General*. Atlanta, GA: U.S. Department of Health and Human Services, Centers for Disease Control and Prevention, National Center for Chronic Disease Prevention and Health Promotion, Office on Smoking and Health.

U.S. Food and Drug Administration. (1996, August 28). *Regulations restricting the sale and distribution of cigarettes and smokeless tobacco to protect children and adolescents: Final rule* (Fed. Reg., 21 C.F.R. Parts 801, 803, 804, 807, 820, and 897, pp. 44396–45318). Washington, DC: U.S. Department of Health and Human Services, Food and Drug Administration.

Wald, M.L. (1996, December 15). A fading drumbeat against drunk driving. *The New York Times*, p. E5.

Weddington, W.W. (1990/1991). Towards a rehabilitation of methadone maintenance: Integration of relapse prevention and aftercare. *International Journal of the Addictions, 25*, 1201–1224.

Zbar, J.D. (1997, June 30). The marketing 100: Revitalift. *Advertising Age, 68*(26), p. s16.

4

Challenges for Marketing Public Health

The challenge for public health practitioners is to market the need for specific public health programs and the need for public health itself in light of diminishing resources, tight budgets, a diversion of potential public health resources to bioterrorism preparedness, and a growing antiregulatory, antigovernment sentiment. The demand for population-based, preventive public health programs among the public and policymakers is low because the perceived benefit (reduction in morbidity and mortality) might not be realized for many years. Programs that can demonstrate an immediate and visible impact are more attractive to policymakers and to the public. Also, the most influential political and economic sectors—business, industry, and powerful special interest groups—are able to convince policymakers of the immediate costs of public health programs. Not only is the demand for public health programs low, but public health practitioners have not traditionally had to compete for public attention and resources. Public health practitioners have not been in the business of self-promotion.

The goal of this chapter is to explain the challenges that practitioners face when promoting public health programs and public health as an institution. These challenges include both redefining the product that public health aims to provide and stimulating demand for this product in a somewhat hostile environment. Understanding and applying marketing principles can provide public health professionals with the power and ability to compete successfully for the survival of public health programs and for public health as an institution.

■ CHALLENGES THROUGHOUT HISTORY

From its inception, public health has had to overcome great obstacles to convince policymakers and the public to invest resources and intervene

73

on behalf of society's interest in preserving health. A brief review of some highlights in public health history reveals the many significant barriers to government adoption of public health programs and institutions.

As early as the 18th century, public health reforms faced fierce, organized opposition. For example, despite the availability of a safe and effective vaccine against smallpox, inoculation efforts in Europe were widely criticized as interfering with God's will and spreading the disease among healthy people (McNeill, 1989). In France, the widespread resistance to inoculation did not crumble until 1774, when Louis XV died from smallpox (McNeill, 1989).

For 42 years after Dr. James Lind's 1753 paper demonstrated the effectiveness of oranges and lemons in preventing and curing scurvy, the British naval administration failed to commit the resources necessary to provide this preventive intervention to its sailors (McNeill, 1989). Even when the British Navy decided to purchase supplies of citrus juice for all sailors, it chose West Indian limes, which contained a much lower dose of vitamin C than the more expensive Mediterranean lemons. As a result, outbreaks of scurvy on British vessels occurred as late as 1875, 122 years after Lind's discovery (McNeill, 1989).

Modern public health arose as a social reform of the 19th century. Society began to recognize illness not only as a sign of spiritual or moral weakness but also of poor social and environmental conditions (Amick et al., 1995; Institute of Medicine, 1988; McNeill, 1989; Rosen, 1958, 1972; Turnock, 1997; Winslow, 1923). "In the absence of specific etiological concepts, the social and physical conditions which accompanied urbanization were considered equally responsible for the impairment of vital bodily functions and premature death" (Institute of Medicine, 1988, p. 59). Sanitation and therefore disease control were then seen as public responsibilities. The control of disease shifted from simply responding to outbreaks of illness to instituting proactive, preventive measures. Thus, public health arose out of the establishment of healthy social conditions as a societal goal and the recognition of public institutions as responsible for achieving this social goal (Institute of Medicine, 1988).

In 1842, Edwin Chadwick documented the high prevalence of infectious disease in England and recommended the establishment of national and local boards of health to develop, implement, and maintain a system of sewage and waste disposal (Amick et al., 1995; Chadwick, 1842/1965; Chave, 1984; Turnock, 1997). Chadwick charged the public with creating the infrastructure necessary to control and prevent the spread of infectious diseases; the public role was accepted and institutionalized in the Public Health Act of 1848. Similar reports published around 1850 by Lemuel Shattuck and John Griscom in the United States laid the foundation for the establishment of a government-directed system of public health surveillance and regulation in this country (Amick et al., 1995; Griscom, 1845/1970; Institute of Medicine, 1988; Rosenkrantz, 1972; Shattuck, 1850;

Winslow, 1923). In 1866, New York became the first large city to establish a permanent Metropolitan Board of Health (Duffy, 1992; Institute of Medicine, 1988; McNeill, 1989; Starr, 1982).

Notably, government action to establish new sanitation systems followed more than a decade of advocacy for such changes by groups of reformers (McNeill, 1989; Turnock, 1997). England's Public Health Act of 1848 was enacted a full 6 years after Chadwick's report. New York City's Metropolitan Board of Health was established 16 years after the Shattuck and Griscom reports.

The initial outbreaks of cholera in the United States in 1832 were met with limited interventions, such as cleaning the streets, caring for the sick, and disposing of the dead (Duffy, 1992). Duffy (1992) noted that "although the cholera epidemic of 1832 shocked the country and literally panicked many citizens, insofar as public health was concerned, its impact was fleeting. . . . Cities and towns, particularly those affected by the outbreak, temporarily remedied the worst sanitary abuses, but within a year or two sanitary conditions were even worse than before. None of the health agencies that came into existence as a result of the epidemic continued to function once the danger was past" (pp. 84, 91).

A reemergence of widespread cholera outbreaks in the United States between 1849 and 1854 led public health advocates to call for sanitary reforms, but their protests were largely ignored. State and local governments did not invest in major changes in societal infrastructure until the mid-1860s, when the nation was threatened by yet another epidemic of cholera. "In almost every American city the cholera outbreaks of the mid-nineteenth century occasioned sanitary surveys and reports. And in almost every case these reports recommended the building of water and sewer systems, the institution of street-cleaning and garbage-collection programs, the creation of strong sanitary measures" (Duffy, 1992, p. 100).

Ultimately, it took the threat of a reemergence of a cholera epidemic in England to precipitate Parliamentary action in 1848 (McNeill, 1989) and the threat of a third wave of approaching cholera to prompt the establishment of a formal and permanent Metropolitan Board of Health in New York City in 1866 (Duffy, 1992; McNeill, 1989; Rosenberg, 1962; Starr, 1982), almost 25 years after Chadwick's report and 15 years after similar reports by Shattuck and Griscom.

One reason for delayed implementation of sanitary reforms was that the early cholera epidemics largely affected the poor and were perceived as a scourge on their filthy living conditions. As Duffy (1992) pointed out, "in New Orleans, where civic leaders insisted that only strangers and the intemperate poor fell prey to pestilential disorders, the city's experience with cholera merely reinforced their belief" (p. 84). Furthermore, the large capital expenditures required to build water and sewage systems would increase taxes for the wealthy. Duffy explained that "the upper classes in general had no desire to tax themselves for the welfare of the poor" (p. 100).

The necessary reforms were finally adopted only when the impending cholera outbreaks threatened to affect all segments of society. During the urbanization and industrialization of the 19th century, infectious diseases began to ravage the entire population, rich and poor alike. In New York City, for example, an 1865 field survey found more than 1,200 cases of smallpox and more than 2,000 cases of typhus in a single tenement district (Institute of Medicine, 1988; Winslow, 1923). Moreover, persons of all social classes were susceptible to these contagious diseases. "Increasingly, it dawned upon the rich that they could not ignore the plight of the poor; the proximity of gold coast and slum was too close" (Institute of Medicine, 1988, p. 59). Whereas disease had previously been viewed as a problem of the underclass, the poor, and the morally flawed, contagion throughout communities of rich and poor alike fostered the view of disease as a societal, not a personal, problem. "Poverty and disease could no longer be treated simply as individual failings" (Institute of Medicine, 1988, p. 59). The implication of this change in the disease paradigm was profound: Disease was a societal problem; thus, prevention and control were societal responsibilities. Social reform gave rise to the establishment of public health agencies (Institute of Medicine, 1988). And because unhealthy social and environmental conditions threatened not only the poor but the entire community, public health came to be seen as a public responsibility (McNeill, 1989; Rosenkrantz, 1972).

Other governments were even slower to respond to the need for sanitary reforms. For example, Hamburg, Germany, held back the necessary expenditures to establish a clean water supply until 1892 when a widespread cholera epidemic affected all social classes in the city (McNeill, 1989).

The public in general and government in particular were relatively apathetic to the welfare of the poor. Public health advocates countered this sentiment to secure funding for many of their programs. "Health and social reformers inveighed against the prevailing social injustices and unsanitary conditions of the times, but the propertied classes had little concern for the welfare of the poor, and without their support little could be done" (Duffy, 1992, p. 118).

The delay in implementing sanitary reforms also was due, in part, to political opposition, especially the firmly held principle of individual freedom and control over one's property (McNeill, 1989). Installation of water and sewer pipes required intrusion onto private property as well as huge capital expenditures. The challenge to public health reformers at the time was not one of finding effective solutions but of convincing policymakers to adopt these solutions. As McNeill (1989) explained, "The problem as it presented itself to sanitary reformers of the 1830s and 1840s was less one of technique than of organization . . . a libertarian prejudice against regulation, infringing the individual's right to do what he chose with his own property was deeply rooted" (p. 239). Duffy (1992) argued that government did not respond more aggressively to the first wave of cholera because it was hesitant to infringe on "individual liberty and private property rights" (p. 84).

Public health measures were perceived as treading not only on individual rights but also on the rights and opportunities of business owners. The development of water and sewer systems was very costly. Other public health measures, such as quarantines, were perceived as interfering with free enterprise and harmful to business and economic development. For example, in 1866, the city of Memphis rejected its board of health's recommendations for preventing a cholera epidemic (Duffy, 1992). "The dominant commercial interests in Memphis reflected the prevailing view in the urban South that the only functions of government were to protect property and preserve the existing social order. That quarantines hindered trade and that sanitary programs cost money only reinforced this assumption" (p. 115).

Paul Starr (1982), in *The Social Transformation of American Medicine*, reinforced Duffy's point:

> The economic boundaries of public health were determined partly by constraints of cost—not simply the direct cost of public health programs to taxpayers, but the indirect cost of such measures to business and to society at large. In the first half of the nineteenth century, some authorities attributed epidemics to contagion and recommended quarantines—an economically damaging measure because of the disruption of commerce. Others ascribed epidemics to miasmas and advised general cleanups of the environment. The environmental approach may have been favored by commercial interest because it was less disruptive than the closing of markets. But wholesale cleanups and quarantines were both costly responses to disease. (p. 189)

Public health measures often have been perceived as interfering not with individual or business rights but with individual behavior. As the Institute of Medicine (1988) explained, "repeatedly, the role of the government in regulating individual behavior has been challenged" (p. 71). Soon after it was formed, Britian's Board of Health was disbanded because Chadwick, its director, "claimed a wide scope for state intervention in an age when laissez-faire was the doctrine of the day" (Chave, 1984, p. 7).

Another reason for the delay in implementing sanitary reforms was that the public seemed interested in public health only during an outbreak—there was little interest in instituting preventive measures. For example, Duffy (1992) explained that despite the widespread second wave of cholera in the United States in the mid-19th century, recommendations of public health reformers were ignored because citizens quickly lost interest after the epidemic disappeared: "Carrying out these recommendations would have required relatively huge capital expenditures and large increases in annual government budgets, but once cholera had disappeared, the average citizen had little interest in public health" (p. 100).

The routine nature of endemic infectious diseases also might explain why government officials did not respond with greater urgency (Duffy, 1971; Leavitt, 1982; Rosenberg, 1962). "The endemic disorders responsible for the high morbidity and mortality rates were all too familiar, and without the stimulus provided by a strange and highly fatal pestilence, the average citizen had little interest in—and even less inclination to spend money for—public health" (Duffy, 1992, p. 179). During the late 1800s, tuberculosis, diphtheria, scarlet fever, and typhoid were the chief killers, but newspapers and the public paid little attention (Duffy, 1992). Instead, "the press and the public worried about Asiatic cholera, which was of no consequence after 1873, and smallpox, which was relatively minor compared to the other epidemic disorders" (Duffy, 1992, p. 179). Why the lack of public concern? According to Duffy (1992), all these endemic disorders "were familiar ones" (p. 179).

Leavitt (1982), discussing the history of Milwaukee's public health system, made a similar point:

> The frightening and dramatic quality of the unexpected provided the first impetus to health reform. . . . When smallpox or cholera threatened Milwaukee, citizens reacted vigorously. Not only were these diseases infrequent visitors, and therefore possibly preventable, they also carried ghastly symptoms and produced perilous outcomes. . . . Because of the fear generated at times of acute distress, epidemics frequently increased the power and authority of the health department. Conversely, chronic diseases, which killed more people than the epidemics, did not easily win the attention of citizen groups or health officials. (pp. 241, 242)

Leavitt (1982) further explained, "The Milwaukee experience abounds with other examples that support the contention that unusual and acute disasters encouraged health reforms more than did the typical endemic problems. Tuberculosis, the city's major killer, received almost no attention until the turn of the twentieth century, in part because it was familiar, its symptoms lacked drama, and the disease took many years to kill its victims" (p. 243).

Even during colonial times, disease was viewed as a burden on society only when it represented something that was not well understood, something mysterious, or something unfamiliar—all conditions that evoke societal fear. As Duffy (1992) noted, malaria was by far the greatest threat to health and life in colonial times, but the epidemics that aroused the most attention during this period were smallpox and yellow fever. Although malaria was far more significant in terms of its public health burden on society, smallpox and yellow fever were less predictable, less well understood, more mysterious, and brought about quicker, more visible, and more graphic death:

> They appeared mysteriously, swept through the community with deadly force, struck down old and young alike, and brought a ghastly death to many of their victims. . . . The constant references in colonial letters, diaries, journals, newspapers, and official records to the two great killer diseases, smallpox and yellow fever, speak more for their dramatic nature than for their actual impact upon colonial health. People have always feared strange and unknown dangers far more than familiar ones, and this holds true for diseases. (Duffy, 1992, p. 23)

A final reason for the delay in implementing public health reforms was organized opposition from the medical profession, which historically has viewed many public health programs as intrusions on its autonomy. As Starr (1982) explained, "extending the boundaries of public health to incorporate more of medicine seemed necessary and desirable to some public health officials, but as one might imagine, private practitioners regarded such extensions as an usurpation. Doctors fought against public treatment of the sick, requirements for reporting cases of tuberculosis and venereal disease, and attempts by public health authorities to establish health centers to coordinate preventive and curative medical services" (p. 181).

Perhaps the most striking example of medical opposition to public health measures was the medical profession's opposition to the proposal for a series of rural health centers in New York State in the 1920s. "When the bill came before the state legislature, it had the backing of public health, social welfare, labor, and farming groups, but was opposed by the medical profession. The doctors' opposition, according to C.E.A. Winslow's account, proved fatal" (Starr, 1982, p. 196).

Starr (1982) summarized public health's perpetual struggle against social forces that oppose government intervention into personal or societal interests: "Much of the history of public health is a record of struggles over the limits of its mandate. On one frontier, public health authorities have met opposition from religious groups and others with moral objections to state intervention on behalf of the officially sponsored conceptions of health and hygiene. On another frontier, public health has met opposition from business and commerce, anxious to protect their economic interests" (pp. 180–181).

The lessons of public health history have three important implications in terms of the marketing environment that public health practitioners face. First, the nature of the public health product puts it in an unfavorable state of demand by the public and by policymakers. Second, the environment in which public health must be marketed is hostile. Third, the type of effort required to market public health involves skills that many public health practitioners have not developed and that are rarely taught to public health students. The reasons that marketing public health is a formidable challenge for the public health practitioner are explored in the following sections.

■ AN UNFAVORABLE STATE OF DEMAND FOR PUBLIC HEALTH PROGRAMS

As was just described, neither the public nor the policymakers have demanded public health programs and policies and public health as an institution. The great public health reforms of the 19th century, for example, took many years of persistent advocacy by public health practitioners before they were adopted. From the foregoing discussion, several major reasons for the low level of public and political demand for public health interventions can be identified. The common denominator is that the benefits of public health programs are remote in time and remote in the mind of the consumer. In contrast, the benefits of medical interventions are usually immediate, both in time and in the mind of the patient. This point is illustrated by comparing and contrasting characteristics of the benefits of medical interventions and public health programs.

The benefits of medical treatment are usually immediate. A patient with appendicitis, for example, will enter the hospital in severe pain and with her life in jeopardy. Within hours of surgery, the patient's condition can be stabilized and her pain will be relieved. On the other hand, the very nature of prevention implies that benefits will not be seen for a long time after intervention, sometimes for many years. For example, cities that invested in new water and sewer systems did not benefit for many years. Although improved sanitation might prevent an epidemic from occurring in the future, it cannot alleviate the epidemic conditions that already exist. Similarly, the benefits of programs that prevent smoking among adolescents, decrease fat intake, or increase physical activity might not be seen until many years later.

Because of the immediate benefits of medical treatment and interventions to control communicable diseases, it is easy to convince policymakers of the need for medical treatment and for infectious disease control programs. When Ebola virus attacks, people die within days, thereby threatening the immediate survival of a community. It is easy to see the benefit of intervening to treat victims of Ebola infection. When an epidemic of smoking affects youth in a community, there is no immediate threat to survival or even to health. The benefits of intervention are not as readily apparent, not as immediate, and not nearly as compelling.

The benefits of public health interventions are remote in time as well as in the mind of the consumer, whereas the connection between a medical intervention and its benefits is much more apparent to the observer.

For example, the benefits of instituting sanitary reforms were not visible when New York City's Metropolitan Board of Health was established in 1866, although it resulted in far better control of the subsequent cholera outbreak. In the public's perception, there simply were fewer victims after the implementation of the reforms.

The remote connection between public health programs and their benefits makes it more difficult to market public health programs to policymakers. Few, if any, policymakers question whether treatment of heart attack victims has a positive impact on their health and survival or whether treatment of victims of infectious diseases is beneficial. Even without scientific demonstration of a positive impact of treatment, a strong and unquestioned link between treatment and outcome is present, leading, for example, to the expenditure of billions of health care dollars on increasing the quantity, but not the quality, of the later years of life. In contrast, the relationship between public health interventions and their effects is often questioned seriously, even when scientific evidence clearly demonstrates a significant effect of the public health program on both longevity and quality of life. Despite a wealth of evidence that public assistance helps to alleviate poverty and to make life more tolerable for the impoverished, policymakers continue to question this link, even suggesting that public assistance causes the poverty. Mikhail et al. (1997) noted that "curative services often have been judged by their perceived value, while preventive services have been held to a more rigorous standard of documentation" (p. 37).

Because the results of public health programs often are invisible, it is much more difficult to develop vocal constituencies around public health issues than around medical treatment issues. As Turnock (1997) explained, "prevention efforts often lack a clear constituency because success results in unseen consequences. Because these consequences are unseen, people are less likely to develop an attachment for or to support the efforts preventing them. Advocates for mental health services, care for individuals with development disabilities, organ transplants, and end-stage renal disease often make their presence felt. But few state capitols have seen candlelight demonstrations by thousands of people who did not get diphtheria" (p. 20).

A major reason for the obscurity of the impact of public health programs, especially those that address chronic disease, is that the outcomes are neither visible nor graphic. The effect of medical treatment (or its absence), however, is highly visible and pervasive in society, especially through the media. Movies such as *Contagion* and *Twelve Monkeys* show the immediate and vividly disturbing consequences of infection with "killer" viruses. Television portrays the immediate impact of treatment in medical emergencies weekly on various shows. Television news stories show vivid images of Hurricane Katrina victims on New Orleans rooftops, prompting an outpouring of concern and money for medical aid. No equally compelling images exist for most public health problems and interventions.

Harvard University researcher Graham Colditz explained, "One of the things we can't get away from is that if you're in a clinic treating patients with cancer, you can count the number treated and the successes. But if you have 10,000 people who increase their physical activity and 10 fewer of them get colon cancer in 10 years, well, those people are not identifiable. That's particularly frustrating when you're trying to lobby for dollars for prevention" (Lauerman, 1997, p. 14).

Mikhail and colleagues (1997) made the distinction between "identified" lives and "statistical" lives and argued that society favors treatment programs over prevention programs because they address the needs of identifiable individuals: "The clear social preference is to provide health care resources to respond to specific and immediate needs of identified individuals. By its very nature, prevention generally deals with amorphous populations; curative care deals with identified personalized lives and thus seems to carry a greater societal ethical imperative for committing resources in response to specific health care needs" (p. 38).

The nature of the demand for public health compared with medical intervention also is different in terms of its urgency. Physicians do not typically go out into the community trying to stimulate demand for medical treatment: When people become sick, they demand medical treatment. This is not the case with public health. The presence of public health problems does not itself imply an immediate demand for intervention. Usually, the demand for public health attention is dormant until a crisis arises. The nature of demand for public health interventions during the 19th century largely followed such a pattern. Although temporary public health programs were established with each of the three waves of the cholera epidemic, demand dissipated when the outbreaks subsided.

Medical interventions often involve technological problems and solutions, whereas public health problems usually require social, economic, and political solutions. Americans tend to view technological challenges as a true test of the nation's strength. Atwood, Colditz, and Kawachi (1997) compared U.S. investment in sequencing the human genome with the limited effort in controlling tobacco use: "Tobacco is responsible for 30% of all cancer deaths, while 5% to 10% can be linked to inherited genetic causes. Yet the tobacco control budget of the National Cancer Institute (NCI) amounted to $60 million in 1996, as compared with the multibillion-dollar research project under way to sequence the human genome" (p. 1604).

■ HOSTILE ENVIRONMENT FOR MARKETING PUBLIC HEALTH PROGRAMS

Because public health interventions often interfere with individual rights or behavior or with the conduct and livelihood of business, marketing public health programs often takes place in a hostile environment. As John Duffy

(1992) noted in *The Sanitarians: A History of American Public Health*, "unfortunately, sanitary and health regulations inevitably infringe on individual rights, a situation compounded by the general American distrust of all laws and regulations. . . . The zealous guarding of individual rights creates major problems for health officials in a democracy" (p. 3).

For this reason public health measures often run up against fierce opposition by many stakeholders, including the public. Regulations against public smoking are criticized on the grounds that individuals have the right to decide when and where to smoke and that infringing on this freedom will lead to regulating other aspects of personal behavior, including eating, drinking, and exercising. In such an environment, public health advocates aiming to reduce tobacco-related mortality are considered zealots seeking prohibition.

Not only do population-based, preventive, public health programs tend to intrude into the lives of individuals, they also often interfere with the autonomy of business and the perceived integrity of the free enterprise system. Public health programs often are seen as intruding into the free market system and placing undue economic burdens on business owners. The debate over public health regulations often is framed in terms of health versus wealth, implying that public health programs are, by definition, economically harmful.

In contrast, medical treatment programs are viewed as providing the individual with personal freedoms and individual rights. Efforts to limit the provision of medical care are attacked as being unfair encroachments on the health care system. Even when medical treatment does affect personal freedom, society often sanctions the treatment on the grounds that it safeguards the rights of other individuals. For example, several states have enacted laws that require pregnant women who are infected with the human immunodeficiency virus to be treated with azidothymidine. Although this interferes far more with individual freedom than do most public health programs, society still views forced treatment as a mechanism to ensure the rights of others—in this case, the unborn child.

The appropriateness of medical treatment interventions also tends to be unquestioned from an economic perspective. Even when their potential cost-effectiveness is not clear, treatment interventions generally are acceptable (Mikhail et al., 1997). Treatment programs are rarely challenged on the grounds that they will adversely affect the nation's economy in spite of the tremendous burden placed on the national economy by the increasing costs of medical treatment.

In addition to interfering with individual rights and business autonomy, public health programs often run up against firmly held social and economic norms. Because the central goal of public health interventions is to change social and economic conditions or policies, these interventions must in some way challenge existing norms. In contrast, medical treatment programs tend to support the established economic norms of the health care system. The more specialists, specialized equipment, and specialized procedures there are, the more deeply entrenched the health care industry becomes as an economic force in society. On the other hand, poorly funded public health agencies have been accused of promoting programs simply to ensure their continued personal livelihood. "Implications for life-style and resource allocation inherent in the modern definition of public health are often in conflict with prevailing social policy or perceived feasibility in an age of growing awareness of scarcity and debate regarding the limits of government" (Ellencweig & Yoshpe, 1984, p. 75).

The presence of opposition groups that fight public health measures that they perceive will harm their economic livelihood creates a hostile environment for marketing public health. In contrast, no established industry opposes medical treatment programs because they perceive them as threats to economic viability. For example, there is no anti-liver transplant industry opposing the extreme medical interventions required to treat liver disease. However, as soon as one proposes regulations on the advertising or sale of alcohol to prevent the need for some liver transplants, one runs into well-funded and well-organized opposition from the alcoholic beverage industry.

Often, public health programs run up against industries whose financial interests are directly affected by the implementation of the program. Public health interventions to reduce alcohol and tobacco use, for example, can be successful only if they reduce alcohol and tobacco sales and, therefore, these industries' profits. In contrast, there are no major special interest groups whose primary purpose is to oppose medical treatment programs. There is no pro-hypertension industry, for example, that opposes treatment of hypertension. However, if public health officials were to propose a federal program to prevent hypertension in the population by regulating the sodium content of foods, a large and powerful food industry would be waiting for them at the Capitol steps. As Ellencweig and Yoshpe (1984) explained, "emphasis upon preventive medicine and environment threatens most prevailing systems of medical care organization and entrenched industrial and professional lobbies" (p. 75).

■ LIMITED CAPACITY OF PUBLIC HEALTH PRACTITIONERS TO COMPETE FOR PUBLIC ATTENTION AND RESOURCES

Because public health practitioners generally are not trained in marketing, communications, political science, and public relations, it might be difficult for them to compete in the battle to secure scarce resources to fund their programs. To gain attention and resources, public health practitioners must be able to work with lawmakers in the legislative process, build constituencies and coalitions, and form collaborative relations with other organizations. Also, to generate public understanding, appreciation, and support, they must employ public relations techniques and marketing and communications principles. The lack of training of public health practitioners in these areas makes the marketing challenge particularly difficult.

Fred Kroger, former director of the Centers for Disease Control and Prevention's Office of Health Communications, summarized as follows:

> When colleagues at the state and local levels try to sell city councils, their boards of supervisors, or their state legislators on the merits of public health, folks are not buying. Some in public health have even admitted publicly that public health has done a singularly poor job of marketing. (Kroger et al., 1997, p. 273)

In addition, public health practitioners generally have not played the same kind of prominent leadership and advocacy roles for themselves, their programs, and their institutions that they have played for the health of their constituents. To promote the continued survival and growth of public health as an institution, public health practitioners must take more prominent leadership and advocacy roles, guided by improved competence in political advocacy.

■ CONCLUSION

Stimulating demand for public health programs is a formidable challenge for the public health practitioner because public health programs (1) tend to have delayed benefits that are not easily recognized and are not visible, (2) are perceived as intruding into individual autonomy and the free enterprise system or as conflicting with established social and economic norms, and (3) face heavy opposition by powerful special interest groups. Fortunately, the strategic application of marketing principles can be a powerful tool in redefining and repositioning public health as a product that is in demand by the public and by policymakers.

References

Amick, B.C., III, Levine, S., Tarlov, A.R., & Walsh, D.C. (1995). Introduction. In B.C. Amick III, S. Levine, A.R. Tarlov, & D.C. Walsh (Eds.), *Society and health* (pp. 3–17). New York, NY: Oxford University Press.

Atwood, K., Colditz, G.A., & Kawachi, I. (1997). From public health science to prevention policy: Placing science in its social and political contexts. *American Journal of Public Health, 87,* 1603–1606.

Chadwick, E. (1965). *Report on the sanitary condition of the labouring population of Great Britain.* Edinburgh, Scotland: Edinburgh University Press. (Original work published 1842)

Chave, S.P.W. (1984). The origins and development of public health. In W.W. Holland, R. Detels, & G. Knox (Eds.), *Oxford textbook of public health: Vol 1. History, determinants, scope and strategies.* New York, NY: Oxford University Press.

Duffy, J. (1971). Social impact of disease in the late 19th century. *Bulletin of the New York Academy of Medicine, 47,* 797–811.

Duffy, J. (1992). *The sanitarians: A history of American public health.* Urbana: University of Illinois Press.

Ellencweig, A., & Yoshpe, R. (1984). Definition of public health. *Public Health Review, 12,* 65–78.

Griscom, J.H. (1970). *The sanitary condition of the laboring population of New York.* New York, NY: Arno. (Original work published 1845)

Institute of Medicine, Committee for the Study of the Future of Public Health. (1988). *The future of public health.* Washington, DC: National Academies Press.

Kroger, F., McKenna, J.W., Shepherd, M., Howze, E.H., & Knight, D.S. (1997). Marketing public health: The CDC experience. In M.E. Goldberg, M. Fishbein, & S.E. Middlestadt (Eds.), *Social marketing: Theoretical and practical perspectives* (pp. 267–290). Mahwah, NJ: Lawrence Erlbaum Associates.

Lauerman, J.F. (1997). Combating cancer: The power of prevention has scarcely been tapped. *Harvard Magazine, 99,* 11–14.

Leavitt, J.W. (1982). *The healthiest city. Milwaukee and the politics of health reform.* Princeton, NJ: Princeton University Press.

McNeill, W.H. (1989). *Plagues and peoples.* New York, NY: Anchor Books.

Mikhail, O.I., Swint, J.M., Casperson, P.R., & Spitz, M.R. (1997). Health care's double standard: The prevention dilemma. *Journal of Public Health Management and Practice, 3,* 37–42.

Rosen, G. (1958). *A history of public health.* New York, NY: MD Publications.

Rosen, G. (1972). The evolution of social medicine. In H.E. Freeman, S. Levine, & L.G. Reeder (Eds.), *Handbook of medical sociology* (2nd ed., pp. 30–60). Englewood Cliffs, NJ: Prentice-Hall.

Rosenberg, C.E. (1962). *The cholera years: The United States in 1832, 1849, and 1866.* Chicago, IL: University of Chicago Press.

Rosenkrantz, B.G. (1972). *Public health and the state.* Cambridge, MA: Harvard University Press.

Shattuck, L. (1850). *Report of the Sanitary Commission of Massachusetts, 1850.* Boston, MA: Dutton & Wentworth.

Starr, P. (1982). *The social transformation of American medicine.* New York, NY: Basic Books.

Turnock, B.J. (1997). *Public health: What it is and how it works.* Gaithersburg, MD: Aspen.

Winslow, C.E.A. (1923). *The evolution and significance of the modern public health campaign.* New Haven, CT: Yale University Press.

CHAPTER

5

Introduction to Marketing Principles

The threats to both the public's health and public health as an institution underscore the need for public health practitioners to improve their abilities to attract attention and resources for issues of importance. One tool that public health practitioners can use to counter these challenges is marketing. This chapter introduces basic marketing concepts the practitioner can and should use to effect change.

The principles of marketing provide a disciplined, audience-focused, research-based process to plan, develop, implement, and assess many different types of initiatives designed to improve the public's health. Marketing can be used to change personal health behaviors directly or to change the environment in which such behaviors take place. Although marketing public health changes and institutions is different from and often more difficult than marketing commercial products and services, the basic goals should be the same: create, communicate, and deliver value. Commercial and social marketers accomplish this goal by understanding the needs, wants, and values of target audience members. Marketers then use that understanding to build relationships with audiences and address the traditional marketing concepts of product, price, place, and promotion. They must adjust these concepts to the environment in which social change takes place.

■ EVOLUTION OF MARKETING SOCIAL CHANGE

The idea of using marketing principles to "sell" social changes as diverse as health practices, recycling, volunteerism, and voting has been around for a long time. In an oft-cited article, Weibe noted in the early 1950s that nonbusiness managers see private sector marketing communications and ask, "Why can't you sell brotherhood like soap?" In 1971, Kotler and Zaltman published their landmark article, "Social Marketing: An Approach to Planned Social Change," in which they defined social marketing as "the design, implementation, and control of programs calculated to influence the acceptability of social ideas and involving considerations of product planning, pricing, communication, distribution, and marketing research" (p. 5).

The first practical public health applications of social marketing took an advertising approach, providing informational or "what to do" messages, such as "stop smoking—it might kill you," but they lacked "here's how to do it" information directed at overcoming barriers or building skills based on research with the audience. The social advertising approach then evolved to social communication—making greater use of personal selling and editorial support in addition to mass advertising—and finally, a true marketing approach. This is characterized by (1) marketing research (commonly referred to as formative research) to understand the potential size of the market, the major groups or segments within it, and their corresponding behavioral characteristics; (2) product development, searching for the best product to meet the need, rather than using a sales approach of trying to sell an existing product; (3) using incentives; and (4) facilitating behavior change by considering ways to make adoption of the behavior easier (Fox & Kotler, 1980).

To change individual health behaviors effectively, it is necessary to consider the historical, cultural, political, and social environments in which change will take place. Often, it is necessary to change aspects of those environments as well; sometimes widespread social change will not or cannot occur until laws, regulations, or other governmental and nongovernmental policies either change to facilitate a particular behavior or add a measure of enforceable behavior change. For example, seat belt use in the United States did not increase significantly until a large number of states passed laws mandating their use. In 1983, seat belt use prevalence was only 15%; by 1995, all but two states had seat belt laws in effect and use prevalence had increased to 67% in 1994 (Nelson, Bolen, & Kresnow, 1998). Similarly, nonsmokers had no real way of escaping cigarette smoke until regulatory changes were widespread, such as bans on smoking on domestic flights and mandates for smoke-free workplaces.

Social marketing scholars have always recognized the frequent need to address the environment in which an individual's behavior occurs as well as the behavior itself. In 1980, Fox and Kotler outlined four broad approaches to producing social change: legal, technological, economic, and informational. Rothschild (1999) described three primary classes of strategic tools available to public health: marketing, education, and law. He noted, "Current public health behavior management relies heavily on education and law while neglecting the underlying philosophy of marketing and exchange" (p. 24). He conceptualized each domain as follows:

- *Marketing:* "attempts to manage behavior by offering reinforcing incentives and/or consequences in an environment that invites voluntary exchange. The environment is made favorable for appropriate behavior through the development of choices with comparative advantage (products and services), favorable cost-benefit relationships (pricing), and time and place utility enhancement (channels of distribution). Positive reinforcement is provided when a transaction is completed" (p. 25).

- *Education:* "messages of any type that attempt to inform and/or persuade a target to behave voluntarily in a particular manner but do not provide, on their own, direct and/or immediate reward or punishment" (p. 25).

- *Law:* "the use of coercion to achieve behavior in a nonvoluntary manner or to threaten with punishment for noncompliance or inappropriate behavior" (p. 25). Rothschild also noted that law can be used to increase (through price subsidies) or decrease (through taxes) the probability of transactions that might not develop as desired through free-market mechanisms.

Often, those working to improve public health may need to use all these strategic tools—marketing, education, and law—in combination. The issue of automobile child safety seats in the United States illustrates this problem. In 1996, almost 80% of child safety seats were used improperly (National Highway Traffic Safety Administration [NHTSA], 1996). Many were not properly secured with seat belts, and many were put in the wrong position in the car, such as in an airbag-equipped passenger seat. Solving this problem involved a combination of approaches. Education provided parents and other caregivers with information on how to install the seats properly; directions are included with the seat itself and with the car. In addition, many federal, state, and local agencies make information available. Many communities also demonstrate proper installation by publicizing days on which police officers will be available to check and, if necessary, correct the installation.

However, technological changes to cars and child safety seats were necessary to address the underlying problem of the seats being excessively difficult to install properly. Bringing about such changes required marketing research: NHTSA and the manufacturers investigated a variety of alternative installation systems and explored which ones consumers could use with the greatest success. They also weighed the costs of various types of systems. The force of law was then used both to allow and to require a new installation system: NHTSA issued a new federal regulation that required specific standardized installation components in vehicles and on child safety seats (NHTSA, 1997).

Even with improved anchorage systems available and laws mandating the use of child restraint systems, ongoing marketing activities are always necessary to inform and persuade new parents and other caregivers to use them, and ongoing educational activities are necessary to teach them how to properly install and use the restraints.

■ USING MARKETING IN PUBLIC HEALTH TODAY

Today, many individuals and organizations interested in public health are working hard to become more marketing driven and are harnessing the power of the marketing mind-set to bring about change, both in personal health behaviors and in the environmental facilitators of and barriers to those behaviors. At the most basic level, any type of change involves an individual taking an action: a member of the public choosing more low-fat foods or getting an immunization; a restaurant chef ensuring plenty of appealing, healthful menu items; a school administrator introducing a policy that increases student and/or staff opportunities for physical activity; a legislator voting for a bill that includes adequate public health funding. To convince any of these audiences to take the desired action, marketers must build a relationship with that audience and create, communicate, and deliver value to the audience, which is the definition of marketing, according to the American Marketing Association (2005). Therefore, marketing can help bring about any of these types of changes.

■ KEY CONCEPTS FROM COMMERCIAL MARKETING

Marketing principles can be used to influence individuals' personal health behavior, to reduce barriers to those behaviors, or to increase benefits of those behaviors in the environments in which the behaviors occur. To apply marketing principles to public health programs successfully, practitioners must first understand the key concepts underlying commercial marketing and distinguishing it from other approaches to social change:

- Exchange
- Self-interest
- Behavior change
- Competition
- Audience orientation and segmentation
- Four Ps: The marketing mix (product, price, place, and promotion)
- Building relationships

Exchange

Marketers believe the notion of exchange plays a central role in the choices people make: A person gives something to get something in exchange. Hastings and Saren (2003) noted that exchange theory "assumes we are need-directed beings with a natural inclination to try and improve our lot" (p. 309) and list five prerequisites for a marketing exchange (citing Kotler, 2000):

- There are at least two parties.
- Each party has something that might be of value to the other party.
- Each party is capable of communication and delivery.
- Each party is free to accept or reject the offer.
- Each party believes it is appropriate or desirable to deal with the other party.

Hastings and Saren also noted that "central to these assumptions is the notion that the exchange must be mutually beneficial" (2003, p. 309). For example, if an individual walks down the street on a hot day and passes a lemonade stand, he might decide to pay one dollar and get a glass of lemonade. Each party benefits from the transaction in obvious ways: The stand owner makes money and the individual gets a glass of lemonade. But each party may also accrue other benefits, and it is those other consumer benefits that are critical to understand, because they often differentiate one offering from another. When engaging in the lemonade transaction, the consumer is actually "buying" a way of quenching thirst—something that was determined to be worth one dollar. The good or service is often merely a means of obtaining the desired benefit.

The same individual walks down the street on that hot day and encounters a convenience store with many types of drinks. To decide which drink to purchase, he weighs the costs of each against the benefits of each. The costs may be more than financial: Calories may be a cost for someone who is watching his weight; therefore, water or a diet soft drink would be a low-cost choice. Benefits beyond thirst-quenching ability are likely to come into play. Perhaps one option is a childhood favorite and thus brings to mind many happy memories but another is 100% fruit juice and therefore has the added benefit of higher nutrient value. But perhaps the 100% fruit juice is also more expensive. Now the consumer must compare the choices and decide what is most important.

As these examples illustrate, regardless of the type of exchange, people go through a process of weighing the tangible and intangible benefits they attach to a product or service against the tangible or intangible costs before making an exchange. The benefits must outweigh the costs for a person to complete the transaction. These mental transactions can become quite complex when people are being asked to replace an existing behavior, which is often the case in public health interventions. In such cases, they must calculate the costs and benefits associated with their existing behavior and the costs and benefits associated with the new behavior and then compare the two before making a decision. The field of behavioral economics provides insights into how factors such as self-control, impulsiveness, and temporal discounting (i.e., valuing a future consequence less than an immediate consequence) can impact the cost-to-benefit equations people construct and therefore their behavior (Bickel & Vuchinich, 2000).

Self-Interest

People act in their own self-interest. From both a marketing standpoint and from the standpoint of the health behaviors, the only relevant costs and benefits are those important to the person. In some instances, one person's cost might be another's benefit. In the previous beverage example, calories were considered a cost by the hypothetical consumer. Another consumer might consider calories a benefit, and a third might not think of them at all when assessing the costs and benefits of different beverages. Failing to consider self-interest can result in the mistaken assumption that benefits to the public's health will be perceived as benefits by individuals being asked to make a change. Often they are not—or are not important enough to affect the balance of a transaction. Rothschild (1999) observed the following:

> In commercial marketing, this self-interest clearly and consistently is acknowledged and pursued. . . . In public health and social issues, managers often ask members of the target market to behave in ways that appear to be opposite of that member's perception of self-interest and are often the opposite of the current manifestation of that self-interest as observed through the member's current behavior. People choose to eat junk food, not exercise, smoke and drink to excess, or engage in unsafe sex because they have evaluated their own situation and environment and made a self-interested decision to behave as they do. (p. 26)

The marketing process is designed to identify the audience's self-interest and then construct an exchange that appeals to and fulfills that self-interest. Marketers

- Get to know the potential audience members to determine their current behaviors and identify the benefits and costs they attach to a particular exchange.
- Make any needed adjustments to the product, its price, or where customers can obtain it to maximize the benefits important to the customer and minimize the costs.
- Promote the exchange to audiences by emphasizing perceived benefits and, when necessary, by illustrating how to minimize or overcome perceived costs.

As Kotler and Andreasen (1996) phrased it, "for the marketer to be successful, the customer must believe that the exchange that the marketer is promoting is better than any reasonable alternative—including doing nothing" (p. 111).

It is nearly impossible to "sell" public health behavior change or public health as an institution if practitioners fail to consider the public's self-interest. Cuts in public health funding are frequently presented as requiring the poor to sacrifice, which inherently implies that the wealthy should sacrifice to help the poor. However, this argument ignores the wealthy's self-interest and does little to garner support of those needed to improve funding. Although no one would argue that the wealthy can better afford the cost, they are unlikely to agree to afford it if it is presented to them as a cost with no offsetting personal benefits. As noted earlier, exchanges need to be mutually beneficial: Emphasizing the benefits everyone, including the wealthy, receives from public health funding can go a long way toward encouraging them to embrace the exchange.

Behavior Change

Kotler and Andreasen (1996) noted that "the bottom line of all marketing strategy and tactics is to influence behavior. Sometimes this necessitates changing ideas and thoughts first, but in the end, it is behavior change we are after. This is an absolutely crucial point. Some nonprofit marketers may think they are in the 'business' of changing ideas, but it can legitimately be asked why they should bother if such changes do not lead to action" (p. 110). Likewise, improving public health requires focusing on behavior change. Sometimes individuals need to change personal behaviors; at other times "upstream" individuals need to make changes to improve the environment in which the personal behavior takes place. For example, a public health initiative aimed at improving children's nutrition can be directed to various audiences. The children themselves may be one audience. However, many others can increase the child's ability or willingness to improve eating behaviors: Parents can send nutrient-rich snacks to school; cafeteria managers can move fruits, vegetables, and other nutrient-rich choices to the front of the lunch line and in easy reach; classroom teachers can refrain from giving candy as rewards; principals can mandate the availability of healthful foods at all gatherings where food is served; and district policymakers can require healthy choices in vending machines and a la carte offerings.

Commercial marketers have an obvious reason for wanting to influence behavior: to increase sales. Typically, the behavior they want to influence is what brand of product or service the consumer buys. Public health goals and objectives are rarely this clear-cut. People can make a variety of behavior changes that would lead to reduced morbidity and mortality. In addition, a direct relationship between the action of an individual and reductions in incidence or death is often lacking; rather, the aggregate actions of a group will lead to morbidity and mortality improvements for the group, which may or may not impact any particular individual in it. Choosing behavior-focused goals and objectives can also be difficult if sponsoring institutions see their role as "disseminating information" or "educating." Similarly, staff within an organization may have been trained in the knowledge-attitudes-behavior paradigm and believe that by increasing people's knowledge or changing their attitudes, behavior change will follow. Noting that interventions changing knowledge or attitudes do not usually result in behavior change, some researchers argue that the knowledge-attitudes-behavior paradigm is too simplistic and does not reflect the best understanding of how to influence behavior (Baranowski, 1997).

This is not to say that social change programs should never make an effort to increase knowledge or change attitudes, as long as behavior change remains the goal. Sometimes more knowledge is necessary before behavior can change—for example, parents are unlikely to immunize their children unless they know they need to do so. However, the information in a campaign to increase immunization rates must relate to the behavioral goal while remaining appropriate for target audience's readiness to change their behavior. In a review of nutrition education interventions, Contento and colleagues (1995) found that many interventions emphasized "how-to" knowledge or skills information when the audience members were not yet ready for such information. They needed motivational information about personally relevant positive or negative consequences of behavior or other motivators of change before they were ready for "how-to" information.

One challenge public health practitioners face is selecting a specific behavior to change. If a variety of behaviors could be changed, they usually can be prioritized according to most significant public health benefits or audience willingness to make the changes. If an organization's mission is to "disseminate information" or "educate," practitioners should question the value of that mission. The organization's mission-writers must expect some change if people have the information or become more educated.

Competition

To craft an acceptable exchange, marketers must understand the competition: alternative behaviors and the benefits they deliver. As discussed earlier, people act in their own self-interest and generally choose the behavior that offers what they perceive to be the most desired benefits. Every proposed behavior change has competition: the existing behavior. Target audiences often have very good reasons for maintaining their behavior patterns. The benefits they receive from their current behavior— or the drawbacks associated with a new behavior—may outweigh the benefits associated with the new behavior. Part of the marketer's challenge is to develop and deliver a bundle of benefits that target audience members perceive to be superior to the benefits they will receive from engaging in any alternative behavior.

Competition can take many forms. When the desired behavior is supporting a public health program or policy, the competition may have to do with resources (other funding needs are more of a priority to the policymaker), philosophy (such as a belief that there are too many government programs already or that government should not intervene in personal decisions), or pressure from interests that are not related to health (e.g., businesses saying that increased regulations to safeguard the public's health would be "bad for business"). Sometimes it is necessary to restructure the public health offering to overcome problems related to competition.

Audience Orientation and Segmentation

To influence an audience, marketers must first understand the audience and the determinants of their behavior. Therefore, marketers make customers the focal point of their efforts and analyze all aspects of the exchange from the customers' viewpoint. Commercial marketers place enormous emphasis on learning all they can about their current and potential customers. Their mission is to know who their customers are, what they want and need, and where and how to reach them.

Marketing is often described as being consumer driven. In commercial marketing, that usually means identifying a consumer need and then developing or positioning a product or service to fulfill that need, although there are instances when a product has been developed or discovered and a "need" is identified later. Public health practitioners often must create need, a fairly difficult task. Even more difficult is selling a product that people perceive as contrary to their self-interest and therefore do not want (negative demand) and then uncovering benefits people can associate with this product to find a way to position it as superior to competing products. The need to uncover these benefits makes research—especially in terms of values and benefits people can associate with a product or behavior change—even more important for public health practitioners than it is for commercial marketers.

Public health organizations using a marketing approach often have difficulty being truly customer driven. One reason for this difficulty is that the structure of most public health organizations is not conducive to the marketing mind-set. Public health institutions are rarely managed by individuals with marketing backgrounds, and priorities are not decided using a marketing or behavior change framework. Unlike commercial marketers, who develop products and services based on what customers are most likely to purchase, public health institutions often allocate resources based on legislative priorities as reflected in mandates or current funding streams (i.e., if tax money or grants are available for tobacco control, then the institution focuses on tobacco control). Rather than driving the effort, marketing is usually only one component of it.

The position of staff within the organization attempting to develop a marketing-based effort contributes to the second factor that inhibits a public health institution's ability to be customer driven. Because staff members are often part of communication or public information departments, they may be unable to influence priorities or institute changes needed to support a marketing approach. Consequently, social change efforts often center on communication activities. Although Andreasen (1995) criticized many social change marketers for effectively defining marketing as communications, the background and organizational position of the staff limit the marketing strategies to communication techniques. For example, a governor announces a new campaign to improve mammography rates among women age 50 and older. The public information staff may use marketing principles to develop the campaign. They start by conducting formative research to identify appropriate audiences, learn the benefits and barriers the audiences associate with mammography, and learn the ideal places to deliver mammograms and messages about them. Then they can develop, pretest, and produce a thorough promotional effort to be delivered through mass media and health care facilities. However, these communication techniques are likely the extent of the marketing strategies the staff will use in this campaign. It is unlikely the public information staff will do anything about the financial cost of a mammogram or about the extent to which insurers will cover the cost. Similarly, they will be unable to overcome accessibility barriers, such as those faced by women who live far away from a mammography facility or who cannot afford to take time off from work to visit such a facility during business hours. Addressing these barriers requires working in partnership with local providers, something that may not be encouraged under the staff's organizational structure.

Another factor that affects many public health institutions' ability to be customer driven is a hesitancy to focus on specific groups of customers because of a mandate to serve everyone. Trying to appeal to everyone is problematic for a number of reasons. It wastes resources because not everyone needs a particular intervention. Often, particular subgroups of the population are reached by other entities, have a very low incidence of the problem the intervention addresses, or have already embraced the behavior being promoted. Furthermore, key to being customer driven is identifying and understanding the customer in question. Even if everyone needs a particular intervention, some subgroups are likely to be closer to changing their behavior than others who may not be ready. Additionally, the public health offerings may be more easily accessed by some groups. Also, different groups will associate different costs and benefits with the behavior in question. An intervention designed for everyone will likely either

- Persuade no one because it is too scattered and resources are wasted promoting costs and benefits to audiences who do not perceive them as the most important costs and benefits, or

- Focus on specific costs and benefits and therefore be relevant only to particular segments of the population (in other words, targeted by default rather than by intention).

By trying to include everyone, no audience group will be reached with any intensity.

Four Ps: The Marketing Mix

In commercial marketing, product, price, place, and promotion are referred to as "the four Ps" and constitute what is termed the marketing mix—the group of independent variables a marketer can alter to influence behavior. Together, these four concepts form the core building blocks of marketing strategy. There has been substantial debate as to how well the four Ps apply to social marketing (Peattie & Peattie, 2003). However, the four Ps terminology continues to be widely used, and in addition to providing a common vocabulary for public health and other social marketers to use when communicating with other types of marketers, it remains a useful framework for thinking through the major variables available to marketers regardless of the type of marketing in which they engage.

People must believe that benefits outweigh costs before they are willing to engage in an exchange. There is a higher likelihood that people will choose a new behavior when benefits increase and/or costs decrease, as **Figure 5-1** illustrates. The four Ps provide a framework for affecting this balance. A brief description of each variable and some of the issues surrounding its conceptualization in social marketing are presented.

Product

Product is often conceptualized as a tangible good, service, or behavior. However, it is most useful to think of product as the bundle of benefits that is exchanged with the target audience for a price. As noted earlier, the bundle of benefits is what the audience actually seeks to obtain when they engage in the exchange. The bundle of benefits will be linked to a specific behavior but may or may not be linked to a tangible product or service. For example, in a family planning program, the desired behavior may be to space pregnancies out rather than having one birth imme-

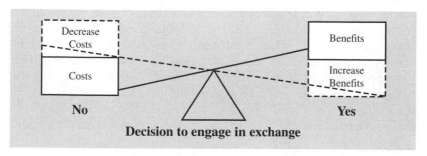

Figure 5-1 Changing the Balance of the Cost-Benefit Analysis

diately after another. Contraceptives are an obvious tangible product likely to be involved in this exchange—even though spacing is what is actually being sold. Similarly, some efforts to improve eating habits encourage increased consumption of particular products, such as fruits and vegetables or whole grains. Other programs, such as those promoting increased physical activity, decreased fat consumption, or violence prevention, often cannot easily tie their behavior changes to a particular product or service.

Sometimes the lack of a tangible product or service causes program planners to get caught up in defining the social change product. The following questions can help marketers clarify the product:

• What are the benefits of the behavior change that members of the target audience value?
• What needs or wants do members of the target audience have that the behavior change can fulfill?
• What is the competition for the behavior?
• What other behaviors can provide benefits the target audience perceives to be equal or superior?

It is vital that public health practitioners define the product in terms of the benefit it will provide to target audience members. The product must satisfy an existing need or want. The benefit delivered must be something the person values enough to engage in the behavior. Some public health programs try to sell long-term public health of social benefits (e.g., reduced risk of cancer, decreased spending on victims of automobile accidents who did not wear seat belts, etc.) rather than short-term individual benefits. Although some people will change a behavior to benefit society if it is at very low cost to them, many will not be sufficiently motivated to change health-related behaviors because society might derive a benefit or because they may derive a benefit in the distant future. They are more likely to change their behavior because they will achieve a short-term benefit from doing so (Backer, Rogers, & Sopory, 1992; Baranowski, Perry, & Parcel, 2002). Behavioral economists assert that short-term benefits are more likely to be chosen because "all behavior occurs in an economic context in which concurrent reinforcers vie for the resources of the consumer" (Madden, 2000, p. 23) and people discount delayed consequences—positive (i.e., reinforcers) or negative (i.e., punishers). In marketing language, at any moment in time a person can choose from a variety of competing benefits. The person is more likely to choose a benefit he or she will obtain immediately, even if the immediate benefit is smaller than what he or she could obtain by waiting. The delay associated with the long-term benefit results in the person discounting that benefit's value.

Price
Price is the cost to the target audience of making an exchange. In commercial marketing, price almost always has a financial component;

if consumers are considering trying a new product or service, the associated risk of change creates a psychological component as well. With health and other social changes, the price may have a financial component but is more likely to be time, effort, lifestyle, or psychological cost. For example, insisting that a sexual partner use a condom has a high potential psychological cost: The partner may reject the one insisting or make assumptions about promiscuous behavior or lack of trust. Being the first policymaker to change from opposing to supporting a policy can create a high psychological or social cost. Many individuals perceive various health behaviors, such as increasing physical activity, as costing a great deal of time. And some behaviors require effort, such as obtaining more nutritious foods if they are not readily accessible. Rothschild (1979) argued that these nonmonetary costs "may be perceived as greater than monetary costs which dominate the price of consumer products" (p. 13).

When the product is a public health program or policy, the perceived psychological price may include an infringement on basic values, such as that resulting from government interference or limitations on freedom. Laws mandating seat belt use and restrictions on smoking are two examples that fit both categories.

Costs, then, are barriers between the target audience and the action that marketers wish them to take. Sometimes they can be easily reduced or eliminated (often by improving place, another marketing variable); at other times they are more challenging. Asking the following questions may help program planners work through the price of their social marketing product:

- What will the behavior change "cost" each target audience member in money, time, effort, and psyche?
- Do target audience members perceive the costs to be a fair exchange for the benefit that is promised in exchange?
- How can marketing efforts reduce costs?

Usually, the only way to answer these questions is through careful formative research.

Place

Place equates to marketing or distribution channels, "a set of interdependent organizations involved in the process of making a product or service available for use or consumption by the consumer or business user" (Kotler & Armstrong, 2004, p. 400). Depending on how they are constructed, distribution channels can allow a marketer to lower an audience's barriers to access, increase utility, or deliver a bundle of benefits to the target audience (Strand, Rothschild, & Nevin, 2004).

Place is often the most difficult commercial marketing "P" to conceptualize in social programs—and the one that can be most difficult to control. Behaviors that involve a tangible product usually have obvious channels of distribution. For example, if the goal is to increase usage of services provided by a health clinic, marketing research can help assess various aspects of the clinic that might create barriers and/or affect the bundle of benefits delivered. These may include issues related to accessibility, cost of services, staff behavior, waiting times, crowding, temperature, cleanliness, and provisions for child care or activities for children while they wait. Other behaviors, such as increasing consumption of certain foods, also have clear distribution channels associated with them. However, unlike their commercial counterparts, social marketers have to consider all distribution channels (e.g., everywhere a target audience member could obtain the food), not just those channels that distribute a specific brand of a specific product.

For other behavioral interventions, place is not as obvious or clearly delineated. For example, consider the many public health programs that encourage lifestyle changes, such as increased physical activity or reducing the risk of acquiring or transmitting a communicable disease. In these instances, no one physical place is associated with the behavior.

In social change programs, place is often conceptualized as message delivery channels. However, it is more useful to define place as the situations in which the behavior does or can occur. Thinking about such situations and their associated channels of distribution can help public health marketers identify opportunities to lower barriers, deliver benefits, or differentiate public health offerings from competitors. Commercial marketers often use place to differentiate their offerings. For example, the experience of purchasing a cup of coffee at Burger King varies from purchasing at Starbucks. Both outlets strive to provide coffee of consistent quality across outlets. But the experience of going to each one is quite different. Burger King is relatively inexpensive, provides few coffee choices, and is fast, bright, utilitarian, and geared to people in a hurry. Starbucks is relatively expensive, offers so many choices the company has run campaigns to increase people's ordering self-efficacy, and, although drinks are delivered quickly, the lighting, comfortable seating, and provision of power outlets encourage lingering.

The following questions can help social marketers think through the opportunities place can provide:

- What are target audience members' perceptions of the situations in which the behavior can take place?
- How can channels of distribution reduce or minimize barriers to the behavior?
- How can channels of distribution create or improve situations so they deliver the benefits target audience members value most?
- How can channels of distribution differentiate the public health offering from competitors' offerings?

- How can channels of distribution be used to create or improve situations so they deliver the benefits target audience members value?
- How can the best channels of distribution for the product and audience be determined and accessed?

As an intervention is developed and specific behavior changes are selected, formative research can help identify situations in which the desired activities do or can take place. Armed with this knowledge, public health marketers can work to change the characteristics of these places and, through promotional activities and materials, provide target audiences with ideas for making their own changes. As the definition at the beginning of this section emphasizes, channels of distribution typically involve multiple interdependent organizations, so creating or improving channels involves identifying and working with the organizations that form or provide the best channels—those that provide access to the audience(s); add value, credibility, and sustainability to the public health offering; deliver immediate and relevant benefits; help overcome the biggest barriers; and counter competition (Strand et al., 2004).

Changing place characteristics often necessitates approaches beyond marketing, such as changes in policy or regulations. For example, widespread smoke-free public places would not have been obtained without changes in local ordinances. Providing children with adequate time to eat a healthful lunch or including sufficient instructional time for health education also requires policy changes at the school level and often at the district or state levels. In situations such as these, a marketing approach can help identify the characteristics of the ideal place, and promotional activities often can support the need for such characteristics. However, techniques other than promotion are necessary to bring about such changes.

An example of using promotional activities and materials to help audiences modify their own places can be found in the early days of the U.S. 5 A Day for Better Health program. Formative research conducted for the program revealed that people were not eating more fruits and vegetables for two reasons: they were not accessible (because vending machines often do not contain them, for example) and people did not think of them (because the fruits and vegetables were at the bottom of the refrigerator in a dark bin). Although the program planners could not control every place that someone might obtain fruits and vegetables, they incorporated simple ideas into promotional activities and materials to help consumers improve their fruit and vegetables places. For example, they included suggestions to make fruits and vegetables accessible during the day, such as packing them into briefcases and lunches, putting them out in a bowl, or placing them on a higher shelf in the refrigerator so people could see them more easily when hunting for something to eat (Lefebvre et al., 1995). More recently, the Produce for Better Health Foundation compiled a National

Action Plan that included many ideas for increasing the availability and accessibility of fruits and vegetables by modifying place, from changing federal, state, and local policies to changing food offerings at restaurants, grocery stores, workplaces, schools, and camps (Produce for Better Health Foundation, 2005).

Promotion

Traditional promotion, for commercial or social marketing, consists of communicating the exchange being offered to the target audience through some combination of advertising, media relations, events, personal selling, and entertainment. When policy change is the goal, promotion often includes techniques such as grassroots advocacy, media advocacy, and lobbying. Some of these techniques use many of the same promotional tools but with a different goal. For example, the media advocacy approach is fundamentally a promotional approach: It relies on media relations and, often, paid advertising. But the purpose is different from using these tools to reach individuals and convince them to change their personal health behaviors:

> The purpose of media advocacy is to promote public health goals by using the media to strategically apply pressure for policy change. It provides a framework for moving the public health discussion from a primary focus on the health behavior of individuals to the behavior of the policymakers whose decisions structure the environment in which people act. It addresses the power gap rather than just the information gap. (Wallack & Dorfman, 1996, p. 293)

All promotional activities have a common goal: to maximize the likelihood that target audience members will take the desired action by reaching them with messages highlighting the exchange's benefits to them and, when necessary, providing methods to overcome the costs. Advertisements are perhaps the most visible form of marketing promotion. The following are examples of other types of promotion activities:

- Framing media coverage through media relations efforts, such as print, audio, and/or video news releases, press conferences, and reporter briefings.
- Community events, such as health fairs.
- Personal selling, such as having physicians or nurses "talk up" a particular behavior related to family planning or the availability of a new vaccine.
- Entertainment, such as integrating public health messages into television series' story lines or producing popular entertainment with a public health message, such as the top-10 Latin American music hits written and produced as part of a U.S. Agency for International Development project (Braus, 1995).

To develop the promotion component of a public health effort, it is necessary to understand product, price, and place and then use that information to develop a communication strategy for each primary and secondary audience. The communication strategy helps managers frame and deliver promotional messages by describing the action being elicited from the target audience, barriers to the action, benefit of the action, and support for the benefit. In addition, the communication strategy identifies the tone the communications should use as well as the channels through which the target audience can be reached.

The communication strategy then guides development of the promotion plan. Key questions that guide development of the communication strategy and promotion plan include the following:

- What action should the audience to take, and what are they doing now?
- What benefit can be promised in exchange for taking that action, and how can that benefit be supported?
- What are the times, places, and states of mind when target audiences can best be reached with materials and activities?
- What promotional materials and activities are appropriate for the message and the openings through which it will be delivered?
- Given limited resources, how can those materials and activities best be delivered to target audience members?

This plan articulates the materials and activities that will form the promotion as well as the timeline for development and implementation.

An Additional P: Partners

Beyond the traditional marketing mix of product, price, place, and promotion, public health efforts often have to consider an additional P: partners. Social change efforts typically gather speed when there is scientific consensus that a particular change will benefit the individual and society. By the time such consensus is reached, many organizations, both public and private, may have an interest in promoting the behavior and, if necessary, in developing technological, educational, and policy changes to facilitate such behavior change. Unfortunately, what often happens is that each organization has different ideas about how to proceed and does not coordinate efforts with the other organizations. Completely separate programs can jeopardize success in a number of ways. First, they can lead to framing the issue in multiple and sometimes counterproductive ways. The public and policymakers may become confused or uncertain as to the actions they should take. Second, resources can be wasted working at cross purposes.

Often, a better solution is for organizations to recognize that others are also interested in bringing about the social change. By combining or coordinating efforts, members of the public, health care providers, policymakers, and other audiences are reached by sources they trust with a consistent, clear message—and resources are maximized. Each organization can perform the activity for which it is best suited. Unfortunately, these types of partnerships and alliances are all too rare. At the conceptual level, they can be difficult because each organization has its own wants and needs. At the operational level, a host of practical difficulties can prohibit progress, including different fiscal years and institutional timetables, restrictions on government agencies working with private sector organizations, and organizational cultures.

Even if strong alliances or perfect partnerships cannot be formed, it is important for organizations to know which other organizations are addressing the same issue and to coordinate activities with them when possible. At a minimum, doing so allows the organizations' efforts to complement, rather than compete with, each other. Often, judicious alliances or partnerships can provide much more, such as access to or added credibility with key target audience segments.

During the planning process, addressing the following questions should provide a starting point for ensuring that social change efforts are planned with potential partners, alliances, and intermediaries in mind:

- What other organizations are addressing the social change?
- What organizations could or do provide something different or provide it better—access to an audience, delivery of key benefits, or reduction or elimination of critical barriers?
- What are the opportunities to work with or complement other organizations?

Exhibit 5-1   Social Marketing Mix

Product

The bundle of benefits exchanged with the audience for a price.

- What are the benefits of the behavior change that members of the target audience will value?
- What needs or wants do members of the target audience have that the behavior change can fulfill?

Price

The total cost (financial and other) to the target audience member of engaging in the behavior.

- What will the behavior change "cost" each target audience member in money, time, effort, lifestyle, and psyche?
- Do target audience members perceive the costs to be a fair exchange for the benefit that is promised in exchange?
- How can marketing efforts reduce costs?

(continues)

Exhibit 5-1 Social Marketing Mix (continued)

Place

The channel(s) through which products are distributed—or situations in which the behavior of interest can or does occur.

- What are target audience members' perceptions of the situations in which the behavior can take place?
- How can channels of distribution reduce or minimize barriers to the behavior?
- How can channels of distribution differentiate the public health offering from competitors' offerings?
- How can channels of distribution be used to create or improve situations so they deliver the benefits that target audience members value?
- How can the best channels of distribution for the product and audience be determined and accessed?

Promotion

A combination of advertising, media relations, promotional events, personal selling, and entertainment to communicate with the target audience about the exchange being offered.

- What action should the audience to take, and what are they doing now?
- What benefit can be promised in exchange for taking the action, and how can that benefit be supported?
- What are the times, places, and states of mind when target audiences can best be reached with materials and activities?
- What promotional materials and activities are appropriate for the message and the openings through which it will be delivered?
- Given limited resources, how can those materials and activities best be delivered to target audience members?

Partners

Other organizations involved with a social change effort or providing channels of distribution.

- What other organizations are addressing the social change?
- What organizations could or do provide something different, or provide it better—access to an audience, delivery of key benefits, reduction or elimination of critical barriers, differentiation?
- What are the opportunities to work with or complement other organizations?

Building Relationships

The need to build relationships is important for a successful marketing campaign. Thinking beyond a specific transaction, campaign, or program to building relationships with the audiences whose behavior marketers want to change can also have profound implications for public health.

First, social marketers . . . frequently deal with behaviors that require long-term effort to change. Giving up an addictive behavior like smoking, for example, typically takes five or six attempts. . . . Similarly, responding to good dietary and exercise advice typically involves lifestyle changes rather than one-off adoption of specific offerings. Such behaviors are likely to be much more susceptible to strategic relationship marketing than traditional transactional thinking.

Second, relational marketing is also vital when social marketers consider the social context and the need to make this conducive to individual healthy behavior. . . . On a general level, critical theory emphasizes the importance of "altering institutions that form the social system within which the individual operates" (Goldberg, 1995). Wallack et al. argue that the media advocacy approach should be seeking to address flaws, not in "the loose threads of the individual," but in the "fabric of society" (Wallack et al., 1993). . . . All this, of course, gels with marketing theory, which makes an important distinction between the immediate environment and the wider social context (Hastings & Haywood, 1991).

Third, relationship building in social marketing can benefit from its noncommercial nature. If, as Morgan and Hunt's (1994) work suggests, commitment and trust are the bedrocks of successful relationship marketing, these could be built more easily when neither party stands to make monetary gains. (Hasting & Saren, 2003, pp. 311–312)

Any encounter a person has with an organization—its physical spaces, its offerings, its communications, its employees—can contribute to building or destroying a relationship. Savvy, successful organizations recognize this simple fact and work to ensure that every encounter is positive. When they ask someone to engage in an exchange, they look beyond the exchange to make sure every aspect of it contributes to building and supporting that relationship. Organizations hope to ensure that the audience member can easily engage in the behavior, that unnecessary costs (time, social, psychological, dealing with unpleasantness, etc.) are eliminated or minimized, and that the audience member has whatever supports may be needed (information, demonstration of behavior, etc.).

Organizations also use branding to help them build relationships by differentiating their offerings from competitors' offerings and conveying a consistent identity.

Everything that a company does—from the way it paints its trucks, to how long it takes to answer your telephones, to what people in your factories tell their friends—communicates with the public.

Strategies beget brands, and brands in today's marketplace transcend products. Brands are much more than what you eat or drink or brush your teeth with. Brand strategy is the summation of all your communications. (Zyman, 1999, p. 41)

On the surface, a brand is "a name, term, sign, symbol, or design, or some combinations of these, which identifies [the goods or services] as the marketer's and differentiates them from competitor's offerings" (Kotler & Andreasen, 1996, p. 374). Initially, brands were used to distinguish products that otherwise could not be differentiated easily. Over time, organizations discovered that a brand has far more powerful functions than simply allowing customers to identify their products. A brand also forms the relationship between the organization or product and its consumer; it has been characterized as a repository, not merely of functional characteristics but of meaning and value (Mark & Pearson, 2001; McDivitt et al., 2003).

A brand is more than a name and a means of identification. It is a set of added values that offer functional and psychological benefits to the consumer, values signaled in consumer products by packaging, price, color, taste, smell, or shape. (Roman, Maas, & Nisenholtz, 2003, p. 13)

Brands can be positioned on product attributes (although this is not advisable because attributes are easily copied), desirable benefits (e.g., Volvo: safety; FedEx: guaranteed overnight delivery; Nike: performance; Lexus: quality), or beliefs and values. The strongest brands are positioned on strong beliefs and values (Kotler & Armstrong, 2004).

The notion of deliberately attempting to build a brand identity makes many in public health uncomfortable, perhaps because doing so seems too commercial or likely to lead to accusations of wasted resources. However, public health institutions have brand identities, whether or not they want to, and unfamiliarity with brand management can lead to mistakes and missed opportunities. Every public health institution has an identity in the mind of funding agencies, potential partners, the media, and target audiences. The identity may be fuzzy or clear, positive, neutral, or negative, but it exists.

A brand is the company's promise to deliver a specific set of features, benefits, services, and experiences consistently to the buyers. It can be thought of as a contract to the customer regarding how the product or service will deliver value and satisfaction. The brand contract must be simple and honest. (Kotler & Armstrong, 2004, p. 293)

Working through branding exercises can help an organization clarify its core mission, prioritize institutional goals, and reconcile internal versus external perceptions. Actively projecting a clear, consistent, and compelling organizational identity can help a public health institution accomplish its mission by building relationships with supporters, partners, and target audiences. For organizations involved in direct product or service delivery, each customer's experience with the organization provides an opportunity to strengthen the relationship. Using brand management techniques to ensure that each interaction communicates a consistent identity and delivers the benefits those customers value can help organizations build stronger relationships. Brand management techniques can be used in similar ways to manage relationships with other organizations.

There has been considerable discussion about whether a particular health behavior can or should be branded in the same way as a commercial product or service (Lefebvre et al., 2003; McDivitt et al., 2003). At a minimum, understanding how commercial marketers use brands to build relationships with audiences can help practitioners design effective interventions. Reflecting on a conference session on using branding in social marketing, Bill Novelli observed that marketers need to think about the brand-related questions in the minds of target audience members, such as "What can you give me that I can't get elsewhere?" and "If I didn't have this brand, I would _____" (Lefebvre et al., 2003). Carol Bryant observed that branding can help practitioners move away from focusing too much on the individual and persuasion and instead take a more expansive view, addressing audiences' values, dreams, needs, and aspirations; in addition, branding reminds practitioners to take time and stick with a concept rather than constantly changing things (Lefebvre et al., 2003).

At times, creating a public health brand may make sense if it is appropriate for the situation and sufficient resources are available. In the United States, the Florida truth® campaign worked to destabilize tobacco companies' relationships with their youth customers by offering youth a replacement brand. Branding also helped the intervention through accumulated awareness: all marketing components built on awareness created by their predecessors (Hicks, 2001). This aspect of branding—making sure all components of an intervention communicate the same identity and therefore build on each other—is always good marketing practice.

■ CONCLUSION

Marketing principles can be used to guide the process of developing, implementing, and refining efforts to improve public health. The cost-to-benefit exchange is essential to the choices people make: A person gives something (cost) in the expectation of receiving something (benefit). Public health, commercial, and other marketers can influence this exchange by altering the marketing mix: the product (benefits), the price (costs), the place (channels of distribution, which can, in turn, decrease costs or increase benefits), and promotion (communications about the cost/benefit exchange).

To influence behavior successfully, all types of marketers must take a number of factors into account, particularly (1) people act in their own self-interest to satisfy wants and needs, so promised benefits must provide something they value, and (2) all proposed behaviors have competition, either from current behaviors or other alternatives. To succeed, the cost-to-benefit exchange of the public health behavior must be more appealing than that associated with any alternative behavior, including doing nothing.

Because the cost-to-benefit exchange can vary significantly for different groups of people, careful segmentation and selection of target audiences is crucial to design and communicate cost-to-benefit exchanges that are relevant to and valued by the target audience and that can be cost-effectively delivered by the marketer, either directly or through alliances, partners, and/or intermediaries.

The marketing framework can be used to design interventions to influence individuals' personal health behaviors or to improve the larger environment in which those behaviors occur so that individuals can more easily engage in the behavior and obtain desired benefits. Marketing principles can help select specific behavior or policy changes on which to focus by first identifying the wants, needs, and values of a target audience—whether that target audience is a member of the public or a policymaker—and then creating and delivering a bundle of benefits to satisfy those wants, needs, and values. Branding and brand management techniques can help ensure that a consistent identity is communicated and delivered to supporters, partners, and target audiences, thereby enabling public health marketers to build strong relationships with all these groups.

References

American Marketing Association. (2005). Definition of marketing. Retrieved November 10, 2005, from http://www.marketingpower.com/content4620.php

Andreasen, A.R. (1995). *Marketing social change: Changing behavior to promote health, social development and the environment.* San Francisco, CA: Jossey-Bass.

Backer, T.E., Rogers, E.M., & Sopory, P. (1992). *Designing health communication campaigns: What works?* Thousand Oaks, CA: Sage.

Baranowski, T. (1997). The knowledge-attitudes-behavior model and defining "behavior changes." In L. Doner (Ed.), *Charting the course for evaluation: How do we measure the success of nutrition education and promotion in food assistance programs? Summary of proceedings* (pp. 26–27). Alexandria, VA: U.S. Department of Agriculture.

Baranowski, T., Perry, C.L., & Parcel, G.S. (2002). How individuals, environments, and health behavior interact: Social cognitive theory. In K. Glanz,

B.K. Rimer, & F.M. Lewis (Eds.), *Health behavior and health education: Theory, research and practice* (3rd ed., pp. 165–184). San Francisco, CA: Jossey-Bass.

Bickel, W.K., & Vuchinich, R.E. (Eds.) (2000). *Reframing health behavior change with behavioral economics.* Mahwah, NJ: Lawrence Erlbaum Associates.

Braus, P. (1995). Selling good behavior. *American Demographics, 17,* 60–64.

Contento, I., Balch, G.I., Bronner, Y.L., Lytle, L.A., Maloney, S.K., White, S.L., ... Swadener, S.S. (1995). The effectiveness of nutrition education and implications for nutrition education policy, programs, and research [Special issue]. *Journal of Nutrition Education, 27,* 279–418.

Fox, K.F.A., & Kotler, P. (1980). The marketing of social causes: The first 10 years. *Journal of Marketing, 44,* 24–33.

Goldberg, M.R. (1995). Social marketing: Are we fiddling while Rome burns? *Journal of Consumer Psychology, 4,* 347–370.

Hastings, G., & Saren, M. (2003). The critical contribution of social marketing. *Marketing Theory, 3,* 305–322.

Hastings, G.B., & Haywood, A.J. (1991). Social marketing and communication in health promotion. *Health Promotion International, 6,* 135–145.

Hicks, J.J. (2001). The strategy behind Florida's truth campaign. *Tobacco Control, 10,* 3–5.

Kotler, P. (2000). *Marketing management* (Millenium ed.). Upper Saddle River, NJ: Prentice Hall International.

Kotler, P., & Andreasen, A.R. (1996). *Strategic marketing for non-profit organizations* (2nd ed.). Upper Saddle River, NJ: Prentice-Hall.

Kotler, P., & Armstrong, G. (2004). *Principles of marketing* (10th ed.). Upper Saddle River, NJ: Prentice-Hall.

Kotler, P., & Zaltman, G. (1971). Social marketing: An approach to planned social change. *Journal of Marketing, 35,* 3–12.

Lefebvre, R.C., Bloom, P., Bryant, C., & Novelli, W. (2003). Emerging innovations: What have we learned? *Social Marketing Quarterly, 9,* 33–38.

Lefebvre, R.C., Doner, L.D., Jonston, C., Loughrey, K., Balch, G., & Sutton, S.M. (1995). Use of database marketing and consumer-based health communications in message design: An example from the Office of Cancer Communications' "5 A Day for Better Health" program. In E. Maibach & R. Parrott (Eds.), *Designing health messages: Approaches from communication theory and public health practice* (pp. 217–246). Thousand Oaks, CA: Sage.

Madden, G.J. (2000). A behavioral economics primer. In W.K. Bickel & R.E. Vuchinich (Eds.), *Reframing health behavior change with behavioral economics* (pp. 3–26). Mahwah, NJ: Lawrence Erlbaum Associates.

Mark, M., & Pearson, C.S. (2001). *The hero and the outlaw: Building extraordinary brands through the power of archetypes.* New York, NY: McGraw-Hill.

McDivitt, J., Schwartz, B., Round, C., Young, E., & Lefebvre, R.C. (2003). Innovations in social marketing conference proceedings session II: Is there a role for branding in social marketing? *Social Marketing Quarterly, 9,* 11–17.

Morgan, R.M., & Hunt, S.D. (1994). The commitment-trust theory of relationship marketing. *Journal of Marketing, 58,* 20–38.

National Highway Traffic Safety Administration. (1996). *Patterns of misuse of child safety seats: Final report* (Rep. No. DOT HS 808-440). Washington, DC: Author.

National Highway Traffic Safety Administration. (1997). Tether anchorages for child restraint systems: Child restraint anchorage system. *62 Federal Register* 7858.

Nelson, D.E., Bolen, J., & Kresnow, M. (1998). Trends in safety belt use by demographics and by type of state safety belt law, 1987–1993. *American Journal of Public Health, 88,* 245–249.

Peattie, S., & Peattie, K. (2003). Ready to fly solo? Reducing social marketing's dependence on commercial marketing theory. *Marketing Theory, 3,* 365–385.

Produce for Better Health Foundation. (2005). National action plan to promote health through increased fruit and vegetable consumption. Retrieved April 4, 2006, from http://www.pbhfoundation.org/pdfs/pulse/action/pbh_nap_book041905.pdf

Roman, K., Maas, J., & Nisenholtz, M. (2003). *How to advertise* (3rd ed.). New York, NY: St. Martin's Press.

Rothschild, M.L. (1979). Marketing communications in nonbusiness situations or why it's so hard to sell brotherhood like soap. *Journal of Marketing, 43,* 11–20.

Rothschild, M.L. (1999). Carrots, sticks and promises: A conceptual framework for the behavior management of public health and social issues. *Journal of Marketing, 63,* 24–37.

Strand, J., Rothschild, M.L., & Nevin, J. R. (2004). Session I: "Place" and channels of distribution. *Social Marketing Quarterly, 10,* 7–13.

Wallack, L., & Dorfman, L. (1996). Media advocacy: A strategy for advancing policy and promoting health. *Health Education Quarterly, 23,* 293–317.

Wallack, L., Dorfman, L., Jernigan, D., & Themba, M. (1993). *Media advocacy and public health.* Newbury Park, CA: Sage.

Weibe, G.D. (1951). Merchandising commodities and citizenship on television. *Public Opinion Quarterly, 15,* 679–691.

Zyman, S. (1999). *The end of marketing as we know it.* New York, NY: HarperCollins.

SECTION

III

Planning the Approach

Adequate planning is at the heart of all marketing—whether for a commercial product or service, a social change, or public health itself. During this stage, the types of changes needed to address a specific problem are identified and prioritized. These changes might include modifications in individual behaviors and lifestyles, reforms to social or organizational policies, and/or other improvements in social and economic conditions.

This section begins with a presentation of the strategic planning process. The remaining chapters describe activities that are used to support the strategic planning process: conducting formative research and developing strategies to frame messages about the public health offering.

CHAPTER

6

Planning Process

Adequate planning is essential to the marketing approach—and essential to achieving social change or the adoption of new public health programs and initiatives. Planning begins with a thorough analysis of the situation at hand: defining the problems, identifying the affected populations, determining the changes the populations can make, recognizing the environmental and social factors that may support the desired behaviors, and considering the types of interventions most likely to be effective under the circumstances. The next step is to set goals and objectives by specifying target audiences and the behaviors, conditions, or policies to be changed. Then planners must develop public health offerings that provide audiences with benefits they value enough to choose to take the public health actions and, if necessary, reduce or overcome barriers to the actions. This is done by addressing all aspects of the marketing mix: product, price, place, and promotion.

■ MARKETING PROCESS

Developing a strong, effective marketing effort is an iterative process. To facilitate understanding, this book presents the process as a series of discrete, sequential activities (**Figure 6-1** and **Exhibit 6-1**), but in reality, the steps often overlap or repeat based on new information or changing conditions. This iteration is a defining characteristic of the marketing approach, providing the flexibility to adapt to different issues, environments, resource levels, and conditions.

As is evident from the number of activities shown in Exhibit 6-1 for each stage, adequate planning is vital to marketing a policy, a health behavior, or a wider social change successfully. Audience and market research are integral parts of the planning process. Allocating sufficient resources to ensure adequate planning and development can prevent costly mistakes and results in a stronger, more effective initiative.

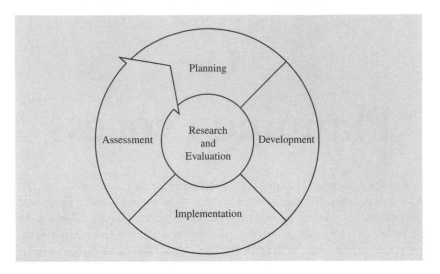

Figure 6-1 Stages of the Marketing Process

Exhibit 6-1 Activities During Each Stage of the Marketing Process

Planning

- Step 1: Analyze the situation:
  - Identify problems and populations affected.
  - Analyze current and possible replacement behaviors.
  - Outline all components of a solution (education, law, marketing).
  - Assess the environment in which change will occur.
- Step 2: Select approaches and determine the role of marketing.
- Step 3: Set goals and objectives: Specify behaviors, conditions, or policies to be changed.
- Step 4: Segment and select target audiences:
  - Determine the target populations for each desired change, and within each population, the audience segment(s) on which you will focus.
  - Identify current and competitive behaviors and how they satisfy needs, desires, and values.
  - Identify barriers to the public health behavior.
- Step 5: Design public health offering(s).
  - Product: Identify and develop a bundle of benefits that you can deliver that differentiates the desired behavior from competitors. Develop any necessary supporting goods and services.
  - Price: Determine how to make costs manageable for target audience members.
  - Place: Determine how you will access channels that deliver the product so that it is easily available to target audience members at prices (financial, time, psyche, social, etc.) they are willing and able to pay.

(continues)

Exhibit 6-1 Activities During Each Stage of the Marketing Process (continued)

 – Promotion: Develop communication strategy to position the public health offering as something consistent with the audience's core values that delivers a key benefit.

- Step 6: Plan evaluation.

Development

- Develop budgets and distribution and promotion plans.
- Develop prototype products, services, and/or communication materials.
- Pretest with target audience members.
- Refine as necessary.
- Build in process evaluation measures.

Implementation

- Produce offerings and materials.
- Coordinate with partners.
- Implement intervention.
- Use process evaluation to monitor implementation.
- Refine offerings, promotions, and distribution channels as needed.

Assessment

- Conduct outcome evaluation.
- Refine intervention as needed.

■ PLANNING PROCESS

The planning process is designed to give project staff the information they need to understand the problem and develop a solution. This model provides a framework in which to identify how marketing can help bring about components of the solution. With that knowledge, marketing strategies can be used to create, communicate, and deliver an offering of sufficient value to target audiences so they engage in behaviors that lead to the solutions outlined in the model.

Although many activities occur along the way, the results of the planning process are summarized into a strategic plan that provides overall guidance for the program. This plan is sometimes called a *marketing plan* or *strategy statement*. **Exhibit 6-2** provides a sample outline of a strategic plan. There are probably as many ways to construct a strategic plan as there are people who write them; the approach presented in this chapter closely follows the planning process outlined in Exhibit 6-2.

The strategic plan should outline how the intervention is expected to work: the audiences it should reach, the actions they are expected to take as a result of the intervention, the exchanges constructed, and how the

---

Exhibit 6-2 Outline of the Strategic Plan

Executive Summary
Background and Mission
Challenges and Opportunities
Goals
Objectives (Measurable Outcomes)
Target Audiences
Strategies
    Developing the Offering (Product)
    Managing Perceived Price
    Improving Access (Place)
    Promotion
Evaluation Design

---

strategies are expected to bring about this action. Once the strategic plan has been completed, it is used as a guide to develop implementation plans for each strategy and evaluation plan. The plan serves not only as a blueprint for the program but as an organization's memory, reminding managers (or informing new staff or partners) of the history and rationale underlying the approaches selected. Strategic plans should be dynamic living documents, revised to reflect changing audiences and environments. In the next few sections, we outline the activities that culminate in the strategic plan.

■ STEP 1: ANALYZE THE SITUATION

The first step of planning is to collect and analyze information to provide an understanding of the problem to be addressed, the environment in which the program will operate, and how marketing activities can contribute to solutions. This process is referred to by various names, including "background review," "market survey," "market audit," "environmental scan," and "situation analysis," the term used here.

A situation analysis can vary in its level of detail, depending on the resources available, time allotted, and scope of the problem. Constructing it is a two-step process: first, information must be collected and, second, it must be analyzed. During the analysis phase, conclusions are drawn and solutions to the problem are recommended. This process may begin with an analysis of either the public health burden or the social environment, depending on whether the organization is trying to determine the public health problems it will address or to develop an initiative to address a particular problem (e.g., cancer, nutrition, drug abuse). If the goal is to determine the problem an initiative (or initiatives) should address, it is best to begin with the social environment and prioritize the problems in that context (e.g., what problems are contributing to the worst, or most pernicious, social problems?). Green and Kreuter (1991) called this the reductionist approach. If, instead, the goal is to understand the social environment in which a particular initiative will be put into place, it is best to begin by looking at the public health burden associated with that problem and then work outward toward understanding the environment around the problem. Green and Kreuter (1991) referred to this as the expansionist approach.

Identify Problems and Populations Affected

In the early information-gathering stages, existing data are reviewed to define the problem, specify populations affected by it (or sometimes causing it), identify potential solutions, and determine what additional information may be needed. For improvements in individual health behaviors, relevant data typically include the following:

- Morbidity and mortality data, including recent trends in the quantities and types of people who already have the condition or are most likely to develop or die from it
- Known risk factors and, if possible, information on the quantities and types of people most like to be affected by these risk factors
- Current behaviors that result in or are associated with the public health problem
- Recommended behaviors that people should do, including those that may involve treatment regimens for existing conditions, screening for early detection of disease, or lifestyle changes or other action to prevent disease or injury

Much of this information comes from the institution sponsoring the program. In the United States, supplementary sources include state and local health department data, epidemiological and surveillance data collected by the Centers for Disease Control and Prevention (CDC), and other large federal studies. In addition, the major health professional organizations and health voluntary agencies often provide information on risk factors, treatment guidelines, and the like. When marketing public health as an institution, the starting point most likely will assess the environment in which marketing efforts will take place (see below under Assessing the Intervention Environment).

Analyze Current and Possible Replacement Behaviors

Constructing a map of the current behavior can help public health groups outline the steps involved in the current behavior and—equally importantly—describe the physical, social, and economic environment in which the behavior takes place. Capturing the benefits and barriers that audience members associate with their current behavior also is important. Formative research often is necessary to complete accurate and complete behavioral maps.

It is helpful to start the behavior mapping process by considering the type of behavior. In general, behaviors can be categorized along two dimensions, frequency and complexity, as shown in **Exhibit 6-3**.

One dimension reflects frequency: Some behaviors occur at one time, whereas others occur continuously. For one-time or episodic behaviors, people generally make a conscious decision to engage in the behavior and then take the steps necessary to perform it (e.g., seeing a physician for an annual exam). In contrast, for behaviors that occur continuously or frequently, people often do not make conscious decisions in advance and then take the steps necessary to implement the decision. For some frequent behaviors, individuals may be confronted with situations that do or could involve the behavior as often as multiple times per day (e.g., eating, wearing seat belts). This frequency can lead people to act somewhat automatically, without making a thoughtful decision to act in a particular way. Other behaviors require certain preplanning actions that a person may be unable or unwilling to take if the situation arises unexpectedly (e.g., having a condom or exercise clothing available, getting home after drinking).

The other dimension is complexity. Some behaviors require one simple action to be taken in a specific situation. Others require a series of actions,

Exhibit 6-3 Dimensions of Behavior

	One-Time or Episodic	Continuous or Frequent
Simple	Getting a flu shot Getting screening tests performed at routine exams	Using condoms Not smoking Not driving after drinking Fastening safety belts
Complex	Getting a colonoscopy Preparing a household for natural disasters and other community emergencies Obtaining and installing a child restraint system in a car	Changing eating habits Engaging in physical activity Lowering risk of contracting communicable diseases

usually over time and often across a variety of settings. As a result, the interventionist's task can range from providing a person with the motivation, opportunity, and ability to engage in one transaction at one time to helping a person integrate motivation, opportunity, and ability into his or her everyday life. Obviously, the interventions required across this spectrum differ dramatically. Although these dimensions apply most readily to individual health behaviors, they can be applied to efforts to bring about policy change as well.

After determining the type of behavior, the next task is to list the steps required to undertake it as well as the (real and perceived) benefits and barriers associated with the behavior. Common barriers can include self-interest (i.e., another behavior provides benefits valued more highly), beliefs, pressures, misinformation, and lack of ability or opportunity to engage in the behavior (i.e., lack of knowledge or lack of physical or financial access).

To prepare a behavior "map" for simple one-time behaviors, planners may need to list only the steps involved in the behavior in one column, with corresponding columns assessing benefits and barriers. For complex frequent behaviors, it may be more useful to diagram the common situations the person would encounter. Whether listing steps or diagramming the behavior, it is important to capture the barriers that might affect opportunity or ability and the competition that might affect motivation.

Mapping physical, social, economic, or cultural factors that influence the behavior can help identify potential intervention targets, some of which may be more amenable to change than others. Beginning with the individual, a person may be receptive or resistant to the behavior change. Regardless of the individual's receptivity, external factors influence whether he or she can engage in the new behavior. Rothschild (1999), building on a model of information processing developed by MacInnis, Moorman, and Jaworski (1991), suggested determining whether the person has motivation, ability, and opportunity to engage in the behavior.

- Motivation is a person's willingness to engage in the behavior; generally, people are motivated to engage in a behavior when they discern that their self-interest will be served by doing so.
- Ability reflects a person's skill or proficiency and self-efficacy (confidence in his or her ability) regarding the behavior.
- Opportunity is provided or prohibited by the person's environment.

Thinking about replacement behaviors in terms of motivation, ability, and opportunity can help planners identify solutions that will lead to the greatest progress toward public health goals. Often, that progress comes from addressing an external factor, such as an opportunity, rather than trying to persuade people to change a behavior when they lack the opportunity or ability to do so.

Choosing a Replacement Behavior

Sometimes the target audience could take a number of actions, and the challenge is to choose one on which to focus. Graeff, Elder, and Booth (1993) suggested first developing a list of "ideal" behaviors. In the context of changing individual health behaviors, they defined ideal behaviors as "the medically prescribed behavioral steps that the target audience should perform in order to prevent or treat the health problem" (p. 65). From this list they recommended selecting target behaviors, which they defined as "the minimum number of behavioral steps essential for the health practice to be effective" (p. 65). Answers to the questions listed in **Exhibit 6-4** can help planners identify an appropriate behavior change. Although Graeff and colleagues developed these questions to assess behaviors related to individual health practices, they can be modified easily to address other types of social changes.

Attempts to reduce drunk driving exemplify the need to choose a replacement behavior carefully. A typical approach is to try to convince people not to get drunk if they are going to drive. This approach meets the first criterion in Exhibit 6-4: If people who planned to drive did not get drunk, there would be fewer drunk drivers. However, the behavioral analysis revealed that this replacement behavior—not drinking before driving—did not meet the second criterion of being feasible to perform, primarily because it was incompatible with the target audience's socio-cultural norms. Another alternative behavior, not driving home, was compatible with criterion one but failed criterion two. However, it failed for a different reason: Not driving home was not feasible because there was no alternative means of transportation. That is a problem marketing could fix: A new product offering could be developed that made not driving home feasible.

The third point in Exhibit 6-4 is particularly important and often is not given adequate consideration by program planners. Some words of advice given to commercial marketers are useful here (Roman, Maas, & Nisenholtz, 2003, p. 22):

> Overambition is the pitfall of most strategies. Don't ask people to change deeply ingrained habits. Behavior can be changed—consumers go to self-service gas stations and many have learned to bank online, but it's generally easier to get people to change brands.

Those trying to improve the public's health are often in the unenviable position of doing what commercial sector counterparts are told to avoid: changing deeply ingrained behaviors. Offering replacement behaviors that are close to existing behaviors makes it easier for target audiences to make changes without disrupting their daily lives and thus makes it more likely they will agree to do so.

Exhibit 6-4 Questions to Select Target Behaviors

---

1. *Does the ideal behavior have a demonstrated impact on this specific health problem?* If not, it should not be selected as a target behavior.

2. *Is the ideal behavior feasible for the audience to perform?* An in-depth understanding of the target audience is essential if one is to understand the environmental constraints that will affect adoption.
   - Does the ideal behavior produce negative consequences for the person performing it?
   - Is the ideal behavior incompatible with the person's current behavior or with sociocultural norms or acceptable practices?
   - Does the ideal behavior require an unrealistic rate of frequency?
   - Does the ideal behavior require an unrealistic duration?
   - Does the ideal behavior have too high a cost in time, energy, social status, money, or materials?
   - Is the ideal behavior too complex and not easily divided into a small number of elements or steps?

3. *Are any existing behaviors approximations to the ideal behavior?* Can these behaviors be shaped into an effective health practice through training and skill development? Communication programs are more likely to achieve behavior change if they build on what people are already doing correctly. If existing behaviors are similar to any of the remaining ideal behaviors, they should be included in the list of target behaviors.

Source: Reprinted with permission from J.A. Graeff, J.P. Elder, and E.M. Booth, *Communication for Health and Behavior Change: A Developing Country Perspective*, p. 67, ©1993, Jossey-Bass Inc., Publishers.

Once the list of possible replacement behaviors is narrowed to target behaviors, planners must map the steps a typical person would have to take to engage in the behavior and then compare it with a map of the current behavior (Sutton, Balch, & Lefebvre, 1995, p. 729):

> A consumer map can help to identify those points in the process where consumers pull away from the recommended health behavior and toward another behavior. . . . What are they doing now, instead of the desired behavior? That action is the competition—the behavior we want to replace. Answers help formulate the intermediate steps that stand between where the consumer currently is and where the science recommends him or her to be.

It is likely that the initial maps of recommended and current behaviors are incomplete. Formative research—whether previously conducted or commissioned specifically for this planning process—can help fill in these blanks.

Role of Theory
The role of theory is to help planners envision how change will occur and the role an intervention can play in facilitating that change. In the early stages of planning, theory can increase the understanding of the current behavior and predict likely reactions to recommended behaviors. Later, theory can help select specific audience segments, determine actions they can take, and develop offerings most likely to reach and motivate those audience segments to take the desired action. Planners can also use theories to set reasonable objectives: If one expects change to occur very quickly and easily, objectives are likely to be quite different from those if one expects change to be gradual and difficult.

No one theory or model will work for every situation. Some theories and models help planners understand individual health behaviors, others predict interpersonal health behaviors, and others explain how a health behavior moves through a community or group. It is not unusual for interventions to be guided by the constructs from different models.

Outline All Components of a Solution

Planners can use the map of current and potential replacement behaviors in combination with the list of internal and/or external factors that lead individuals to their current behaviors instead of the replacement behaviors to create a model of how the problem can be addressed. This model helps everyone involved clearly see what types of changes are necessary to lessen or control the problem and what types of tools—education, law, marketing—are useful to bring about these changes. If multiple organizations are working together, for example, as a coalition, it is usually wise for representatives from all groups to work together on this process.

Figure 6-2 contains the beginning of a model of change; in this case, the goal is to increase the percentage of child safety seats that are properly installed in passenger cars. It was developed from information presented in **Exhibit 6-5**.

Determining Types of Approaches: Education, Law, and Marketing
The MOA (motivation, opportunity, ability) framework for thinking about recommended behaviors, illustrated in **Figure 6-3**, can be used to determine the types of tools needed to bring about change in individual health behaviors—education, law, and/or marketing. For example, if the audience is motivated and has both opportunity and ability (cell 1), an educational approach is appropriate. In contrast, if the audience is motivated and has ability but lacks opportunity, a marketing intervention that focuses on providing that opportunity and communicating its availability is the approach to use. With other problems, a combination of approaches may be most effective. If, for example, the audience has the ability to engage in the public health action but has neither the opportunity nor the motivation to do so (cell 4), then a marketing offering may be able to create both opportunity and motivation. However, if motivation remains insufficient, law may be necessary.

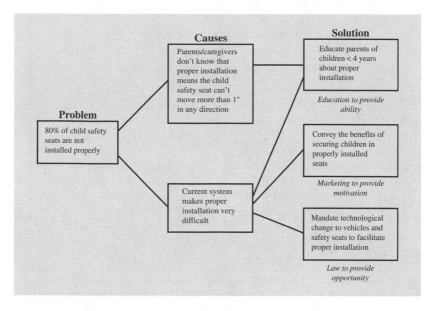

Figure 6-2 Modeling the Child Safety Seat Initiative

Exhibit 6-5 Key Aspects of the Child Restraint System Situation Analysis

Problem

- Child restraints are 71% effective in reducing the likelihood of death in motor vehicle crashes. However, actual average effectiveness of restraints in use is 59%, due to
  - Incorrect use, and/or
  - Vehicle seat and/or seat belt incompatibility issues
- Consumer frustration with installation and compatibility may lead to eroding confidence in the safety of child restraint systems and decreased usage of the systems.

Causes

- Incorrect use. A 1996 four-state study found that 80% of participants made at least one significant error in installation: 72% did not use a locking clip when necessary, or used it incorrectly; 17% used the vehicle seat belt incorrectly.
- Vehicle seat and seat belt incompatibility. Advances in seat and seat belt design features to protect older children and adults have led to increased difficulty with child restraint installation. In consumer clinics (somewhat similar to focus groups) conducted in the United States and Canada, virtually all participants expressed high levels of dissatisfaction with conventional means of attaching child restraints in vehicles.

Source: Reprinted from L. Doner and M. Siegel, *Using Marketing in Public Health.* In L. Novick & G. Mays (Eds.), *Public Health Administration*, p. 489, © 2001, Aspen Publishers. Data from *Federal Motor Vehicle Safety Standards: Child Restraint Systems: Child Restraint Anchorage systems*, 64 Fed. Reg. 10785, 1999, National Highway Traffic Safety Administration.

MOTIVATION	Yes		No	
OPPORTUNITY	Yes	No	Yes	No
ABILITY — Yes	1 Prone to behave Education	2 Unable to behave Marketing	3 Resistant to behave Law	4 Resistant to behave Marketing, Law
ABILITY — No	5 Unable to behave Education, Marketing	6 Unable to behave Education, Marketing	7 Resistant to behave Education, Marketing, Law	8 Resistant to behave Education, Marketing, Law

Source: Rothschild, M.L. (1999). Carrots, sticks and promises: A conceptual framework for the behavior management of public health and social issues. *Journal of Marketing,* 63, 24–37.

Figure 6-3 Modeling the Child Safety Seat Initiative

This framework can be used first to identify whether education, law, marketing, or a combination should be used to change individual health behaviors. A second level of analysis may help identify interventions needed to enable or force some other group to act in a way that will result in increased motivation, opportunity, or ability to support the individual behavior change. To illustrate, in the child safety seat example in Figure 6-2, some parents and other caregivers had motivation but did not have opportunity or ability; they would be in cell 6. Education could be used to improve skills for installing existing seats in existing cars. However, before marketing could be used to provide an improved product and therefore opportunity, legal changes were necessary: Regulations had to be changed to both enable and require manufacturers of child safety seats and automobiles to use a different installation system.

Factors to Consider

Sometimes, a variety of possible solutions is needed to address a particular problem. Thinking about these approaches from a number of different perspectives may help prioritize them and narrow them down to the ones that best fit the problem, the organizations seeking to address it, and currently available resources. Considering the following questions may help.

Will an increase in demand or adjustment of supply be more effective? When the focus is trying to get individuals to take actions that improve their personal health, increasing demand for that behavior is necessary. Sometimes, progress toward health objectives is achieved much more quickly by adjusting supply: Rather than (or in addition to) trying to persuade the people who need to improve their health to change, planners can use marketing to persuade (or, in some instances, legal approaches to mandate) suppliers of a product or service necessary for the health behavior to make a change. For example, adding folate to grain products is a regulatory approach to reducing birth defects. Instead of focusing solely on persuading women who are or might become pregnant to increase their folic acid intake (to decrease neural tube defects), requiring that food processors fortify certain grain products with folate allows women to increase their intake, in some instances without even realizing they are doing so. Supply-side adjustments can also be brought about through marketing voluntary changes, such as persuading restaurants and other food outlets to decrease portion sizes or the amount of fat or sodium in their foods and convincing fast food restaurants to offer fruit as an alternative to french fries or milk or juice as alternatives to soft drinks.

What type of demand exists? Kotler and Roberto (1989) divided social changes into the type of product or service that must be developed—new, superior, and substitute—depending on the state of demand. New products fill a latent demand; target adopters have an unfilled need the product addresses. In contrast, superior products are appropriate when there is underfilled demand—the current product or its accessibility does not satisfy target adopters' needs. Finally, substitute products or behaviors must be developed to address the unwholesome demand that occurs when target adopters are engaging in harmful behaviors, such as drug abuse. The challenge in this instance is to "de-market" the existing behavior and provide a substitute that the target adopters will accept.

Is a tangible good or service tied to the product? Kotler and Roberto (1989) divided behavior changes into those tied to a tangible product, such as family planning and contraceptives, versus those that involve the behavior change alone. They argued that if a behavior is tied to a tangible good, the marketer must market both the behavior and the product, a situation they characterized as dual demand. They noted that dual demand can take a number of forms, each requiring a different strategy. First, the tangible good may already be embraced by the target adopters for reasons other than the behavior change on which the program is focusing (e.g., condoms may be used to prevent disease but not as a method of family planning). Second, the behavior change may have been adopted but the particular good or service has not been. Third, both good or service and behavior change are at the same stage of adoption.

Is this a one-time or a frequent behavior? For one-time or periodic behavior changes, such as getting a flu shot or donating blood, Kotler and Roberto (1989) noted that demand is irregular—the change only needs to happen at certain times or under certain conditions. Therefore, the marketing task is to convince people to do something once. Community tragedies sometimes create a different sort of irregular demand: The public and policymakers suddenly clamor for a public health program previously thought to be unimportant. In contrast, with continuous or frequent behaviors the marketing task is to help individuals fit the behavior into their daily life processes. Building and maintaining a relationship with target audience members is likely to be critical to success. With sustained behavior changes, marketers who have successfully convinced target adopters to try the behavior will eventually face a faltering demand situation when compliance with the behavior drops. This situation can occur with individual health behaviors and with the policies that facilitate those behaviors. Those marketing disease or injury prevention frequently experience the ramifications of faltering demand among policymakers: When prevention programs are successful, the attention-grabbing poor outcomes stop occurring and policymakers are often tempted to reallocate the prevention resources to burgeoning crises.

Do the solutions need to occur in a particular order, or can they happen simultaneously or in any order? Sometimes, changes must be made to product, price, or place so people have sufficient opportunity before any significant behavior change can occur. Also, sometimes legal or educational approaches are required to make these changes before marketing can be of use. At other times, two solutions can move forward in tandem, as was true with the child safety seats example discussed earlier. Education to tell people how to install existing child safety seats correctly and marketing to persuade them to do so took place while a regulatory approach was pursued. Once new child restraints and new anchorage systems were available, education and marketing efforts were modified to address the new systems as well.

Which focus would benefit the largest number of people? Although sometimes it is important to address those most in need, regardless of whether they are the largest group, at other times choosing the approaches that would benefit the greatest numbers is the ethical and appropriate decision.

Which focus is the best match for the sponsoring organization? Based on the organization's mission, expertise, and resources, some approaches may be a better fit than others. One approach may have the best funding potential, which is important if outside funds need to be raised. Assuming that likely contributions to the public health problem are equal, success is more likely with an approach that attracts more funding.

When analyses are complete, planners can then consider the mandates, resources, and restrictions of the organization(s) and make an objective assessment of what roles the organization(s) can play in the solutions and what roles will have to be played by others. If an organization cannot implement all necessary approaches, the environmental assessment (described in the next section) should provide sufficient information to determine if other approaches can be implemented by other organizations (Kotler, Roberto, & Lee, 2002, p. 97):

> The best focus would then have a high potential for behavior change, fill a significant need and void in the marketplace, match the organization's capabilities, and have a high funding potential.

Assessing the Intervention Environment

Once planners have determined the education, law, and marketing approaches appropriate for the public health problem and identified some possibilities for the organization, they should evaluate the environment in which the intervention will be implemented to gain further guidance on how to focus the organization's efforts. An environmental assessment will likely encompass reviewing past attempts to address the problem and their results and identifying current complementary and competing activities. It also may include analyzing how the problem or its potential solutions are currently framed in the media, thereby providing insight into the public and policy agendas.

Reviewing Past Activities and Results

Information can be collected on previous programs, their target audience(s), goals, products, services, distribution channels, promotional approaches, and results. Identifying approaches from programs that have and have not worked well and environments in which they were used can help focus current efforts on solutions that may be more likely to be effective. Ideally, past approaches will include sufficient process and outcome evaluation measures to provide such information. If not, insight can be gleaned by talking to people involved with implementing the program.

Identifying Complementary and Competing Activities

Competition for a public health initiative is anything that limits its resources, diverts attention from it, or calls for contrary behaviors. Identifying competition allows planners to position and focus a program appropriately and differentiate its offerings from others.

Social changes unrelated to the public health initiative can compete with planners' work. Although multiple social changes can occur at the same time in history because they build on each others' momentum, they also compete for media coverage, political capital, and audience attention. In some instances, groups may be promoting a product, message, or practice in conflict with each others' goals or solutions to the problem.

Often, multiple organizations address the same public health issue or problem. Though it may seem counterintuitive, this is a source of competition because the organizations must compete for limited resources. Identifying other groups' activities can facilitate cooperation instead of competition by promoting synergy and preventing duplication of effort.

If one organization is doing a sufficient job of addressing a problem, a second organization may not need to get involved at all. In other instances, where one group already has adequate plans to cover a particular target audience, a second group can work with them to address the same audience, which may maximize both groups' resources. Perhaps materials can be shared or responsibilities can be divided up among the partners.

A third major source of competition is commercial entities. Although many industries promote healthy behaviors, some public health activities, such as preventing or stopping tobacco use, have a direct commercial opponent encouraging the very behavior public health practitioners are trying to stop. More often, there are commercial institutions that emphasize behaviors or choices that are detrimental if not moderated or balanced by other behaviors. For example, data show that most food advertisements seen by both children and adolescents are for foods of poor nutritional value (Powell et al., 2007). Similarly, popular media tend to portray characters engaging in violent or risky behaviors. With the possible exception of physical activity, the media rarely picture everyday healthful behaviors such as using condoms or wearing seat belts.

Identifying "competing" activities helps program planners make informed decisions about how to proceed, such as whether to oppose unfriendly competitors, whether to create an alliance with friendly competitors, whether to do nothing (either because other groups are already addressing the problem sufficiently or because the unfriendly competition is such that progress is exceedingly unlikely without substantially greater resources), and so on.

Program planners often know of complementary or competing activities being conducted by other groups. Some activities also can be identified by contacting likely organizations, through web searches, and through reviews of media coverage to determine if and how other organizations are addressing a particular issue.

■ STEP 2: SELECT APPROACHES AND DETERMINE THE ROLE OF MARKETING

After planners have assessed the environment, they must make realistic decisions about what solutions to pursue. If all critical solutions cannot be pursued, they must decide whether it is worthwhile to devote resources to the problem. The first step is to examine trends and determine the potential opportunities and challenges as well as the types of approaches to change that may be necessary (e.g., education, law, and marketing). A common way to do this is to conduct a strengths, weaknesses, opportunities, and threats (SWOT) analysis. In the SWOT approach, the strengths and weaknesses of both the organization that sponsors the intervention and of the social change itself are assessed. This information is then used to identify opportunities for an intervention to make a difference. At the same time, potential threats to the success of the intervention are identified. This process helps point the intervention in promising directions and, hopefully, minimizes time wasted on efforts that are not likely to succeed. Early identification of threats to success allows program managers to address many of these threats or at least factor them in when setting expectations and objectives.

The SWOT analysis can be used to evaluate the solutions previously outlined in the MOA–Approaches to Behavior Management framework (Figure 6-3) and make decisions regarding which approaches will be pursued by the organization. **Exhibit 6-6** summarizes some challenges to accomplishing social change, particularly when marketing approaches are used.

■ STEP 3: SET GOALS AND OBJECTIVES

When general approaches have been selected, planners can set measurable goals and objectives for specific target audiences and then proceed to develop market offerings. If necessary, they can also plan educational and legal approaches, although here we focus on market offerings

---

Exhibit 6-6 Some Challenges to Social Change

Obstacles associated with using a marketing approach in a noncommercial setting:

- Audience data are more difficult to obtain and often of poorer quality.
- Financial cost may be outside the marketer's control, so managers must rely on changing other costs (i.e., psychological, time, effort, or lifestyle costs).
- Contributions of marketing efforts are often difficult to measure.
- Organizations may not be marketing-savvy and/or control all components of the marketing mix.

Obstacles associated with changing ingrained behaviors:

- Negative demand—the target audience may oppose the change being advocated.
- Legal and regulatory changes may be required to support or facilitate individuals' behavior change.
- The change may involve highly sensitive issues or may conflict with culture.
- The costs of the behavior change often exceed tangible benefits.
- The benefits may accrue to third parties, rather than to the individual making the change.
- Early adopters risk ostracism (for individuals) or losing a competitive standing in the marketplace (for companies).
- Change may take a long time.

and activities. Although we divide "setting goals and objectives" and "selecting target audiences" into two steps for clarity, these decisions must be made together in reality.

Goals translate a program's mission into specific behavioral outcomes (Andreasen, 1995). For example, the goal of the National Fruit & Vegetable Program (formerly known as the 5 A Day for Better Health program) is to promote health through increased fruit and vegetable consumption (CDC, 2011).

Objectives quantify the goals and describe the specific intermediate steps necessary to make progress toward them. In the private sector, objectives are typically defined in terms of product or service trial, brand awareness, or sales. Public health efforts often include health objectives (such as reductions in morbidity or mortality) and corresponding behavioral objectives that address how the health objective will be achieved.

Objectives should be measurable, solidly linked to a behavioral outcome, associated with a specific target audience, and associated with a specific time period. As Green and Kreuter (1991) noted, "objectives are crucial; they form a fulcrum, converting diagnostic data into program direction" (p. 118). They noted that objectives should answer these questions:

1. Who will receive the program (health objective) or make the change (behavioral objective)?
2. What health benefit should be received or action taken?
3. How much of that benefit or action should be achieved?
4. By when should it be achieved?

Exhibit 6-7 presents some possible behavioral objectives for a mammography program targeting women age 50 and older. The goal of this hypothetical program is to increase the rates of screening mammography among older women, as research has shown that rates decrease with age (Marchant & Sutton, 1990). In this example, many of the supply-side changes necessary to support increased use of mammography had already been implemented in the United States. For example, Medicare and other insurance reimbursements for mammograms had been established.

The first objective in Exhibit 6-7 is actually a product trial objective: Get women who have never had a mammogram to do so once. The second objective is to increase population compliance with the recommended schedule of annual mammograms. The third objective addresses the behavior of a secondary audience: physicians. This objective illustrates one aspect of the iterative nature of the marketing process: Research conducted during the planning phase of a program can result in objectives and audiences that may not have been considered at the outset. In this instance, secondary research had shown that three-fourths of women went for a mammogram because their physician

Exhibit 6-7   Sample Objectives for Mammography Program

1. By 2015, increase by x% the number of women age 50 or older who received their first mammogram in the past year.

2. By 2015, increase by x% the number of women age 50 or older who received a mammogram in the past year.

3. By 2015, increase by x% the number of general practitioners, family practitioners, and internists who discuss mammography at all office visits by female patients over age 50 and provide them with a referral if necessary.

recommended it (Marchant & Sutton, 1990) and that overall visits to physicians increased with age (unpublished data from the National Center for Health Statistics, 1990).

However, although women got mammograms because their physicians recommended them and older women were more likely to see a physician, screening rates were lower for older women. A survey of women revealed two factors that likely played a role: (1) Obstetricians/gynecologists are more likely to recommend mammograms than are other physicians, but visits to these specialists are less frequent for older women, and (2) women who went for a checkup were more likely to get mammograms than those who went for a specific problem, which suggests that physicians were less likely to discuss screening tests with women who were there only for a problem (Sutton & Doner, 1992). Therefore, increasing the percentage of physicians who recommend mammograms to all female patients, regardless of whether the office visit is for a checkup or a specific problem, is likely to increase the percentage of women who get them.

To measure progress toward objectives, baseline and follow-up data must be available. Previously conducted studies often supply baseline data, which help program planners set reasonable objectives by examining current behavior and, with any luck, recent trends over time. In other instances, a custom study must be conducted. When objectives are set, evaluation plans should be developed that spell out how progress will be measured against the objectives.

Green and Kreuter (1991) also outlined a number of other factors that planners should consider when setting objectives:

1. Progress toward meeting objectives should be measurable.
2. Individual objectives should be based on relevant, reasonably accurate data.
3. Objectives should be in harmony across topics and levels.

This third factor is particularly important; occasionally programs will inadvertently establish two objectives that conflict with one another.

When setting behavioral objectives, planners should consider the type of change most likely to result in progress toward a health goal. That is, if the health goal is to reduce by $x\%$ the number of people who die in car accidents each year, a behavioral objective might be to increase by $x\%$ the number of people who wear seat belts. That might be supplemented by a regulatory/legal objective of increasing by $x\%$ the number of states with primary seat belt laws. It is important to assess what can be accomplished, given the program's resources, and to refrain from setting objectives the program cannot possibly address or attain. A thorough situation analysis coupled with a sound theoretical framework for the intervention should help avoid such problems.

In setting objectives to change individual health behaviors, the biggest challenge public health practitioners confront is choosing objectives that are reasonable for the audience to achieve. In general, practitioners should choose behavioral objectives that are as similar to existing behavior as possible to minimize the changes audience members will need to make. Asking people to engage in more of some behavior they already do is easier than asking them to begin an entirely new behavior.

Interventions that ask people to make changes only in some settings can also keep objectives manageable and more likely to be attained. For example, an HIV prevention program might craft an objective such as "Within 1 year, increase by $x\%$ the proportion of men who have sex with men who use a condom the first time they have sex with a new partner," rather than, "Within 1 year, increase by $x\%$ the proportion of men who have sex with men who use a condom every time they have sex." The costs associated with the first behavior (such as occasionally experiencing decreased pleasure) are likely to be less than those associated with the second (chronic decreased pleasure and perceived lack of trust).

Selecting objectives for public health policy audiences can be clear-cut or challenging, depending on the nature of the initiative. When the time frame is clearly defined and the goal is to get the audience to take some specific action now, not to continue taking it for the rest of their lives, the objective is often obvious. For example, the objective for voters might be to get a certain percentage of "undecided" voters to vote for (or against) a referendum, or to contact a public official to support (or oppose) a specific policy. The desired action for a food company might be to decrease the amount of salt or fat in its processed foods.

When the time frame is less clearly defined or the behavior changes are more complex or involve more people, the initial action can be difficult to identify and somewhat removed from the ultimate goal. For example, initial efforts to persuade schools to adopt a coordinated approach to school health typically focus on building support among parents and community members. The action might be asking them to show support by contacting a school board member. Later efforts might build on that support by forming a school health committee of parents and school representatives, which might then introduce specific changes to the school.

■ STEP 4: SEGMENT AND SELECT PRIMARY AND SECONDARY TARGET AUDIENCES

Identifying population groups who could benefit from a specific health behavior is typically a straightforward process. However, identifying specific audience segments to which programs will market can involve nearly as much judgment as science. This tends to be an iterative process. As additional secondary and primary research is conducted, more is learned and the audiences are refined—or new audiences may be introduced.

A program's primary target audience is the group that needs to take a specific action. That action might be to engage in a particular health behavior (e.g., add some physical activity each day, eat two more servings of fruits and vegetables, use a condom with a new partner), or the action might be doing something that increases the ability or opportunity of others to engage in the health behavior (e.g., legislators or elected or appointed public officials might be the primary target audience if the goal is public policy change; employers might be the target if the goal is worksite changes; health insurers might be the target if the goal is changes in covered medical services, etc.). There can be more than one primary target audience, although each should form a distinct group. If everyone who has certain broad characteristics (e.g., American adults, policymakers) needs to make the change, then program planners need to identify a subset of this group that is most willing to make the change, most easily reached by the intervention, or most likely to impact overall public health by making the change.

Secondary target audiences are those who can help the primary target audience(s) make the change or influence them to do so. For example, family members of persons with hypertension can help them adhere to treatment regimens. Health care providers can counsel patients about various behavioral risk factors or recommend tests for early detection of disease. Health teachers or school food service personnel can help students change their eating habits. Constituents can help policymakers understand the importance of a particular initiative.

Segmentation

The process of dividing the population into groups based on one or more variables is termed *audience segmentation*. The goal of audience segmentation is to identify subgroups whose members are similar to each other and distinct from members of other groups along dimensions that are meaningful in the context of the behavior to be changed. Audiences can be segmented on a variety of dimensions, such as demographic, geographic, behavioral, or lifestyle characteristics. Target audiences are then selected from these subgroups.

The best starting point for identifying target audiences is to segment the population of interest based on the behavior the program seeks to change. Dividing the population into those who already practice the behavior (doers) and those who do not (non-doers) provides some of the information needed to set goals and objectives and to define specific program target audiences. For example, planners of an intervention to address youth smoking might divide children and teens into "never smoked," "tried it," and "current smoker." If the audience is policymakers, dividing them into those who have supported similar initiatives and those who have not is a logical starting point.

If non-doers are sufficiently homogeneous, a program may target the whole group. More often, non-doers are further segmented on dimensions such as how close they are to the recommended behavior (e.g., their current amount of physical activity or their current consumption of specific foods, drinks, or other substances), differences in real or perceived barriers to the behavior, or differences in perceived benefits.

Selection

A number of factors must be considered when choosing audience segments, such as the size of each segment, the extent to which the group needs or would benefit from the behavior change (if the goal is to get them to change individual health behaviors), how well resources can reach each group, and the extent to which the segment is likely to respond to the marketing offering.

Profiling

Once audiences have been selected, the task is to learn enough about them to design, communicate and deliver an appealing offering. The behavioral maps constructed in step 1 provide a good starting point but generally need to be augmented based on the specific audience selected. Public health data sources may provide some information on knowledge and attitudes, but they almost never include information that helps determine how to reach an audience, such as media habits and leisure activities. Public health data also usually do not include information on the benefits and barriers people associate with the proposed behavior. When professionals or policymakers are the target audience, even less information is likely to be available. For health care providers, sometimes government or academic studies are available on knowledge, attitudes, or practices. For public policymakers, obtaining material produced by them, their staff members, or their political parties can help assess how they are likely to think about an issue, as can reviewing media coverage for their comments.

The next step is to identify sources of information that could help further segment the target audience or answer some of these questions once the target audience is refined. Sources of additional information on public and patient target audiences and some professional audiences can include the following:

- Past situation analyses or target audience profiles (prepared for an organization or for others addressing the same topic; federal agencies, voluntary health agencies, professional societies, and trade associations are also possible sources)
- Government data sources (in the United States, these include the National Health Interview Survey, the Behavioral Risk Factor Surveillance System, the National Health and Nutrition Examination Survey, and others)
- Syndicated commercial market research studies, for information on demographics, lifestyle, media habits, product purchase behavior, and leisure activities (in the United States, the two largest are conducted by Mediamark Research, Inc., and Simmons Market Research Bureau)
- Public opinion polls (many U.S. polls are archived at the Roper Center for Public Opinion Research at the University of Connecticut)

Although many of these sources are national, they can be useful for local programs when no local data are available.

In addition to a demographic description of potential audiences, planners need detailed information on target audiences' knowledge, attitudes, practices, and behaviors related to the public health problem. They also need information on target audience members' media habits, lifestyles, leisure activities, and general outlook to identify how best to construct and deliver offerings they find appealing and relevant.

■ STEP 5: DESIGN PUBLIC HEALTH OFFERING(S)

Once target audiences have been selected and goals and objectives set, it is time to develop the marketing mix strategies. This involves deciding what the product offering will be, determining how price will be managed, identifying the channels through which offerings will be available, and developing a promotion strategy. A strategy is "the broad approach that an organization takes to achieving its objectives" (Andreasen, 1995, p. 69). Strategies are usually long term; they are developed with the intention of using them for 3 to 5 years or more. Once strategies have been determined, the tactics—short-term, detailed steps used to implement each strategy—can be developed for each strategy.

- *Strategies are relatively abstract:* for example, provide an alternative ride for drunk drivers, reduce embarrassment involved in obtaining condoms, make fruits and vegetables available throughout the day, communicate how to add two daily servings of fruits and vegetables easily

- *Tactics are concrete:* create a community ride service, persuade retail outlets to locate condoms where customers do not have to ask for assistance, implement policies requiring fruits and vegetables at all eating occasions (meals, snacks, classroom treats) at school, create and place a subway poster showing easy ways to add two servings of fruits and vegetables during the day

All four components of the marketing mix—product, price, place, and promotion—must work together to create, communicate, and deliver a public health offering superior to all alternative behaviors. The product—the benefits one will obtain by engaging in the public health action—is the core of the marketing mix. Pricing and distribution strategies are designed to increase product appeal and accessibility by increasing the benefits or decreasing the costs associated with the product. Promotion's role is to make the audience aware of the product and position it in their minds as superior to all alternatives, including doing nothing.

Factors to Consider

Planners must consider a number of factors when developing the marketing mix for a public health offering, including maximizing self-interest, the ethics of the intervention, and sustainability.

Maximizing Self-Interest

People voluntarily choose to engage in a marketing exchange if they believe it is in their self-interest to do so. Therefore, products must be designed and distributed in such a way that it is in the person's best interest to engage in the replacement behavior—and promotions must make a compelling case for how self-interest will be satisfied.

Ethics

Because marketing fundamentally involves trying to persuade someone to do something, it is inherently fraught with ethical decisions. Some believe any use of marketing is unethical; some advocates of free choice strongly oppose trying to pass laws or regulations that affect the incentives or penalties a person receives as a result of a behavior. In the context of developing a public health offering, the decisions with ethical dimensions are choosing a replacement behavior and designing the marketing mix.

In *choosing a replacement behavior* for an individual's health, one must carefully consider the target audience's culture as well as the ramifications to its members and others of engaging in the behavior. For example, in the previously discussed drunk driving example, many public health and community leaders were initially troubled by the focus on providing rides home rather than trying to reduce alcohol consumption. However, planners considered the audience culture and the likelihood of success for each replacement action and concluded that although excessive drinking can have serious self-destructive consequences, the culture and motivation of the target audience was such that they were very unlikely to be persuaded to drink less. In contrast, providing rides home would better serve the public good by getting intoxicated young people out from behind the wheel, therefore decreasing the societal costs, both of death and injury among innocent bystanders and the financial costs associated with the crashes. In this program, planners also chose a replacement behavior that lent itself to a marketing offer that could become self-sustaining: Ride services have a source of income.

Careful consideration should also be given to the length of time the market offering can be provided or can be provided at a cost target audience members can afford. Particularly when working with extremely vulnerable populations, it is unethical to design a market offering, persuade them to make the behavior change, and then eliminate or greatly increase the cost of supply. One example of this might be demonstration projects that devote considerable resources to providing a good or service but make no effort to create a self-sustaining entity or identify an existing entity that can continue availability after the project ends.

Designing the marketing mix involves several factors. Often, it is unethical to focus on stimulating demand for a particular behavior, product, or service if there are substantial environmental factors inhibiting the target audience's ability to engage in the behavior or access the good or service (such as high cost or distance or lack of availability of tangible goods and services). It is more ethical to focus on improving opportunity or ability. In the child safety seat example discussed above, it would have been unethical for the National Highway Traffic Safety Administration (NHTSA) to focus only on persuading parents and other caregivers to use safety seats and educating them on how to do so properly without mandating changes to vehicles and safety seats to support the new behavior. It is unethical to encourage people to seek particular health services without addressing barriers like affordability and accessibility.

Sustainability

Some marketing efforts are inherently short term, and so sustainability is not an issue. For example, efforts to get a particular law or referendum passed or policy implemented are often in this category. However, many times public health practitioners are addressing an ongoing public health need, such as immunization, changing lifestyles, or maintaining funding for core programs. Even if the mandate or funding is short term (a few months to a couple of years) in planning market offerings, consideration should be given to how the marketing offering will continue to be made available to the target audience and how they will continue to be aware that it is. Involving stakeholders in the design and development of product offerings and indicating they are being asked to come up with permanent changes encourages them to integrate the solutions into their typical business practices. This may increase the likelihood that solutions will be available over the longer term.

Product

The product is the bundle of benefits the target audience receives in exchange for taking the public health action. It may or may not be bundled with a tangible good or service. It is imperative for planners to understand the benefits a target audience can or does associate with the replacement behavior and how they are likely to value those benefits, especially in relationship to costs they associate with the behavior. A successful product is one that

1. The initiative can easily and cost-efficiently deliver
2. Clearly differentiates the initiative's offering from its behavioral competition
3. The target audience believes offers more and greater benefits than those associated with the current behavior

Including the target audience in product development greatly increases the chance of achieving success. Target audience input should always be sought through formative research, but an advisory group of target audience members also can be helpful in multiple ways. At a minimum, they can suggest ideas for the form, pricing, distribution, and promotion of the product. In some instances, advisory group members can serve as the early adopters and champions, spurring audience adoption of the innovation. As Roman and colleagues summarized, "people don't buy products—they buy expectations of benefits" (2003, p. 20). In deciding what bundle of benefits to offer, the following questions may help:

1. Are the benefits associated with the replacement behavior similar to those the target audience associates with the current behavior?
2. Are the replacement behavior's benefits clear to the target audience? Decreasing the likelihood of contracting influenza is an attribute of the flu shot; the benefit is likely to be avoiding suffering or missing work or, for parents inoculating kids, feeling like they are being responsible parents and caring for their children.
3. To what core values (freedom, autonomy, control, fairness, etc.) does the replacement behavior appeal?
4. What immediate, tangible benefits does the replacement behavior provide? Immediate, tangible benefits are particularly important for continuous/frequent behaviors in which the possibility of a long-term health benefit has to compete with the certainty of a short-term pleasurable benefit.

People place greater value on benefits they will obtain immediately and discount those they may attain at some point in the future (Simpson & Vuchinich, 2000, p. 194):

Behavior patterns that promote long-term health frequently lose the competition with more immediately rewarding choice options.

This phenomenon is due to opposing short- and long-term preferences and because the value of a specific benefit or cost is influenced by its temporal proximity (Simpson & Vuchinich, 2000). As a result, a smaller benefit can be valued more highly than a larger benefit if the smaller benefit is obtained sooner. People place greater (negative) value on immediate costs and discount those that will occur in the future. This means the cost-to-benefit equation associated with a particular behavior changes over time. For many health behaviors, choosing "smaller sooner rewards" (pleasure of fatty foods or watching TV rather than working out) can lead to "larger later costs" (poor health), whereas choosing "larger later rewards" (good health) may mean "smaller sooner costs" (i.e., forgoing the smaller sooner rewards; Simpson & Vuchinich, 2000).

This competition between the "larger later reward" of good health and the "smaller sooner reward" provided by certain behaviors has been termed "the tyranny of small decisions." This is a "behavioral pattern in which an individual opts to engage in behavior that is desirable at the present time, but is less than desirable and perhaps even harmful at some future point in time" (Bickel & Marsch, 2000, p. 341). In other words, one may choose the donut rather than whole-wheat toast or choose to sit on the couch and watch TV rather than exercising because, at that moment, the poor choice offers immediate benefits that the healthy choice does not. Bickel and Marsch argued that environment and culture contribute to this problem by selecting for "shortened temporal horizons"—aspects of culture promote placing greater value on immediate benefits over longer-term ones (**Table 6-1**).

In instances where a poor choice's "smaller sooner benefits" trump a healthy choice's "larger later rewards," the public health practitioner must provide some other immediate reward for engaging in the health behavior. Behavioral economists noted as follows (Simpson & Vuchinich, 2000, p. 211):

> It would not appear to be necessary, at least initially, that these additional rewards be directly related in any way to health, only that they control behaviors that are necessary for its accrual . . . it would be beneficial to develop a better understanding of the valued nonhealth rewards to which health behavior maintenance and good health potentially allow access. Interventions that focus relatively less attention on increasing health and relatively more attention on increasing access to the immediately available, tangible activities and rewards to which optimal health allows access potentially will provide the most powerful and lasting interventions.

This perspective is validated by experience: Backer, Rogers, and Sopory (1992) found that health campaigns "are more effective if they emphasize current rewards rather than the avoidance of distant negative consequences" (p. 30).

Table 6-1 Summary of Temporal Horizon in Modern Society

Factors Promoting Short Temporal Horizon in Modern Society	Related Behavioral Principles
Cultural factors	
Culture of immediate gratification-leisure	High availability of low-cost reinforcers; low effort needed to obtain reinforcer; immediate reinforcement (little delay)
Economic deterioration and destabilization	Unpredictable environments-reinforcers
Community factors	
Erosion of civic-community bonds	Lack of behavioral surveillance with contingencies; high availability of low-cost reinforcers
Erosion of religious or moral training	Lack of behavioral surveillance with contingencies
Family-individual factors	
Erosion of the nuclear family	Lack of behavioral surveillance with contingencies; unpredictable environments-reinforcers

Source: Bickel, W.K., & Marsch, L.A. (2000). The tyranny of small decisions: Origins, outcomes, and proposed solutions. In W.K. Bickel & R.W. Vuchinich (Eds.), *Reframing health behavior change with behavioral economics* (p. 355). Mahwah, NJ: Lawrence Erlbaum.

Price

Price is the cost the target audience associates with taking the public health action. Costs may be monetary or nonmonetary. Nonmonetary costs include time, effort, and energy, as well as real or perceived psychological, social, or physical discomforts.

Managing price is a two-step process. First, planners must identify the monetary and nonmonetary costs associated with the public health behavior. The behavioral analysis described in step 1 and the target audience profile should help identify key costs impeding an audience's willingness, ability, or opportunity to take action. Then planners should determine whether the initiative should focus on

1. Decreasing target audience costs
2. Increasing benefits
3. Doing a bit of both

The discussion above, under "Product," of behavioral economics and the differences in how people value short- and long-term costs and benefits should be helpful in developing a pricing strategy.

A common example of choosing between immediate and delayed costs occurs when deciding whether to go to the dentist. Going to the dentist is hardly pleasant, but the costs associated with dental visits are small relative to the long-term costs of poor dental care and hygiene. Thus, the choice is between seeing the dentist and incurring a little pain and monetary costs now or not seeing the dentist and incurring a lot of pain and monetary costs later. . . . At times distant from both a dental visit and later dental problems, the smaller cost of visiting the dentist is preferred. Thus, the individual will make a dentist appointment. As the time of the appointment approaches, however, the values of the [smaller sooner costs] and the larger later costs change at different rates. Immediately before the appointment, seeing the dentist becomes more aversive than the later dental problems, and the appointment may be canceled. (Simpson & Vuchinich, 2000, p. 198)

It is also helpful to think about the kinds of costs people experience when adopting the replacement behavior. Kotler and colleagues (2002) noted that costs may be associated with abandoning the old behavior as well as associated with adopting the new behavior.

Some public health behaviors involve monetary costs. A variety of tactics can be used to decrease these costs, including discount coupons, cash discounts, quantity discounts, seasonal discounts, promotional pricing (temporary price reductions), and segment pricing (e.g., different pricing for different geographic locations; Kotler et al., 2002). Sometimes these costs are within the public health marketer's control (e.g., the public health marketer is responsible for setting the price at which the good or service is sold). However, often the monetary price is set by an entity or entities other than the public health marketer (e.g., safety equipment, foods, exercise equipment, etc.), and efforts to manage monetary costs may need to be collaborative. In other situations, the goal may be to increase monetary costs of undesirable behaviors, as is done through taxes on tobacco products and alcoholic beverages.

A variety of tactics can be used to decrease nonmonetary costs as well. For continuous and frequent behaviors, planners should start by examining the costs target audience members encounter and then thinking of how those can be reduced and how the behavior can more easily fit into daily life processes. For example, for some behaviors time can be decreased through "embedding" the behavior into present activities, such as suggesting that people floss their teeth or exercise while watching TV (Kotler et al., 2002; citing Fox & Kotler, 1980).

The following example presents multiple approaches to managing price within one marketing effort. It is drawn from an example developed by Kotler and colleagues (2002) of changes in a mammography facility to manage the costs women associated with getting a mammogram.

- Offer new or improved tangible goods or services. In their example, mammography plates were heated to decrease the physical costs women experienced as a result of cold equipment.
- Improve distribution of existing goods and services. Time costs were reduced in two ways: wait time at appointments was decreased, and volunteers were used to provide valet parking so women would not have to arrive early to look for a difficult-to-find parking spot.
- Lower associated monetary costs. A sliding fee scale was used for the mammograms themselves, and free child care was provided.

Another approach to managing price is to use incentives, either to increase benefits or to increase costs. If they are used to increase benefits, engaging in the behavior earns the incentive. For example, companies that pay part or all of the cost of a fitness club or a weight-reduction program if employees demonstrate a certain level of participation are using an incentive to increase benefits. When an incentive is used to increase costs, changing to the replacement behavior earns the incentive. For example, health insurance policies that charge more for smokers offer people an incentive to stop smoking. Incentives are most often monetary but can be nonmonetary, such as contests, public recognition, or other indications of social approval. McKenzie-Mohr and Smith (1999) outlined the following suggestions for using incentives:

- Pair the incentive and the behavior closely in time.
- Use incentives to reward positive behavior.
- Make the incentive visible—an incentive will have little or no impact if people are unaware it exists.
- Be cautious about removing incentives. Incentives are external motivations to engage in a behavior. Sometimes incentives replace whatever internal motivation some people may have had to engage in the behavior. As a result, when the incentive is discontinued, those who may originally have had an intrinsic internal motivation to engage in the behavior will stop.
- Prepare for people's attempts to avoid incentives that work by raising the costs of not engaging in the behavior. For example, McKenzie-Mohr and Smith described actions that solo drivers take in order to use the carpool lane (such as installing a well-dressed mannequin in the passenger seat).

Place

Place refers to the situations in which the target audience does or can perform the health behavior and the outlets through which the target audience does or can obtain any tangible goods or services necessary for the health behavior. The goal of most place strategies is to make engaging in the behavior as convenient as possible for as many members of the target audience as possible—by putting together the most useful channels of distribution. In some instances, place can be used to differentiate the public health offering from its competitors.

Place is often overlooked as a strategy for social change initiatives. Strand, Rothschild, and Nevin (2004, p. 10) noted as follows:

> The "good" behavior social marketers promote tend to lose out to "bad" behaviors because we are stuck on messaging while the "bad" products are developing better channels. Availability is a strong competitive advantage.

Developing a place strategy starts with reviewing the behavioral analyses and looking for ways in which the replacement behavior can be made more accessible or convenient (National Cancer Institute, 1993):

- Can planners increase the number of locations at which a tangible good or service is available? Ideally, any needed tangible goods or services will be available every time and any time the audience has an opportunity to engage in the behavior—hence attempts to put condoms not only in pharmacies but also in school clinics, 24-hour retail outlets, restrooms in bars and dance clubs, and so on.
- Can the locations that provide services be moved so they are closer to the target audience (mammography vans, for example), better match operating hours to clients' availabilities, address other barriers (e.g., by providing child care during visits), or make the location more appealing?
- Can the intervention help individuals improve their own distribution channels? For example, the 5 A Day for Better Health program suggested that people move fruits and vegetables to a bowl on the counter and move them higher in the refrigerator so when they walk into the kitchen looking for something to eat, they quickly see produce.

Place strategies are typically more challenging for public health and other social marketers to implement because they typically have little control or power over the organizations that form the channels (unlike commercial marketers). This makes it particularly important to identify and deliver meaningful benefits to channel members.

At times, a place strategy may include making the current behavior less accessible or convenient. Access to cigarettes can be reduced by banning cigarette vending machines near places where children gather without supervision. Alcohol use can be limited by restricting the hours of opening and by limiting the quantity and type of alcohol that can be purchased in rural communities (Donovan & Henley, 2003).

Promotion

Promotion involves the communication of the exchange being offered to the target audience, typically through some combination of advertising, media relations, events, personal selling, and entertainment. Promotional messages should always communicate the product (bundle of benefits), how it differs from competitive products, and the action the target audience should take. Messages may also address pricing and access strategies that the planners will use to help overcome audience members' barriers.

Once the public health offering has been designed, it is time to determine the best way to promote it. The first step is to develop a communication strategy that identifies the target audience(s), the action they should take, and the benefit they will receive for doing so. In addition, the strategy should describe how to package and deliver the message so it will reach and motivate the target audience. Messages and promotional materials can then be developed in accordance with the strategy.

■ STEP 6: PLAN EVALUATION APPROACHES

Evaluation planning takes place in conjunction with planning interventions. Planning both together can result in early identification of unrealistic objectives and ensures that results of the intervention will be as measurable and as affordable as possible. While planning objectives and outlining strategies, planners should also create plans for evaluating progress against those objectives. Typically, process evaluation is used to track when, where, how, and with whom specific tactics were used; the resulting information is used to monitor progress and, most importantly, to make refinements to intervention offerings or implementation. Outcome evaluation is used to determine if objectives are met and whether the intervention succeeded in changing behaviors.

■ CONCLUSION

Thorough planning is essential to using strategic marketing in public health successfully. It begins with a systematic analysis of the situation: defining problems; identifying the populations they affect; analyzing current and possible replacement behaviors in terms of motivation, opportunity, and ability; outlining all possible components of a solution, including education, marketing, and law; and assessing the environment in which the intervention will compete.

Once a role for marketing has been determined, the next step is to set goals and objectives and select target audience segments based on the specific behaviors, conditions, or policies to be changed. To design an effective intervention, target populations must be thoroughly researched. In particular, the needs, desires, values, and barriers they associate with their current behaviors and the replacement behaviors must be understood.

The final step in the planning process is designing the public health offering and marketing mix strategies. The goal is for planners to use all four components—product, price, place, and promotion—and deliver a public health offering superior to all alternative behaviors.

It is important that planners include evaluation strategies as part of the marketing plan. A well-planned evaluation framework, developed in tandem with the project itself, results in activities that are well targeted, resource efficient, and more likely to result in the desired outcomes.

References

Andreasen, A.R. (1995). *Marketing social change: Changing behavior to promote health, social development, and the environment.* San Francisco, CA: Jossey-Bass.

Backer, T.E., Rogers, E., & Sopory, P. (1992). *Designing health communication campaigns: What works?* Thousand Oaks, CA: Sage.

Bickel, W.K., & Marsch L.A. (2000). The tyranny of small decisions: Origins, outcomes, and proposed solutions. In W.K. Bickel & R.W. Vuchinich (Eds.), *Reframing health behavior change with behavioral economics* (pp. 341–392). Mahway, NJ: Lawrence Erlbaum.

Centers for Disease Control and Prevention. (2011). Fruits & veggies: More matters. Retrieved October 6, 2011, from http://www.fruitsandveggiesmatter .gov/qa/index.html

Donovan, R.J., & Henley, N. (2003). *Social marketing: Principles & practice.* East Hawthorn, Victoria, Australia: IP Communications.

Fox, K.F.A., & Kotler, P. (1980). The marketing of social causes: The first 10 years. *Journal of Marketing, 44*(4), 24–33.

Graeff, J.A., Elder, J.P., & Booth, E.M. (1993). *Communication for health and behavior change: A developing country perspective.* San Francisco, CA: Jossey-Bass.

Green, L.W., & Kreuter, M.W. (1991). *Health promotion planning: An educational and environmental approach* (2nd ed.). Mountain View, CA: Mayfield.

Kotler, P., & Roberto, E.L. (1989). *Social marketing: Strategies for changing public behavior.* New York, NY: Free Press.

Kotler, P., Roberto, N., & Lee, N. (2002). *Social marketing: Improving the quality of life* (2nd ed.). Thousand Oaks, CA: Sage.

MacInnis, D.J., Moorman, C., & Jaworski, B.J. (1991). Enhancing and measuring consumers' ability, motivation, and opportunity to process brand information ads. *Journal of Marketing, 55*(4), 32–33.

Marchant, D.J., & Sutton, S.M. (1990). Use of mammography: United States, 1990. *Morbidity and Mortality Weekly Report, 39,* 621–630.

McKenzie-Mohr, D., & Smith W. (1999). *Fostering sustainable behavior: An introduction to community-based social marketing.* Gabriola Island, British Columbia, Canada: New Society Publishers.

National Cancer Institute. (1993). *5 A Day for Better Health: NCI media campaign strategy.* Bethesda, MD: Author.

National Center for Health Statistics. (1990). *Medical care survey.* Unpublished raw data.

Powell, L.M., Szczypka, G., Chaloupka, F.J., & Braunschwig, C.L. (2007). Nutritional content of television food advertisements seen by children and adolescents in the United States. *Pediatrics, 120,* 576–583.

Roman, K., Maas, J., & Nisenholtz, M. (2003). *How to advertise* (3rd ed.) New York, NY: St. Martin's Press.

Rothschild, M.L. (1999). Carrots, sticks and promises: A conceptual framework for the behavior management of public health and social issues. *Journal of Marketing, 63,* 24–37.

Simpson, C.A., & Vuchinich, R.E. (2000). Temporal changes in the value of objects of choice: Discounting, behavior patterns, and health behavior. In W.K. Bickel & R.E. Vuchinich (Eds.), *Reframing health behavior change with behavioral economics* (pp. 193–215). Mahway, NJ: Lawrence Erlbaum.

Strand, J., Rothschild, M.L., & Nevin, J.R. (2004). Place and channels of distribution. *Social Marketing Quarterly, 10*(3), 8–13.

Sutton, S.M., Balch, G.I., & Lefebvre, R.C. (1995). Strategic questions for consumer-based health communications. *Public Health Reports, 110*(6), 725–733.

Sutton, S.M., & Doner, L.D. (1992). Insights into the physician's role in mammography utilization among older women. *Women's Health Issues, 2,* 175–179.

CHAPTER

7

Formative
Research

Formative research is at the core of the marketing approach. At the outset, it is used to help define health problems, delineate their causes, and identify potential solutions. Next, it helps determine the audiences who can bring about needed changes to the physical, economic, or policy environment and/or segments of the public who can change their individual health behaviors. As audiences are selected, formative research helps create, communicate, and deliver exchanges that target audiences will value by identifying competition and helping to shape products, pricing strategies, selecting or developing distribution channels, and developing promotional strategies and tactics. Depending on the nature of the research questions, quantitative and qualitative research techniques, systematic observations, and experimental and quasi-experimental designs are used.

This chapter begins with a general discussion of the roles of formative research. This provides a foundation for subsequent discussions of how formative research can be used to select audiences and shape individual health behavior and policy change initiatives.

■ ROLE OF FORMATIVE RESEARCH

Formative research can be used in many ways during the planning and development stages. At times, it is used as a situation analysis tool to help define the problems an initiative could address, such as lack of motivation, ability, or opportunity to engage in a health behavior. It is essential for identifying the most appropriate audiences for a program to reach and understanding their wants and needs. It can also help determine the actions that target audience members are most amenable to taking to help them make the most progress toward addressing the public health problem. Formative research helps to identify the benefits and barriers audience members associate with each action, as well as the environmental changes, goods, services, distribution channels, or information they may need to take an action. As an intervention begins to take shape, formative research helps shape product offerings, pricing strategies, distribution channels, and promotional materials by gathering feedback on possibilities from target audience members.

As an example, formative research can be used in a situation in which immunization rates are lower than recommended for a particular disease. First, public health practitioners would identify why immunization rates are low. Learning more about the target audience members' thoughts and motivations can help public health groups increase rates. Do people have objections to vaccines in general or this specific one? Are target populations aware they or their children need immunization? Is the vaccine available in sufficient supply? Is the vaccine affordable? Is the vaccine available at nearby locations? Armed with answers to these questions, public health professionals can begin marketing an intervention.

Formative research also provides information to help assess what action the target audience can reasonably take and the benefits and barriers they associate with possible actions. This in turn can help planners design, deliver, and communicate offerings that satisfy audience wants and needs. A useful analogy is that of an interstate highway: The desired behavior is at the end of the highway, but as a person embarks on his or her journey, there may be roadblocks and/or attractive exit ramps before the destination.

Formative research can identify the roadblocks that must be dismantled or develop an attractive detour. In the immunization example, if the roadblock is lack of awareness, telling the target audiences about the vaccine and where they can get it may improve rates. Alternatively, the roadblock may be that health care providers are averse to the vaccine, so addressing their concerns is necessary. Perhaps the vaccine is in short supply, only available at distant providers, or too expensive. In these cases, planners can work with partners to increase supply, improve convenience, or decrease price, respectively.

Formative research can also help planners identify who is being led astray and at what exit ramps. Then it can increase understanding of why those ramps (competitive behaviors) are more appealing than the destination (desired behaviors) so planners can reconfigure the destination accordingly. For behaviors that people engage in frequently, formative research allows planners to make a data-based decision about whether to ask target audience members to avoid the exit ramps on every trip or only under certain conditions. For example, HIV prevention efforts targeting men who have sex with men almost universally choose a risk prevention approach: "Use a condom every time you have sex." However, men may find it impossible to comply with this guideline, so they may not bother to use a condom at all. Adequate formative research may have helped program managers realize that a risk reduction approach is more likely to be successful: "Use a condom in certain situations, such as with a new partner."

The remaining sections of this chapter discuss the following:

- Formative research to support health behavior change
- Formative research to support nonlegislative policy changes
- Formative research to support public health policy initiatives
- Pretesting

■ FORMATIVE RESEARCH TO SUPPORT HEALTH BEHAVIOR CHANGE

Initiatives seeking to change individual health behaviors typically use formative research in three ways. First, it is used to identify one or more target audiences and develop an understanding of their current practices, needs, wants, and values vis-à-vis the health behavior and any competing behaviors. In this way, it can help planners determine if they need to increase motivation, provide more or better opportunities for the behavior, or increase audience members' ability to engage in it. Second, formative research is used to determine what bundle of benefits will be most compelling (e.g., how the behavior change can be positioned as fulfilling the audience's needs or wants and as consistent with their values) and how the bundle of benefits can best be made available. Finally, formative research is used to develop and test product offerings, delivery systems, promotional strategies, messages, and materials designed to support the behavior change.

Segmenting and Selecting Target Audiences

Segmentation is a key aspect of effective communication and marketing. As Slater (1995) noted when discussing segmentation for health communication efforts, "success might not be assured by segmentation—there are too many other contingencies regarding resources, quality of implementation, and the inherent difficulty of the task. *Poor or nonexistent segmentation of audiences, on the other hand, is likely to doom public communication or education programs* [italics added]" (p. 186).

Types of Audience Segmentation

Audiences can be segmented based on a variety of dimensions, including demographic, geographic, lifestyle, or behavioral characteristics. The goal should be to segment on variables that influence whether people will change the behavior of interest. Slater (1995) noted that these variables can "include attitudinal beliefs and perceptions of relevant social norms (Ajzen & Fishbein, 1980); self-efficacy and presence of behavioral models (Bandura, 1986; Strecher et al., 1986), salience of, and involvement with, the health behavior (Chaffee & Roser, 1986; Grunig & Hunt, 1984); perceived preventability and costs of alternatives (Maiman & Becker, 1974) and constraints regarding the behavior" (Slater, 1995, p. 189).

Unfortunately, many initiatives rely on what Slater (1995) calls short-cuts to segmentation. These shortcuts are taken for a number of reasons. First, identifying the antecedents of behavior is a complex process. Second, even if the antecedents are identified, segmenting based on them often requires an expensive quantitative study and a great deal of time. Finally, there may be a lack of behavioral science background among some practitioners.

A popular shortcut is demographic segmentation, or grouping people on characteristics such as gender, age, income, education, or race/ethnicity. As Slater (1995) noted, the potential flaw with demographic segmentation is that it often groups people together based on variables that are meaningless in the context of changing the behavior in question: Two people can be demographically identical and yet lead totally different lives in terms of health behaviors and the factors that determine them. For example, consider two 23-year-old White men. They may have the same income and education levels, be single, live alone, and have similar jobs. Suppose one is straight and regularly practices unprotected sex with a variety of partners, whereas the other is gay and has been in a mutually monogamous relationship for 5 years. Demographic segmentation would offer little help to a manager aiming to identify and understand the target audience member for a new HIV prevention program.

Sometimes geographic characteristics (i.e., whether a person lives in an urban, a suburban, or a rural environment or the region, state/province, postal code, or neighborhood in which he or she resides) are combined with demographic and lifestyle information (e.g., product purchases, leisure activities, media habits, attitudes, interests, and opinions) to identify distinct neighborhood types. This process is referred to as *geodemographic segmentation* or *geoclustering* and is based on the assumption that people who live near each other have similar attitudes, interests, and behaviors. This type of segmentation strategy can help in planning community outreach activities and services and in delivering targeted messages through the mail. In the United States, commercial geodemographic clustering systems include Claritas Corporation's PRIZM (Potential Rating Index by Zip Markets).

Although there are no hard-and-fast rules, for many public health programs the population should first be segmented based on current behavior. At a minimum, dividing the population into "doers" and "nondoers"—those who do and do not engage in the desired behavior—allows identification of determinants of behavior and other characteristics that distinguish the two groups. Individual groups can then be further segmented based on readiness to change or psychographic characteristics. **Exhibit 7-1** presents a case study from a 5 A Day for Better Health program describing one application of this type of segmentation.

Exhibit 7-1   Segmenting and Profiling the Audience for the 5 A Day for Better Health Media Campaign

Background

The national 5 A Day for Better Health program helps Americans to increase their consumption of fruits and vegetables in order to decrease their risk of developing certain cancers, heart disease, and other conditions. When the National Cancer Institute (NCI; one of the U.S. Department of Health and Human Services' National Institutes of Health) was developing the initial national media campaign, rather than spending their limited resources on a general effort targeting all consumers, planners chose to follow marketing practice and segment the audience to maximize impact. The discussion below is based on the process outlined in NCI's media campaign strategy document (NCI, 1993) and in a chapter reviewing the campaign (Lefebvre et al., 1995).

Method

The first step was to segment based on behavior. A nationally representative baseline survey conducted in 1991 indicated that the average number of servings of fruits and vegetables consumed daily was about 3.5. Because this average intake is a point around which most people cluster, planners looked at this group in selecting a target audience. They then looked to the transtheoretical model of stages of change for guidance. Planners decided they wanted to first influence the largest number of people possible who would be open to the message (i.e., most ready to increase their fruit and vegetable intake) and who had not yet reached the objective of eating five or more servings daily. Therefore, they defined their target audience as people who were already trying to increase their consumption of fruits and vegetables (those in the contemplation or action stages of the transtheoretical model) but who had not yet achieved the minimum of five servings a day.

Next, they used two different marketing databases to profile the psychographic and demographic characteristics of the target audience. The first database came from MRCA Information Services and linked information on demographics, food consumption (based on food diaries), dietary habits, attitudes, interests, media habits, and other lifestyle characteristics through an annual study of 2,000 households demographically balanced to represent the U.S. population. MRCA data were used to compare two groups. The target audience group was defined as those age 18 or older who reported increasing their consumption of both fruits and vegetables and who currently averaged two servings a day (range of 1.5 to 2.5). This group constituted about 14% of the total population. The comparison group was adults who were already eating 3.5 or more servings of fruits and vegetables per day.

The second database was DDB Needham's 1993 Life Style study, an annual survey of 4,000 consumers who are members of a mail panel. Life Style includes nearly 1,000 questions related to attitudes, opinions, interests, activities, media habits, and demographics. Life Style results are demographically balanced to reflect the U.S. population, but as with all panel studies, the sample tends to underrepresent the very poor, the very rich, minorities, and transient populations. Two groups were again compared, but they were defined somewhat differently due to differences in the questions asked. The target group was adults who ate or drank two to three servings of fruits and vegetables on the previous day; desire to increase consumption

(continues)

> **Exhibit 7-1   Segmenting and Profiling the Audience for the 5 A Day for Better Health Media Campaign (continued)**
>
> could not be measured because the survey did not include such a question. Thus defined, the target group was about 50% of the population. The comparison group was adults eating five or more servings of fruits and vegetables on the previous day.
>
> Findings from the two studies were consistent overall: The target audience was younger, married with children, employed full time, and generally concerned with good health. The comparison group was older, likely to be retired, and more concerned with a healthier diet. The Life Style profile provided additional insights into the target audience's psychographic profile: Target audience members tended to lead a faster-paced life and had less spare time; were more likely to suffer from stress-related conditions such as headaches, lack of sleep, and indigestion; and tended to be "impulse" buyers. In terms of media habits, target audience members tended to watch local news, news interview shows, and prime-time movies, and listened to soft rock, classic rock, easy listening, and country-western music. They were not as involved in volunteer and community activities as the comparison group.
>
> The target audience profile was built from the information in the two databases, coupled with previous qualitative research. However, planners did not know what the image, or personality, of the campaign should be. To find out, they sent a short questionnaire to members of the MRCA consumer panel who met the target audience definition. The questionnaire asked respondents to rate 29 adjectives in terms of how well the adjectives described themselves and then how well the adjectives described someone who eats five fruits and vegetables a day. Target audience members tended to describe themselves as dependable, sensible, concerned, and careful. In contrast, they viewed "5 A Day eaters" as smarter, more disciplined, healthier, and more fit.
>
> **Results**
>
> Results were used to flesh out and shape the communication strategy for the program.

Sources of Segmentation Data

Ideally, audience segmentation and profiles involve a custom quantitative study; however, time and resources often are not available for such endeavors. The usual starting point is to look at existing data sources that are relevant for the health behaviors of interest. In the United States, federal data sources that may help include the National Health Interview Surveys, the National Health and Nutrition Examination Surveys, the Behavioral Risk Factor Surveillance System, and the Youth Risk Behavior Survey.

In addition to measures of health behaviors, these studies include demographic information about respondents. With the exception of the National Health and Nutrition Examination Surveys, all the studies measure self-reported (not observed) behavior. Public-use data sets are available from the National Center for Health Statistics for most of the studies, so custom analyses can be conducted.

Unfortunately, although these sources provide useful behavioral and demographic data, they often provide very little information on respondents' lifestyles, leisure time activities, and media use habits—information needed to design effective marketing efforts. In some instances, a commercial marketing study can fill the gap if it contains items that allow appropriate behavior-based segmentation. In the United States, two well-known commercial marketing studies are the twice-yearly surveys conducted by Mediamark Research, Inc., and Simmons Market Research Bureau. These surveys include hundreds of items that assess people's leisure time activities: what they read, watch, and listen to—and when they do it—and what products and services they buy—and how much they buy. These studies also contain full demographics for all respondents.

Audience Segmentation Process

In some instances, other completed studies may allow initial target audience profiling; at other times, it may be necessary to design and conduct one or more studies to collect the information needed. The following steps may be involved:

Step 1: Review the literature to identify (1) variables likely to be determinants of the behavior and (2) other studies that may have segmented the population based on these variables.

Step 2: Consider conducting a qualitative study to help identify or explore behavior determinants. Even if likely determinants have been identified, there may be determinants affecting behavior in a specific setting or group that past research did not include. For example, a focus group study identified the perceived shortage of available Black men as a significant obstacle to HIV prevention among certain Black female university students (Slater, 1995).

Step 3: If custom analyses need to be conducted, determine the segmentation approach. As noted earlier, a good starting point is "doers" versus "non-doers." Will a qualitative or quantitative approach be taken? Often, the ideal is to start with a qualitative study to explore and identify the differences between doers and non-doers and then follow with a quantitative study to quantify those differences and isolate the most common and presumably most critical. However, budget and timing do not always permit both.

Step 4: Collect—or analyze—the data and segment the audiences. Segmentation is often iterative; it must be revised as necessary until the segments make sense. This process also involves building profiles of each segment—their activities, lifestyles, and personalities. Segments need to be distinct from one another along these dimensions, or it will be impossible to target an intervention to reach them.

Step 5: Select the segment(s) to target with the program. The section below titled "Factors Influencing Target Audience Selection" provides some guidance on this process.

Choosing a Segmentation Strategy

This section discusses a number of segmentation strategies; in practice, every segmentation must be customized to fit the problem at hand, and the resulting process is often a combination of approaches. As Slater (1995) noted, "The crucial point here is that it is more efficient, in terms of maximizing impact with given resources, to identify people who are similar in important respects and tailor communication content and delivery to them" (p. 187). To help assess potential segmentation strategies, Kotler and Andreasen (1996) identified six characteristics of an optimal segmentation strategy:

1. *Mutual exclusivity*: That is, each person or organization fits the definition of only one segment.
2. *Exhaustiveness*: Every member of the population is included in a segment (even if not all segments are targeted by the program).
3. *Measurability*: Membership in a segment can be readily measured.
4. *Differential responsiveness*: Each segment should respond to different marketing strategies. If segments respond to the same approaches, then the segmentation strategy is not helping reach a particular audience.
5. *Reachability*: This is the degree to which the segments can be effectively reached and served.
6. *Substantiality, or size*: Segments should be large enough to be worth pursuing.

The last two characteristics apply to making decisions about which segments to target and are discussed in more detail in the next section.

Factors Influencing Target Audience Selection

Once the population has been segmented, it is time to select target audiences. One of two approaches can be used: interventions can be tailored to each audience segment, or one or more audience segments can be chosen as the target audience(s). The approach used depends on the objectives of the program and on available resources because tailoring interventions for many audiences can be an expensive proposition. Distinct interventions for each audience segment are most often used if most of the intervention will take place one on one; for example, hotline callers might receive different materials depending on the audience segment to which they belong. Programs taking more of a mass approach, in which aspects of the intervention will be delivered to groups of people, usually select one or two audience segments and develop intervention components specifically for those segments. When comparing different segments, a number of factors can be used to assess each group's suitability as target audience, as shown in **Exhibit 7-2** and described in more detail below.

Exhibit 7-2 Factors Influencing Selection of Target Audiences

- Audience size
- Extent to which the group needs or would benefit from the behavior change
- How well available resources can reach the group
- Extent to which the group is likely to respond to the program
- Extent to which secondary audiences influence primary audiences

---

The first factor is audience size. If an overall goal is population-wide improvement, targeting larger audiences will yield large changes—assuming they are provided with the motivation, opportunity, or ability they need to engage in the behavior. Sometimes program planners select a very small audience—often those most at risk or in need of a particular change. This approach can make it more difficult to show population-wide change. In addition, the program may not be able to effect all the environmental changes the audience would need to engage in the behavior. Individuals most in need are often defined as those farthest from the recommended behavior; this may be because they confront the most barriers—some of which may be difficult to address with limited resources. Before choosing a small, in-need audience, it is imperative that public health groups are able to develop an intervention that will adequately address its motivation, opportunity, and ability to engage in the behavior.

The second factor is the extent to which the group needs or would benefit from the behavior change. Some populations may be less amenable to behavior change because the group would derive little benefit from it. For example, it can be difficult to identify the benefits of early detection of breast or prostate cancer for very elderly people. In other instances, the group is already very close to the target behavior and may not see it as different enough from their current behavior to be worth changing.

The third factor is how well available resources can reach the group. The greatest marketing successes often result from using product, pricing, or distribution strategies to increase an audience's opportunity to engage in the behavior. For each audience segment, planners should consider how easy or difficult it is to implement the changes they need, either directly or through a relationship with other organizations. This includes having sufficient resources to deliver messages using mass media, the ability to translate materials into the target audiences' languages, and access to goods and services necessary for the intervention. For example, if the goal is to increase fruit and vegetable consumption, interventionists must be sure fruits and vegetables are available to audience members in the places where they eat throughout the day. If they are not available, then the nearby stores must be convinced to provide more fruits and vegetables or the audience must be persuaded to travel farther to purchase fruits and vegetables.

The fourth factor is the extent to which the group is likely to respond to the program. If the group has no interest in the behavior change, the program will have to work much harder. Current behavior often can provide some insights into group members' likely interest or level of motivation. For example, if the 5 A Day for Better Health program had chosen to target people who currently eat no more than one serving of fruits and vegetables per day, it would have been targeting people who either did not like fruits and vegetables or could not eat them for some specific reason, and the program would be far less likely to achieve its goal. Instead, the program selected a group that already eats about three servings a day—an indication that they are not averse to the behavior in question, thereby increasing the chance of success.

The fifth factor is the extent to which secondary audiences influence primary audiences. Sometimes the best way to convince someone to change his or her behavior is to have someone else do the convincing. This is often true of behavior involving patient interactions with health care providers. Often, people are most likely to get an immunization or screening test or start treating a medical condition when their physician tells them to do so. Secondary audiences can also form useful bridges to primary audiences for programs promoting the diagnosis of previously undiagnosed conditions or in circumstances when secondary audience members are more motivated to address a health problem than is the person with the problem.

Shaping Intervention Components

Once the audiences have been segmented and selected, managers should know who they are addressing, what needs to be provided, and how to reach the audience. As they begin to design the components that will constitute the intervention, additional formative research is used to shape each component.

Developing Strategies and Tactics

One of the first tasks for formative research is to identify the specific replacement behaviors that are likely to be successful. Qualitative techniques can help at this point because they can identify obstacles specific to the behavior. When possible, the issues identified in qualitative studies can be quantified with surveys.

Formative research can provide similar insights into product development or improving service delivery. For example, focus groups or even informal conversations with clinic users may reveal many reasons they do not make more use of services: Perhaps they find staff rude, perhaps hours are inconvenient, or perhaps they must travel too far. A training program can address the first problem; clinic hours might be adjusted to address the second problem. The third problem is a more difficult one, but in some instances it might be resolved by adding new locations, perhaps by using a mobile van if services could be delivered appropriately that way.

Creating Messages

The target audience profiles built as part of the segmentation process can be used in developing a communication strategy. However, they often do not include sufficient information about exactly what benefit to promise, how to support it, or what image to convey. Qualitative research is often used to explore these topics. Ideally, this research will then be quantified. The case study in Exhibit 7-1 (5 A Day) describes different methods of obtaining some of this information. Additional information is provided below, under Pretesting.

■ FORMATIVE RESEARCH TO SUPPORT NONLEGISLATIVE POLICY CHANGES

Many entities have policies that can affect public health, largely by making it easier or more difficult for people to take actions that maintain or improve their health. The following are examples:

- Employers can affect employee wellness by how they price and construct health insurance offerings, whether they provide or support on- or off-the-job physical activity and other wellness offerings, and so on.
- Schools can impact students' health through their policies on the types of food and beverages available during school meals and other occasions; frequency, duration, and content of recess, physical education, and health education; provision of vision and hearing screenings; availability of health services, and so on.
- Food establishments can help or hinder their clientele's ability to maintain healthy weight through policies regarding portion size, cooking oils, inclusion of fruits and vegetables as side items, and so on.

Formative research can be used to develop a marketing approach to improve these types of policies. First, it can quantify the content and prevalence of various types of policies that impact health behaviors. Next, qualitative techniques can be used with policymakers to uncover the reasoning behind policies and to explore the benefits and barriers they may associate with changing the policy. This information can then be used to craft an exchange policymakers would value and to develop a marketing plan. Formative research may again play a role in pretesting or pilot testing the resulting marketing effort. There are many techniques to conduct the formative research necessary for these types of changes.

■ FORMATIVE RESEARCH TO SUPPORT PUBLIC HEALTH POLICY INITIATIVES

Enabling people to improve their health often involves changing an existing public policy or introducing a new program or policy. Formative research plays the same roles in initiatives to promote a public health program or policy as it does in campaigns to promote a change in health behavior. It helps to identify and understand the most appropriate audiences for the initiative to reach, and it helps to develop an initiative that is relevant and motivates the target audience.

Segmenting and Selecting Target Audiences

In contrast to efforts to change individual health behaviors in which the target audience usually consists of the people whose health behavior needs to change or those who influence them, the target audience for policy initiatives consists of three diverse groups. One audience is composed of policymakers, those with the power to enact the public health program or policy. Policymakers are often elected government officials, such as town selectmen, city council, county board members, or state or federal legislators. At other times, they may be appointed government officials, such as the heads of government agencies and some school boards, or career administrators, such as city managers and school superintendents. The policymaker audience also includes the people most likely to influence them: staff members, lobbyists, political party leaders, and so on.

A second audience group includes members of the general public who can exert a strong influence on policymakers. The third group is the mass media, which can strongly influence the opinions of policymakers and the general public.

Wallack et al. (1993) explained that the policy agenda, issues considered important by policymakers, is shaped by both the public agenda, topics relevant to the general public, and the media agenda, subjects covered by the print and electronic news media. The media agenda can influence the policy agenda directly or by placing an issue on the public agenda. An example of the media agenda directly influencing the policy agenda occurred in 1995 when *The Washington Post* reported that U.S. President Bill Clinton had called for all states to enact legislation that lowered the legal blood alcohol limit for youth drivers to 0.02 mg/dL. The issue of more stringent youth drunk-driving laws was directly placed on the policy agenda in all 50 states (Harris, 1995). Policymakers could not ignore the issue once the president had embraced it and the national news media reported on it. In contrast, media coverage of the death of a teenage boy who was killed by a drunk driver in Gloucester, Massachusetts, put the issue of stronger drunk-driving legislation on the public agenda but not on the policy agenda (Langner & Laidler, 1993, Murphy, 1994).

Only after a widespread public outcry did state legislators decide to do something about the problem (Wong, 1994a, 1994b).

Because of the diverse nature of the three target audience groups, the nature of public health policy initiatives is also diverse. Varying activities are needed to influence each audience. Lobbying, visiting elected officials, and testifying at hearings may all be necessary to influence legislative policymakers. Grassroots educational activities and the effective use of the mass media can help reach the general public. Meeting with editorial boards, writing op-ed pieces, and staging special events can shape the media.

For each of these activities, a clear understanding of the audience is necessary to craft the most effective messages. But first, careful segmentation within each of these audiences is necessary.

Policymakers

Policymakers may be segmented based on their likely position on the public health policy or program. For example, policymakers can be segmented into three groups: those who definitely support the policy, those who definitely oppose the policy, and those who are in the middle. Focusing efforts on the third group is often the best use of resources: the first group needs no convincing, and the second group may never be influenced no matter how many resources are used. For example, in a campaign to promote a mandatory motorcycle helmet law, it may be a waste of time to focus lobbying efforts on a legislator who is a strong civil libertarian who has opposed all health behavior regulations in the past on ideological grounds. It may be equally wasteful to focus on a legislator who has repeatedly sponsored motorcycle helmet legislation in the past.

Formative research can answer several important questions about the policymakers' backgrounds. What are the legislators' current positions on the bill in question? How have they voted on similar legislation in the past? What are their ideological views, especially as they relate to the proposed legislation?

Identifying elected officials who hold key positions of influence, such as chairpersons of committees to which a bill is likely to be referred, is imperative. At the state and national levels, the speaker of the house and senate majority leader are almost always in a position to influence legislation. At the local level, the mayor or first selectman is almost always in a critical position of influence on ordinances. Leaders of the minority party and legislative caucuses may be important to reach. For example, the tobacco caucus in Congress would be expected to play a critical role in any federal tobacco legislation.

In addition, it is important to identify potential sources of influence on critical policymakers. These may be powerful individuals, institutions, and other organizations in a particular legislator's district. Business groups or key businesses in a district may be able to persuade a legislator's support for or against a public health policy campaign. Policymakers' friends and family members may be effective liaisons for the health coalition. Finally, campaign contributors can also have sway over legislators. For example, in promoting policies to regulate alcohol, tobacco, or firearms, knowledge of campaign contributions to legislators from the alcohol industry, tobacco industry, or the National Rifle Association may help to expose the degree of outside influence on the policy process.

There are many potential sources of this information. In U.S. state legislatures and Congress, library reference sections have guidebooks that list legislators, describe their districts, outline their committee positions, identify their political parties, and provide addresses and telephone numbers. An increasing number of states have detailed information of this type on their websites, as does the U.S. Congress. Voting records and campaign contribution sources are usually available to the public.

Perhaps the best method to obtain information is to meet with each legislator, his or her staff, or both. This approach has the dual purpose of providing coalition representatives with an opportunity to tell the legislator their positions as well as learn about the legislator's standpoint. Too often, public health coalitions wait until late in a process to meet with legislators. At this point it may be too late, and important information that could have guided the development of the initiative has been missed. Andreasen (2006) recommended identifying a set of target policymakers and then preparing a matrix that lists, for each policymaker, the benefits, costs, others who support the initiative or its objectives, and self-assurance issues.

The Public and Influential Members of It

It is particularly important to segment the general public, because a small number of individuals or groups usually have a disproportionate amount of influence on public opinion and, in turn, on legislators. Mothers Against Drunk Driving, in its *How To Compendium* (1991), a policy manual for public health advocates, describes the importance of what it calls community analysis. Mothers Against Drunk Driving's description is a useful summary of many important formative research questions for promoting a public health policy (p. 138):

> Know your community inside out, so that as you set goals and build an action plan, you can gauge the probable reactions of various constituencies, estimate your chances for success and build the power base you need to win. Community analysis means much more than being in command of facts about geography and governmental structures, ethnic and socioeconomic data. It means finding out what the power structure really is, not just what the table of organization says it is. It includes hard information on political make-up and party strength. It looks at the community for residential, business and industry concentrations and asks, "Who really runs

which parts of town?" It searches out the ethnic, religious and organizational alignments, the loyalty groups, formal and informal. It finds out who's influential about what and with whom—maybe the local bank president at the state capital, the public works commissioner in the city council, it could even be the rock station disc jockey with his or her devoted listeners. . . . It is imperative to identify the hidden power structure affecting any specific issue you're working on, to line up allies within that power structure but also to spot opposition early in the game. . . . A careful community analysis can help eliminate the surprise and prepare the legislative committee to take the offensive.

RoperASW has found that about 10% of the adult population of the United States qualifies as Influential Americans®—socially and politically active individuals who are highly engaged and active in their personal lives, their workplaces, and their communities (Keller & Berry, 2003, p. 124):

The most engaged Americans, Influentials are conduits of information for their community and the nation. Their activist bent, many connections, and active minds, as well as the sheer force of their personalities—their clear sense of priorities, belief in growth and change, passionate approach to life, and infectious sense of confidence—make the Influentials natural intersections for intelligence. They tend to know more than others, to hear about things first, and to broadcast what they know to many people.

If planners successfully reach and convince the influentials, they will reach other members of the population and motivate them. Compared with the general public, they use more information sources, so good, high-quality data may have a strong impact. They are particularly likely to value word of mouth. They were most likely to say they get information on ways of improving health from other people (32%), magazine articles (31%), family (25%), newspaper articles (24%), TV programs (21%), and friends (18%; Keller & Berry, 2003).

RoperASW has developed 12 questions to help identify individuals who can be considered to be influentials (Keller & Berry, 2003). These questions assess whether an individual has done any of the following: written or called a politician to express a position on an issue, attended a political event, such as a rally or protest, attended a public meeting on local policy, held a political office or run for office, served on a committee for a local organization, served as an officer for an organization, written a letter to the editor or called into a live radio or television show, signed a petition, volunteered to help a candidate run for election, made a political speech, written an article for a magazine or newspaper, and been active in a group trying to influence public policy (Keller & Berry, 2003).

Generally, influentials will have done three or more of the items on the list other than having signed a petition. This item is included to give everyone something to answer affirmatively to satisfy the human need to say they are doing things they believe they should.

Another reason why influentials are pivotal in reaching other members of the population is that they often hold central positions within social networks. A social network is a group of individuals who are connected by social ties, usually familial ties or friendships. An impressive body of research by Christakis and Fowler has demonstrated that many health behaviors and conditions spread not randomly through individuals, but systematically through social networks (Christakis & Fowler, 2007, 2008). For example, by analyzing social networks of individuals in the Framingham study, they demonstrated that smoking initiation and cessation tend to occur simultaneously among members of a social network (Christakis & Fowler, 2008). Rather than individuals randomly quitting smoking, entire groups of people who are closely tied together within a social network quit smoking together. As a result, over time, clusters of nonsmokers and smokers tend to form. Strikingly, the same result held for the spread of obesity. People tended to become obese together in social networks, rather than in a random pattern of individual weight changes over time (Christakis & Fowler, 2007).

Malcolm Gladwell, in *The Tipping Point* (2000), provided another way of identifying the type of people most important to reach. He noted that "the success of any kind of social epidemic [e.g., when an idea or behavior moves through a population in a manner similar to a disease epidemic] is heavily dependent on the involvement of people with a particular and rare set of social gifts" (p. 33). He identified three types of people who play important roles in social epidemics:

- *Connectors*: People who know lots of people (often four or five times as many as others) spanning many different social groups. They actively pass information on to the appropriate people and are listened to when they do so.

- *Mavens*: People who collect detailed information, are socially motivated to share that information, and are viewed by others as expert sources. They "have the knowledge and the social skills to start word-of-mouth epidemics" (Gladwell, 2000, p. 67). For example, market mavens may collect detailed information on many different products, prices, or places and have a strong desire to be of service and influence to others.

- *Salespeople*: People who are very persuasive, generally through subtle and nonverbal cues that draw people into their physical and conversational rhythms and dictate the terms of the interaction.

Gladwell noted that social epidemics typically involve all three kinds of people.

When trying to move something up on the public and political agendas, it is clear that reaching RoperASW's Influentials or Gladwell's mavens can be important. Both crave information, collect it from many sources, and share it with others. Identifying influentials or mavens who are interested in the health behavior or policy makes this process easier. For example, if the goal is to improve Medicare's coverage of prescription drugs, marketers can start by identifying influentials and mavens among senior citizens and then aim public education and advocacy efforts at this segment of the population.

The general public may also be segmented based on the way they are likely to vote on an issue; those who are undecided or not fully entrenched in their positions are often the best group to reach. For example, in opposing a referendum to end affirmative action, it may be important to study the opinions of women, persons of color, and liberal and conservative White men. It may be, for example, that liberal, White men are the key swing group whose votes will determine the ultimate fate of the referendum. Public education and advocacy efforts could then be conducted most efficiently by focusing on reaching this demographic group. With limited resources, it would not make sense to spend large amounts of money trying to influence the opinions of minority communities, who are likely to support affirmative action anyway.

Mass Media

The mass media should be segmented based on the results of the above formative research, which identifies key policymakers and segments of the general public. By studying the geographic and sociodemographic reach of each media outlet, planners can select those outlets most likely to reach the target audiences for media advocacy efforts. In most U.S. states and at the local level, most of the public is reached by one or two major media markets, so efforts can be concentrated on them. It would be inefficient, for example, to run ads on every television station in Massachusetts, when television stations in Boston and Springfield reach the majority of state residents. If a particular legislator is important, then the media market that covers his or her district is essential.

Once planners select the appropriate media market(s), they can decide which specific channel(s) would be most useful (e.g., newspaper, radio, or television). Within each channel, it is important to identify the specific outlet(s) with the greatest reach and influence. It may be more efficient to meet with editorial boards of the three or four most important outlets than to try to visit every outlet in the media market. Information on the reach and audience composition of various media outlets is available through standard public relations and advertising resources. In the United States, these include online and print media directories, Standard Rate and Data Service (for profiles of all media outlets; www.srds.com), Arbitron (for radio station ratings as well as audience size and composition; www.arbitron.com), and Nielsen Media Research (for similar information on television stations and programs; www.nielsenmedia.com).

To be most effective, public health practitioners should segment their target audience down to the level of the individual reporter. It is important to identify which reporters' beats include the topic of the public health policy in question and which reporters have taken an interest in this issue in the past. When planning a media event to promote the policy, the press release should be sent specifically to these reporters, and follow-up calls should be made directly to them rather than to a general news desk. One formative research technique that is very easy, especially because most newspapers now have news archives that can be searched online, is to identify the authors of past news stories on the health topic of interest.

Shaping the Policy Initiative

Once audiences have been segmented, additional formative research is often needed to understand what actions audiences can take, what barriers need to be overcome, and what benefits should be communicated to persuade target audience members to take action. Sometimes this information can be gathered at the same time as the information used to segment the audiences; at other times it is gathered separately.

No one formative research technique is best for use in developing a public health policy campaign. For example, focus groups can serve as a valuable tool to explore a wide variety of potential messages, which can then be narrowed down and tested with the population as a whole in a survey. Ideally, formative research methods will be used in concert to assess the level of support for a policy and the effectiveness of various ways of shaping arguments for and against the policy. **Exhibit 7-3** describes how formative research was used to shape a campaign against a ballot initiative in California.

■ PRETESTING

Pretesting should be conducted as planners develop components that will form the initiative. Pretesting involves assessing how target audiences react to proposed goods, services, distribution channels, packaging, messages, and/or materials. It can help identify what needs to be changed before final production or implementation, or it can help determine which of a number of alternatives is likely to work best. Common methodologies for pretesting include central-site interviews, in-depth interviews, and telephone or web surveys. When possible, it is best to use a quantitative method.

Planners should ask themselves the following questions to design and conduct a successful pretest:

- *What is being tested?* Certain methodologies are appropriate for specific materials. For example, if an ad is being tested, a focus group

---

**Exhibit 7-3 Using Formative Research to Frame Messages Against
a Ballot Initiative**

Background

The use of formative research in developing a policy campaign was illustrated by the California coalition that successfully defeated Proposition 188 in 1994. Proposition 188 was a ballot initiative sponsored by Philip Morris that would have repealed all 270 local antismoking ordinances in California, as well as the state's new law eliminating smoking restrictions (Macdonald, Aguinaga, & Glantz, 1997). Most damaging, the initiative would have preempted the ability of cities and towns to enact more stringent regulation of smoking in the workplace in the future. Although the initiative was sponsored and promoted by the tobacco industry, the industry hid its involvement in the campaign from the public. Philip Morris used a public relations firm—the Dolphin Group—to run the campaign and formed a front group, Californians for Statewide Smoking Restrictions, to disguise its involvement and to mislead the public into thinking that this was an antismoking referendum. Using deceptive billboards that read "Yes on 188—Tough Statewide Smoking Restrictions—The Right Choice," the industry gathered enough signatures to qualify Proposition 188 for the California ballot in November 1994.

The public health community was in a difficult position. The anti-Proposition 188 coalition had only about $1.2 million to spend, compared to the $18 million spent by the tobacco industry to promote the referendum (Macdonald et al., 1997). The health coalition needed to be extraordinarily efficient in its campaign: It had to find the single most effective argument that would sway the most crucial voters. The coalition turned to basic marketing principles—and to formative research.

Method

The coalition conducted a public opinion poll to determine the baseline level of support for Proposition 188 and to test the effectiveness of various framing strategies for and against the initiative. The choice of a framing strategy to defeat the initiative was not intuitive. Many arguments could be made in opposition to the proposal: (1) It would set back public health by repealing local antismoking ordinances. (2) It would create weak statewide standards that were not adequate to protect nonsmokers from secondhand smoke. (3) It would prevent cities and counties from enacting more stringent secondhand smoke regulations in the future. (4) It would help the tobacco industry protect its profits.

The anti-188 coalition could have simply chosen one or more of the arguments to use as the basis of a campaign. But would such a theme have resonated widely with voters? The tobacco industry–funded front groups promoting the initiative were making three arguments that could have swayed voters, even in light of the above arguments against the initiative: (1) Proposition 188 completely prohibits smoking in workplaces and restaurants unless strict ventilation requirements are met; (2) Proposition 188 replaces the crazy patchwork quilt of local ordinances throughout the state and replaces them with one tough uniform state law, and (3) The uniform restrictions are stronger than 90% of the local ordinances currently in place—90% of communities in California would see an immediate increase in secondhand smoke protection as a result of passage of Proposition 188 (Macdonald et al., 1997).

(continues)

Exhibit 7-3 Using Formative Research to Frame Messages Against a Ballot Initiative (continued)

Instead of relying on intuition to choose its campaign theme, the anti-188 coalition conducted extensive formative research. Public opinion polls were conducted to assess the reaction of voters to many alternative ways of framing the debate over Proposition 188 (Hypotenuse Inc., 1994; Marttila & Kiley, Inc., 1994). The results were striking. The initial support for the initiative was strong: About 60% of California voters supported Proposition 188. Although specific arguments about the negative impact of the initiative on protections against secondhand smoke did sway some voters, they did not change enough votes to predict defeat of the initiative. However, the poll revealed that simply mentioning that the initiative was sponsored by Philip Morris was enough to turn the vote around completely. In fact, when told that Philip Morris was behind the initiative, 70% of California voters stated that they would vote against it.

Results

The coalition chose "Stop Philip Morris" as its campaign theme. It then conducted a coordinated campaign that included grassroots advocacy, media advocacy, and paid advertising focused on this single theme. The goal was simply to educate voters about who was really behind Proposition 188, not to worry about making detailed arguments about why the initiative was bad for public health.

The coalition conducted periodic public opinion polls throughout the 3-month campaign period to assess how well its approach was working. By mid-July, the initiative was ahead 52% to 38% (Macdonald et al., 1997). By mid-September, voters were about equally divided on Proposition 188. Seeing the dangerous level of support for Proposition 188, the health coalition stepped up its efforts to educate the public about the initiative's sponsor. The coalition hired Jack Nicholl to produce television advertisements using former Surgeon General C. Everett Koop as a spokesperson and paid to air these ads in the major California media markets during the last week of the campaign. The ads highlighted the deceptive nature of the pro-188 campaign, exposing that Philip Morris was behind the initiative and how Californians for Statewide Smoking Restrictions was trying to cover up this important fact. It was, in fact, the discouraging September poll results that convinced the national American Cancer Society and American Heart Association to make substantial contributions to the anti-188 campaign that allowed the Koop spots to be aired (Macdonald et al., 1997).

On November 8, Proposition 188 was defeated by an overwhelming margin of 71% to 29%. The coalition's strategy had succeeded. Careful formative research and subsequent tracking allowed the coalition to develop an effective campaign, to monitor its progress, and to make necessary refinements along the way to increase the campaign's effectiveness.

---

setting is unrealistic. People usually do not see an ad and then spend 2 hours discussing it with a group of people. A one-on-one interview provides a more realistic setting: The interviewer (or web survey) can show the material to the participant for a fixed amount of time (e.g., take back a printed piece after 1 minute or play a video or audiotape once) and then ask him or her a series of questions about it. Although this situation is still unrealistic because it forces participants to think more about the material than they otherwise might, it is less unrealistic than forcing them to discuss it with others.

- *Why is it being tested?* Planners must have a specific research question in mind before pretesting. Methodologies will be different if they are seeking an overall assessment of a new program or if they are concerned about particular aspects, such as the hours of a new clinic, ease of completing an application form for a new service, the packaging for a new product, or the details—voices, music, actors— of a new video. It is important to know how audience members will obtain, use, or distribute the product, service, or material as well as how they react to it. The answers to all these questions help shape the methodology.

- *With whom does it need to be tested?* Generally, planners are interested in target audience members' reactions. In other cases, they want to gauge influentials' reactions. Once the pretest subjects are selected, planners need to think about the best ways to recruit enough participants. The audience may be easily recruited at a central location, such as a shopping mall, or it may need to be reached some other way if the behavior of interest is rare.

- *In what geographic locations does it need to be tested?* If the initiative is local, this question may not arise. For regional or national programs, sometimes it is important to obtain reactions from people in different parts of a state or the country.

- *When are results needed?* Obtaining results by mail usually takes the longest amount of time, particularly if packages are sent and returned via regular mail rather than by express services or fax. Individual in-depth interviews can also take a long time. Once the topic guide has been developed and potential participants have been identified, interviews usually take at least 2 to 3 weeks to schedule and conduct, and analysis can easily take an additional 2 weeks or more. Results from mall-intercept interviews can be available as quickly as a week after the questionnaire and materials are ready if the population is relatively large, although mall-intercept firms usually prefer to have at least two weekends to field a questionnaire and may need longer depending on the population. Results from telephone or web surveys can be available within a week if omnibus studies are used.

- *What decisions will be made with the results?* Pretesting can help planners address questions and concerns that others (including opponents) may have raised regarding the campaign. Results can also be used to refine aspects of the campaign, including decisions about which channels to use or how to present the benefits.

Pretesting Messages

As marketers begin planning their campaign, messages are developed and explored. Often, multiple prospective messages are tested. Sometimes reactions are explored using qualitative research techniques, messages are refined, and then messages are tested using central-site interviews or a telephone or web survey. It is unwise for planners to explore reactions to messages and test promotional materials containing the message at the same time, because it is extremely difficult (and often impossible) to determine whether the participants are reacting to the message or its execution.

Regardless of methodology, the goal of pretesting messages and materials is to assess message appeal, recall, and comprehension; sources of confusion or offense; and motivation to act. When messages are tested, they are usually presented as statements. Audience members' reactions can be assessed if they are asked to

- Sort the messages from most compelling to least compelling. (This approach works best if the respondents are interviewed in person.)
- Indicate how much they agree or disagree with each statement using a scale of responses.
- Rate each statement on dimensions such as believability, relevance, and importance to them using scaled responses.

One useful way to pretest messages is to prepare each message as a separate title or headline and ask participants which they would be most likely to pick up and why. If such a process is used, everything should be identical except the message—the same type, colors, graphics, and so on should be used.

Pretesting Materials

Once a message approach has been selected, materials that will deliver it can be tested. Materials that are often pretested include advertisements, brochures, booklets, audiotapes, videotapes, and websites. Sometimes only one version of the material is tested; at other times different approaches that convey the same basic message may be tested against each other. Although materials pretests cannot predict exactly how materials will perform, they will identify any "red flags" in terms of unintended interpretations and/or details that need changing (typeface, type size, colors, music, voices, timing, etc.). Pretesting also can help "sell" the materials internally by providing information on target audience reactions to counter criticism from nontarget audience members.

Materials being pretested can be in various stages of readiness; the most common formats are discussed here. **Exhibit 7-4** lists some topics commonly covered in pretests; the exact wording of questions addressing each topic depends on the method used for the pretest. *The Handbook of*

Exhibit 7-4 Topics Commonly Included in Materials Pretests

General Topics

- What is the main idea of the (ad, booklet, etc.)?
- What, if anything, was particularly liked?
- What, if anything, was particularly disliked?
- Was anything offensive? (What? Who would it offend?)
- Was anything hard to understand? (What?)
- Was anything hard to believe? (What? Why?)
- Who is this (ad, booklet, publication, etc.) for? Who would get the most out of it?
- What, if anything, should be changed, added, or deleted?
- Which option would be most likely to induce the desired action?

Topics for Long Publications and Websites

- How was the amount of information—was it too much, about right, or too little? Are there particular sections that should be longer or shorter?
- Were there topics you expected to see covered that were not? Were topics covered that you think are unnecessary?
- Do you have any additional questions about the subject that were not answered?
- What do you think about the layout? How easy or hard was it to find information? What do you think about the amount of white space used?
- What do you think about the type? Was it too large, about right, or too small? How easy or hard was it to read?
- What do you think about the language used? How easy or hard was it to understand?
- What do you think about the (photos or style of illustration)? How easy or hard was it to understand the diagrams? Are there places where diagrams or illustrations would clarify the text? Are there places where they are unnecessary?
- What do you think about the use of color? What types of people do these colors appeal to? (Certain colors have different meanings in different cultures; probe for cultural sensitivity if necessary.)
- Are there any other changes that you would make?
- Where would you expect to find the publication/find out about the website?
- For professional audiences: How would you use this information in your work?

Marketing Scales provides examples of scales that have been developed to measure specific areas of reactions to ads (Bearden & Netemeyer, 1999).

Print materials are most often tested in a form that looks final because of today's desktop publishing capabilities. Headlines and text are final (unless changes need to be made as a result of the pretest), and the layout and typeface(s) used are those planned for the final product. Stock photos that are similar to those planned for the final version are generally used.

If different headlines or tag lines are being tested against each other, all other elements of the ad, poster, or brochure (layout, typeface, type size, etc.) should be identical if possible.

Radio ads and other audio products are most often recorded by program or agency staff rather than by the talent that will be used in the final version. They do not have music or sound effects included unless they are critical to comprehension.

Videos and television ads can be represented as storyboards (similar to a cartoon strip, with separate frames depicting each scene and the script typed or written underneath), animatics (basically the storyboard is videotaped; the dialogue is also taped, and each scene changes to match the dialogue), or prefinished products (scenes are videotaped and the actual audio track is included, although final music may not be included). The form in which video products are tested depends largely on the available budget and, to a lesser degree, on the characteristics of the final product. Each format is progressively more expensive. Storyboards almost always test much worse than the other versions because they are not as visually interesting and are often more difficult to follow. Additionally, if the interviewers read the script, each will read it differently, resulting in a less consistent test. Animatics are often used if the visuals include text, because it is difficult for someone to read the type and the script at the same time.

Prefinished products are obviously the best format to test because they are closer to the final version, but they are prohibitively expensive and rarely tested unless there is some reason they must be tested in that format (i.e., if there is no other way to communicate what the final product will be like). If a prefinished version is tested, one way to assess memorability of and attention to ads is to embed the material being tested in a few minutes of other advertising and then begin the test by asking the respondents what ads they remember seeing.

Pilot Tests

Sometimes the best way to test a new material, service, or policy is to implement it, or a number of possible versions, and study what happens. For example, advertisers can do this through split runs in publications, cable systems, or web advertising. A health clinic could try adding a new service or adjusting an existing one for a few months, such as evening hours one night a week, and then assess usage versus cost. A school system might implement a new recess policy, different food offerings, or wellness activities open to the public at a few schools for a few months or a school year and then examine the reactions among students, faculty, staff, and, if appropriate, the community. Policymakers can then decide whether and how to continue the new policy. Pilot tests most often use an experimental or quasi-experimental design.

Professional Review

For many public health organizations, another important component of pretesting is professional review. Asking community leaders and other professionals in the field to review proposed goods, services, messages, promotional materials, or distribution channels serves a number of purposes. First, the process can identify potential problems that planners may not have considered. Second, it provides an opportunity to obtain buy-in early in the process. Third, it can identify potential objections to the content or structure of program components, which can be assessed when conducting audience pretests: If the objections are raised by audience members, they should be addressed; if they are not, the planners can explain to reviewers that in fact such concerns were not raised by the audience. For messages and materials, professional review helps to ensure that the information presented is sound and can enhance the credibility of messages or materials with other stakeholders.

Professional reviews can be obtained a number of ways. Two common methods are to mail or e-mail a questionnaire and prototypes (or representations of prototypes) to reviewers or to conduct review in conjunction with an already scheduled meeting. The latter approach increases the likelihood that reviews will be completed.

■ CONCLUSION

Formative research is central to the marketing approach. It is critical to building strong relationships with targeted audiences and other constituencies because it helps create, communicate, and deliver the value that forms the cornerstone of those relationships. Lefebvre and Flora (1988, p. 305) noted as follows:

> [I]n an arena characterized by lower levels of funding, the importance of formative research cannot be overemphasized. Although budget-minded persons might view the additional costs of such research as frivolous, it will prove to be money well spent. Not only can such research suggest changes in program content or delivery that will enhance its reach and/or effectiveness, but it can also circumvent a costly and ill-fated intervention before it receives broad exposure.

The formative research activities discussed in this chapter will help proponents of public health develop and use a marketing mind-set. This mind-set can be used to improve public health offerings and policies, thereby building stronger relationships with beneficiaries of those offerings and allowing the institutions to demonstrate greater value to all constituencies, such as taxpayers, community leaders, and elected officials. The marketing mind-set also helps public health proponents compete with marketing-driven industry efforts that are detrimental to public health.

References

Ajzen, I., & Fishbein, M. (1980). *Understanding attitudes and predicting social behavior*. Englewood Cliffs, NJ: Prentice-Hall.

Andreasen, A.R. (2006). *Social marketing in the 21st century*. Thousand Oaks, CA: Sage.

Bandura, A. (1986). *Social foundations of thought and action*. Englewood Cliffs, NJ: Prentice-Hall.

Bearden, W.O., & Netemeyer, R.G. (1999). *Handbook of marketing scales* (2nd ed.). Thousand Oaks, CA: Sage.

Chaffee, S.H., & Roser, C. (1986). Involvement and the consistency of knowledge, attitudes, and behaviors. *Communication Research, 13*(3), 373–399.

Christakis, N.A., & Fowler, J.H. (2007). The spread of obesity in a large social network over 32 years. *New England Journal of Medicine, 357*, 370–379.

Christakis, N.A., & Fowler, J.H. (2008). The collective dynamics of smoking in a large social network. *New England Journal of Medicine, 358*, 2249–2258.

Gladwell, M. (2000). *The tipping point*. Boston, MA: Little-Brown.

Grunig, J.E., & Hunt, T. (1984). *Managing public relations*. New York, NY: Holt, Rinehart & Winston.

Harris, J.F. (1995, June 11). Clinton urges "zero tolerance" for young drinking drivers. *The Washington Post*, p. A6.

Hypotenuse Inc. (1994). *Bullet poll: California smoking research*. Verona, NJ: Author.

Keller, E., & Berry, J. (2003). *The influentials*. New York, NY: The Free Press.

Kotler, P., & Andreasen, A.R. (1996). *Strategic marketing for non-profit organizations* (5th ed.). Upper Saddle River, NJ: Prentice-Hall.

Langner, P., & Laidler, J. (1993, December 14). Traffic deaths restart debate: 3 fatalities fuel push for new laws. *The Boston Globe*, pp. 37, 38.

Lefebvre, R.C., Doner, L.D., Johnson, C., Loughrey, K., Balch, G.,& Sutton, S.M. (1995). Use of database marketing and consumer-based health communications in message design: An example from the Office of Cancer Communications' "5 A Day for Better Health" program. in E. Maibach & R.L. Parrott (eds.), *Designing health messages: Approaches from communication theory and public health practice* (pp. 217–246). Thousand Oaks, CA: Sage.

Lefebvre, R.C., & Flora, J.A. (1988). Social marketing and public health intervention. *Health Education Quarterly, 15*, 299–315.

National Cancer Institute. (1993, December). *5 A Day for Better Health: NCI media campaign strategy*. Bethesda, MD: Author.

Macdonald, H., Aguinaga, S., & Glantz, S.A. (1997). The defeat of Philip Morris' "California Uniform Tobacco Control Act." *American Journal of Public Health, 87*, 1989–1996.

Maiman, L.A., & Becker, M.H. (1974). The health belief model: Origins and correlates in psychological theory. *Health Education Monographs, 2*, 384–408.

Marttila, L.A., & Becker, M.H. (1974). The health belief model: Origins and correlates in psychological theory. *Health Education Monographs, 2,* 384–408.

Mothers Against Drunk Driving. (1991). *How to compendium.* Irving, TX: Author.

Murphy, S.P. (1994, January 21). Gloucester couple seeks tougher drunken driving law. *The Boston Globe,* pp. 17, 25.

Slater, M.D. (1995). Choosing audience segmentation strategies and methods for health communication. In E. Maibach & R.L. Parrott (Eds.), *Designing health messages: Approaches from communication theory and public health practice* (pp. 186–198). Thousand Oaks, CA: Sage.

Strecher, V.S., DeVellis, B.M., Becker, M.H., & Rosenstock, I.M. (1986). The role of self-efficacy in achieving health behavior change. *Health Education Quarterly, 13,* 73–91.

Wallack, L., Dorfman, L., Jernigan, D., & Themba, M. (1993). *Media advocacy and public health: Power for prevention.* Newbury Park, CA: Sage.

Wong, D.S. (1994a, March 25). Drunken driving bill OK'd by House: Tough rule could allow cars to be forfeited. *The Boston Globe,* pp. 29, 34.

Wong, D.S. (1994b, May 26). Tough bill on drunken driving OK'd: Blood alcohol limit lowered; Weld expected to sign package. *The Boston Globe,* pp. 1, 34.

CHAPTER

8

Framing and Reframing

Public health practitioners must market changes in behavior, societal conditions, and social policy in the absence of significant demand among the public and policymakers for these changes. They must also market the need for public health itself in hostile and competitive political and social environments. The strategic use of marketing principles can help public health practitioners effectively confront these challenges. To succeed, public health practitioners must abandon the traditional approach in which they decide what they want the public and policymakers to buy and then attempt to sell this product to an audience that has little demand for it. Instead, public health practitioners must first identify the needs and desires of the audience and then define, package, position, and frame the product in such a way that it satisfies an existing demand among the target audience. Public health practitioners must be able to offer benefits that the audience appreciates and demands and to communicate an image of public health programs or the public health institution that reinforces the target audiences' core values.

Although public health practitioners aim to improve health conditions, they must recognize that the core value of health may not resonate with the target audience. To discover more salient core values, practitioners must understand more about people's desire for health. This requires practitioners to acknowledge benefits that people associate with health.

■ DEFINING THE PRODUCT: IMPORTANCE OF CORE VALUES IN PROMOTING AND OPPOSING HEALTH BEHAVIORS

A large body of sociological research has revealed that health is of value to the individual not intrinsically but because it ensures a certain degree of personal freedom, independence, autonomy, and control (Conrad, 1987; Glaser & Strauss, 1968; Kleinman, 1988; Mishel, 1984; Mishel et al., 1984; Molleman et al., 1984; Weitz, 1994). In fact, it is not really health itself

177

that people value most. Rather, it is the freedom, independence, autonomy, and control over their lives that come with being healthy for which people have the most fundamental need and desire.

If public health practitioners fail to make this subtle, yet critical, distinction in how they define and then market their product, they are unlikely to be successful. As Salmon (1989) noted, public health campaigns "represent only one social force among many driving and restraining forces. For every campaign message intending to dissuade consumers from illegal drug use or cigarette smoking, there are literally dozens of forces . . . espousing competing philosophies, similarly at work" (pp. 44, 45).

Public health practitioners face this challenge when confronting alcohol consumption. As Winett and Wallack (1996) suggested, "given the social value placed upon recreational alcohol consumption, the availability and accessibility of alcoholic beverages, the environmental cues encouraging social drinking, and the pleasurable physical effects people often experience while drinking—the social marketing campaign designed to dissuade people from excessive drinking by teaching them of the health risks faces a profoundly difficult task" (p. 179).

Although public health practitioners have not traditionally conducted marketing research to identify and understand the needs and desires of their target audiences, their opponents have long used marketing research to find out what consumers want, what is important to them, and what values are most salient, influential, and held most deeply by consumers. As a result, public health practitioners traditionally have relied solely on the individual's inherent value for health, whereas their opposition has taken advantage of more compelling core values to sell their harmful products.

The tobacco industry, for example, conducted extensive research into the desires, needs, and values of adolescents and young adults. The consistent finding of this research was the importance of the themes of independence, freedom, autonomy, control, self-reliance, and rugged individualism. These themes have formed the basis for many of the tobacco industry's promotional campaigns during this century. As former Surgeon General Joycelyn Elders concluded, "United States advertisers, too, have long thought that individualism and the stimulating notions of independence, self-reliance, and autonomy are important strategic concepts in ad development" (U.S. Department of Health and Human Services [USDHHS], 1994, p. 177).

As early as 1929, Edward Bernays, a public relations consultant for the American Tobacco Company, organized a group of women to smoke publicly in the New York Easter Parade and to carry placards identifying their cigarettes as "torches of liberty" (Bernays, 1965; Schudson, 1984; USDHHS, 1994). This strategy was based on the work of consulting psychoanalyst A. A. Brill, who advised the company to promote cigarettes as "symbols of freedom" (Bernays, 1965; USDHHS, 1994, p. 165).

Young and Rubicam conducted a series of motivational interviews of smokers in the 1950s (Smith, 1954; USDHHS, 1994). These studies revealed the importance of the themes of freedom and escape to smokers (USDHHS, 1994). They suggested that appeals based on health claims would offer only transient results, but to increase the cigarette market, companies would have to "tap the driving force of the real psychological satisfactions of smoking" (USDHHS, 1994, p. 171).

Imperial Tobacco Limited of Canada conducted research on adolescents that revealed "the adolescent seeks to display his new urge for independence with a symbol, and cigarettes are such a symbol" (USDHHS, 1994, p. 175). The research also found that young males in particular are "going through a stage where they are seeking to express their independence and individuality under constant pressure of being accepted by their peers" (USDHHS, 1994, pp. 176–177). Another Imperial Tobacco Limited study provided guidelines "for the effective display of freedom and independence in advertising imagery" (USDHHS, 1994, p. 177) and recommended that cigarette brands designed for youth show someone "free to choose friends, music, clothes, own activities, to be alone if he wishes," who "can manage alone" with "nobody to interfere, no boss/parents" (USDHHS, 1994, p. 177). The research described the importance of developing imagery to tap into four core adolescent values: independence, self-reliance, autonomy, and freedom from authority (USDHHS, 1994).

Indeed, the Surgeon General noted that "the brands most successful with teenagers seem to be those that offer adult imagery rich with connotations of independence, freedom and authority, and/or self-reliance" (USDHHS, 1994, p. 176). Marlboro, the most popular brand among adolescents, epitomizes the stereotype of American independence. As the Surgeon General noted, the Marlboro man is "usually depicted alone, he interacts with no one; he is strikingly free of interference from authority figures such as parents, older brothers, bosses, and bullies. Indeed, the Marlboro man is burdened by no one whose authority he must respect or even consider" (USDHHS, 1994, p. 177). R. W. Murray, former president and chief executive officer of Philip Morris, observed that "the cowboy has appeal to people as a personality. There are elements of adventure, freedom, being in charge of your destiny" (as cited in Trachtenberg, 1987, p. 109). Jack Landry, a key advertising executive behind the Marlboro Man campaign, described the cowboy as "a perfect symbol of independence and individualistic rebellion" (as cited in Meyers, 1984, p. 70).

Marlboro ads tell kids that smoking will make them free and independent, like cowboys. Teens see adults smoking in bars and other places where they are not allowed, which conveys a message that smoking is a symbol of maturity and autonomy. The cigarette companies themselves, through campaigns that portray smoking as an adult decision and encourage youths to listen to their parents, tell kids that smoking is a way to exert independence from their parents and to give them—not adult authority figures—control over their own lives. These are deeply ingrained American core values. On the contrary, public health practitioners try to convince adolescents not to smoke by appealing to their desire for health, a far less salient value.

Although public health practitioners rarely do so, strong core values can be used to market health products. When corporate marketers sell health products, they do not generally rely on the benefit of health to sell their products. Health clubs and exercise equipment are marketed to consumers not based on their ability to improve long-term health outcomes and prevent disease but based on their ability to give people a feeling of control over how they look, how they feel, and how attractive they are to others. Ads for these products and services do not cite medical evidence about the benefits of physical activity in preventing chronic illness. Instead, these ads show attractive people who seem to be in control of how they look, how they feel, and how others think of them.

Public health practitioners can use these same approaches to promote changes in behavior. Using formative research techniques, public health practitioners can determine what consumers want and what core values resonate most strongly. Then practitioners can redefine, repackage, reposition, and reframe the product in such a way that it satisfies an existing demand among the target audience and appeals to their core values.

■ DEFINING THE PRODUCT: IMPORTANCE OF CORE VALUES IN PROMOTING AND OPPOSING PUBLIC HEALTH POLICIES

Two major audiences for promoting a public health program or policy are policymakers and the public. Too often, the benefit that public health practitioners attempt to sell is that of improved health for individual members of society. Historically, however, the intrinsic presence of disease among the population has not motivated policymakers to adopt major public health programs, policies, and reforms. On the contrary, fear of the political and economic consequences of losing control over the spread of disease has prompted policymakers to enact change. The prospect of disease is dreaded not because it signifies that individuals are sick or suffering, but because it represents a threat to a society's freedom, independence, autonomy, and control. Just as freedom, independence, autonomy, and control underscore the value that individuals place on health, these same core values are held by policymakers, which explains their desire to exert some control over the spread of disease in society.

Therefore, in defining the public health product in a campaign to promote a public health program or policy, practitioners may need to go beyond simply offering health as the benefit to society. Public health practitioners must redefine the product and its benefits. The product is not health for society's members but something more basic, more compelling, and more at the core of the American policymakers' values system. The product is the preservation of freedom, independence, autonomy, and control for society.

Although public health practitioners traditionally have based their public health campaigns solely on what they believe should be important—that is, health—their opponents have used marketing principles to define their campaign themes. They determine what the public or policymakers want and then design, package, and position the product so it satisfies the need. Often, this leads to campaigns based on themes that have little to do with health.

An example of the use of marketing research to defeat a public health campaign was the insurance industry's effort to defeat President Clinton's proposed health care reform initiative in 1994. The Coalition for Health Insurance Choices, an insurance industry front group, conducted a carefully crafted media and grassroots lobbying campaign based on extensive research (Stauber & Rampton, 1995). Stauber and Rampton (1995) described how the coalition used formative research to identify campaign themes that would resonate with voters: "Instead of forming a single coalition, health reform opponents used opinion polling to develop a point-by-point list of vulnerabilities in the Clinton administration proposal and organized more than 20 separate coalitions to hammer away at each point" (p. 96). Campaign organizer Blair Childs emphasized the importance of formative research: "in naming your coalition . . . use words that you've identified in your research. There are certain words that . . . have a general positive reaction. That's where focus group and survey work can be very beneficial. 'Fairness,' 'balance,' 'choice,' 'coalition,' and 'alliance' are all words that resonate very positively" (Stauber & Rampton, 1995, pp. 96, 97).

Using careful, formative research, the coalition framed Clinton's health reform proposal in a way that conflicted with the core values of American voters, generating subsequent opposition to the proposal. The coalition identified a fear among Americans that government-sponsored health care would "bankrupt the country, reduce the quality of care, and lead to jail terms for people who wanted to stick with their family doctor" (Stauber & Rampton, 1995, p. 97). Clinton's proposal was framed as the archetypal example of government-sponsored health care, which would take away all individual choice, put health care into a helpless bureaucracy, hurt small businesses, and eliminate America's position as the international leader in quality of medical care. These messages appealed to the American core values of independence, autonomy, self-determination, free choice, free enterprise, capitalism, economic stability, and the democratic principle. With these core values at the heart of its arguments, it is no surprise that the insurance coalition's campaign was so effective.

A now-legendary television spot vividly illustrated to the public how the Clinton plan would affect them personally. In it, a middle-class couple named Harry and Louise lamented "the complexity of Clinton's plan and the menace of a new 'billion-dollar bureaucracy,' . . . 'Harry and Louise' symbolized everything that went wrong with the great health care struggle of 1994" (Stauber & Rampton, 1995, p. 97). Harry and Louise became a symbol for the entire campaign and effectively suggested that the Clinton plan represented the opposite of everything for which America is supposed to stand. A pro–health care reform campaign that relied primarily on the arguments that millions of Americans lacked health insurance, that the costs of health care were increasing, and that the insurance and pharmaceutical industries were acting irresponsibly (White House Domestic Policy Council, 1993) simply could not compete against a campaign for the hearts and minds of the American people.

Another excellent example of the use of marketing research to defeat a public health campaign is the tobacco industry's successful effort to defeat a proposed Montana ballot initiative to raise the state cigarette excise tax in 1990. The tobacco industry did not restrict itself to the health-oriented aspects of the proposed cigarette tax in fighting this initiative. It also did not design its campaign based on the public health community's definition and packaging of the product (Moon, Males, & Nelson, 1993). Instead, the tobacco industry conducted marketing research to identify the basic needs and desires of the Montana voters, messages that would and would not appeal to the voters, and the core values influencing their voting intentions. The industry then redefined the product and reframed the discussion over the product's benefits and costs such that voting against the initiative would be perceived as fulfilling the identified needs and desires and as reinforcing the most influential core values of Montana voters. Specifically, freedom, security, and fairness were targeted by tobacco interests as campaign messages to discourage voters from supporting the tax increase.

First, the tobacco industry argued that the ballot initiative would interfere with the core value of security by causing cigarette smuggling problems: Gang members would bootleg cigarettes from nearby states with lower taxes. Second, the industry showed how the proposal conflicted with the core values of fairness and equality: Poor families would be harder hit by the cigarette tax than wealthier families. Third, the industry explained that the initiative would take control away from the voters: Bureaucrats would take the taxpayers' money and use it however they saw fit. Fourth, the proposed cigarette tax interfered with the core values of freedom and autonomy: The proposal represented an effort on the part of special interest groups to override the concerns of the people of Montana and to manipulate voters into establishing programs favored by these special interest groups. At the most basic level, the tobacco industry was not selling opposition to the initiative; it was selling freedom and independence, fairness, security, control over one's life, individual rights, and the democratic ideal.

In contrast, the public health coalition in Montana did not conduct extensive marketing research studies. Because of the lack of adequate resources, only one poll was conducted during the campaign. The coalition defined and positioned the initiative based on its health content alone and on speculation about the health benefits that would be most important to the voters: reducing the number of smokers, preventing children from starting to smoke, reducing exposure to secondhand smoke, and establishing better prenatal care programs for poor families.

A third example of how opponents of public health policies use marketing principles to fight reform comes from the environmental health movement. Stauber and Rampton (1995) explained how corporations that pollute the environment also use marketing principles to prevent significant policy reforms that could hurt their profits. Many corporations hire sophisticated public relations, marketing, and advertising firms to determine what the public thinks about them and about environmental policy issues. In this way they learn how to frame environmental policy issues so citizens perceive increased environmental regulation as conflicting with their core values. Joanna Underwood, president of one environmental research firm, explained the importance of talking to people to find out how they think: "Companies must have some vehicle for knowing what the intelligent public thinks about their products and processes. If they want to understand sophisticated outside views of environmental issues affecting their companies, they would do well to have someone in the room" (Stauber & Rampton, 1995, pp. 127, 128). Too often, public health practitioners attempt to design policy campaigns without having anyone else "in the room."

The key strategy of corporate polluters, according to Stauber and Rampton (1995), is to frame environmental issues so the blame is shifted from corporations to the individual. In other words, these corporations rely on the core American value of rugged individualism, convincing people that individual actions are at the root of environmental problems. "In place of systemic analysis and systemic solutions to social problems, they offer an individualistic and deeply hypocritical analysis in which 'all of us' are to blame for our collective 'irresponsibility.' If we would all just pick up after ourselves . . . the problems would go away" (Stauber & Rampton, 1995, p. 132).

About 200 companies funded an organization called Keep America Beautiful, the "industry's most organized proponent of the belief that individual irresponsibility is at the root of the pollution" (Stauber & Rampton, 1995, p. 133). Although these companies produce products that are estimated to account for about a third of the material in U.S. landfills, Keep America Beautiful's message to consumers is that they are responsible for the trash problem in this country. Although Keep

America Beautiful has used more than half a billion dollars of donated advertising time and space to encourage guilty consumers to "put litter in its place," the organization's leadership "opposes a national bottle bill that would place a deposit on glass and metal drink containers" (Stauber & Rampton, 1995, p. 133). These companies are strategically applying basic marketing principles to reframe the issue of environmental pollution so responsibility for the problem shifts from the corporation to the individual.

Although Americans certainly value health, they also hold other values, which tend to be more important, more salient, and more influential on individual behavior. The traditional public health approach to policy change simply tries to reinforce the value of health, but in the process it conflicts with other deeply held values that are stronger and more influential. Just as the industries that oppose public health programs and policies use marketing principles to convince the public that these policies are detrimental, public health practitioners must begin to use marketing principles to promote them. The key is to redefine the public health product and its benefits in a way that appeals to the most compelling core values of the target audience. Public health practitioners must use formative research to determine what the public and policymakers want and to identify the arguments, messages, themes, and values that are highly salient and influential among these target audiences.

■ PACKAGING AND POSITIONING THE PRODUCT: FRAMING HEALTHY BEHAVIORS, PROGRAMS, AND POLICIES

Public health programs and policies must be defined such that their goals will satisfy the needs and desires of the public. To do so, public health practitioners need to package and position the program or policy to communicate its benefits in a way that reinforces the core values of the public—both general citizens and policymakers. Public health practitioners must provide support for the promised benefits and must communicate a compelling image for the product. Framing is the process of packaging and positioning a public health program or policy so that it reinforces core values.

Framing: Definition and Examples

A frame is a way of packaging and positioning an issue to convey a certain meaning (Andreasen, 2006; Chapman & Lupton, 1994; Entman, 1993; Gamson & Lasch, 1983; Gamson & Modigliani, 1989; Iyengar, 1991; Kaniss, 1991; Ryan, 1991; Schon & Rein, 1994; Wallack & Dorfman, 1996; Wallack et al., 1993). Framing has been described as the emphasis placed around particular issues "that seeks to define 'what this issue is really about'" (Chapman & Lupton, 1994, p. 12) and as "the process by which someone packages a group of facts to create a story" (Wallack et al., 1993, p. 68). Schon and Rein (1994) defined frames as "the broadly shared beliefs, values, and perspectives familiar to the members of a societal culture and likely to endure in that culture over long periods of time, on which individuals and institutions draw in order to give meaning, sense, and normative direction to their thinking and action in policy matters" (p. xiii).

In 1922, political pundit and author Walter Lippmann wrote that people see the world through certain frameworks and that these frameworks affect what a person sees. Lippmann wrote, "We do not first see, and then define, we define first and then see" (Steel, 1981, p. 181). Steel (1981) expanded on the point: "We define, not at random, but according to 'stereotypes' demanded by our culture. The stereotypes, while limiting, are essential. . . . But if stereotypes determine not only how we see but what we see, clearly our opinions are only partial truths. What we assume to be 'facts' are often really judgments" (p. 181).

The concept of framing was formally introduced as early as 1954 (Tannen, 1993). Gregory Bateson theorized that "no communicative move, verbal or nonverbal, could be understood without reference to a metacommunicative message, or metamessage, about what is going on—that is, what frame of interpretation applies to the move" (Tannen, 1993, p. 3). Tversky and Kahneman (1982) showed that minor changes in the way decision problems are framed may influence people's decisions: "Systematic reversals of preference are observed when a decision problem is framed in different ways" (p. 3). The concept of framing has important implications for individuals' opinions and attitudes. On the most basic level, the framing of questions influences responses to attitude surveys and public opinion polls (Krosnick & Alwin, 1988).

On a broader level, the framing of an issue forms "the basis by which public policy decisions are made" (Wallack et al., 1993, p. 68; see also Nelkin, 1987). Framing not only defines the issue, it also suggests the solution: "If we alter the definition of problems, then the response also changes" (Wallack et al., 1993, p. 82; see also Ryan, 1991; Watzlawick, Weakland, & Fisch, 1974). As Wagenaar and Streff (1990) pointed out, "how questions are worded is related to how policy advocates and opponents shape and present policy options to legislators and other opinion leaders, as well as to the general public" (p. 203).

The effect of framing has been demonstrated in studies of public opinion on alcohol policies (Wagenaar & Streff, 1990), mandatory seat belt laws (Slovic, Fischoff, & Lichtenstein, 1982), affirmative action (Fine, 1992), environmental policy (Vaughan & Seifert, 1992), and welfare policy (Smith, 1987). Message framing has been shown to influence not only public opinion but individual behavior as well (Meyerowitz & Chaiken, 1987; Rothman et al., 1993; Vookles & Carr, 1993; Wilson, Purdon, & Wallston, 1988; Wilson, Wallston, & King, 1990).

Ryan (1991), one of the developers of framing theory and its applications in public policy advocacy, argued that a frame is defined by a core value or principle that underlies it. Ryan, adapting previous work done by Gamson and Lasch (1983), further characterized frames by their core positions, metaphors, images, catch phrases, attribution of responsibility for the problem, and the solution implied by the frame. Ryan and Gamson, through the work of their Media Research and Action Project in the Sociology Department at Boston College, adapted a useful framing matrix that can be used by public health practitioners to identify and outline the frames used by supporters and opponents of public health policy issues (see Ryan, 1991; also see Gamson & Lasch, 1983; Gamson & Modigliani, 1989).

For example, one frame used in debates over citywide smoking restrictions in restaurants is the "level playing field" frame (**Table 8-1**). The core position of this frame is that restricting smoking in restaurants in one city creates an unlevel playing field: Customers will shift their business to restaurants in nearby cities that allow smoking, resulting in a loss of business for restaurants in the affected city. The metaphor suggested by this frame is that of an unlevel playing field that favors one team over another. The core values, or principles, to which this frame appeals are fairness, equality, justice, and economic opportunity. It is simply unfair

Table 8-1 Level Playing Field Frame Used by the Tobacco Industry to Fight Local Smoke-Free Restaurant Ordinances	
Frame	**Level Playing Field**
Core position	Restricting smoking in restaurants in one city creates a selective advantage for restaurants in nearby cities
Metaphor	An unlevel playing field in a sports event, favoring one team over another
Images	An unlevel playing field in a sports event
Catch phrases	"Level playing field," "unfair advantage," "discrimination"
Attribution of responsibility	The government, which is creating a selective advantage for some businesses
Implied solution	Maintain a level playing field by banning smoking in all restaurants nationwide or do nothing
Core values	Fairness
	Equality
	Justice
	Economic opportunity

Source: Adapted from Ryan (1991), following the work of Gamson and Lasch (1983) and Gamson and Modigliani (1989).

for the government to create an advantage for restaurants in one city over those in another city.

Importance of Framing in Behavior Change Campaigns

As previously discussed, salient core values such as freedom and control generally have a strong impact on individuals' behaviors. Often, maintaining, rather than changing, an unhealthy behavior supports these values. If an individual has firmly established a behavior in the first place, the behavior must fulfill some core value for the individual. If the individual is aware that the behavior has undesirable health consequences, that awareness is less potent than the pull of the other values. To effect behavior change, public health campaigns must demonstrate how the new behavior enhances, rather than diminishes, an individual's freedom and control.

For example, a youth antismoking campaign might focus on the adolescent core values of freedom, independence, control, identity, and rebellion (**Table 8-2**). Focus group research conducted by the Centers for Disease Control and Prevention's (CDC's) Office on Smoking and Health revealed that "the desire of teenagers to gain control over their lives would make them responsive to a counteradvertising strategy aimed at exposing the predatory marketing techniques of the tobacco industry" (McKenna & Williams, 1993, p. 85). The CDC research found that teens place a high value on "self-determination and being in control" (p. 87) and concluded that "teenagers' rebellion can be viewed as a manifestation of

Table 8-2 Repackaging, Repositioning, and Reframing the Public Health Product: Strategic Use of Marketing in a Smoking Prevention Campaign	
Core Value	**Message**
Freedom	By not smoking, you can remain free of captivation by the addictive power of nicotine.
Independence	By not smoking, you can remain independent of the tobacco industry, which is trying to control you by fooling you into becoming a nicotine addict.
Control	By not smoking, you can maintain control over your social image, preventing being made a fool of by the tobacco industry.
Identity	Only the most mature youth are able to resist the tobacco industry's attempt to capture them; smoking is something that kids do because they are not mature enough to understand.
Rebellion	Rebel against an industry that is trying to deceive you, lie to you, manipulate you, seduce you, addict you, and kill you.

asserting their independence from adults' influence and control" (p. 87). The CDC researchers suggested that the important adolescent values of independence and control could be used to frame an antismoking message: "If you smoke, you are not in control; you are being manipulated by the tobacco industry" (p. 87).

The results of formative research like this were used to develop a successful youth smoking prevention campaign in Florida (Hicks, 2001). The campaign, which emphasized to youths how they were being manipulated by the tobacco companies to start smoking, aimed to reframe the issue of independence and autonomy from something provided by smoking to something conferred to a youth by rejecting tobacco industry influence to attempt to get them to smoke. The campaign was successful in reducing 30-day smoking prevalence among middle-school students from 18.5% to 11.1% and among high school students from 27.4% to 22.6% in just the first 2 years of the program (Bauer et al., 2000).

The potential effectiveness of such a reframing of the antismoking message can be seen in the success of tobacco prevention initiatives among Black youth. In 1992, the percentage of Black high school seniors who smoked was 8.2%, four times lower than the percentage who smoked two decades earlier (33.7% in 1974), whereas smoking prevalence among White youth during this period remained essentially unchanged at 30% to 34% (USDHHS, 1994). One explanation for this difference is the development, in the Black community, of social norms that view smoking as an infringement of individual freedom and view promotion of tobacco as an effort to control and enslave Blacks. Several campaigns in the Black community, including successful efforts to end the tobacco industry's marketing of X cigarettes and Uptown cigarettes, both directed specifically at young Black people, infused the community with a spirit of rebellion against an industry that was portrayed as trying to enslave it. As Cass Sunstein (1997) described it, the antismoking campaign was "symbolized most dramatically by posters in Harlem subways showing a skeleton resembling the Marlboro man lighting a cigarette for a black child. The caption reads, 'They used to make us pick it. Now they want us to smoke it'" (p. 33).

Not only must public health practitioners demonstrate to the audience how the behavior change will fulfill basic needs and desires, but they must also show that the alternative (maintaining the unhealthy behavior) will conflict with basic needs and desires. Thus, it is not enough merely to promote the behavior change in isolation. The public health practitioner must research the reasons the population maintains the unhealthy behavior, the alternative messages being communicated, the sources of these messages, and the core values to which these messages appeal. Part of the process of packaging, positioning, and framing the public health product is finding a way to demonstrate to the target audience that the desired behavior change will fulfill important core values, while maintaining the behavior is actually conflicting with these values. "Any program seeking to moderate or eliminate this destructive behavior must recognize that it meets important needs and wants of the target audience. To change the behavior, the social marketer must understand those needs and wants and show how the proposed behavior can either also meet those needs and wants or can meet other needs and wants that are subordinate" (Andreasen, 1995, p. 80).

For example, to promote increased physical activity, public health professionals must not only show why being physically active will fulfill some important needs and desires but how remaining inactive will conflict with important needs. Not only must public health professionals offer benefits for adopting the desired behavior change, but they must identify and understand contradicting messages and confront them directly. Andreasen (1995) explains that marketers "recognize that every choice of action on the consumer's part involves giving up some other action. Thus campaigns must keep in mind not only what the marketer is trying to get across but also what the customer sees as the major alternatives. Many times social marketers can bring about change as much by showing the deficiencies of an alternative as they can by emphasizing the benefits of the approach the marketer favors" (pp. 17, 18).

Importance of Framing in Public Policy Debates

In the late 1980s, the tobacco industry shifted its strategy from a focus on challenging the scientific evidence about the health effects of tobacco to a focus on discussing non–health-related frames: civil liberties, government interference, individual rights, and discrimination. This was not a lucky guess but the result of public opinion research showing that these frames resonated well with American voters. For example, in 1988, a Tobacco Institute poll appraised the strength of various core values as well as alternative campaign messages and arguments. This poll assessed the extent of antiregulatory sentiment among American voters to determine whether an antigovernment interference theme might be effective in generating opposition to tobacco policy proposals (Roper Center at University of Connecticut, 1989). In addition to assessing voter attitudes concerning specific tobacco policies, the poll also asked questions about government regulation of the use, transportation, and disposal of toxic chemicals (Roper Center at University of Connecticut, 1989; **Exhibit 8-1**). The tobacco industry's strategy has been quite successful because of the extent to which the core values of its messages are an inherent part of American thinking (Jacobson, Wasserman, & Raube, 1993, p. 807):

> The concept and symbolic importance of individual freedoms are deeply ingrained in American myth, culture, and law. Antismoking advocates may have underestimated how powerfully the idea of personal autonomy for lifestyle choices resonates among legislators, especially when used creatively to obscure the tobacco industry's goals. As the tobacco industry has correctly calculated, the individual

---

Exhibit 8-1   Sample Questions from a 1988 Tobacco Institute Public Opinion Poll

---

1. The U.S. Agriculture Department currently inspects food processing plants to make sure they are sanitary. Do you believe these inspections should be made more strict than they are now, made less strict than they are now, or should they be left about as they are now?

2. The Federal Aviation Administration now places restrictions on the number of commercial flights that can be scheduled in and out of major airports. Do you believe these restrictions should be made more strict than they are now, made less strict than they are now, or should they be left about as they are now?

3. The Environmental Protection Agency now requires companies using toxic chemicals to follow certain procedures in the use, transportation, and disposal of those chemicals. Do you believe those procedures should be made more strict than they are now, made less strict then they are now, or should they be left about as they are now?

Source: Data from Roper Center at University of Connecticut (1989).

---

liberties arguments are seductive when framed as unfair restrictions on private social behavior, even in the presence of compelling scientific evidence on the adverse health effects from smoking.

In their case studies of antismoking legislation in six states, Jacobson et al. (1993) found that the tobacco industry "attempted to shift the nature of the debate from the credibility of the scientific evidence to personal freedoms" (p. 800). Moreover, they observed that "antismoking forces fare better when public health issues dominate and that the tobacco industry benefits when personal freedoms arguments are predominant. . . . [L]egislative outcomes favored antismoking advocates during the time that public health dominated the debate. Once the debate shifted to personal freedoms, statewide antismoking legislation stalled" (p. 801). Jacobson and colleagues (1993, p. 802) described it as follows:

[The tobacco industry] shifted its opposition to smoking restrictions to a broadly conceived argument equating smoking behavior with other personal liberties, such as freedom of speech and protection against racial discrimination. This argument involves three interconnected concepts; first, governmental interference—that smoking restrictions should be determined by private economic arrangements, not by governmental fiat; second, smokers' rights—that smokers have certain rights and autonomy in pursing personal social behavior; and third—nondiscrimination—that smokers cannot be discriminated against for their smoking behavior, particularly in employment, for smoking during nonworking hours.

The findings of Jacobson and colleagues (1993) suggested that although health is an important core value, personal freedoms, civil liberties, and individual rights may be even more compelling values for the public. When the debate is framed in a way such that antismoking legislation is seen as conflicting with these values, smoking advocates must directly confront the opposition frames. They must develop their own frames that appeal to the same compelling core values being tapped by the opposition. The development of these frames should be guided by market research, not by mere conjecture.

Wallack and associates (1993) argued that, in a sense, debates over public health policy issues represent a battle for framing the issue in the eyes of the public. It is not necessarily the relative merits of various arguments for and against a proposal that most influence its legislative fate. Rather, it is the relative success of proponents and opponents in framing the overall terms of the debate. For example, in tobacco control, "the battle for framing is evident in how the tobacco industry uses symbols and images to promote itself as a good corporate citizen, defender of the First Amendment, protector of free choice, and friend of the family farmer. The industry paints antitobacco people, on the other hand, as zealots, health fascists, paternalists, and government interventionists" (Wallack et al., 1993, p. 71). As Jacobson and associates (1993) argued, "how the issue of smoking restrictions is framed is an important component of the legislative debate and outcome" (p. 806). Similarly, Schon and Rein (1994) explained that in a policy controversy, "two or more parties contend with one another over the definition of a problematic policy situation and vie for control of the policy-making process. Their struggles over the naming and framing of a policy situation are symbolic contests over the social meaning of an issue domain, where meaning implies not only what is at issue but what is to be done" (pp. 28, 29).

The public's perception of how an issue relates to its needs, wants, and values most influences public opinion. The way in which a debate is framed has important implications for how the public relates the issue to its needs and core values. The battle over public health programs and policy initiatives, then, can be viewed not only as a battle over specific facts and arguments but as a battle over the framing of the overall issue—not solely as a battle over policy, but as a battle over the packaging of that policy into symbols, images, and themes.

In their discussion of "the framing of debate," Chapman and Lupton (1994) emphasized the need to understand "how issues need to be reframed in order to steer public and political support in the desired directions" (p. 18). The authors stated that "political battles are seldom won only on the elegance of logic or by those who can best assemble rational arguments. These are mere strategies within a wider battle front. The real issue is which are the overall framings of debates that best succeed in capturing public opinion and political will" (p. 125). Similarly, Schon and

Rein (1994) saw policy controversies as "disputes in which the contending parties hold conflicting frames. Such disputes are resistant to resolution by appeal to facts or reasoned argumentation because the parties' conflicting frames determine what counts as a fact and what arguments are taken to be relevant and compelling" (p. 23).

Kaniss (1991), too, emphasized the importance of the "symbolic framing of the proposal," concluding that "the way in which new initiatives are presented and framed for the media is particularly important" (pp. 182, 183). She stressed that symbols play a critical role in the framing of policies and showed how the battle for the symbolic framing of a policy issue in a way that best appeals to the media is the central battle over a public health policy.

Framing can be viewed as the packaging and positioning of a public health policy or program so it appeals to deeply ingrained, widely shared principles held by the target audience. Framing is an integral part of developing a strategy to market public health programs and policies.

Developing Public Health Frames

In developing frames, public health practitioners must identify how to define, position, and package an issue in ways that (1) present a unified, coherent core position; (2) evoke desired visual images; (3) use recognizable "catch phrases"; (4) suggest appropriate metaphors; (5) attribute responsibility for the problem to society, rather than merely to the individual; and (6) imply as a solution the program or policy being marketed by the practitioner (**Exhibit 8-2**). All these individual objectives must work together effectively to reinforce the deeply ingrained, widely held principles and values of the target audience.

In a case where a public health coalition is supporting a local ordinance to protect the health of restaurant workers by eliminating smoking in restaurants, the coalition may instinctively frame its arguments using

---

Exhibit 8-2   Key Objectives in Development of Framing Strategy for Public Health Programs and Policies

1. Present unified, coherent core position on the policy or program that is consistent with the core values of target audience.

2. Evoke visual images that appeal to the core values.

3. Develop catch phrases (verbal images) that appeal to the core values.

4. Suggest appropriate metaphors that evoke themes and images that appeal to the core values.

5. Attribute responsibility for the public health problem to society (including government), not merely to individuals.

6. Imply as a solution the program or policy being marketed.

health as a core value. However, instead of defining the product of an antismoking ordinance campaign as a law to protect the health of non-smokers and offering health for restaurant customers as a benefit, the coalition might develop four frames based on more salient core values of freedom, independence, control, and fairness. This would entail redefining the product and benefits as the freedom to work in an environment free of health hazards, the right to make a living without being involuntarily exposed to carcinogens, creating a level playing field for all workers by affording restaurant workers the same protection that is provided to almost all other workers, helping business by preventing huge liability risks for damages caused by secondhand smoke, preventing discrimination against blue-collar workers by extending to all workers the protection that almost all white-collar workers have from secondhand smoke, and protecting the livelihood of workers in small restaurants by ending the suffering they endure from exposure to a hazardous working environment (**Table 8-3**).

Table 8-3 Core Values and Messages That Appeal to These Values for Several Public Health Policies

Public Health Policy	Core Value	Message
Eliminate smoking in restaurants	Freedom/ Free enterprise	What could possibly be a more basic freedom to Americans than the freedom to make a living and support one's children without having to be exposed to dangerous working conditions?
		What is a more basic civil liberty than the right to work in a safe environment?
		Forcing employees to breathe in carcinogens in order to make a living is a violation of the free enterprise principle.
	Independence/ economic opportunity	Liability risks posed by allowing employees to be exposed to secondhand smoke (workers' compensation, disability, etc.) could hurt business owners. Illnesses and deaths will cause a loss of jobs, productivity, and sales.
	Control	How can workers pursue a livelihood and support children if they are too sick to work or suffer (can't breathe) at work?

(continues)

Table 8-3 Core Values and Messages That Appeal to These Values for Several Public Health Policies (continued)

Public Health Policy	Core Value	Message
	Fairness/Equality	Excluding restaurant workers from health protection that all other workers take for granted is not fair; it represents discrimination against a certain class of workers; this is a class issue.
Increase cigarette tax	Freedom	Voting for the tax is a way to assert freedom from tobacco industry influence. Rejecting the tax is just playing into the hands of the industry and letting it dictate state policies.
	Independence	Without a higher tax, parents cannot effectively keep children from smoking, cannot effectively fight the tobacco industry's pressure on their children to smoke.
	Control	Voting for the tax allows you, not the tobacco industry, to decide the fate of your children's health.
	Democracy	Voting for the tax preserves the democratic ideal by keeping government in the hands of the people, not in the hands of a powerful, greedy, special interest group that has intruded into our state.
Adopt stricter environmental regulations	Control	Regulations will allow society to retain control over the unknown consequences of regulations of environmental destruction.
	Economic opportunity	Regulations will help preserve livelihoods and economic opportunity by protecting tourism; rejecting the regulations will lead to economic devastation of the community.
Adopt needle exchange	Freedom	The program will allow society to remain free of the scourge of acquired immunodeficiency syndrome (AIDS); without it, AIDS may spread from the drug-using population to the general population.

(continues)

Table 8-3 Core Values and Messages That Appeal to These Values for Several Public Health Policies (continued)

Public Health Policy	Core Value	Message
	Control	If AIDS spreads to the general population, the epidemic may soon be out of control.
Adopt mandatory seat belt law	Fairness	It is not fair for taxpayers to have to pay medical bills for people seriously injured because they were irresponsible and failed to wear seat belts.
	Economic livelihood	The medical costs of accidents involving individuals not wearing seat belts are wreaking havoc on the budget and the economy and increasing taxes for everyone.
		The law will create savings that will translate into lower taxes and increased economic livelihood.
Adopt tuberculosis (TB) screening and treatment program in drug treatment clinics	Freedom	The program will prevent the epidemic scourge of TB that threatens to affect all of us, as TB spreads from drug users into the general population.
	Control	The program will allow society to retain control over the unknown consequences of the spread of multidrug-resistant TB into the general population. The consequences are unknown, but could be devastating to society.

Note: This framing matrix model was adapted from Ryan (1991), following the work of Gamson and Lasch (1983) and Gamson and Modigliani (1989).

Similarly, instead of framing an initiative to increase the cigarette tax simply as a measure to reduce cigarette consumption and improve health, supporting the initiative could be framed as a way for voters to remain free of the tobacco industry's influence, raise their children independent of the pressure being placed on their children to smoke, maintain control of the health of their communities, and preserve the principles of democracy (Table 8-3). Programs to adopt measures such as stricter environmental regulations, needle exchange programs, mandatory seat belt laws, and screening and treatment programs also could be framed to appeal to the core values of freedom, independence, economic opportunity, autonomy, control, fairness, and equality (Table 8-3).

Reframing Public Health Issues

In addition to developing their own frames, public health practitioners must also learn to confront the frames developed by opponents of their proposed policies and programs directly. Public health advocates can use two approaches to confront opposition framing. For example, when the level playing field frame is used to fight local smoking regulations (Table 8-1), advocates can simply ignore the opposition frame and emphasize that this is a health issue. The success of this approach depends on policymakers perceiving the policy's conflict with the value they place on fairness and equality. As Jacobson and colleagues (1993) noted, this approach may be successful, but only if advocates are able to make the public health frame the dominant one.

An alternative approach is to reframe the issue so that supporting the policy reinforces rather than conflicts with the core values being tapped by the opposition frame. In other words, public health advocates must develop a new frame that shows policymakers how a local restaurant smoking ordinance is necessary to preserve fairness and equality for the city's residents.

One way the issue could be reframed is to demonstrate how denying restaurant workers the protection from secondhand smoke that is afforded most other workers is unfair (**Table 8-4**). The real unlevel playing field is the singling out of restaurant workers as the one occupational group not deserving of basic public health protections that most other workers take for granted and consider to be their right. A second way to reframe the issue might be to show how the failure to protect citizens in the city would perpetuate an unlevel playing field by denying citizens in that city a basic right guaranteed to the citizens of more than 200 cities throughout the country—the right to work in an environment free of hazards (Table 8-4). In both frames, the core values are the same: fairness and equality. However, in the opposition frame, voting for the ordinance would conflict with these values, whereas in the proponent frame, voting for the ordinance would reinforce these values.

Another excellent example of the technique of redefining public health issues so the desired program reinforces rather than opposes core values was provided by former Surgeon General Joycelyn Elders. In 1994, public health practitioners in Baltimore proposed a program to offer Norplant—a system of long-term contraception that involves the surgical insertion of a slow-release hormone delivery device under the skin of the upper arm—to teenage girls at a city health department clinic. The plan was condemned on the grounds that it would interfere with the autonomy and freedom of the young women and restrict their reproductive rights. In response, Dr. Elders redefined the Norplant program as a method to free young women from the enslaving grip of unwanted pregnancies: "If

Table 8-4 **The Level Playing Field Frame: Reframing for Use by Public Health Advocates in Promoting Local Smoke-Free Restaurant Ordinances**

Frame	Level Playing Field—Reframe 1	Level Playing Field—Reframe 2
Core position	Singling out restaurant workers as the one occupational group not deserving of the basic health protection already afforded to nearly all other workers creates an unlevel playing field for these workers.	Failing to protect citizens in this city from secondhand smoke when more than 200 cities nationwide have already afforded these protections to their workers creates an unlevel playing field for our residents.
Metaphor	An unlevel playing field in a sports event, favoring one team over another	An unlevel playing field in a sports event, favoring one team over another
Images	An unlevel playing field in a sports event	An unlevel playing field in a sports event
Catch phrases	"Level playing field," "unfair," "disadvantage," "discrimination"	"Level playing field," "unfair," "disadvantage," "discrimination"
Attribution of responsibility for problem	Government, which is selectively protecting workers in typical offices, but excluding restaurant workers from protection	Government, which is selectively excluding our city's residents from protection that many residents in other cities have
Implied solution	Extend smoke-free working environment protections to all workers	Extend smoke-free working environment protections to workers in our city
Core values	Fairness	Fairness
	Equality	Equality
	Justice	Justice
	Economic opportunity	Economic opportunity

Note: This framing matrix model was adapted from Ryan (1991), following the work of Gamson and Lasch (1983) and Gamson and Modigliani (1989).

you're poor and ignorant, with a child, you're a slave. Meaning that you're never going to get out of it. These women are in bondage to a kind of slavery that the Thirteenth Amendment just didn't deal with" (Gaylin & Jennings, 1996, p. 16). As Gaylin and Jennings (1996) explained, Surgeon General Elders framed the use of Norplant as "a liberating factor from the veritable 'slavery' of teenage pregnancy" (p. 16).

Beauchamp (1976) discussed how public health practitioners can use the core value of justice to redefine public health problems in ways that will gain public support and motivate the public and policymakers to collective action. "In building these collective redefinitions of health problems, however, public health must take care to do more than merely shed light on specific public health problems. . . . This means that the function of each different redefinition of a specific problem must be to raise the common and recurrent issue of justice by exposing the aggressive and powerful structures implicated in all instances of preventable death and disability, and further to point to the necessity for collective measures to confront and resist these structures" (p. 10).

The process of reframing public health programs and policies effectively can be aided by considering the nature of societal core values. In particular, two characteristics of these core values are most salient. First, the deeply ingrained core value of freedom represents both the absence of interference from others (negative liberty) and the presence of control over one's life and destiny (positive liberty). Special interest groups that oppose public health programs tend to emphasize their infringement on negative liberty. Public health practitioners can often reframe the debate by pointing out how the program or policy will actually enhance positive liberties. For example, men may perceive wearing a condom as an infringement on their personal lives and their privacy. But the behavior itself may help to ensure positive liberty for the individual by keeping him in control of his future and allowing him, not AIDS, to make his decisions. Similarly, whereas a law that limits individuals' ability to drink and drive may be perceived as interfering with personal freedom, public health practitioners can market such a law by pointing out that it actually preserves individual autonomy by protecting society's members from being killed by drunk drivers and therefore preserves their ability to control their lives.

Second, core values such as freedom, independence, autonomy, and even justice have tended to be interpreted with an individualistic perspective. Civil rights laws, for example, usually have been interpreted as protecting the rights of individuals. But Gaylin and Jennings (1996) argued that "nothing inherent in civil rights laws . . . requires that they be interpreted in individualistic terms; their meaning could easily be construed in terms of nondiscrimination or equality" (p. 53). In other words, public health practitioners may be able to reframe public health programs and policies in a way that highlights how they will promote a communitarian or societal advancement of civil rights. For example, a law that eliminates smoking in bars could be promoted as a necessary measure to ensure equality of occupational safety protections for all workers. A smoke-free ordinance is simply an expression of a societal interpretation of civil rights.

Gaylin and Jennings (1996) suggested that in America, civil rights have become "a framework for individual claims against others," but that they could just as easily become "a framework for social solidarity" and a means of "building a moral community of equal citizens" (p. 53). Etzioni (1993) even claimed that a communitarian perspective of rights is not only consistent with, but is necessary for, the preservation of individual liberty. "Neither human existence nor individual liberty can be sustained for long outside the interdependent and overlapping communities to which all of us belong. . . . The exclusive pursuit of private interest erodes the network of social environments on which we all depend and is destructive to our shared experiment in democratic self-government. For these reasons, we hold that the rights of individuals cannot long be preserved without a Communitarian perspective" (pp. 253, 254).

Sunstein (1997) wrote that the government effort to change social norms is often necessary to advance individual autonomy (pp. 37, 55, 59):

> In fact, there are many reasons why a legal system might seek to alter norms, meanings, and roles. The most important reason is that the resulting reforms might enhance autonomy. . . . Obstacles to autonomy and to good lives can also come from bad roles, norms, and meaning. . . . In some cases, existing norms undermine people's autonomy, by discouraging them from being exposed to diverse conceptions of the good and from giving critical scrutiny to their own conceptions, in such a way as to make it impossible for them to be, in any sense, masters of the narratives of their own lives.

Thus, in reframing public health programs and policies, public health practitioners can confront antiregulatory sentiment by positioning these reforms as necessary to eliminate obstacles to individual freedom and autonomy. "It should be clear that social norms, meanings, and roles may undermine individual autonomy. Above all, this is because norms can compromise autonomy itself, by stigmatizing it. . . . In such cases, autonomy cannot exist without collective assistance, people are able to produce the norms, meanings, and roles that they reflectively endorse only with governmental involvement. Something must be done collectively if the situation is to be changed" (Sunstein, 1997, p. 62).

In general, public health practitioners can confront the antiregulatory sentiment in the nation by reframing public health issues to show that government action is necessary precisely to preserve the societal interest in individual freedom and autonomy. Sunstein (1997, pp. 20, 30, 31) wrote as follows:

> [M]ore broadly, a democratic government should sometimes take private preferences as an object of deliberation, evaluation, and even control—an inevitable task in light of the need to define initial entitlements—and precisely in the interest of welfare and autonomy. . . . The interest in liberty or autonomy does not call for government

inaction, even if that were an intelligible category. Indeed, in many or perhaps all of the cases, regulation removes a kind of coercion. . . . The view that freedom requires an opportunity to choose among alternatives finds a natural supplement in the view that people should not face unjustifiable constraints on the free development of their preferences and beliefs. . . . Liberalism does not forbid citizens, operating through democratic channels, from enacting their considered judgments into law, or from counteracting, through the provision of opportunities and information, preferences and beliefs that have adjusted to an unjust status quo. Ironically, a system that forecloses these routes—and that claims to do so in the name of liberalism or democracy—will defeat many of the aspirations that gave both liberalism and democracy their original appeal, and that continue to fuel them in so many parts of the world.

Perhaps the best example of reframing social policy so as to reinforce the core values of freedom and autonomy is the description offered by Sunstein (1997, p. 28) of the rationale for government programs to address poverty:

Poverty itself is perhaps the most severe obstacle to the free development of preferences and beliefs. Programs that attempt to respond to the deprivation faced by poor people—most obviously by eliminating poverty, but also through broad public education and regulatory efforts designed to make cultural resources generally available regardless of wealth—are fully justified in this light. They should hardly be seen as objectionable paternalism or an unsupportable redistribution. Indeed, antipoverty efforts are tightly linked with traditional efforts to promote security and independence in the interest of creating the conditions for full and equal citizenship.

The strategic use of issue framing to redefine the public health product and package and position it so it supports the most compelling core values of the public and policymakers can play an important role in helping public health practitioners deal with the unique marketing challenge they face. Evidence suggests that issue-framing strategies derived from marketing and public opinion research can help promote support for public health policies. For example, a 1988 survey funded by the Coalition for a Healthy California explored the effectiveness of various issue-framing strategies for a state cigarette tax initiative and was used in developing the campaign that led to the passage of Proposition 99 (Marr, 1990; Traynor & Glantz, 1996). A 1991 survey funded by the Massachusetts division of the American Cancer Society played a key role in developing the campaign that led to the passage of a cigarette tax initiative in

1992 (Marttila & Kiley, Inc., 1991). Similar marketing research helped a public health coalition in Arizona promote the passage of a cigarette tax initiative in 1994 (Ross, 1996).

Despite the promise of issue framing in marketing public health programs and policies, more research must be done in this area. Chapman and Lupton (1994, p. 12) suggested four specific questions to address in such research:

(1) Are there important differences in the framings favored by those working in public health, and those that hold most public and political appeal?; (2) Are there methodologies that are sufficiently sensitive to be reliably used in pretesting different framings used in advocacy?; (3) What examples are there, where dominant framings that run against the interests of public health appear to have been successfully reversed?; (4) Are there principles that characterize such reversals, which can be applied in practical ways in future debates?

Providing Support for the Public Health Promise

In marketing terms, the message that a particular behavior, public health program, or policy will provide a set of benefits as defined by a frame is called the "promise." Part of demonstrating that a behavior will reinforce core target audience values is providing support to back up the promise. Traditionally, public health practitioners have relied on scientific evidence of the health benefits of a new behavior, policy, or program to support the promise of improved health from the intervention. In contrast, successful corporate marketers tend to rely on much more compelling support for their promises. Nike, for example, backs up its offer of control over one's life with solid documentation: video footage of elite athletes in action or images of everyday people (wearing Nike gear of course) reaching personal fulfillment through physical activity. Almost never does one see a corporate marketer offer statistics and data to support the promise of particular benefits from the use of a product.

Public health practitioners, too, must learn to provide equally compelling documentation to support their promises. Although it is natural for public health practitioners to rely on data and statistics to accomplish this, this tendency is unlikely to be effective. Statistics and data are not terribly effective at influencing policymakers. But frames, images, and emotional appeals to core values are.

One way to bring frames, images, and core value appeals together in an emotional and compelling way is through the use of stories. In many ways, the successful telling of a story of one affected individual can be far more compelling than providing data and statistics that document the thousands of people affected by a particular health condition or disease. Public health practitioners need to learn how to tell and deliver effective and emotional stories to provide support for their promised benefits rather than to simply rely on data and statistics.

Branding

One way to put together the repositioning, repackaging, and reframing of the public health program or policy product is through the concept of branding. The concept of branding has been introduced into public health marketing (Andreasen, 2006) and has served as a useful framework for the development of a number of effective public health communication campaigns.

Public health practitioners need to think of the policy or program they are promoting (or even of public health itself) as a brand, similar in many ways to the brands offered to consumers by marketers of consumer products. As such, brands need to convey the personality of a program or policy. The idea is to build a relationship with the policymaker, not merely to promote a one-time transaction. "In recent years, marketers have come to realize that the best way to influence behavior is not through one-time transactions, but by building ongoing relationships with their customers" (Hastings, 2003, p. 15).

By focusing on developing their brand's personality for their public health policy or program product offering, public health practitioners can unify their promotional campaign around a single brand identity, which can ensure that all aspects of the public health communication—the object, the promise, the benefit, the support, and the image—work together to convey an identity to which the target audience can relate and to which it aspires. In this way, branding can serve as an ideal concept around which to incorporate the repackaging, repositioning, and reframing of a public health program or policy.

After all, a brand not only forms the relationship between the organization or product and its consumer, but it has also been characterized as a repository of functional characteristics as well as meaning and value (Mark & Pearson, 2001; McDivitt, 2003). It is that meaning and value (such as standing for freedom, independence, and autonomy), not merely the functional characteristics of the desired public health program or policy (such as improving health and reducing disease or death), that are most closely tied to individual behavior.

Hicks (2001) described how branding was used in the truth[SM] youth smoking prevention campaign in Florida to make not smoking an identity to which youth would aspire: "In a search to define one's identity, brands (like piercing, haircuts, and even tobacco use) serve as a shorthand way for youth to identify themselves to the world. If we wanted youth to really embrace our anti-tobacco effort, it made sense that we should deliver it just like other successful U.S. youth products, such as Adidas, Fubu or Abercrombie—in a branded form they understood" (p. 5).

■ CONCLUSION

To advocate successfully for public health policies and programs and to promote the survival of public health as a societal institution, public health practitioners must adopt two basic marketing principles:

1. The first step in developing campaigns to promote a public health policy or program is not to decide how to convince the public or policymakers to support the program, but to use market research to identify the basic needs, desires, and core values of the target audience.

2. When referring to public health, practitioners must define the product they are selling based on the results of formative research. Public health practitioners must acknowledge that they cannot always effectively sell public health programs. They must begin to sell basic values such as freedom, independence, control, and the democratic way. Public health must be positioned, packaged, and framed in such a way that it will be perceived as fulfilling the needs, desires, and values of the target audience. And then the message must be reinforced and supported by compelling, emotional stories and images, not merely by statistics and data.

In the new view of public health presented in this chapter, epidemiologic research and formative research combine to form a basic foundation. Epidemiologic research helps identify the most effective programs and policies to solve public health problems. Then, based on the findings of formative research, the most important needs, desires, and values of the target audience (policymakers and/or the public) can be identified. Next, the public health practitioner must define the product so it offers as a benefit the fulfillment of these desires and needs. Finally, the practitioner can package, position, and frame the product in an effort to demonstrate to the audience how it will indeed fulfill these desires and needs (**Figure 8-1**).

This model differs from traditional models of public health practice because it includes two intermediate steps not generally included in other models. Most models begin with step A and jump immediately to the final step D, running the campaign. In this model, before the actual planning, implementation, and evaluation of the public health campaign, there are two additional steps: formative research (understanding the consumer's needs, desires, and values) and strategic marketing for public health (using the results of formative research to effectively define, package, position, and frame the public health program or policy being promoted).

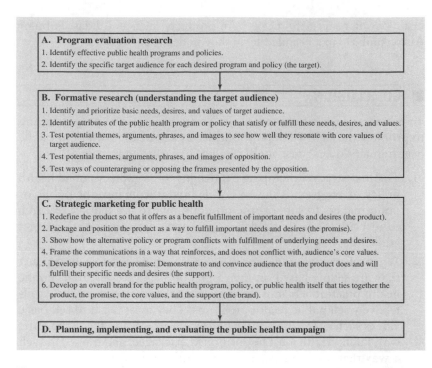

Figure 8-1 A New Marketing Strategy for Public Health: Confronting Threats to the Survival of Public Health

References

Andreasen, A.R. (1995). *Marketing social change: Changing behavior to promote health, social development, and the environment.* San Francisco, CA: Jossey-Bass.

Andreasen, A.R. (2006). *Social marketing in the 21st century.* Thousand Oaks, CA: Sage.

Bauer, U.E., Johnson, T.M., Hopkins, R.S., & Brooks, R.G. (2000). Changes in youth cigarette use and intentions following implementation of a tobacco control program: Findings from the Florida Youth Tobacco Survey, 1998–2000. *Journal of the American Medical Association, 284*(6), 723–728.

Beauchamp, D. (1976). Public health as social justice. *Inquiry, 13*(1), 3–14.

Bernays, E.L. (1965). *Biography of an idea: Memoirs of public relations counsel Edward L. Bernays.* New York, NY: Simon & Schuster.

Chapman, S., & Lupton, D. (1994). *The fight for public health: Principles and practice of media advocacy.* London, England: BMJ Publishing Group.

Conrad, P. (1987). The experience of illness: Recent and new directions. *Research in the Sociology of Health Care, 6,* 1–31.

Entman, R. (1993). Framing: Toward clarification of a fractured paradigm. *Journal of Communication, 43,* 51–58.

Etzioni, A. (1993). *The spirit of community: Rights, responsibilities, and the communitarian agenda.* New York, NY: Crown.

Fine, T.S. (1992). The impact of issue framing on public opinion toward affirmative action programs. *Social Science Journal, 29*, 323–334.

Gamson, W.A., & Lasch, K.E. (1983). The political culture of social welfare policy. In S.E. Spiro & E. Yuchtman-Yaar (Eds.), *Evaluating the welfare state: Social and political perspectives* (pp. 397–415). New York, NY: Academic Press.

Gamson, W.A., & Modigliani, A. (1989). Media discourse and public opinion on nuclear power: A constructionist approach. *American Journal of Sociology, 95*(1), 1–37.

Gaylin, W., & Jennings, B. (1996). *The perversion of autonomy: The proper uses of coercion and constraints in a liberal society.* New York, NY: The Free Press.

Glaser, B.G., & Strauss, A.L. (1968). *Time for dying.* Chicago, IL: Aldine.

Hastings, G. (2003). Social marketers of the world unite, you have nothing to lose but your shame. *Social Marketing Quarterly, 9*(4), 14–21.

Hicks, J.J. (2001). The strategy behind Florida's 'truth' campaign. *Tobacco Control, 10*, 3–5.

Iyengar, S. (1991). *Is anyone responsible? How television frames political issues.* Chicago, IL: University of Chicago Press.

Jacobson, P.D., Wasserman, J., & Raube, K. (1993). The politics of antismoking legislation. *Journal of Health Politics, Policy and Law, 18*, 787–819.

Kaniss, P. (1991). *Making local news.* Chicago, IL: University of Chicago Press.

Kleinman, A. (1988). *The illness narratives: Suffering healing, and the human condition.* New York, NY: Basic Books.

Krosnick, J., & Alwin, D. (1988). A test of the form-resistant correlation hypothesis: Ratings, rankings and the measurement of values. *Public Opinion Quarterly, 32*, 526–538.

Mark, M., & Pearson, C.S. (2001). *The hero and the outlaw: Building extraordinary brands through the power of archetypes.* New York, NY: McGraw-Hill.

Marr, M. (1990, April). *Proposition 99: The California tobacco tax initiative, a case study.* Berkeley, CA: Western Consortium for Public Health.

Marttila & Kiley, Inc. (1991). *A survey of voter attitudes in Massachusetts: Benchmark survey.* Boston, MA: Author.

McDivitt, J. (2003). Innovations in social marketing conference proceedings. Session II: Is there a role for branding in social marketing? *Social Marketing Quarterly, 9*(3), 11–17.

McKenna, J.W., & Williams, K.N. (1993). I. Crafting effective tobacco counter-advertisements: Lessons from a failed campaign directed at teenagers. *Public Health Reports, 108*, 85–89.

Meyerowitz, B.E., & Chaiken, S. (1987). The effect of message framing on breast self-examination attitudes, intentions, and behavior. *Journal of Personality and Social Psychology, 52*, 500–510.

Meyers, W. (1984). *The image-makers: Power and persuasion on Madison Avenue.* New York, NY: New York Times Books.

Mishel, M.H. (1984). Perceived uncertainty and stress in illness. *Research in Nursing and Health, 7*, 163–171.

Mishel, M.H., Hostetter, T., King, B., & Graham, V. (1984). Predictors of psychosocial adjustment in patients newly diagnosed with gynecological cancer. *Cancer Nursing, 7*, 291–299.

Molleman, E., Krabbendam, P.J., Annyas, A.A., Koops, H.S., Sleijfer, D.T., & Vemey, A. (1984). The significance of the doctor-patient relationship in coping with cancer. *Social Science and Medicine, 18,* 745–480.

Moon, R. W., Males, M.A., & Nelson, D.E. (1993). The 1990 Montana initiative to increase cigarette taxes: Lessons for other states and localities. *Journal of Public Health Policy, 14,* 19–33.

Nelkin, D. (1987). *Selling science: How the press covers science and technology.* New York, NY: Freeman.

Roper Center at University of Connecticut. (1989). Public opinion online. Tobacco Institute sponsored survey conducted by Hamilton, Frederick, and Schneiders, November 23–December 6, 1988.

Ross, M. (1996). *Tobacco tax campaigns: A case study of two states.* Washington, DC: Advocacy Institute.

Rothman, A.J., Salovey, P., Antone, C., Keough, K., & Martin, C.D. (1993). The influence of message framing on intentions to perform health behaviors. *Journal of Experimental and Social Psychology, 29,* 408–433.

Ryan, C. (1991). *Prime time activism: Media strategies for grassroots organizing.* Boston, MA: South End Press.

Salmon, C.T. (1989). Campaigns for social improvement: An overview of values, rationales, and impacts. In C. Salmon (Ed.), *Information campaigns* (pp. 19–53). Newbury Park, CA: Sage.

Schon, D.A., & Rein, M. (1994). *Frame reflection: Toward the resolution of intractable policy controversies.* New York, NY: Basic Books.

Schudson, M. (1984). *Advertising, the uneasy persuasion: Its dubious impact on American society.* New York, NY: Basic Books.

Slovic, P., Fischoff, B., & Lichtenstein, S. (1982). Response mode, framing, and information-processing effects in risk assessment. In R.M. Hogarth (Ed.), *Question framing and response consistency* (pp. 21–36). San Francisco, CA: Jossey-Bass.

Smith, G.H. (1954). *Motivation research in advertising and marketing.* New York, NY: McGraw-Hill.

Smith, T. (1987). That which we call welfare by any other name would smell sweeter: An analysis of the impact of question wording on response patterns. *Public Opinion Quarterly, 51,* 75–83.

Stauber, J., & Rampton, S. (1995). *Toxic sludge is good for you! Lies, damn lies and the public relations industry.* Monroe, ME: Common Courage Press.

Steel, R. (1981). *Walter Lippmann and the American century.* New York, NY: Vintage Books.

Sunstein, C.R. (1997). *Free markets and social justice.* New York, NY: Oxford University Press.

Tannen, D. (Ed.). (1993). *Framing in discourse.* New York, NY: Oxford University Press.

Trachtenberg, J.A. (1987). Here's one tough cowboy. *Forbes, 139*(3), 108–110.

Traynor, M.P., & Glantz, S.A. (1996). California's tobacco tax initiative: The development and passage of Proposition 99. *Journal of Health Politics, Policy and Law, 21*(3), 543–585.

Tversky, A., & Kahneman, D. (1982). The framing of decisions and the psychology of choice. In R.M. Hogarth (Ed.), *Question framing and response consistency* (pp. 3–20). San Francisco, CA: Jossey-Bass.

U.S. Department of Health and Human Services (USDHHS). (1994). *Preventing tobacco use among young people: A report of the Surgeon General.* Washington, DC: Author.

Vaughan, E., & Seifert, M. (1992). Variability in the framing of risk issues. *Journal of Social Issues, 48,* 119–135.

Vookles, J., & Carr, J. (1993). The effects of message framing manipulations on AIDS preventive behavior. *AIDS Weekly,* p. 16.

Wagenaar, A.C., & Streff, F.M. (1990). Public opinion on alcohol policies. *Journal of Public Health Policy, 11,* 189–205.

Wallack, L., & Dorfman, L. (1996). Media advocacy: A strategy for advancing policy and promoting health. *Health Education Quarterly, 23,* 293–317.

Wallack, L., Dorfman, L., Jernigan, D., & Thomba, M. (1993). *Media advocacy and public health: Power for prevention.* Newbury Park, CA: Saga.

Watzlawick, P., Weakland, J., & Fisch, R. (1974). *Change: Principles of problem formation and problem resolution.* New York, NY: Norton.

Weitz, R. (1994). Uncertainty and the lives of persons with AIDS. In P. Conrad & R. Kern (Eds.), *The sociology of health & illness: Critical perspectives* (4th ed., pp. 138–149). New York, NY: St. Martin's Press.

White House Domestic Policy Council. (1993). *Health security: The President's report to the American people.* New York, NY: Touchstone.

Wilson, D.K., Purdon, S.E., & Wallston, K.A. (1988). Compliance to health recommendations: A theoretical overview of message framing. *Health Education Research: Theory and Practice, 3,* 161–171.

Wilson, D.K., Wallston, K.A., & King, J.E. (1990). Effect of contract framing, motivation to quit, and self-efficacy on smoking reduction. *Journal of Applied Social Psychology, 20,* 531–547.

Winett, L.B., & Wallack, L. (1996). Advancing public health goals through the mass media. *Journal of Health Communication, 1,* 173–196.

IV

Developing and Implementing the Approach

Once a strategic plan has been drafted, the components that will comprise the intervention must be developed and implemented. This section discusses that process. Specifically, Chapter 9 addresses the best ways to translate formative research findings into communication strategies. Chapter 10 introduces the tools and materials that marketers and practitioners can use to deliver the message.

CHAPTER

9

Communication Strategies and Tactics

A strong communication strategy is necessary to create an effective marketing campaign. The communication strategy describes how the behavior or issue will be framed and positioned in the minds of target audience members. It describes the target audience(s), the action(s) they should take, the benefits they will receive, and how best to reach them. It is based on a thorough understanding of the audience and their wants, needs, and values coupled with knowledge of the types of appeals likely to work in a given situation. Once a communication strategy has been developed, message concepts are devised to present that positioning to the audience and assess whether it is believable, compelling, and relevant. In addition to determining how best to communicate with an audience about taking a specific action, communication strategies help to build and maintain a relationship with audiences over time.

Public health marketing efforts rely on communication to inform, educate, and persuade. Communication can be used to model new behaviors or reinforce existing ones. It can call on cultural symbols and icons to frame an issue, an organization, or public health itself in a variety of ways. People are exposed to a barrage of health information every day. They hear it on the radio or TV, read it in newspapers or magazines, see it on the Internet, and learn more from friends, family members, and health care providers. Many feel overwhelmed by all the often conflicting advice and perspectives. The challenge is to break through the clutter and reach target populations with persuasive, actionable messages that convey a consistent identity. Messages that address behaviors and policies must be both scientifically sound and audience oriented. This chapter outlines a process for crafting a communication strategy and developing message concepts based on it.

■ COMMUNICATION STRATEGY

A communication strategy frames the issue in a particular way and thus positions the social change in the audience's mind. It must address the following points:

1. *Target audience*: The people the communication should reach
2. *Action*: What they should do after exposure to the communication
3. *Key benefit*: What they will gain that they value by taking the action
4. *Support*: How they will be convinced that they will receive the benefit
5. *Openings*: When and how the audience can best be reached with the communication
6. *Image*: The tone and personality conveyed by the communication

The activities conducted to develop an overall strategic plan can be used to develop a solid communication strategy. However, target audiences for various communications may have to be refined and/or may require separate communication strategies depending on the action they should take as a result of exposure to the communication. The target audience might be composed of members of the public, patients, health professionals, policymakers, voters, reporters, or some other groups.

The communication strategies developed for public health efforts include the same components as their commercial sector counterparts. The consumer-based health communications process outlined by Sutton, Balch, and Lefebvre (1995) is an excellent example of modifying the commercial communication strategy development framework specifically to the needs of public health practitioners. It is used as the basis for the approach outlined here.

Role of Theory

As with development of the overall intervention, the development of communication strategies should be guided by the theories or models of how change is expected to occur. For example, Maibach and Cotton (1995) developed what they term a "staged social cognitive approach to message design" (p. 41) in which they use the concepts of social cognitive theory to determine the most appropriate types of messages for people in each of the transtheoretical model's stages of change. They recommend the following types of messages to help people move from one stage to the next:

- For people in the precontemplation stage (those with no intention to change behavior in the foreseeable future: unaware of risk, will not acknowledge risk, or some other reason):
  - Enhance knowledge of and expectations about the consequences— good or bad—of the risk behavior

- Personalize the risk
- Emphasize the benefits of the new behavior and encourage a reevaluation of the costs and benefits (or outcome expectancies) that includes the new benefits.
- For people in the contemplation stage (those considering the need to change behavior but with no specific plan):
  - Encourage gaining experience with the new behavior (e.g., through trying the new behavior or trying to refrain from the risk behavior)
  - Continue promoting new expectations of positive consequences and reinforce existing positive expectations
  - Consider disputing commonly believed but untrue negative consequences and suggesting ways to minimize bona fide negative consequences, though it is typically easier to promote advantages than to challenge perceived disadvantages
  - Enhance self-efficacy by identifying how to overcome barriers to change effectively.
- For people in the preparation stage (those making the decision to change behavior):
  - Encourage people to restructure their environments—and instruct them on how to do so—so that important cues for practicing the new behavior are obvious and supported socially
  - Encourage people to identify and plan solutions to the relevant obstacles they are most likely to face
  - Help people to maintain their motivation by encouraging them to set a long-term goal and instructing them on appropriate ways to set short-term goals to keep them progressing to the long-term goal
  - Increase self-efficacy to cope with specific situations and other obstacles that people are likely to encounter in their change efforts
  - Model social reinforcement of appropriate behaviors.
- For people in action (those beginning to perform the behavior consistently):
  - Encourage refining skills, especially those that will help avoid relapse and that allow productive coping with setbacks to prevent full relapse
  - Bolster self-efficacy for dealing with new obstacles and setbacks in the behavior change process
  - Encourage people to feel good about themselves when they make progress, especially in the face of temptation
  - Make explicit or reiterate the long-term benefits of the behavior change.

Strategic Questions

Crafting a communication strategy should begin with collecting data to answer most or all of the questions shown in **Exhibit 9-1**. Much of this information would have been collected when the intervention's strategic plan was prepared. The answers to all the strategic questions must fit together; changing one answer often necessitates changing others. Each question is discussed in more detail below. As answers are developed, consideration should be given to the issues raised in the section "Message Content and Construction: Additional Factors to Consider" at the end of this chapter.

Who Is the Target Audience, and What Are They Like?

Although many public health agencies have a mandate to serve the public, decisions to target "the general population" do not make for good communications. As Sutton and colleagues (1995) noted, any communication will appeal to some groups more effectively than others, based on executional details (i.e., language used, type of people portrayed, color, music, etc.) if nothing else. It is a far better use of resources to take a proactive approach, carefully identifying the most appropriate audience(s) and then developing communications specifically to address their needs, perceptions, and values. For example, for initiatives seeking to bring about policy change, there are usually at least three audiences: policymakers, some segment of the public, and members of the media. Some public health initiatives may communicate with segments in each of the three audiences; others may restrict their efforts to one or two, depending on how the initiative is expected to work. The promotion strategy developed as part of the strategic plan should outline overall audiences, but additional segmentation may be required in some instances for communication efforts.

Once each audience has been identified, communication planners should get to know its members. Thinking of the audience as one person rather than as a group is useful and leads to more focused, relevant communications. One way to do this is to write a profile of the person

---

Exhibit 9-1 Questions to Guide Communication Strategy Development

- Who is the target audience, and what are they like?

- What action should they take—and what are they doing now?

- What barriers stand between the audience and the action?

- What is the benefit to the audience of engaging in the action?

- What is the support for that benefit, that is, what will make it credible to the audience?

- What are the best openings for reaching the audience, and are the channels available appropriate for conveying the message?

- What image should communications convey?

based on formative research. Some creative teams go as far as drawing a picture of a typical audience member. Demographic characteristics (age, marital status, presence of children, ethnicity, political leanings, etc.) are just a starting point. Understanding the person's values and possible motivating factors as well as his or her feelings, attitudes, and beliefs about the behavior change and its benefits and barriers is also important (Sutton et al., 1995).

What Action Should They Take, and What Are They Doing Now?

To persuade audience members to take a particular action, communication planners must understand exactly what they are willing and able to do. First, planners must know what people are doing now so they know what they want to change. The behavior analyses conducted as part of strategic planning may provide most of the needed information, though sometimes communication efforts focus on a more narrow audience or slice of time, and thus behavior analyses may need to be refined. For example, to increase child safety restraint usage, the initial action parents and caregivers were asked to take would be related to installing car seats properly with the challenging seat belt installation systems. Later, when new technology was available, the action might be modified, for example, to encourage parents and caregivers to use the new systems.

Selecting an action is a critical—and difficult—decision to make. Planners should avoid the trap of focusing on a very narrow audience and persuading them to make a complicated behavior change. This sometimes happens with individual health behaviors because there is usually a group of at-risk people far from the ideal behavior and, therefore, most in need of change. Often a better strategy—from the viewpoint of both communication success and change in health status—is to address the easier changes first. Targeting the group most willing or able to make the change often leads to two accomplishments. First, the population makes progress toward the public health objective. Second, as that group makes the change, members of it may begin communicating about it through their social networks, thereby directly encouraging adoption of the change by others and creating a climate in which others are more willing to (and indeed may feel pressure to) make changes.

What Barriers Stand Between the Audience and the Action?

This question is not explicitly addressed in many communication strategy frameworks (see, for example, Sutton et al., 1995; also see Roman, Maas, & Nisenholtz, 2003); however, knowing what real or perceived barriers stand in the way of taking action is an invaluable aid to developing communication strategies. Understanding barriers helps communication planners select an action audiences are most likely to take and determine what obstacles the communications need to help audiences overcome or circumvent. Barriers may be physical, social, or economic. The extent to which any given barrier may impede behavior change may change depending on whether a person is choosing a behavior right now or at some point in the future.

Planners can begin to understand obstacles by identifying how public health policies are currently being framed on the public agenda. This can be accomplished by analyzing media coverage of the issue and preparing a framing memo that outlines the various ways the issue has been positioned, or framed, by the media.

What Is the Benefit to the Audience of Engaging in the Action?

This is a crucial point and an area in which many communication planners make mistakes. The challenge is to promise a benefit that outweighs the costs the audience associates with the action and the benefits the audience might obtain from any alternative behavior. Immediate, high-probability benefits are most compelling, especially when they are connected to strong core values. In general, good health generally is neither an immediate, high-probability outcome nor a salient core value.

For example, from a public health standpoint, the major benefit of smoking cessation is decreased risk of developing heart disease, various cancers, and a host of other diseases. But from the standpoint of the person deciding whether to try to quit, "decreased risk" is not a guarantee that he or she will not develop these illnesses, and even if lack of illness were guaranteed, a change in health status would not occur in the near future. An immediate and, therefore, more highly valued benefit may be ceasing to cough in the morning or no longer smelling like smoke.

Identifying high-impact benefits also improves success when policymakers are the target audience. Policymakers may not be motivated by funding programs that mostly benefit the not politically powerful poor or by a possible improvement in the public's health that may not be realized for decades; however, they usually do want to be perceived as contributing to their community's or the nation's economic or physical security.

The challenge is to identify and focus on one key benefit from the myriad possibilities. Often, people have a number of motivations for engaging in a particular behavior, and understanding the needs and values underlying the current and desired behaviors is critical. The greatest need or strongest core value generally provides the most meaningful, compelling benefit. Identifying those basic values can be accomplished in a number of ways and can be incorporated into formative research. One approach is to ask qualitative research participants why particular attributes are important. Another approach that can be used in qualitative or quantitative settings is to ask participants to rate a set of adjectives in terms of how well each describes themselves and then to rate how well each describes people who engage in the desired behavior. What they do—and do not—put in each list speaks volumes about the values they are looking for, and associate, with each behavior. The Rokeach Value Survey (Rokeach, 1973) is an example of a scale often used to identify values important to a target audience segment. It is important to note that the benefit is "promised" in communications. Often, it is never explicitly stated. Rather, it is a conclusion that people draw after exposure to the communication. Sutton and colleagues (1995) recommended using the following sentence to link desired and current behavior with a benefit: "If I (action) instead of (current behavior), I will (benefit)."

For example, for the early 5 A Day media campaign the action–benefit statement was "If I add two servings of fruits and vegetables the easy way instead of making it hard, then I will feel relieved and more in control of my life" (Lefebvre et al., 1995; Sutton et al., 1995). An action–benefit statement for California's campaign against Proposition 188 (which would have repealed local antismoking ordinances) might have been "If I oppose Proposition 188 instead of supporting it, I will keep Philip Morris from exerting control over my state." This approach helps to position the new behavior as superior to the old by implicitly showing that maintaining the old behavior will conflict with the target audience's basic needs and desires.

What Is the Support for That Benefit, That Is, What Will Make It Credible to the Audience?

The support convinces the audience that the benefit outweighs the barriers. It can take many forms, such as hard data, demonstrations of how to perform the action, or demonstrations of the valued benefits to the action (e.g., a person feeling more in control after taking steps to improve eating habits). It can be emotional, factual, or both. Support is provided through aspects of the message's execution. The degree to which models are like target audience members and how they look, talk, dress, and behave, as well as music, colors, background, design, typeface, and paper stock, can all support or detract from the promised benefit (Sutton et al., 1995). In the terms of the action–benefit statement introduced above, support is the "because" (Sutton et al., 1995): "If I (action) instead of (current behavior), I will (benefit) because (support)."

Signorielli (1993) criticized the antidrug "just say no" campaign that ran in the United States in the 1980s, in part because it lacked support (p. 155):

> This campaign is problematic because it fails to take the basic principles of adolescent psychology and functioning into consideration. This campaign preaches and tells young people (and the rest of society for that matter) what to do. It does not provide information about why or even how teens, in the face of strong (or not so strong) peer pressure, can "just say no."

Public health communicators often are tempted to use scientific facts as support; however, they should do so with caution. Hard data can work, provided they are understandable, relevant, and believable to the target audience. However, practitioners should bear in mind that many members of the public place little credence in scientific data. They recall too many instances when those data later changed or were debunked by yet another new study. In addition, people often do not understand science, particularly intangible concepts such as relative risk, and so personal decisions may be based on faulty reasoning (National Cancer Institute, 1989). Furthermore, it can be difficult for hard data to compete with an emotional appeal to core human values. This problem is illustrated in the case study on affirmative action presented later in this chapter.

What Are the Best Openings for Reaching the Audience, and Are the Channels Available Appropriate for Conveying the Message?

First, planners must determine the times, places, and situations when the audience will be most attentive to, and able to act on, the message. Then they must assess (1) whether the message lends itself to delivery via the channels that can be used to reach that time and place and (2) whether the program can access or reasonably afford those channels.

For example, most mass media are best suited to providing simple information. With the exception of print media and some interactive Internet applications, they cannot be used effectively to convey complex information and cannot take the place of one-on-one education and monitoring. Used alone, they can induce behavior change only under limited circumstances. However, they can frame a public health issue, raise awareness of a behavior change, provide cost-effective support and reinforcement for the change, and stimulate discussions of more complex information in the appropriate setting. Bellicha and McGrath (1990) provided examples of how mass media can be put to effective use within a larger social change initiative. They discuss how mass media are used to help educate patients, health professionals, and the public about high blood pressure and cholesterol as part of efforts to reduce morbidity and mortality caused by heart disease.

Thorough target audience research is critical to identifying the best openings. The ideal opening allows the target audience to hear or see the message and immediately take action. Researchers should consider when a typical target audience member would be most receptive to and most able to act on messages about the behavior. Depending on the audience and the desired change, the best times may be parts of the day, week, or year. Alternatively, the best openings may occur at teachable moments when the target is thinking about the benefit.

Once planners identify the best openings, they must decide which channels to use. The best channels will reach these openings and deliver the message in the most compelling, understandable manner. **Figure 9-1** depicts this balancing act. In general, a combination of interpersonal and mass communication channels leads to a more effective campaign (Backer, Rogers, & Sopory, 1992).

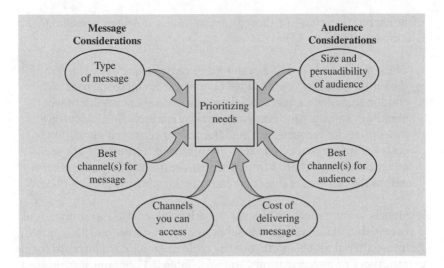

Figure 9-1 Balancing Message, Audience, and Resource Considerations to Select Channels

If there is a conflict between the best channels for the message and the best channels for the audience, the preferable resolution is to examine the message and see if it can be modified to suit the channels. Likewise, if there is a conflict between the channels that will best reach the audience and the channels an initiative can access, planners should look for another way to access the other channels, perhaps through a partner or intermediary.

What Image Should Communications Convey?
Image is often thought of as the personality of the communication and the action. Image is what makes the communication speak to the target audience. It is also critical to developing brand identity and relationships with audiences and so should be carefully selected and then remain stable over time. An audience member must believe that the communication—and by extension, the action—is designed for someone like them or like the person he or she wants to be. The goal is to portray the behavior as something target audience members can see themselves doing and something consistent with their core values. "All but the newest behaviors already have an image—a set of expectations and associated feelings among consumers. . . . Developing or changing an action's image involves creating a look and feel for the action that makes it accessible, inviting, distinctive, and compelling" (Sutton et al., 1995, p. 732).

The symbols, metaphors, and visuals linked to the behavior or positioning of an issue convey image, as do the types of actors, language, and/ or music used. Image taps into what has been termed *cultural code*, or *cultural frame of reference*—the associations, expectations, and strategies of interpretation that are shared throughout a culture (Hirschman & Thompson, 1997, p. 45):

> The cultural code provides a shared understanding of how to read the symbolic meaning embedded in mass media images. From early childhood, individuals are socialized into a deep knowledge of what meanings specific products embody. For example, in U.S. culture, pickup trucks are generally understood to represent rural, blue-collar transportation, whereas chauffeured limousines are seen as representing urban, affluent transportation. Most consumers within the culture are fluent in reading multiple forms of this code.

Hence, communicators can use a variety of symbols and images as a sort of shorthand and, as Hirschman and Thompson (1997) noted, "can use shared understanding of the code to entice consumers to form certain types of interpretations" (p. 45). **Table 9-1** contains a scale used in commercial marketing to discern and compare brand personalities—"the set of human values associated with a brand" (Aaker, 1997, p. 347).

Table 9-1 Brand Personality

Trait (item)	Facet	Dimension
Down-to-earth Family-oriented Small-town	Down-to-earth	Sincerity
Honest Sincere Real	Honest	
Wholesome Original	Wholesome	
Cheerful Sentimental Friendly	Cheerful	
Daring Trendy Exciting	Daring	Excitement
Spirited Cool Young	Spirited	
Imaginative Unique	Imaginative	

(continues)

Table 9-1 Brand Personality (continued)

Trait (item)	Facet	Dimension
Up-to-date Independent Contemporary	Up-to-date	
Reliable Hard-working Secure	Reliable	Competence
Intelligent Technical Corporate	Intelligent	
Successful Leader Confident	Successful	
Upper-class Glamorous Good-looking	Upper-class	Sophistication
Charming Feminine Smooth	Charming	
Outdoorsy Masculine Western	Outdoorsy	Ruggedness
Tough Rugged	Tough	

Source: From Aaker, J. (1997). Dimensions of brand personality. *Journal of Marketing Research, 34,* 354. © 1997 by the American Marketing Association. Reprinted with permission.

"The brand personality scale has five dimensions and 15 facets that encompass 42 items. Items are scored on 5-point Likert-type scales ranging from not at all descriptive (1) to extremely descriptive (5) for each brand rated. Item scores are summed within each dimension, and then divided by the number of items within a dimension, to form scores for each dimension that can theoretically range from 1 to 5" (Bearden & Netemeyer, 1999, p. 232).

The section "Using Branding Effectively" later in this chapter provides additional discussion relevant to communicating an image.

Symbols and metaphors are used extensively when public health issues are framed; identifying the exact symbols and images used to frame a public health issue is key to properly positioning the public health perspective. **Exhibit 9-2** illustrates how a framing memo can provide a useful framework to evaluate the metaphors, symbols, and images used to package the offer. Also, it can frame the benefits being offered to the target audience by proponents and opponents of a policy, the support used to back up the benefit, and the strength of the core values to which the promised benefit appeals.

Exhibit 9-2 Framing the Affirmative Action Debate

Background

Woodruff, Wallack, and Wallis prepared a framing memo to guide the development of more effective strategies for promoting affirmative action programs (Woodruff, Wallack, & Wallis, 1996). They used the Lexis/Nexis database to search nine major newspapers for mention of "affirmative action," "racial preference," "California Civil Rights Initiative," or "CCRI" in the first three paragraphs of articles. They identified 221 placements that included news articles, editorials, op-ed pieces, and letters to the editor. Each item was coded for its news type, subject matter, and position(s) on affirmative action. From the articles, the authors identified frames in support of and in opposition to affirmative action. They analyzed each frame for its core position, metaphor, symbols, catch phrases, images, and appeal to principle. The analysis revealed 11 distinct frames on the issue of affirmative action: 5 pro–affirmative action (**Table 9-2**) and 6 anti–affirmative action (**Table 9-3**).

Results

The analysis revealed that "those seeking to eliminate affirmative action have done an excellent job of using drama to capture and frame the news coverage. They are very adept at personalizing their argument by putting a face on it. A highly qualified young white girl is turned away from a selective public high school; her father leaves a prestigious law practice to seek justice for her. This is the stuff of high news drama" (Woodruff, Wallack, & Wallis, 1996, p. 11). In contrast, "the pro–affirmative action groups have simply not yet captured the necessary drama to put forth their argument. The benefits of affirmative action tend to be framed not in personal but in social terms, which don't have the same impact. The gentle, gradual progress toward a more just society does not pack the dramatic wallop of a single sympathetic individual denied a deserved opportunity because of affirmative action" (p. 11). "Those supporting affirmative action have some difficulty in putting a face on the benefit. While there are some examples of a woman or person of color acknowledging that affirmative action policies opened a door and gave him or her a fair chance, in the world of aggressive American individualism this is not a very interesting argument. When government helps people, the story is less dramatic and compelling than when someone is shut out because of a government policy gone bad" (p. 12).

Use of Symbols and Images

Woodruff and colleagues found that both sides of the affirmative action debate effectively used symbols and images of the civil rights movement and appealed to the core values of "fairness, justice, equality, and protecting the American dream . . ." (p. 12). "However, evocative images of discrimination and civil rights are being used in opposition to affirmative action. These symbols resonate because most Americans support the concept of civil rights; it is a strongly held, shared value. . . . Proponents of affirmative action do not effectively highlight the fact that imagery of the civil rights movement is being applied to measures that could undo the gains of the past" (p. 12).

(continues)

Exhibit 9-2 Framing the Affirmative Action Debate (continued)

Woodruff and colleagues also found that proponents of affirmative action failed to invoke the most powerful image of civil justice: Dr. Martin Luther King and his "I have a dream" speech. On the contrary, anti–affirmative action groups adopted Dr. King's message as a call for a color-blind society and as an argument against affirmative action.

Perhaps more problematic, Woodruff and colleagues found that supporters of affirmative action were relying on communitarian rather than individual values, and communitarian values tend to be less salient and influential than individual values (p. 13):

> Many of the symbols used by the supporters of affirmative action tend to evoke idealistic values that put community above individuals. The call for "open doors" and a "level playing field," the description of affirmative action as "the medicine American must take for the ills of inequality," and the picture of a multicultural "rainbow community" where diverse groups get along: these images all appeal to a concept of the social good that simply may not resonate to the extent that the opposition messages does. On the other hand, the image of individual achievers in formerly white fields—female firefighters, black doctors—may appeal by putting a face on the successes of affirmative action.

Message Consistency and Types of Appeals

Two other conclusions of the framing memo were quite revealing. First, anti–affirmative action groups delivered a strong and consistent message by relying on a few simple and consistent arguments: 70% of the anti–affirmative action messages used were either content of one's character or reverse discrimination. In contrast, the pro–affirmative action groups used many different arguments. No single message accounted for more than 10% of all pro–affirmative action arguments used. The authors concluded that "this argumentative overkill by supporters of affirmative action may dissipate the power of these frames" (p. 13).

Second, the anti–affirmative action frames tended to use more emotional appeals, whereas the pro–affirmative action frames tended to rely more on facts. In other words, the support for the benefit promised by affirmative action groups tended to be scientific documentation, whereas the anti–affirmative action groups backed up their promised benefit with stronger and more compelling documentation: human emotion.

Based on their findings, Woodruff and colleagues offered six concrete suggestions to affirmative action advocates. They recommended that advocates (1) "simplify their arguments, focusing on one or two frames that are most likely to sway voters," (2) "create more dramatic stories that put faces on the success of affirmative action efforts," (3) "counter the 'reverse discrimination' theme by involving white males in message delivery," (4) "reclaim Dr. Martin Luther King Jr.'s language and other dramatic symbols of the civil rights movement," (5) "stress that quotas are already illegal and are not part of current affirmative action programs," and (6) "emphasize that measures like prop. 209 are radical approaches that go too far and would eliminate successful, worthwhile programs" (Woodruff, Wallack, & Wallis, 1996, pp. 14, 15).

Table 9-2 Pro–Affirmative Action Frames

Frame	Core Position	Symbol/Metaphor/Visual Image	Catch Phrases and Quotes	Source of Problem	Appeal to Principle
Keep the doors open	We must maintain gains of the civil rights and women's movements to keep opportunities available.	Level playing field Open doors CCRI is a "U-turn toward exclusion." Women in traditionally male jobs Minorities in professional positions Rights are "a valued heirloom women have fought for."	CCRI would take women back to a second-class status.... "We won't go back." "At PG&E, we don't have preferential treatment and never have. We don't have quotas and never have. But we do have affirmative action, that is, affirmatively reaching out and ensuring equal opportunity for everyone." "We should mend, not end, affirmative action."	White men trying to slam the door on further progress Fearful White men who are insecure	American Dream—the land of opportunity Maintain/protect civil rights gains
Necessary medicine	Affirmative action is a necessary remedy for historical and continuing discrimination.	Legacy of racism and slavery The symbols of continuing racism: Rodney King beating, power and wealth gulf, glass ceiling	"The reality is that without affirmative action, 230 years of official spoils system based on race, ethnicity, and the like will continue." "Prejudice against minorities and White women continues to be the single most important barrier to their advancement." "In order to treat some people equally, we must treat them differently."	Historical racism, sexism, and White male privilege Persistent inequality in housing, education, and jobs	Justice Correcting historical inequities

(continues)

Table 9-2 Pro–Affirmative Action Frames (continued)

Frame	Core Position	Symbol/Metaphor/Visual Image	Catch Phrases and Quotes	Source of Problem	Appeal to Principle
Political football	Anti-affirmative action forces are playing the politics of divisiveness.	Affirmative action as a wedge issue that divides Democrats. Building walls. Dirty politics. Playing the quota card. Political bargaining chip	"Anger has become the emotional gold of American politics."	Cynical, manipulative politicians	Common sense to see through political manipulation
Benefits of diversity	Affirmative action recognizes that the diverse community is of value to all. We must recognize a wider definition of "merit" than mere test scores.	Multicultural society richness of diverse experience	"Diversity is a 'compelling interest' of educational institutions." All students benefit from a diversity of experiences in the classroom. "The issue is not a person's race-based characteristics; it is experience. And any judge who thinks Black Americans have not had a different experience is blind."	Institutions not adequately responding to shift in demographics. Fear of difference. Failure to understand benefits of diversity	Value of inclusiveness. Difference as a strength rather than a weakness
Preference the privileged	Admissions and hiring processes are already full of preferences for privileged classes.	"Athletics is the largest preferential program in existence." Preferences extended to "musicians and cheerleaders, athletes of questionable academic potential and dull offspring of alumni." Back room admissions "Old boys'" network	"I needed all the help I could get. . . . I mean, this is America. It's not what you know. It's who you know." "Does it make sense to give consideration to an African American man to allow him to dribble a basketball but not to become a teacher or doctor?"	Rot at the top. Corruption, hypocrisy, influence peddling	Fairness. No special privilege for the rich. Equality

Source: Adapted with permission from *Framing Memo: The Affirmative Action Debate*, September 1996, Woodruff, Wallack, & Wallis, © 1996, The Advocacy Institute.

Note: This framing matrix model was adapted from Ryan (1991), following the work of Gamson and Lasch (1983) and Gamson and Modigliani (1989).

Table 9-3 Anti–Affirmative Action Frames

Frame	Core Position	Symbol/Metaphor/Visual Image	Catch Phrases and Quotes	Source of Problem	Appeal to Principle
Content of one's character	People should be judged on their character and merit, not the color of their skin or their gender.	MLK Jr. "I have a dream" speech Color-blind society	Treat people as individuals. "It's your ability that counts, not your disability." Reward merit, not skin color/gender.	Sense of group entitlement Lack of individual initiative	Equality Merit
Reverse discrimination	You can't solve discrimination with more discrimination. Affirmative action lowers standards by admitting the undeserving.	Color-blind constitution Qualified White males denied opportunities Level playing field Quotas	"Equal rights for all, special privileges for none." "Racial discrimination is not the way to end racial discrimination." Government-sponsored discrimination	Unconstitutional preferences Misguided overcompensation for past wrongs	Fairness
Hurts those it intends to help	Affirmative action is demeaning to minorities and women; people internalize low expectations.	The stigma of being an affirmative action recipient Affirmative action infantilizes/coddles minorities Affirmative action squelches ambition	It's wrong to have every single minority tarred with the notion that they're less qualified "Affirmative action is . . . instilling in (minorities) a permanent sense of dependency and inferiority." "You don't want people to think you only go in here because you're Black."	People live up—or down—to society's expectations. Reducing expectations squelches human potential.	Respect for all Equal expectations

(continues)

Table 9-3 Anti–Affirmative Action Frames (continued)

Frame	Core Position	Symbol/Metaphor/Visual Image	Catch Phrases and Quotes	Source of Problem	Appeal to Principle
No longer needed	Affirmative action is unnecessary because discrimination is no longer a barrier.	Connerly, Thomas, and others who overcame adversity and pulled themselves up by their bootstraps without affirmative action The playing field has been leveled.	"Legally sanctioned racism is a thing of the past." "Affirmative action is a strong-arm tactic that has outlived its time." "If I made it, anyone can."	Confusing real racism of the past with isolated slights of today	Work ethic Honor for the struggles of the past
Divides, doesn't unify	Affirmative action pits groups against each other and increases racial tension and divisiveness.	Affirmative action leads to the Balkanization of America around racial lines. Voluntary resegregation Black against White	"Americans pitted against Americans" Affirmative action "undermines tolerance and mutual respect."	Lack of primary identity as Americans	National unity Patriotism Community Cohesiveness
Wrong solution	Focusing on affirmative action diverts us from the real problem.	Affirmative action is compared to forced busing as a misguided policy. Racial numbers game	"Affirmative action is an obsession with racial balance as an end in itself." The affirmative action debate is an unfortunate "subterfuge" for a discussion about race, one that "demonizes" African American men, who have barely benefited from affirmative action programs.	Affirmative action distracts from more effective policies.	Courage and commitment to tackle the tough real issues

Source: Adapted with permission from *Framing Memo: The Affirmative Action Debate,* September 1996, Woodruff, Wallack, & Wallis, © 1996, The Advocacy Institute.

Note: This framing matrix model was adapted from Ryan (1991), following the work of Gamson and Lasch (1983) and Gamson & Modigliani (1989).

Process for Communication Strategy Development

The following provides a systematic way planners can go about developing the communication strategy and obtaining buy-in from key stakeholders at the same time:

1. Develop preliminary answers to the communication strategy questions using the information gathered for the situation analysis. For public health policy initiatives, the framing memo is a key part of developing a preliminary strategy.

2. Convene a workshop of experts on the public health issue (often internal and external to the sponsoring organization) and expert communication practitioners. There should be no more than about 10 people total, including internal and external people. During the workshop, work through the strategic questions and determine what additional information is needed to develop answers that work together.

3. Obtain additional information needed by locating additional sources of secondary research and/or conducting primary research.

4. Revise the answers to the strategic questions based on research results.

5. Reconvene the group to review the answers. This is best done interactively and, ideally, in person.

6. Develop *message concepts* based on the communication strategy. A message is the thought or belief audience members should have after they have been exposed to communications, either through the mass media or directly from materials or events. Messages should stimulate action; for example, an audience member should change his or her mind, vote a different way, or substitute one behavior for another as a result of the message. A message is different from a slogan, a theme line, or a sound bite; each of these is a way of packaging a message to make it accessible to the audience.

7. Share the message concepts with target audience members to explore whether the positioning is relevant, appealing, and motivating to them. Message concepts are often explored using qualitative research techniques, which provide an opportunity to gather insights into all aspects of the communication strategy. In some situations, message concepts can then be tested through quantitative techniques, such as a public opinion poll.

8. Revise the communication strategy, if needed, based on the research results.

9. Prepare a creative brief, a one- or two-page summary of the communication strategy that is given to the creative team to use for guidance when developing the program materials. (See **Exhibit 9-3** for a sample creative brief for the 5 A Day for Better Health media campaign.)

Exhibit 9-3 Creative Brief for the 5 A Day for Better Health Media Campaign

Target Audience

People increasing their fruit and vegetable consumption but eating less than the minimum of five or more servings each day (particularly people currently eating two to three servings). Audience members tend to be 25- to 55-year-olds who lead busy, hectic lives and are strongly motivated by the need to be in control. They are anxiety ridden about nutrition but do not feel urgency to eat healthier. They believe fruits and vegetables taste good and know they should eat more but believe doing so is not easy because preparation takes time and they don't think about it. They lack the knowledge and skills to fit in more services.

Action

Add two or more servings of fruits and vegetables a day "the easy way" instead of making it hard.

Benefit

I will feel more relieved and in control of my life.

Supports

- Illustrations of how fruits and vegetables can fit into busy lives.
- A great number of studies have shown that a diet rich in fruits and vegetables has a protective effect against cancer.
- Fruits and vegetables taste great.
- People keep hearing the phrase "5 A Day for Better Health."
- This information is coming from the National Cancer Institute, a credible source of health information.

Openings

- Times when people are preparing shopping lists or shopping, choosing foods at a restaurant or take-out, or are in transition between activities.
- Places such as the dinner table; by the TV; in stores or restaurants; in the car, train, or bus; and in the kitchen.
- Situations when people are hungry, thinking about what to eat, starting to relax, and/or reflecting on their day or planning for tomorrow.

Image

People who eat five servings of fruit and vegetables each day can be responsible, balanced, and warm.

Source: Data from the National Cancer Institute. (1993). 5 A Day for Better Health. Data from Sutton, S.M., Balch, G.I., & Lefebvre, R.C. (1995). Strategic questions for consumer-based health communications. *Public Health Reports.* 110, 725–733.

The creative brief should be used by anyone developing promotional materials for the initiative to ensure that every communication reflects the strategy. For example, if the program goal is to increase mammography rates among older women, program components may include both outreach to women and physician education materials. Individuals developing the physician materials should refer to the creative brief, identify the strategies that work best for persuading women to get mammograms, and incorporate those strategies into the physician materials.

Some organizations prepare longer documents that summarize the communication strategy but also provide the rationale for the communication effort and include more detail on target audience research and specific message points. These documents are useful for partner organizations and coalition members; they provide insights about communicating with the target audience, and they extend the reach of the sponsoring organization by providing an opportunity for others to develop materials using the same communication strategy. **Exhibit 9-4** summarizes some potential problems that might arise when developing communication strategies.

■ MESSAGE CONTENT AND CONSTRUCTION: ADDITIONAL FACTORS TO CONSIDER

Constructing health messages is a complex art. The final message a target audience member receives is a combination of the communication strategy, how the message is executed in the materials, and how it is processed by the receiver. In this section, we discuss some of the common types of message appeals used in health communications and provide some insights into how to increase the amount of attention people pay to messages.

Exhibit 9-4 Pitfalls to Avoid When Developing Communication Strategies

- Focusing on very small audiences
- Targeting too many or too diverse audiences
- Including multiple actions or framing an issue multiple ways rather than focusing on one
- Focusing on a long-term benefit when a short-term benefit is more compelling
- Focusing on public health benefits when personal benefits are more compelling
- Appealing to noncritical values (e.g., good health) rather than core values (freedom, autonomy, control, independence)
- Supporting the message with facts alone when an emotional appeal would be more compelling
- Using mass media to convey complex messages
- Developing strategies for different audiences that conflict or send mixed messages

Common Types of Appeals

Traditionally, messages have been divided into rational and emotional appeals. Using a rational argument to convey a message is said to be using a rational appeal. In contrast, emotional or affective appeals are those that attempt to elicit some emotional response—feeling good, laughter, fear, and so on—from the message receiver. As Monahan (1995) noted, some "analyses find most messages utilize, or at least are perceived by audiences as utilizing, both rational and affective appeals" (Stewart & Furse, 1986, p. 83). In fact, most commercial messages probably do contain both types of appeals, because marketers have learned that people make decisions for emotional reasons but want rational justifications for those decisions.

Rational approaches can be further divided into one-sided and two-sided messages. One-sided messages usually present a major benefit but do not directly address any major drawbacks. Two-sided messages address both drawbacks and benefits. Kotler and Roberto (1989) noted that each type of message is appropriate for different audiences: "Studies have identified that one-sided messages appear to work best with people who are already favorably predisposed to an idea or practice and who have a low level of education but that two-sided messages work best when people are not predisposed to the product and have a higher level of education" (p. 196).

Emotional appeals can be positive or negative. In general, positive appeals are considered to be more effective. Backer and colleagues (1992) concluded that campaigns that emphasize positive behavior change and/or current rewards are more effective than those that emphasize negative consequences of current behavior or avoiding future negative consequences. Behavioral economics provides some insights into why this happens based on how people value short-term versus long-term costs and benefits and how these values change depending on the temporal proximity of taking the action. In commercial advertising, positive emotional appeals are most often used for a simple reason: "Research consistently shows advertisements that arouse positive emotions result in more positive feelings toward the product and greater intent to comply with the message" (Monahan, 1995, pp. 81–82, citing Thorson & Friestad, 1989, as an example).

Positive Emotional Appeals

Monahan (1995) divided positive emotional appeals into two types: emotional benefit and positive heuristic appeals. Emotional benefit appeals combine emotional and rational appeals to portray the benefits the message recipients will reap by complying with the message. Positive heuristic appeals try to make recipients feel good about the product through executional detail rather than describing the benefits they could derive from complying with the message.

In general, public health communicators will find that emotional benefit appeals are more useful than rational appeals. Monahan (1995) recommended using such appeals in the form of comparisons, demonstrations, satisfaction, and testimonials when the audience is unfamiliar with an issue, and she noted that emotional benefit appeals are an excellent strategy when the audience is undecided or confused. She also noted that positive appeals can help reframe an issue. She recommended stressing positive rather than negative outcomes and control rather than helplessness as a way to increase compliance.

Monahan (1995) recommended using positive heuristic appeals when message recipients are familiar with an issue or campaign; however, few public health interventions reach audience members with enough frequency to assume they attain sufficient familiarity. Finally, Monahan cautioned against using positive heuristic appeals in an attempt to change strongly held negative attitudes.

Threat (Fear) Appeals

Public health campaign planners are often tempted to use fear appeals to scare the audience into changing their behavior. There is enormous debate among practitioners and scholars about whether, and under what circumstances, this type of negative appeal is effective.

A number of researchers suggested that part of the reason for the apparently conflicting evidence about effectiveness is in the definition of a fear appeal and that these types of appeals might better be called threat appeals (Donovan & Henley, 1997; Hale & Dillard, 1995; LaTour & Rotfeld, 1997; Strong, Anderson, & Dubas, 1993). LaTour and Rotfeld (1997) discussed the distinction between threats and fear: "Threats illustrate undesirable consequences from certain behaviors, such as car damage, injury, or death from unsafe driving, or bad health, illness, or cancer from cigarette smoking. However, fear is an emotional response to threats, and different people fear different things" (p. 45).

They further explained: "A threat is an appeal to fear, a communication stimulus that *attempts* to evoke a fear response by showing some type of outcome that the audience (it is hoped) wants to avoid. Fear is an actual emotional response that can impel changes in attitude or behavior intentions (e.g., toward auto safety issues or toward the energy crisis) and consumer actions (e.g., cessation of cigarette smoking or more careful driving habits)" (LaTour & Rotfeld, 1997, p. 46, emphasis in original). They noted that some threat appeals (i.e., appeals intended to arouse fear) may in fact arouse other emotions in some audience members.

There are three main independent variables to consider when developing or assessing fear appeals (Witte & Allen, 2000):

- Fear, which as noted above is an emotional response
- Perceived threat, which has two dimensions:
  - Perceived susceptibility: the degree to which one feels at risk of experiencing the threat
  - Perceived severity: magnitude of harm expected from the threat

- Perceived efficacy, which also has two dimensions:
  - Perceived self-efficacy: one's confidence in one's ability to take the recommended action
  - Perceived response efficacy: one's belief that the recommended action will in fact avert the threat

Successful appeals to fear communicate both a severe threat and high efficacy (Hale & Dillard, 1995; Witte & Allen, 2000).

Decisions to use a threat appeal should be considered carefully, and the appeal should be tested thoroughly before implementation. Hastings and MacFadyen (2002) argued that, at a minimum, using fear appeals can negate an initiative's ability to build a relationship with the audience and therefore may not be a good solution over the longer term. In their meta-analysis of fear appeals, Witte and Allen (2000) noted that "much more information is needed on how people process fear appeals, as well as what triggers danger control and fear control responses" (p. 604). Witte and Allen (2000) recommended the following regarding practitioners:

1. Increase references to the severity of the threat and the target population's susceptibility to the threat.
2. Create messages that make a health threat appear serious and likely to happen to increase motivation (i.e., strong severity and susceptibility messages).
3. Pair strong fear appeals with equally strong efficacy messages. Strong efficacy messages make the target audience believe:
   a. They are able to perform the recommended response (i.e., strong self-efficacy). To increase self-efficacy, identify barriers (lack of skills, costs, beliefs, emotions, etc.) that inhibit the audience's perceived ability to perform the action, and directly address these barriers in messages.
   b. That the recommended responses will work in averting or minimizing a threat. Clearly outline how, why, and when a recommended response eliminates or decreases the health threat.
4. Do not address individual differences, such as personality traits or demographic characteristics, in communications because they do not appear to influence processing of fear messages.
5. Assess danger control responses (attitude, intention, and behavior changes) and fear control responses (denial, defensive avoidance, and reactance) in evaluation. If a campaign fails, this assessment can determine whether the campaign simply had no effect (in which case perceptions of threat may need to be increased to motivate action) or whether it contained insufficient efficacy messages and thus activated fear control responses rather than danger control responses.

Common wisdom is that death threat appeals are ineffective in young people, particularly young men, because they feel immortal. However, Henley and Donovan (2003) exposed smokers in two age groups (16–25 and 40–50) to one of two messages about emphysema, either a premature death message or a disablement message. Finding that younger smokers responded equally to both messages and expressed a higher level of response than older adults to both, they concluded that death threats can be effective with young people and they do not feel immortal. They also found that women in the older age group responded significantly more to non–death threats than did men in that age group. They concluded that "death is not invariably the most effective threat. Non–death threats can be at least as effective for most people and apparently more effective for some" (Henley & Donovan, 2003, p. 12).

Humorous Appeals

Humor is another popular emotional approach that must be used carefully. If used, humor should convey the main message; otherwise, people are likely to remember the humor and forget the message. "If you can remove your product, but the joke remains intact, chances are that it has nothing to do with the key benefit" (Roman et al., 2003, p. 104). The advertising literature is littered with examples of very funny, entertaining ads that did not sell products. Kotler and Roberto (1989) offered several guidelines for using humorous appeals. They noted that humor is most appropriate for simple messages, humorous appeals cannot be used repeatedly or they will become more irritating than effective, and humorous messages have a greater impact when other communications on the topic are not humorous.

Breaking Through Inattention

Parrott (1995) laid out a number of content and linguistic factors that can increase the attention people give to health messages, based on Louis and Sutton's (1991) model of "switching cognitive gears." The following recommendations for marketers are based on Parrott's analysis:

- Use novel messages, settings, and media to increase chance of success. For example, rather than producing a skin cancer brochure that begins with a standard factual approach, such as, "Know the signs of cancer," marketers should try a positive emotional appeal, such as, "Safeguard your health by knowing the signs of skin cancer." Alternatively, they can explicitly state a motive to pay attention: "You can avoid a serious health problem by knowing the following signs of skin cancer so you can detect any unusual skin conditions." Another possibility is to invoke a sense of personal responsibility: "You can help friends and family detect skin cancer early by knowing the following signs." (Examples are modifications of Parrott's.)

- Present unexpected content or present it in an unexpected place. New recommendations, particularly if they run contrary to past recommendations, are one form of unexpected content. Parrott's example is the recommendation to stay out of the sun, when for years sunlight was promoted as health enhancing. An unexpected place can be anywhere people do not expect to receive health messages.
- Instruct the audience to pay more attention by using phrases such as "Now hear this" or, less directly, "Is everyone listening for information about . . . ?"
- Use language that conveys immediacy and personal relevance:
  - Use "your" rather than third person or passive constructions
  - Use "this," "these," and "here" rather than their more spatially distance counterparts "that," "those," and "there"
  - Use active, present-tense verbs
  - Avoid qualifiers (e.g., perhaps, may, maybe, possible, it could be, it might be).

Using Branding Effectively

Many public health practitioners shy away from learning about brand management, believing it is too commercial and that using it is likely to result in public criticism. Another misconception is that branding is not relevant to an industry that is often marketing a product category (e.g., fruits and vegetables, whole-grain or low-fat foods, public health) rather than a specific brand within the category or a behavior not tied to any particular good or service (e.g., physical activity, not driving drunk).

However, branding has much to offer public health practitioners. At its most basic, branding taps the cultural code to communicate meaning and value. Consistent use of the same carefully constructed brand identity allows an organization to build a relationship with its audiences through the characters and stories that are part of that shared cultural code. Building a brand can help create more effective communications, differentiate product offerings, and build relationships with target audiences—all of which are arguably more important to public health initiatives than commercial groups, given the small size of their budgets.

Public health practitioners can think about the product offering in terms of archetypes that reflect core values and fulfill core needs. Archetypes are forms or images of a collective nature that occur practically all over the earth (Mark & Pearson, 2001). Mark and Pearson (2001) presented a system for "finding the right stories" for commercial brands through the use of archetypes; **Table 9-4** presents some of their examples. (Our apologies to readers outside the United States who may be unfamiliar with some of the brands mentioned.) **Table 9-5** illustrates

Table 9-4 Archetypes and Their Primary Functions in People's Lives

Archetype	Helps People	Brand Example
Creator	Craft something new	Williams-Sonoma
Caregiver	Care for others	AT&T (Ma Bell)
Ruler	Exert control	American Express
Jester	Have a good time	Miller Lite
Regular guy/gal	Be okay just as they are	Wendy's
Lover	Find and give love	Hallmark
Hero	Act courageously	Nike
Outlaw	Break the rules	Harley-Davidson
Magician	Effect transformation	Calgon
Innocent	Retain or renew faith	Ivory
Explorer	Maintain independence	Levi's
Sage	Understand their world	Oprah's Book Club

Source: From Mark and Pearson (2001). Reprinted with permission of The McGraw-Hill Companies. Copyright © 2001 by Margaret Mark and Carol S. Pearson.

Table 9-5 Archetypes and Motivation

	Motivation			
	Stability & Control	Belonging & Enjoyment	Risk & Mastery	Independence & Fulfillment
	Creator	Jester	Hero	Innocent
	Caregiver	Regular guy/gal	Outlaw	Explorer
	Ruler	Lover	Magician	Sage
Customer Fear	Financial ruin, ill health, selling out, chaos	Exile, orphaning, uncontrolled powerlessness, engulfment	Ineffectuality	Entrapment, impotence, abandonment, emptiness
Helps People	Feel safe	Have love/ community	Achieve	Find happiness

Source: From Mark and Pearson (2001). Reprinted with permission of The McGraw-Hill Companies. Copyright © 2001 by Margaret Mark and Carol S. Pearson.

how archetypes "mediate between products and customer motivation by providing an intangible experience of meaning" (Mark & Pearson, 2001, p. 17). Identifying a target audience's concerns and values and then thinking about them in terms of the archetypes can provide insight into an appropriate image and identity to communicate.

Archetypes can also be useful in helping practitioners understand and position against a behavior or organization's competition. In formative research, audience members can be given brief descriptions of each archetype and asked which best characterizes the people who engage in each behavior or, for organizations, the archetype that best characterizes each organization or type of organization.

Importance of Core Values

Perhaps the most important step in designing an effective public health campaign is to ensure that all elements of the campaign's communication are tightly wrapped around one or two salient and compelling core values that are deeply held by the target audience. The core values form the basis or cornerstone for the entire communication. The more strongly held the core value, the more effective the communication is likely to be.

Some examples of compelling core values that are deeply held by the public are freedom, independence, autonomy, control, acceptance, justice, rights, and fairness (**Table 9-6**). Health itself is not a particularly strong core value. One of the most common flaws in public health interventions is that they tend to rely on health, a weaker core value, rather than on stronger core values such as freedom or independence. In contrast, successful commercial marketers almost always rely on the strongest core values.

For example, Nike's "Just Do It" campaign has little to do with the quality of the athletic shoes it sells. Instead, the communication

---

Table 9-6 Examples of Strong Core Values

Freedom
Independence
Autonomy
Control
Acceptance
Fairness
Justice
Individual rights
Security
Money
Sex
Youthfulness
Strength/vitality
Hope

campaign is based on the core value of control. The Marlboro advertising campaign relies on core values of freedom, independence, control, and rugged individualism, all represented perfectly the by Marlboro cowboy.

Public health practitioners need to find ways to craft their communication campaigns around the most compelling core values. This often means rejecting messages that are based on promises of improved health and, instead, using messages that promise to fulfill people's more basic aspirations, such as their desire for freedom, autonomy, and control over their lives. By reframing health issues in this way, public health practitioners can ensure that the core values underlying their campaigns are strong enough to uphold the entire communication strategy.

■ CONCLUSION

Crafting a solid communication strategy is critical to framing messages and positioning a social change. The strategy describes the target audience, the action they should take, and how they will benefit from it. In addition, the strategy details how to reach audience members—the times, places, and situations in which they are receptive and the image to use so they identify the message as relevant to them. The strategy should be based on a theory or model of how change is expected to occur.

Developing a solid communication strategy is an iterative process involving extensive formative research. Two of the most difficult decisions involve selecting the action that audience members should take as a result of the communication and determining the benefit to promise them for doing so. Knowing what will resonate with the audience is crucial to crafting persuasive messages. Asking and answering strategic questions can help planners create a communication strategy that is focused, believable, and compelling to the target audience.

Another decision planners must make involves selecting the appeals that will work best in a given situation. Different types of rational and emotional appeals can be used to create behavior changes; however, marketers must weigh the appeals' strengths and weaknesses when choosing an approach. Branding strategies can also help practitioners identify the best emotion to convey or elicit and can convey meaning and build relationships with audiences by using symbols, images, and metaphors from a shared cultural code. Finally, marketers should carefully consider the language they will use. Language that conveys immediacy and personal relevance can help increase the amount of attention paid to the message. Presenting a novel message in unusual or unexpected settings also is effective.

References

Aaker, J. (1997). Dimensions of brand personality. *Journal of Marketing Research, 34,* 354.

Backer, T.E., Rogers, E.M., & Sopory, P. (1992). *Designing health communication campaigns: What works?* Thousand Oaks, CA: Sage.

Bearden, W.O., & Netemeyer, R.G. (1999). *Handbook of marketing scales* (2nd ed.). Thousand Oaks, CA: Sage.

Bellicha, T., & McGrath, J. (1990). Mass media approaches to reducing cardiovascular disease risk. *Public Health Reports, 105*(3), 245–252.

Donovan, R.J., & Henley, N. (1997). Negative outcomes, threats and threat appeals: Widening the conceptual framework for the study of fear and other emotions in social marketing communications. *Social Marketing Quarterly, 4,* 56–67.

Gamson, W.A., & Lasch, K.E. (1983). The political culture of social welfare policy (pp. 397–415). In Spiro, S.E. & Yuchtman-Yaar, E., eds. *Evaluating the welfare state: Social and political perspectives.* New York: Academic Press.

Gamson, W.A., & Modigliani, A. (1989). Media discourse and public opinion on nuclear power: A constructionist approach. *American Journal of Sociology, 95*(1), 1–37.

Hale, J.L., & Dillard, J.P. (1995). Fear appeals in health promotion campaigns: too much, too little, or just right? In E. Maibach & R.L. Parrott (Eds.), *Designing health messages: Approaches from communication theory and public health practice* (pp. 65–80). Thousand Oaks, CA: Sage.

Hastings, G., & MacFadyen, L. (2002). The limitations of fear messages. *Tobacco Control,* 11, 73–75.

Henley, N., & Donovan, R.J. (2003). Young people's response to death threat appeals: Do they really feel immortal? *Health Education Research, 18*(1), 1–14.

Hirschman, E.C., & Thompson, C.J. (1997). Why media matter: Toward a richer understanding of consumers' relationships with advertising and mass media. *Journal of Advertising, 26*(1), 43–60.

Kotler, P., & Roberto, E.L. (1989). *Social marketing: Strategies for changing public behavior.* New York, NY: Free Press.

LaTour, M.S., & Rotfeld, H.J. (1997). There are threats and (maybe) fear-caused arousal: Theory and confusions of appeals to fear and fear arousal itself. *Journal of Advertising, 26*(3), 45–58.

Lefebvre, R.C., Doner, L.D., Johnston, C., Loughrey, K., Balch, G., & Sutton, S.M. (1995). Use of database marketing and consumer-based health communications in message design: An example from the Office of Cancer Communications' "5 A Day for Better Health" program. In E. Maibach & R.L. Parrott (Eds.), *Designing health messages: Approaches from communication theory and public health practice* (pp. 217–246). Thousand Oaks, CA: Sage.

Louis, M.R., & Sutton, R.I. (1991). Switching cognitive gears: From habits of mind to active thinking. *Human Relations, 44,* 55–76.

Maibach, E.W., & Cotton, D. (1995). Moving people to behavior change: A staged social cognitive approach in message design. In E. Maibach &

R.L. Parott (Eds.), *Designing health messages: Approaches from communication theory and public health practice* (pp. 41–64). Thousand Oaks, CA: Sage.

Mark, M., & Pearson, C.S. (2001). *The hero and the outlaw: Building extraordinary brands through the power of archetypes.* New York, NY: McGraw-Hill.

Monahan, J.L. (1995). Using positive affect when designing health messages. In E. Maibach & R.L. Parrott (Eds.), *Designing health messages: Approaches from communication theory and public health practice* (pp. 81–98). Thousand Oaks, CA: Sage.

National Cancer Institute. (1989). *Making health communication programs work: A planner's guide* (NIH Pub. No. 89-1493). Bethesda, MD: Author.

Parrott, R.L. (1995). Motivations to attend to health messages: Presentation of content and linguistic considerations. In E. Maibach & R.L. Parrott (Eds.), *Designing health messages: Approaches from communication theory and public health practice* (pp. 7–23). Thousand Oaks, CA: Sage.

Rokeach, M. (1973). *The nature of human values.* New York, NY: Free Press.

Roman, K., Maas, J., & Nisenholtz, M. (2003). *How to advertise* (3rd ed.). New York, NY: St. Martin's Press.

Ryan, C. (1991). *Prime time activism: Media strategies for grassroots organizing.* Boston: South End Press.

Signorielli, N. (1993). *Mass media images and impact on health: A sourcebook.* Westport, CT: Greenwood Press.

Stewart, D.W., & Furse, D.H. (1986). *Effective television advertising: A study of 1,000 commercials.* Lexington, MA: Lexington Books.

Strong, J.T., Anderson, R.E., & Dubas, K.M. (1993). Marketing threat appeals: A conceptual framework and implications for practitioners. *Journal of Managerial Issues, 5,* 532–546.

Sutton, S.M., Balch, G.I., & Lefebvre, R.C. (1995). Strategic questions for consumer-based health communications. *Public Health Reports, 110,* 725–733.

Thorson, E., & Friestad, M. (1989). The effects of emotion on episodic memory for television commercials. In P. Cafferata & A. Tybout (Eds.), *Cognitive and affective responses in advertising* (pp. 305–326). Lexington, MA: Lexington Books.

Witte, K., & Allen, M. (2000). A meta-analysis of fear appeals: Implications for effective public health campaigns. *Health Education & Behavior, 27*(5), 591–615.

Woodruff, K., Wallack, L., & Wallis, K. (1996). The affirmative action debate. Framing memo for The Certain Trumpet program. Washington, DC: The Advocacy Institute.

CHAPTER

10

Promotional Materials and Activities

Most—possibly all—efforts to change individual health behaviors, implement public health policies, or increase support for public health as an institution include promotional materials and activities. To communicate the strategic positioning and a common identity, all such activities and materials should build on and reinforce each other and help build relationships with target audience members.

Once a strategic plan has been developed, the materials and activities most suited for effective implementation are chosen and developed. They should be easily used or adapted by partners or intermediaries and provide maximum progress toward achieving objectives for the resources invested. All these components should communicate the initiative's core positioning and reflect its identity or brand. In this chapter, we focus on some of the most common promotional venues: mass media, meetings and conferences, special events, print materials, websites, and social media. Entire books have been written on how to develop and implement many of the tactics discussed here. This chapter merely provides an introduction to some of the practical issues involved with designing and using each type of tactic and some suggestions for assessing potential materials and activities in terms of their utility, cost, and contribution to the initiative's objectives.

■ ESTABLISHING IDENTITY

A consistent identity helps build recognition and relationships between target audiences and products, services, social change efforts, or public health institutions. Branding techniques can be used to develop this identity. To craft promotional materials and activities that convey a common identity and build on each other, the creative team can develop a set of visual and aural standards to be used on all materials. These standards typically include the following:

- Campaign or program names, logos, and theme lines, and details about where and how they will be used
- Two or three basic colors that are used on websites and all materials—from press releases, packaging, and advertisements to t-shirts, sides of trucks, office or event signs, and so forth
- Three or four typefaces as well as formats and layout elements for websites, other electronic communications, and printed documents (and paper stocks for the latter)
- Music, if many audio/visual products are produced

Standards of this sort are particularly helpful in situations where many organizations may be developing campaign components as part of an alliance or coalition or when promotions must be developed very quickly in response to competing information (such as in the heat of a legislative or referendum battle). Establishing standards also streamlines the review process by confining it to the content and unique elements of each new item. Those working under tight time deadlines or in committee situations appreciate the ability to avoid making decisions about typefaces, color, and logo placement each time a new material is presented. In addition, providing creative teams or graphic artists with the standards can help control costs by avoiding situations where they have to start over because the initial concepts were inconsistent with other materials or with the program's image. Large organizations may have existing standards (particularly relating to websites or print reproduction costs) that may apply to the initiative.

■ PLANNING DEVELOPMENT TIME

Campaign planners are often unrealistic about the amount of time required to develop, test, and produce the many elements that comprise a multifaceted promotional effort. Planners who recognize the sheer number of steps needed as part of a promotional effort are more likely to have reasonable timelines and, therefore, to complete the steps. Most commonly, planners will complete the following steps:

1. Determine types and quantities of materials to be developed based on the audience, the message, the desired reach and frequency, and the amount of time the campaign is expected to last. Determine how each material will be distributed. For websites, determine the number and complexity of the pages and whether they will form a new site or be added to an existing one.

2. Develop initial concepts (designs and copy points) for each material. For short materials, such as posters or advertisements, often two or three potential concepts are developed.
3. Prepare prototypes.
4. Pretest and submit the prototypes for peer or professional review.
5. Revise designs and copy to incorporate pretest recommendations.
6. Obtain commitments from directors, talent, photographers, and so forth. If existing artwork, audio, or video material will be incorporated, obtain necessary permissions and releases.
7. Prepare and submit an approval and/or clearance package that includes all necessary forms, pretest results, and revised prototype materials; revise the designs and copy to address the clearance comments.
8. Obtain final preproduction approval.
9. Produce rough cuts of audio and video materials and camera-ready versions of print materials; obtain approvals. For websites, develop all content and layouts and thoroughly test the site to make sure all links work properly.
10. Make final edits and obtain final approval.
11. Oversee production of the quantities required.

■ ASSESSING PROPOSED MATERIALS AND ACTIVITIES

Planners and organizers should ask themselves the following questions to assess the utility of any proposed material or activity:

- Is the approach and content accurate and consistent with the communication strategy? It is good practice to check all materials and activities before production to ensure they contain the appropriate messages, speak to the audience, communicate a relevant and appealing identity, and are delivered through openings likely to reach audience members. When materials undergo extensive edits before production, accuracy or identity sometimes slips away.
- Is this the best solution for the least cost? Public health efforts often have minuscule amounts of funding, so every material and every activity needs to work hard.
- Does it complement and reinforce other aspects of the social change effort? Materials and activities that reinforce each other in tone, look, and content are more effective because each additional time an audience member is reached, the new contact can build on the identity established before.
- Is it easily reproducible and customizable by partners or collaborating organizations? Considering customization and reproduction costs

when materials and activities are designed makes it more likely that the final products can be used as intended. For example, if it is likely that intermediaries will photocopy a brochure or classroom materials, printing in dark inks on a standard paper size ensures that copies will be readable. Allowing for customization can increase use of an initiative's materials and enhance their credibility with intended target audiences.

Subsequent sections of this chapter present issues to consider for specific types of materials and activities.

■ MASS MEDIA

Public health initiatives can use mass communication tactics in a variety of ways. Perhaps most important, mass media can frame public discussion of an issue in terms of core values. They can also be used to increase knowledge, promote specific behaviors, provide sources of tangible goods or direct service delivery, and repeat and reinforce the messages target audience members receive in other forums.

Campaigns that are more effective use multiple media to deliver a single focused message multiple times (Backer, Rogers, & Sopory, 1992; Hornik, 1997, 2002). Planners of public health initiatives can use news coverage, advertisements, entertainment programming, or a combination of all three to reach their audiences through the mass media. The mix appropriate for a particular initiative depends on many factors: program goals, communication objectives, the media environment, competition, and available resources all play a part. **Table 10-1** describes some of the major characteristics of mass media channels and the Internet.

Role of Mass Media

The mass media, including newspapers, magazines, television, radio, and the Internet, influence what and how the public thinks. The media agenda plays a powerful role in setting the public agenda (people's perceptions of what issues are important) and the policy agenda (priorities of legislators, other government officials, and policy influencers such as political parties, lobbyists, think tanks, etc.).

Research on the media's influence on what the public thinks began in earnest with McCombs and Shaw's (1972) landmark study of the media's role in the 1968 presidential election. They calculated the media agenda by analyzing the content of the main mass media reporting on the election and measured the public agenda by surveying undecided voters—and found an almost perfect correlation in the rankings of issues on the media agenda and the public agenda.

The mass media can influence how the public thinks about issues by the way in which they frame their coverage. Andreasen noted, "Different framing results not only in different interpretations of data but in the ranking of social problems and in the solutions proposed for problems we might care about. Simple labels for social problems can have powerful impacts on the debate about solutions" (2006, p. 47). His examples included U.S. debates over gun control versus gun safety and "a woman's right to choose" versus "protecting the rights of the unborn."

The attributes of an issue that are emphasized in media coverage can have a demonstrable impact on public opinion and behavior. McCombs and Shaw (1993) observed that "even when multiple attributes of an issue are included on the news agenda, there is likely to be a perceptible set of priorities" (p. 63). As the authors noted, many studies have demonstrated that this set of priorities is communicated to the public and reflected in what they deem to be important. These media and public agendas can in turn put pressure on the policy agenda (Andreasen, 2006).

Wallack and colleagues (Wallack & Dorfman, 1996; Wallack et al., 1993) argued that the media tend to frame health issues in terms of individual health behaviors. Part of the job of social change initiatives is to work to reframe these issues in terms of public policy. Part of the reason the public—and policymakers—tend to be complacent about health issues is likely that the media, when they portray health problems at all, do not portray them as threatening strong core values like freedom, independence, autonomy, and control.

It is difficult to measure exactly how much the media influence people's perceptions of a given issue; many variables undoubtedly come into play. Some evidence suggests that the media influence perceptions more when alternative sources of information are not available. For example, a 1975 study by Tipton, Haney, and Baseheart found that agenda setting is less likely to occur in local than in national campaigns, whereas in 1977, Palmgreen and Clarke reported that less agenda setting occurs when members of the public interact on local issues. Nonetheless, the combination of the inaccurate way in which media (particularly television) portray health behaviors and issues coupled with the media's ability to set the public's agenda by what is or is not covered (and how it is covered) means mass media can play an important role in many social change efforts.

Editorial Coverage

In this text, *editorial coverage* refers to any content appearing in traditional media (newspaper, magazine, radio, or television) or on a news organization's website that is not an advertisement and, for television and radio, not an entertainment program. Editorial coverage includes all the content under the control of an editor, such as news and feature stories, columns, editorials, op-ed pieces, and letters to the editor.

Table 10-1 Characteristics of Mass Media Channels and the Internet

	Television	Radio	Magazines	Newspapers	Out-of-Home	Internet
Reach	Potentially largest, but audiences are increasingly fragmented.	Various formats offer potential for audience targeting.	Can target specific audience segments; audiences are increasingly fragmented.	Can reach broad audiences rapidly. Daily readership in decline. (Sunday readership growing.)	Can target specific neighborhoods; can achieve high frequency with one placement.	Offers many opportunities for targeting.
Openings for messages (other than ads)	News and talk shows; entertainment programming.	News and talk shows; disk jockey chatter; letters to editor.	Feature stories; regular columns; letters to editor.	News stories; feature stories; regular columns.	—	Websites; list servers; chat rooms; blogs; emerging formats.
Use of public service announcements (PSAs)	Deregulation ended government oversight of PSA use and public affairs content; weak requirements for "educational" broadcast stations.	Deregulation ended government oversight of PSA use and public affairs content.	No requirements for public service/public affairs use; PSAs more difficult to place than on TV or content on radio.	No requirements for use; few larger papers use PSAs.	No requirements for use; limited PSA space available.	No requirements for use; PSA space available on some sites.
Appropriate messages	Primarily short and simple; viewers usually can't refer back to message.	Primarily short and simple; listeners can't refer back to message.	Can be short and simple or can provide more detail on complex health issues and behaviors.	Can be short and simple or can provide more detail on complex health issues and behaviors.	Outdoor: very short, simple. Inside trains and buses: can provide more detail.	Ranges from short and simple to detailed information on complex health behaviors.

(continues)

Table 10-1 Characteristics of Mass Media Channels and the Internet (continued)

	Television	Radio	Magazines	Newspapers	Out-of-Home	Internet
Characteristics of medium	Visual and audio make emotional appeals powerful. Easier to demonstrate a behavior.	Opportunity for direct audience involvement via call-in shows.	Audience can clip, reread, and contemplate material and share it with others.	Can convey health news/breakthroughs more thoroughly than radio and faster than magazines.	Frequent viewership; retain control of TV message content.	Permits instantaneous updating; can retain control of message content.
Type of audience interaction	Mostly passive; active possible with call-in shows.	Generally passive; active interaction possible with call-in shows. Requires attention when aired.	Permits active consultation. May pass on. Read at reader's convenience.	Same as magazines but short life limits rereading and sharing with others.	Passive; attention may be fragmented or complete.	Permits active interaction; audience can easily search out additional information.
Production costs	Ads and video news releases are expensive.	Live copy: very inexpensive. Produced spots: much cheaper than TV.	Ads are inexpensive. Distribution is inexpensive.	Ads are inexpensive.	Costs are higher than with print.	Depends on site design.
Editorial placement issues	Requires contacts and may be time-consuming.	Feature placement requires contacts and may be time-consuming.	Long lead time; relatively little control of timing (often determined by editorial calendar).	Newsworthiness is needed for news coverage; little control over timing of feature.	—	Varies by format.

Source: Some information adapted from *Making Health Communication Programs Work,* National Cancer Institute, 1989.

Many mass communication specialists believe an advantage of embedding messages within editorial content (e.g., in a news story) is that these messages are perceived by target audience members as credible, especially in comparison with messages delivered through advertising. The major drawback of editorial coverage is the loss of control over message content. A few stations and publications will run a news release or suggested story exactly as written, but reporters often alter the material as they see fit. Key messages can easily become distorted or lost in this process. Another shortcoming of using editorial coverage is the loss of control over reach and frequency. To obtain news coverage of an initiative, planners must understand how to (1) build relationships with members of the media, (2) determine newsworthiness, (3) frame a topic, (4) attract news coverage, and (5) find coverage opportunities in each medium.

Building Relationships with the Media

The first step in effectively using the mass media is building relationships with the reporters, editors, and producers who determine what stories get covered. Many people are understandably uneasy about interacting with members of the media, but learning how to do so can facilitate accomplishment of an initiative's goals. Some organizations have separate press offices or public information departments that can provide support. This office may not be able to handle all media relations needs because of other responsibilities or limited experience in "pitching" the media (trying to get them to cover a particular story).

Reading current newspapers, magazines, and websites or watching and listening to recent news shows can give planners a sense of what is covered, how it is covered, and who is covering it. A number of media directories can help identify media to target. In addition to listing reporter and editor names and contact information, the directories provide statistics on circulation and audience size, information on the editorial profiles of publications and programs, editorial calendars, and types of press materials accepted.

Once the media list is developed, planners can send a package introducing themselves, describing their initiatives, and emphasizing the initiatives' relevance to the community (or region or nation, as appropriate). One of the goals of building relationships with reporters and producers is for planners to position themselves as important, reliable sources of information so reporters will call them when they are running a story on that topic. When reporters call or e-mail, it is important to understand the parameters within which they work, particularly as follows:

- *Planners must be ready.* Frame the topic and have short, pithy "sound bites" developed to support this positioning.
- *Planners must be sensitive to deadlines.* If reporters want additional information, ask what their deadline is and then make sure to get them whatever they need before then.

- *Planners must be available.* Make a list of who can talk to the press, and make sure someone on that list is always available—and that everyone else in the office knows who those people are and how to reach them.
- *Planners must be aware of the "rules" of talking to reporters.* With some reporters, it is possible to go "off the record" (i.e., say something that cannot be published or cannot be attributed to a specific source), but it is wise to do so only after establishing trust with the reporter.

Determining Newsworthiness

To gain coverage of a social change initiative, it is important for planners to understand the goals of journalists, producers, and editors. In general, they want to appeal to the broadest audience possible, and they want to tell a story that is novel, timely, relevant, and compelling. Television producers need a visual aspect to the story as well.

The following quote from an interview with Edwin Chen, at the time a science writer for the *Los Angeles Times*, on the role he has played in health communication campaigns illustrates the journalist's perspective:

> The U.S. surgeon general might say that smoking is bad or eating fatty food is detrimental for health, and heart disease prevention might be featured in a campaign by a government agency. But the *L.A. Times* does not see itself involved as a partner with, or part of, such education campaigns for health. The job of the *L.A. Times* is to cover the news. The newspaper might handle campaign press releases and promotional materials or report on the statements of different media campaign officials as long as such material is considered *newsworthy* . . .
>
> Editorial decisions are made to do certain stories, projects, or a series about some specific issue. . . . For example, the paper might write news stories on how to lose weight or measures to reduce the likelihood of AIDS transmission, but it does not see itself as part of a campaign to combat AIDS or other health problems. . . . The newspaper also seeks to inform its readers about what the government and government officials, other agencies, and concerned people are doing or not doing in combating AIDS or other health issues. (As cited in Backer et al., 1992, p. 58, emphasis in original)

Exhibit 10-1 lists some common questions journalists may ask themselves to determine whether a story is newsworthy.

Framing a Topic

As Wallack and colleagues (1993) noted, "media attention on health tends to be framed in terms of personal, individual issues that revolve

---

Exhibit 10-1 Elements of Newsworthy Stories

- Breakthrough: What is new or different about this story?

- Controversy: Are there adversaries or other tensions in this story?

- Injustice: Are there basic inequalities or unfair circumstances?

- Irony: What is ironic, unusual, or inconsistent about this story?

- Local peg: Why is this story important or meaningful to local residents?

- Personal angle: Who is the face of the victim in this story? Who has the authentic voice on the issue?

- Celebrity: Is there a celebrity already involved with or willing to lend his or her name to the issue?

- Milestone: Is this story an important historical marker?

- Anniversary: Can this story be associated with a local, national, or topical historical event?

- Seasonal: Can this story be attached to a holiday or seasonal event?

Source: Wallack et al. (1993). © 1993 by Sage Publications, Inc. Reprinted by permission of Sage Publications, Inc.

---

around life-style, disease, and medical breakthroughs" (p. 56). Journalists often frame their stories from the vantage point of the individual's plight. Wallack and colleagues argued that this perspective creates problems when the goal is to stimulate policy changes, because it leads to an emphasis on what individuals should do to avoid a problem rather than a discussion of changes that need to be made to address the underlying social or environmental conditions. One of the examples they cited is a crime story that focuses on what individuals can do to improve their safety (in reaction to a woman being kidnapped, raped, and murdered) rather than on what could be changed to improve the safety of the environment (e.g., better lighting, more security). Planners can reframe the content of coverage so it better addresses the social issues rather than personal problems.

One approach that public health practitioners can take is to sponsor a study that frames the issue in a striking way. The Center for Science in the Public Interest (CSPI) has mastered this technique. Its studies often generate enormous media coverage and stimulate product changes by creating news that applies pressure to business leaders. For example, CSPI commissioned an analysis comparing the nutrient content of movie popcorn to fast food and ice cream (Hurley & Liebman, 2009). This study illustrated the key components of CSPI's approach: frame a critically important public health issue (the fat content of the American diet) in terms of a product many people use (broad appeal), at least some of whom probably select it because it is supposed to be "healthier" (irony and loss of control). In addition, CSPI presented the nutritional information as a comparison with commonly consumed foods rather than as a technical construct (e.g., percentage of calories from fat or grams of fat).

The latter part of the CSPI approach is something referred to as *social facts* or *social math*—the art of making numbers, especially large numbers, meaningful. Social math can be a valuable tool. It can help persuade a journalist to cover a story by increasing the perceived news value or providing a new angle, and it can make the story more compelling. Wallack and colleagues (1993), citing Petschuk and Wilbur, described three approaches to making large numbers meaningful: localization, relativity, and effects of public policy. Localization involves taking a large national number (e.g., tobacco causes 400,000 deaths in the United States each year) and applying it to a particular state or community. Relativity is what the members can easily identify. A variation is to make numbers smaller and more familiar. "You might want to remember that $1 billion a year translates into roughly $2.7 million per day, $114,000 per hour, and $1,900 per minute" (Wallack et al., 1993, p. 109).

Attracting News Coverage
Promoters of public health initiatives, issues, policies, and institutions can choose from a range of tactics to generate news coverage and influence how an issue or topic is framed on the public agenda. News releases, press kits, press conferences, and media tours are some of the most common. Regardless of the tactics used, promoters must be able to summarize their issues using compelling sound bites, "short, concise summaries of your issue or position that can be conveyed in a few sentences or less than 10 seconds" (Wallack et al., 1993, p. 112).

News Releases
The heart of many efforts to gain editorial coverage is the news release. A health organization might issue news releases to announce a variety of newsworthy topics, such as the availability or implementation of infection control measures during a disease outbreak, the release of new study results, the opening of a new facility, or an upcoming special event. News releases also provide an opportunity to communicate and reinforce an organization's identity through the consistent use of a tagline or descriptive statement.

Traditional written press releases are inexpensive and can be distributed to all types of media; audio and video news releases are more expensive to produce—especially video news releases—but can provide the interviews and sound bites (and, for television, video footage) that radio and television producers need to put together a story.

Written press releases should use the inverted-pyramid structure that journalists normally use: Who, what, where, when, why, and how should be covered, with the most important information at the beginning of the story, followed by progressively less important information. With this structure, it is more likely that reporters will cover the important details as they may not have time to read the complete release.

As with any communication, press releases can help—or hinder—efforts to build a relationship with a particular reporter. By carefully identifying the reporters who cover a particular topic and e-mailing the press release only to them, an organization gives credit to those reporters. When possible, planners should follow up with a short phone call referring to the reporter's recent coverage and explaining why they thought he or she might be interested in this story.

Audio or video news releases are typically about 90 to 120 seconds long and designed as stand-alone news stories, conforming to the broadcast news style conventions of each medium. They frequently include an interview with someone authoritative, such as a physician or researcher, and often a target audience member as well. Video news releases can also include footage of the initiative "in action," for example, shots of a new clinic department or an event that took place as part of the initiative.

There are a host of technical factors to consider when designing and producing broadcast news releases; the help of a producer skilled in broadcast news production is a must. Before distribution, video news releases can be encoded with an electronic marker so their use can be tracked and their reach and frequency estimated.

Press Kits

The content and format of a press kit are determined in part by how it will be used. It can be simple or elaborate. If a press kit is distributed in conjunction with or immediately after an event, the kit will generally include the event agenda, a press release, background information on the program, relevant photos, audio, or video, and (if applicable) speaker biographies. If the kit is sent separate from any event, it often includes a news release or cover letter, sample story ideas, and artwork or photographs (or b-roll for television producers).

For print and Internet media, quizzes and "top 10" lists can communicate key messages in a format many editors like and are disinclined to alter. Startling or unusual data presented in a graphically interesting fashion are also useful. Some editors like to include mentions of materials their readers can order or links to websites with more information.

Press Conferences

Press conferences are usually convened to announce a new initiative or plans for managing a disease outbreak or other public health crisis; to unveil study findings or a new product, service, or treatment; or to discuss the availability—or lack thereof—of a product, service, or treatment. Press conferences can be useful for framing an issue through media coverage. However, they have some potential drawbacks. Most notably, there is a very real risk that no (or few) members of the media will attend—either because they do not consider the issue newsworthy or because some other breaking news story is more important.

If a press conference is held, it should be limited to 30 minutes, be in a location easily accessible to the media, and should include visuals and handouts. Speakers should be the highest-level, most visible individuals available. To attract television coverage, the conference needs to include something visually interesting. Providing footage (b-roll) of activities relevant to the press conference can also help increase television coverage.

Demonstrations are another means of attracting the press. They can take many forms. For example, Wallack and colleagues (1993) discussed how tobacco-control advocates used an embargo on Chilean grapes to gain access to the media. The grapes were embargoed after cyanide was found on them. At press conferences, advocates stacked several bushels of grapes next to a pack of cigarettes to illustrate the quantity of grapes needed to equal the cyanide in one pack of cigarettes and the difference in government policy on fruit versus cigarettes.

Media Tours

An alternative to a press conference is sending spokespeople on a virtual or real media tour by scheduling interviews with news outlets at predetermined times. Interviews with print and radio reporters can take place over the phone; television interviews can be conducted via satellite uplinks from a local television studio, hotel conference room, convention center, or other location.

Finding Coverage Opportunities in Each Medium

Traditional media such as print, radio, and television as well as nontraditional media all structure their news coverage somewhat differently and hence provide opportunities for different types of coverage. The following sections introduce some of the characteristics to weigh as tactics are planned.

Print

Newspapers and magazines (both online and hard copy formats) typically offer three main ways of reaching target audience members (other than through advertising): news coverage, a feature story, or a letter to the editor. Newspapers also offer the op-ed (opposite the editorial page) option. Beyond these basic similarities, each medium differs in terms of lead times, ratio of news stories to feature stories, and geographic area of interest. For the most part, newspaper reporters write tomorrow's story today, and with the exception of some special feature sections, newspapers contain mostly news. In contrast, reporters and editors at monthly magazines may start writing stories for July in January, February, or March, according to a predetermined editorial calendar. The news-to-feature ratios and closing deadlines of weekly news magazines (e.g., *Time, Newsweek, U.S. News and World Report*) fall between these extremes.

In newspapers, news coverage is often considered the most desirable because people, especially policymakers, tend to read the news section more than other sections of the paper. Health-related feature stories often appear in the lifestyle or health sections, although there are times when newspapers run feature stories that take more of a social justice perspective in the news section. Letters to the editor and op-ed pieces are useful because the writer retains control over the message and op-ed pieces are widely read by policymakers. However, these items often run in response to previous coverage of a specific issue. Wallack and colleagues (1993) recommended meeting with the newspaper's editorial board as an important way to ensure that the paper at least considers the perspective of the initiative. They noted that sometimes such meetings can result in an editorial in support of an initiative's position; at other times, such a meeting may at least moderate the newspaper's criticism of the position.

Radio

Many practitioners believe radio is underused by social change initiatives (Backer et al., 1992; Wallack et al., 1993). Radio coverage of an initiative can include news programs, call-in shows, a station's special promotion, or entertainment-education programming. News coverage often results from a written press release or media tour; sometimes audio news releases are used. Some initiatives make their experts available for interviews by station reporters during specific times, often in conjunction with an event.

Call-in shows are a chance to hear community reactions to a proposed social change but also provide an opportunity for callers (or the host of the show) to disseminate messages that are decidedly off strategy. Before attempting to place a speaker on a call-in show or accepting an invitation to appear, practitioners should listen to a few shows to get a sense of the host and the audience.

Television

Television provides a number of openings to reach audiences with social change messages: news programs, talk shows, and entertainment programming. (Entertainment programming is discussed in more detail below, under in the "Entertainment-Education.") For local television news, there is intense competition for high ratings in most markets; therefore, producers generally select stories they believe will be most shocking or intriguing when used on news promos throughout the day. Because television "wraps every story in pictures" (Wallack et al., 1993, p. 56) and news segments are short, stories must be visually striking and simple.

Television talk shows run the gamut from completely news-oriented to completely entertainment-oriented programs. Morning talk shows can provide a forum to frame an issue or raise awareness of an upcoming special event. Appearing on talk shows requires contact with the producer, a celebrity spokesperson, or a very newsworthy development coupled with an articulate, photogenic expert. Luck is also a factor: The segment will get bumped if a story comes along that the producers believe is more likely to attract viewers.

Nontraditional Media

Local print and e-mail newsletters are among the most commonly used nontraditional media. They can reach some target audiences through unexpected channels:

- *Employer newsletters*: Some large employers publish periodic newsletters (in print or electronically) that may include a health or wellness column.
- *Bulletins and newsletters produced by churches and other religious institutions, community groups, and civic and homeowners' associations*: Although these are unlikely to include a health/wellness column, they might mention an upcoming event in which members could participate (e.g., immunization or screening drive).
- *School system and parent-teacher organization newsletters*: Many schools distribute electronic or print newsletters to parents periodically and might include upcoming public health activities that would benefit parents (and especially children). Some also regularly include health and wellness information.

Entertainment-Education

Entertainment-education is the process of embedding social change messages in entertainment media (i.e., movies, television programs other than news, some radio programs, books, novellas, comic books, interactive games). It is sometimes called "edutainment" or "infotainment." Backer and colleagues (1992) noted that effective campaigns use educational messages in entertainment contexts.

There are a number of reasons to include entertainment-education as part of a social change effort. First, the media can influence people's perceptions of reality, and the entertainment media may not accurately depict health issues without input from public health practitioners. Second, it is important to reach audience members multiple times through multiple channels—and entertainment vehicles are additional channels and a means of reaching people who might not pay attention to a health program or product. Third, the audience may already have a "relationship" with the television series into which health stories are being integrated; therefore, sensitive topics can be addressed more quickly as the trust does not need to be newly developed.

A report by the Henry J. Kaiser Family Foundation (2004) provides examples of how the entertainment-education approach has been used:

- The Harvard Alcohol Project's National Designated Driver Campaign helped to incorporate the concept of "designated driver" into more than 160 prime-time television storylines from 1988 to 1992.
- The UCLA School of Public Health along with the California Department of Health Services worked to increase awareness about the importance of immunizations by integrating stories about vaccines into more than a dozen television shows from 1996 to 1998.
- The Robert Wood Johnson Foundation established the Last Acts Writers Project to provide experts on end-of-life care and terminal illness to television and movie writers and producers to improve the accuracy in the ways in which these issues are portrayed.

The entertainment-education approach can involve developing custom products or working with others who develop programming and materials to incorporate health messages. In the United States, developing custom print and Internet products may be helpful to many initiatives, particularly for some audiences (e.g., comic books or a comic strip format for young people, novellas when working with Latin American audiences, websites). For television, working with producers and writers of existing programming generally is the most useful and cost-efficient approach for most initiatives.

Entertainment-education approaches can support a social change effort in many different ways:

- Model skills and appropriate behaviors. Simple behaviors can be portrayed, such as wearing seat belts, making healthful food choices, engaging in physical activity, taking blood pressure medication, or scheduling a mammogram. More complex skills can be illustrated, such as the negotiation or refusal skills needed to manage sexual encounters.
- Educate about realistic consequences of health-related actions and medical conditions. For example, incorporate concern about becoming pregnant or contracting HIV in storylines that include unprotected sexual encounters or add characters with chronic conditions such as asthma or more serious illnesses such as breast cancer.
- Influence social norms by highlighting appropriate behavior, commenting on unacceptable behavior, or portraying a range of acceptable options, especially if some of them are likely to be new to the audience.

When approaching writers or producers with suggested storylines, planners should consider the constraints under which they work. First, the ideas have to be consistent with the work's storyline and characters. For example, two episodes of "ER" dealt with the emotional and medical needs of a character who was dying—a natural outgrowth of the existing storyline that furthered the Robert Wood Johnson Foundation's goal of changing expectations about the kind of care seriously ill patients should receive by increasing their knowledge of the possibilities (Bronner, 2003). Second, producers of commercial programming are unlikely to highlight any behavior that will make advertisers unhappy. The Harvard Alcohol Project managed this constraint by addressing drunk driving, not alcohol consumption per se (Backer et al., 1992).

Advertising

Compared with editorial placement efforts, advertising allows total control over message content and can include very effective emotional appeals. It can be used by a social change initiative in many ways, ranging from helping to frame an issue to modeling simple behaviors. However, the brief and fleeting nature of many advertisements (e.g., 30-second television and radio spots) makes them best suited for reminders or simple messages that require little context or explanation. Only print and some out-of-home advertising provide the space to develop ideas in greater detail.

> Advertising is not generally the powerful force in moving consumers to act as many people think it is. Rather, it is a subtle force that must be skillfully planned and carefully deployed to maximize its effectiveness. (Tellis, 2004, pp. 16–17)

Characteristics of Effective Advertising

In an extensive review of more than 50 years of advertising research, Tellis (2004) identified characteristics of effective advertising. Novelty—in message, media, target segment, and product—is more likely to result in increased sales than increasing media weight (e.g., running new advertisements, running them in different media, or targeting a new audience is more likely to increase sales than is spending more on advertising in a particular time period). Emotional appeals are more likely to be effective than arguments (using evidence or force of logic) or endorsements (perhaps because emotional appeals are more interesting and thus can more easily cut through clutter and grab attention, because they require less concentration, and/or because they are more vivid and better remembered). In the same review, Tellis (2004) reported the following:

• Advertising is a subtle force and its effects are not entirely instantaneous (either because consumers take time to think about the ad and become convinced, because they are convinced only after discussing it with someone else, and/or because they may not make the purchase until they are out of stock or feel the need for the product), though carryover effects are generally short, due to noise from competing ads, poor attention to ads, and competition from newer messages.

- Advertising is more effective for new than for mature products.
- Advertising affects loyal users and nonusers differently (loyal users need relatively low levels of advertising for brands to which they are loyal and become saturated with repetitive advertising sooner than nonusers; in contrast, nonusers are more likely to be affected by heavy repetition).
- Advertising is effective early or never: If effects are not seen in the first few weeks, the campaign is likely to be ineffective.
- Ads reach their peak effectiveness almost immediately and wear out rapidly, perhaps in 6 to 12 weeks, although wear-out may take longer if an ad is complex, uses an emotional appeal, or is run less frequently.

These findings resulted primarily from the study of consumer packaged-good advertising; however, they are relevant for those developing and monitoring advertising campaigns to support policy or individual behavior changes. One thing planners should consider is the need to change target audience segments, media choices, and creative executions frequently. In addition, planners must identify their target audience as either familiar or unfamiliar with the policy or behavior because this determines the appropriate level of advertising (media weight). Finally, they must be flexible: Desired effects may not occur instantly, but if they are not observed within a few weeks, they are unlikely to occur and the advertising may need to be changed.

Basic Principles of Advertising

Some basic principles can be used to guide the development of all advertising, regardless of medium and whether placement will be paid or provided as a public service:

- Advertising messages should be consistent across media and consistent with messages delivered through other channels.
- The goal of advertising should be to sell, not entertain. There is no correlation between entertainment value and sales (Roman & Maas, 1992).
- Advertisements should focus on the benefit the audience will receive, not the product, service, behavior, or sponsoring organization.
- Messages that involve threat appeals or scare tactics are more likely to work with some audiences than others, must provide a resolution the audience believes they can perform that eliminates or substantially minimizes the threat, and must be carefully tested before use. Planners should resist the temptation to scare the audience into performing the desired behavior.

- Humor can work but should be used carefully. It can relax an audience and make them receptive to a message, distract them from counterarguing, and help attract and retain attention to the ad (Tellis, 2004). Humor should deliver the key benefit; otherwise, people may remember the joke but forget the action they are being asked to take. In addition, humorous commercials wear out fast, so planners will need more spots than with other approaches (Roman, Maas, & Nisenholtz, 2003).

- Celebrity spokespeople should be used with care; generally, it is not a good idea to build an entire campaign around a particular celebrity. Celebrities can be effective if target audience members believe their involvement is authentic, the topic has personal relevance to them (e.g., they actually have the health condition or truly believe the social change is important), and they are not just doing it because they are getting paid for it. For campaigns relying on donated airtime, celebrity involvement can increase airplay. However, celebrities can also overwhelm the message (people remember them but forget the product or service being advertised). Equally important, celebrities can do something embarrassing to the organization, such as hawking an "unhealthy" product or getting arrested.

Suggestions for Assessing Advertisements

One's initial reaction to a message is a good first step in assessing an advertisement and determining if it is on strategy. The following questions may help planners examine specific aspects of any ad:

1. "Is the key consumer benefit the central and most compelling idea . . . ?" (Roman et al., 2003, p. 94).
2. Is the ad focused and single-minded?
3. Does the ad reflect the organization's strategic positioning and desired image?
4. Does the ad capture the audience's attention early?
5. Is the dramatic approach best for the communication objective? There are four major dramatic approaches (Roman et al., 2003):
   a. Demonstrations can model a skill or show a product/service/behavior advantage.
   b. Testimonials or endorsements from ordinary people, experts, or celebrities can help make a claim believable and are particularly useful when an advantage cannot be visualized.
   c. Slice-of-life involves actors telling a story, such as setting up a problem for which the product, service, or behavior is the solution.
   d. Animation can be especially effective when talking to children but also can be a solution to other problems, such as simplifying

complex ideas (often in demonstrations) or treating abstract (or even distasteful) subjects.

6. Do the executional details—clothing, jewelry, music, regional accents, props, sets, and so on—convey the image outlined in the communication strategy?

Table 10-2 presents suggestions for assessing advertisements in specific media. It incorporates ideas from Roman and colleagues (2003), who cover each medium in considerably more detail. As advertising researchers have noted, "the relative success of an advertisement depends not only on the rational merits of the message being promoted, but also on how well it appropriates desirable mass media images, styles, and cultural icons to its promotional purposes" (Hirschman & Thompson, 1997, p. 44, citing Jhally, 1987; McCracken, 1989; Scott, 1990; Sherry, 1987).

Paid Versus Public Service Placement

Generally, it is not a wise use of resources to spend substantial chunks of a budget to produce advertisements but then rely on donated time and space to run them. Most organizations obtain much greater reach and frequency with their target audiences—and progress toward communication objectives—by paying for placement. "The fact that some people refer to PSAs as 'people sound asleep' instead of 'public service announcements' reflects the concern that they will not be very effective" (Kotler, Roberto, & Lee, 2002, p. 312).

Practitioners can increase the affordability of paid advertising placement in a number of ways:

- Develop fewer ads or use media with lower production or placement costs. The cost of placing advertising varies enormously by medium: Television is most expensive, and radio, newspapers, and the Internet are least expensive. Within a medium, cost varies widely depending on various factors (e.g., how many people are reached by a particular channel and who is reached—some target audiences are more desirable and thus advertisers are willing to pay more to reach them). If practitioners are considering the use of advertising but are unfamiliar with placement costs, they might consider inviting a media planner from a local advertising agency to speak.

- Explore media or corporate partners. By cultivating a partnership, an organization can negotiate specific placement in exchange for the partner's exclusive right to sponsor the media component—and garner broader coverage because the media outlet will involve itself in other ways, such as sponsoring contests. Corporate partners can donate some of the advertising space they buy. Because they buy specific spaces (particular television shows, particular times of day on radio, and

Table 10-2 Suggestions for Assessing Advertisements for Various Media

	Radio	Television	Magazines/ Newspapers	Out-of-Home	Internet
Description	Prerecorded spots or announcer-read scripts of 15, 30, or 60 seconds; 60-second lengths most commonly sold in the United States.	Prerecorded spots of 15, 30, or 60 seconds; 30-second spots are most common in the United States.	Can range in size from multiple pages to a single page, half-page, quarter-page, or smaller.	"Outdoor" encompasses billboards, posters, dioramas, train stations, exteriors of buses and other vehicles, and so on. "Indoor" includes interiors of buses and trains, grocery carts, bathroom stalls, and so on.	Banner ads, pop-ups, text presence on relevant search engine listings.
How to Assess	Play it in your car so you evaluate it the way listeners are likely to hear it.	Look at the pictures first: Do they tell the story? Typically, a storyboard is reviewed first; it looks like a comic strip, with each frame illustrating the action and a written description of what the viewer will see and hear underneath.	Ask to see the ad pasted in a likely editorial environment.	If an ad will be seen in motion, look at it quickly, then look away or put it down.	On a website, as it will appear.

(continues)

Table 10-2 Suggestions for Assessing Advertisements for Various Media (continued)

	Radio	Television	Magazines/Newspapers	Out-of-Home	Internet
Look for . . . (in addition to the list provided in the text)	Engaging the listener by using voices and sound to evoke pictures.	Something that grabs viewers' attention within the first 5–10 seconds.	The message in the headline or visual, ideally in both.	Outdoor ads need to communicate one very simple message instantly—people are moving when they see them. Copy should be seven words or less.	See "magazines/newspapers."
	A focus on one idea; radio listeners have too many distractions to grasp or remember more.	A key visual or one frame that sums up the message.	Whether the reader can "get" the message from the headline alone; often it is all that is read. "Every headline has one job: it must stop the reader with a believable promise" (Roman & Maas, 1992, p. 45).	Indoor ads provide the opportunity for more complex messages and can include tear-off pads to deliver coupons, messages, or "send for more information" request forms.	If animation is used, is it just to get attention or does it help tell the story? "You cannot annoy the consumer into buying your product or service" (Roman et al., 2003).
	Conveying to target audience members why the ad is for them early on.	Communicating the message through both senses—sight and hearing.	Visuals are often the most important part of the ad.		When the consumer clicks on the ad, does the page that loads deliver on the ad's promise?
		60-second ads should not add points; they should tell the same story as 30s but with more time, detail, and repetition.	Photos usually are more compelling than artwork, and fewer is better; many small pictures lead to cluttered layouts.		
			Appropriate copy length depends on the message		

(continues)

Table 10-2 Suggestions for Assessing Advertisements for Various Media (continued)

	Radio	Television	Magazines/Newspapers	Out-of-Home	Internet
Look for . . . (in addition to the list provided in the text)			and layout; some very successful ads have a lot of copy.		
Consider . . .	Radio commercials are inexpensive, quick to produce, and underused in health initiatives. Radio is a very targeted medium; there are more than 140 radio formats (all news, all talk, many kinds of music, etc.) in the United States. Different versions of a spot may need to be made—with different background music or other changes—for different formats.	TV commercials are the most complicated and expensive to produce—and hardest to assess prior to production.	Investing in an advertising copywriter. Writing print ads requires special expertise that other writers are unlikely to have. Whether the ad will be reproduced in a range of sizes and paper stocks. What looks good and readable on a full page—or on glossy paper—may be lost if the ad is reduced or printed on newsprint. Design ads that will work everywhere or re-design for different environments. For example, crop photos to suggest what appears in the larger version.		Creating fewer banner ads but increasing their reach and frequency. Banner ads have been shown to be more effective when target audience members are exposed to fewer executions (different ads from the same campaign) across many pages and websites (Manchanda et al., 2006).

particular locations within print media), a willing corporate partner can provide a way to execute a particular media placement schedule.

- Negotiate free spots or insertions for certain numbers of paid spots or insertions.

If practitioners wish to pursue public service placement, they must (1) build relationships with community affairs staff, who decide what public service ads a station or publication will run; (2) find media organizations interested in the issue; and (3) provide high-quality advertisements (Kotler et al., 2002). Newspapers and magazines have no obligation to accept public service advertising. Many newspapers do not; many magazines run them only if they have unfilled advertising space. Because radio and television stations lease the airwaves from the public, they are regulated by the Federal Communications Commission and are supposed to serve the needs of their communities. Although broadcasting deregulation in the early 1980s seriously weakened community service requirements, radio and television stations remain the largest users of public service advertising. Part of the job of each station's community affairs director is to determine what public service advertisement to use.

Services exist that handle public service placement for an initiative, but the cost can be high, and often it is to an initiative's advantage for staff to build their own relationships with community affairs directors. To do so, it is important to understand the environment in which community affairs directors work. McGrath (1995) outlined the following aspects of the community affairs directors' realities, based on presentations and discussions at four annual meetings of the National Broadcast Association for Community Affairs:

- Their activities are expected to generate or enhance revenues for the station.
- They strive to find a unique position for their station in their market.
- They work in a pressure-cooker environment and are always in a time crunch.
- They are more receptive to people and organizations they know on a personal basis.
- They are committed to their communities and to the organizations working to make these communities a better place to live.

McGrath (1995) made several recommendations for working with community affairs directors, based on Grunig and Ripper's (1992) situational theory. First, organizations can help community affairs directors recognize the issue as a problem in the community, perhaps by providing information on the number of people affected and what the consequences in terms of individual or family suffering cost, reduced wages or purchasing power in the community, and so forth. Next, they should identify the constraints the community affairs director faces, most commonly (1) a perception that the issue does not affect enough people, which can be resolved by noting the profound impact on these people and their families; (2) a perception that there are other, more serious issues, which can be resolved by suggesting that the directors can address multiple issues; and (3) the station is promoting another issue this year, which can be resolved by identifying similarities between the issues.

■ MEETINGS AND CONFERENCES

Many social change initiatives develop standard exhibits and presentations to communicate their core messages. Establishing a speaker's bureau—a service for placing initiative spokespersons at events—provides an additional way to spread program messages and to increase the visibility of the organization and its contributions. A speaker's bureau can be primarily reactive, responding to requests for speakers, or it can be a proactive component of the initiative, designed to spread program messages by seeking out appropriate venues. The latter form of a speaker's bureau can be designed to address groups within the general public or professional audiences.

To create a smoothly functioning speaker's bureau, organizers should provide both the speaker and the contact person for the group the speaker will address with a form (e-mailed or printed) that includes all details: group name; expected audience size and composition; date, time, location, and directions; audiovisual equipment needed; length, nature, and style of presentation; group's expectation of topic; and names and phone numbers of the group contact person and the speaker (Lewton, 1991). Lewton also advised providing each contact person with a confidential evaluation form. This form allows the performance of individual speakers to be monitored and addressed if necessary and provides an opportunity to improve future talks by assessing how relevant the information was to the group and what additional information they would like to have had presented.

■ SPECIAL EVENTS

Public health initiatives may use special events to generate media coverage or to reach target audience members, either to deliver messages or to help them engage in a particular health behavior. Some common events for health topics include conferences for professional audiences, health screenings (often at partner sites, such as a worksite, a shopping mall, or other areas where people congregate), or exhibits in conjunction with events sponsored by partners or intermediaries. If the initiative includes providing some type of service, a tour (for press or for potential users of the service) of new facilities can be a good way to attract attention.

When developing plans or reviewing ideas for a special event, organizers may want to consider the following questions:

1. Is this event consistent with the initiative's positioning and strategy?
2. Is the event a cost-effective way of reaching the target audience(s)?
3. What other community, regional, or national activities might impact the attention or attendance the event receives?
4. What date, time, and location will best reach the intended audience?
5. What "take-away" can be provided to attendees to reinforce a behavior or to share with a nonattending target audience member to extend the initiative's reach?
6. Do all the event details—refreshments, signage, location, and so on—reflect the initiative's positioning and image?

■ PRINT MATERIALS

Throughout the life of a social change initiative, many types of print publications and materials may be used. Brochures, newsletters, manuals, and posters often play a role, as well as a host of other materials, such as signs, packaging, folders for meetings or press kits, calendars, letterhead, and envelopes. Each provides an opportunity to convey key messages (through the use of a theme line or initiative name if nothing else), and all convey an image. Using the graphics standards discussed earlier in this chapter can help ensure that all printed materials communicate the right image for the initiative.

When selecting designs and formats, organizers should consider the purpose of the piece, the image to be conveyed, how it will be distributed, how it will be reproduced, and how much various choices will cost. For brochures, posters, and other print materials that will deliver messages, review the criteria presented above under "Advertising." For all print materials, thinking through the following questions may help:

- How will the material be used? If a material will have a short life (i.e., posters to be used in conjunction with a 1-day event), using lightweight (and inexpensive) paper stock probably makes sense. If, on the other hand, it is a booklet or newsletter that people could keep and reference over a long period, a heavier (but more expensive) stock ensures that the item holds up over time.
- Is the image conveyed consistent with the communication strategy? Many aspects of a printed piece convey image: size, type of paper

stock (i.e., matte or glossy, heavy or light, recycled or not), use of color (particularly the number of colors used) and photos, special effects (i.e., die cuts, foil stamping, embossing), and the graphic standards (typeface, layouts) discussed earlier in this chapter.

- How easy is it to read? Color, type size and style, and line justification can all affect readability. Black, dark blue, and other dark-colored inks on light backgrounds are easiest to read. Reverse type (light type on a dark background) is very hard to read, as is type that has been printed over a photo or illustration. All capital letters are more difficult to read than a mixture of upper case and lower case. Serif typefaces are easier to read than sans serif. (This sentence is in a serif typeface; the tables are sans serif.) Ideally, type size should be 12 points or larger and definitely no smaller than 10 points. Type that is set ragged right (ending wherever the words end, rather than adding spaces or hyphenation to fill each line) is easier to read. The way in which the text is laid out on the page also affects readability. Layouts that are simple and open are more inviting than those with densely packed text, as are those that break up large amounts of text with visuals.

- Is the writing style appropriate for the audience? In general, text that is as simple, short, and jargon-free as possible is best. However, some professional audiences interpret simple language as an indication that a publication is designed for laypeople, so organizers must strike a balance.

- Is sufficient identifying information included? Date of publication or publication number (in tiny type at the bottom or on the back) can save endless headaches when people call to request a copy of a material, as requests often come years after the publication was first produced. Depending on the design and purpose, most print materials also include some or all of the following: the organization's name, complete mailing address, phone number, e-mail, and website address.

- How many colors are used, and are they all necessary? Color can be very powerful, and it can be very expensive. For pieces that are printed rather than photocopied, every additional ink color used increases the cost.

- Are there any special effects that are increasing cost? For example, bleeds (printing to the edge of the paper rather than leaving a margin), die cuts, embossing, and special folding all add costs. Set-up charges for special effects can be substantial and are the same for small or large press runs. If a publication or material (such as poster or tabletop card) is intended to serve as a model that will be customized and printed in relatively small quantities by collaborating organizations, avoiding special effects set-up charges reduces printing costs significantly.

- Do the materials make full use of standard-size press sheets? Some odd-sized publications may not take up the whole sheet, resulting in wasted paper.
- Can the same paper stock be used for several materials so quantity discounts can be obtained? Is there a comparable paper stock that is less expensive?
- What are the mailing cost ramifications of the proposed design? Lewton (1991) offered a number of suggestions for reducing mailing costs: using standard-size envelopes (odd sizes cost extra postage) or self-mailers (the latter also eliminate the cost associated with purchasing envelopes and assembling their contents) and mailing using bulk-rate permits rather than first-class postage. Reviewing and updating mailing lists regularly can also help control costs by eliminating duplications.
- How can reproduction costs be minimized? One of the first steps is to determine whether a particular item should be printed or photocopied. Often, if 2,000 or more copies are needed, printing is less expensive (even for black-and-white reproductions). Other methods of stretching a budget include printing lengthy documents such as manuals or reports on both sides of the page (saving paper and mailing costs) or printing newsletter mastheads or folders in color (and in large quantities to reduce the cost per piece) and then printing or photocopying onto them in black or some other single color when they are actually used (Lewton, 1991).

Once a material's design and content have been approved and it is being readied for printing, a few final checks can prevent a lot of headaches. Have someone other than the writer read all copy, checking it for typographical and other errors before it is sent to the printer. Once the printer is ready to go, ordering proofs and checking them carefully often reveals mistakes. When the job is on the press, having someone there to do a press check is a final step that can detect errors and ensure a high-quality product.

■ WEBSITES

Websites can play a number of roles in public health, depending on how efforts to bring about change are structured. A website can be any or all of the following:

- A communication medium, delivering news, entertainment, and/or advertisements
- A distribution channel, augmenting or replacing "brick-and-mortar," telephone, fax, or mail channels

- A customer service interface, providing an alternative to telephoning for information.

In all of these roles, an Internet presence should reflect and reinforce an initiative's or institution's positioning and communication strategy.

As a communication medium, websites can combine the multisensory power of audio and video with the flexibility of print. They permit the user to determine the order in which information will be accessed and the amount of time spent on particular sections of information. Websites can also help people model healthful behaviors and/or take specific actions in a way that is not possible in other media. For example, the website of a group trying to bring about policy change can include a sample letter to policymakers that users can quickly customize and send it to the appropriate policymaker. This integrated approach avoids many of the usual barriers that impede letter-writing campaigns: The target audience member does not have to compose the letter, identify the appropriate policymaker, locate the address, find an envelope, find a stamp, and then mail the letter.

As a distribution channel or customer service medium, websites allow people to identify the product, service, or information they want and obtain it at a time and place convenient for them. Well-designed sites can provide distribution and customer service transactions that are faster and of more consistent quality than alternative channels.

Website Design

The best websites are designed from the target audience's point of view and make it easy for site visitors to get the information they are looking for or take the action the initiative wants them to take. When planning a site, organizers should consider the following:

- How will people access the site? Common access points are personal computers, mobile phones, and other handheld devices.
- Where are they likely to be at the time? If they are at work, most will not appreciate background music or other audio that automatically starts playing.
- What are they likely to be seeking?
- How do they want to access or take away information? Different formats include HTML pages, PDFs, PDA downloads, and MP3 files.

Carefully selecting site design elements such as graphics, layout, and audio/visual components can improve readability and use.

Graphic identity can be established by using the same colors, fonts, backgrounds, and signature icons throughout the site; these should be consistent with initiative's overall identity standards. To reduce eye fatigue (which occurs when the eyes have to refocus constantly), designers should limit screens to four non-neutral colors and avoid complementary colors and red–blue combinations. When assigning colors to various screen elements, organizers should keep in mind that users assume objects of the same color are related. Selecting one or two font families and sticking with them provides a consistent, noncluttered look. As with printed publications, words in all capital letters are more difficult to read. Although background patterns are a way to create unique identity, care should be taken in their use because strong background patterns can render text unreadable.

The best layout for a particular site depends on its content. However, some technical aspects of site design can determine the degree to which the site is friendly (or unfriendly) to use. For example, including a search capability or index on the home page helps users locate the information they want, as does following common conventions, such as having "About us" and "Contact us" pages.

Sites that regularly add menu items run the risk of becoming disorganized and unwieldy over time. A general rule of thumb is to limit lists to seven choices, breaking longer lists into smaller groups. Frequent visitors appreciate a "last updated" date next to menu items; this feature lets them avoid waiting for a screen to load only to discover there is no new information. Adding hyperlinks to partner sites and resources provides site users with access to more information and increases a site's perceived value.

Contact information for the organization sponsoring the site is also important to include. People may have comments on the site itself, or they may have questions about the initiative or want to know if more information is available on a particular topic. Providing both electronic and traditional addresses and telephone numbers is helpful, because some people will access the site to find out how to contact the organization through traditional means. Similarly, if the site includes suggestions on actions to take (such as contacting a policymaker), information should be provided on how to contact the appropriate parties (e.g., name, e-mail and mailing address, phone number).

Audio and visual components are part of a website's appeal, because these help bring ideas to life and simplify complex information through illustrations, photographs, and streaming audio or video. However, every image added to a page increases the time it takes for the page to load, and some systems take quite a bit of time to begin playing audio or video. While a target audience member is waiting for the organization's information to load, he or she may get bored and decide to go somewhere else. These components must be optimized to load quickly or they will be counterproductive.

Testing the Site

One of the most important steps in website design is testing the site after it is constructed. Sites are often built and tested using state-of-the-art setups: large monitors, the most current versions of software, and, most important, the fastest modes of access. However, a site that is intended to provide information to members of the public should be evaluated through their eyes and their computers. Some aspects organizers should consider when testing the site include the following:

- How long do pages take to load using access methods likely to be used by target audience members? Users are typically unwilling to wait more than 20 or 30 seconds. Some techniques can make the wait seem shorter (because images are materializing on the screen). Site designers can put up brief descriptions that users can click on to proceed before the images load; this is another way to retain user interest and let them make progress—and to let them know what is on the screen if they have graphics turned off. Some sites give a "text-only" option.

- What do pages look like when viewed with different browsers, smaller monitors, or lower-end graphics settings? For example, do the pages still deliver the message if they are viewed with a text-only browser or one with deactivated graphics? What happens if the monitor is set to fewer colors or a lower resolution than that of the screen on which the site was developed? How does the site look when viewed over a mobile phone or PDA?

- How user-friendly is the menu structure? If users have to wade through huge lists, they may get frustrated and quit looking before they find what they need. On the other hand, if they have to navigate through a series of menus, each with two or three choices, they may also get frustrated and stop before they reach their destination. Every screen they have to go through increases the chance that they will get bored and go elsewhere.

- If pages are part of a larger site, what steps would users have to take find the pages relevant to the initiative? Most users look for content, not departments, yet many large organizations create websites that are arranged according to their organizational structure. This schema may work for the employees, but it has the effect of burying information on social change initiatives unless a search option is part of the site's home page.

■ SOCIAL MEDIA

Although they are newer than activities and materials previously discussed, social media are increasingly used in both commercial and public health marketing efforts. Tools like social networking sites (e.g., Facebook, MySpace), blogs, and microblogs (e.g., Twitter) are growing in popularity and provide new avenues through which marketers can reach their target audiences. These media allow marketers to disseminate information instantly, reach a broad audience, and increase public engagement.

In 2011, the Centers for Disease Control and Prevention created "The Health Communicator's Social Media Toolkit" to help organizations incorporate social media into health campaigns. Various social media tools have different strengths and, as such, can be used for different purposes.

Social Networking Sites

Facebook and other social networking sites serve as a means through which to provide program information to the target audience immediately. To reach the target audience, however, members must be "friends" or "fans" of the organization; otherwise, the updates will not reach them. One way an organization can increase traffic to its page is to partner with other organizations that share a target audience. Organizations may also consider a separate page for each initiative, which may help them attract more appropriate audience segments. For example, a county public health department may want the Facebook page for a campaign to increase childhood vaccination rates to be separate from a page for a campaign to improve prostate cancer screening. The former campaign may be able to capitalize on partnerships with parent-teacher associations, because they share a target audience. The latter may partner with local sports teams—which already have large followings—to reach more men.

Blogs

Web logs, more commonly known as "blogs," are online forums where individuals or organizations post information about various topics. Some blogs function as personal journals, whereas others provide commentary and updates on specific issues. Each blog entry can be tagged with key words, making it easier for users to find information they want.

Unlike a standard website, blogs allow readers to comment on posts, thereby increasing the connection between the creator and the user. The interactive nature gives bloggers a sense of the audience's reaction to specific issues. However, organizations should be careful not to assume the comments represent the general public's feelings on an issue: often, only those who strongly agree or vehemently disagree with an idea respond in this public way (even if given the opportunity to post anonymously).

The Centers for Disease Control and Prevention (2011) provided the following suggestions for public health groups using blogs:

- Treat blog entries like press releases. Drafting strong headlines and keeping posts short increase readership.
- Provide links to relevant websites.
- Tag entries with relevant key words so users can easily find information they want.
- Review comments to ensure they are appropriate. The blog can create a policy that does not allow inappropriate or derogatory comments.

However, bloggers should not delete comments merely because they disagree with the post. Doing so will make readers feel censored and likely decrease readership.

Microblogs

Twitter and Tumblr are the most widely used microblogging services. Like standard blogs, these allow individuals or organizations to disseminate information quickly. Microblogs often have character limits (e.g., Twitter allows tweets to be 140 characters in length). Therefore, microblogs may be most effectively used to convey simple information or reminders, such as "Get your flu shot today" or "Join us at the rally at the Capitol today at 2 p.m." A tweet can also direct audience members to a blog where they can read more about a given topic.

■ CONCLUSION

A broad range of activities can be used to draw attention to a public health initiative, including obtaining coverage in the mass media, establishing a presence on the Internet, speaking at various forums, creating special events, and using social media. Strong promotional efforts use a mix of tactics to maximize the number of target audience members reached, the number of times they are reached, and the number of channels reaching them. The tactics used in a specific situation depend on the communication objectives, the audience(s) to be reached, the message(s) to be delivered, and the available time and resources. All activities should reflect and reinforce the initiative's identity.

References

Andreasen, A.R. (2006). *Social marketing in the 21st century.* Thousand Oaks, CA: Sage.

Backer, T.E., Rogers, E.M., & Sopory, P. (1992). *Designing health communication campaigns: What works?* Thousand Oaks, CA: Sage.

Bronner, E. (2003). The foundation's end-of-life programs: Changing the American way of death. In S.L. Isaacs & J.R. Knickman (Eds.), *To improve health and healthcare* (pp. 81–98, Vol. VI). San Francisco, CA: Jossey-Bass.

Centers for Disease Control and Prevention. (2011). The health communicator's social media toolkit. Retrieved April 25, 2012, from http://www.cdc.gov/socialmedia/Tools/guidelines/pdf/SocialMediaToolkit_BM.pdf

Grunig, J., & Ripper, F. (1992). Strategic management, public, and issues. In J. Grunig (Ed.), *Excellence in public relations and communications management* (pp. 117–157). Hillsdale, NJ: Lawrence Erlbaum Associates.

Henry J. Kaiser Family Foundation. (2004, Spring). Issue brief: Entertainment education and health in the United States. Retrieved April 25, 2012, from http://www.kff.org/entmedia/upload/Entertainment-Education-and-Health-in-the-United-States-Issue-Brief.pdf

Hirschman, E.C., & Thompson, C.J. (1997). Why media matter: Toward a richer understanding of consumers' relationships with advertising and mass media. *Journal of Advertising, 26*(1), 43–60.

Hornik, R. (1997). Public health education and communication as policy instruments for bringing about changes in behavior. In M.E. Goldberg, M. Fishbein, & S. E. Middlestadt (Eds.), *Social marketing: Theoretical and practical perspectives* (pp. 45–58). Mahwah, NJ: Lawrence Erlbaum Associates.

Hornik, R.C. (Ed.). (2002). *Public health communication: Evidence for behavior change.* Mahwah, NJ: Lawrence Erlbaum Associates.

Hurley, J., & Liebman, B. (2009, December). "Big: Movie theaters fill buckets . . . and bellies." *Nutrition Action Healthletter,* pp. 2–5.

Jhally, S. (1987). *The codes of advertising.* New York, NY: St. Martin's Press.

Kotler, P., Roberto, N., & Lee, N. (2002). *Social marketing: Improving the quality of life.* Thousand Oaks, CA: Sage.

Lewton, K.L. (1991). *Public relations in health care: A guide for professionals.* Chicago, IL: American Hospital Publishing.

Manchanda, P., Dube, J., Goh, K.Y., & Chintangunta, P.K. (2006). The effects of banner advertising on internet purchasing. *Journal of Marketing Research, 43*(2), 98–108.

McCombs, M.E., & Shaw, D.L. (1972). The agenda-setting function of mass media. *Public Opinion Quarterly, 36*(2), 176–185.

McCombs, M.E., & Shaw, D.L. (1993). The agenda-setting research: Twenty-five years in the marketplace of ideas. *Journal of Communication, 43*(2), 58–67.

McCracken, G. (1989). *Culture and consumption: New approaches to the symbolic character of goods and activities.* Bloomington: Indiana University Press.

McGrath, J. (1995). The gatekeeping process: The right combinations to unlock the gates. In E. Maibach & R.L. Parrott (Eds.), *Designing health messages: Approaches from communication theory and public health practice* (pp. 199–216). Thousand Oaks, CA: Sage.

National Cancer Institute. (1989). *Making Health Communication Programs Work.* Washington, DC: Author.

Palmgreen, P., & Clarke, P. (1977). Agenda-setting with local and national issues. *Communication Research, 4,* 435–452.

Roman, K., & Maas, J.M. (1992). *How to advertise* (2nd ed.). New York, NY: St. Martin's Press.

Roman, K., Maas, J., & Nisenholtz, M. (2003). *How to advertise* (3rd ed.). New York, NY: St. Martin's Press.

Scott, L. (1990). Understanding jingles and needledrop: A rhetorical approach to music in advertising. *Journal of Consumer Research, 17,* 223–226.

Sherry, J.F. (1987). Advertising as a magic system. In J. Umiker-Sebeok (Ed.), *Marketing and semiotics: New directions for the study of signs for sale* (pp. 441–452). Berlin, Germany: Mouton de Gruyter.

Tellis, G.J. (2004). *Effective advertising: Understanding when, how, and why advertising works.* Thousand Oaks, CA: Sage.

Tipton, L., Haney, R.D., & Baseheart, J.R. (1975). Media agenda-setting in city and state election campaigns. *Journalism Quarterly, 52*, 15–22.

Wallack, L., & Dorfman, L. (1996). Media advocacy: A strategy for advancing policy and promoting health. *Health Education Quarterly, 23*, 293–317.

Wallack, L., Dorfman, L., Jernigan, D., & Themba, M. (1993). *Media advocacy and public health: Power for prevention.* Newbury Park, CA: Sage.

V

Assessing Progress and Measuring Impact

Organizers must incorporate multiple types of evaluation into their initiatives. Often, public health professionals focus exclusively on outcome evaluation, which is used to determine whether the program met its goals. However, if the program was not successful, outcome evaluation results may not be able to explain why. For example, a program may be unsuccessful either because it was based on inappropriate theories or because it was poorly implemented. To gather this information and determine how to improve the program in the future, organizers can use process evaluation. Process and outcome evaluations can encompass a wide range of activities depending on the complexity of the social change effort. This section outlines common process and outcome evaluation activities used to monitor and assess initiatives.

Process evaluation is an ongoing, iterative process that should occur as the communication strategies, tools, and materials are developed and implemented. These tactics are introduced in Chapter 11. Chapter 12 is dedicated to outcome evaluation, which occurs at the end of a campaign—or maybe at the end of a specific stage—and is equally important.

CHAPTER
11
Process Evaluation

Proper program execution is necessary for success, and process evaluation can help identify ways in which planners can improve or refine initiatives to ensure optimal execution. Evaluation findings will be most helpful if the tactics are planned and implemented in tandem with the initiatives, because this allows planners to make midcourse corrections if needed. For example, if the target audience is inadequately exposed to the messages, the program may fail. In this instance, process evaluation can be used to measure message delivery and reception by tracking material distribution and surveying target audience members, and the implementation can be adjusted on an ongoing basis.

Process evaluation "verifies what the program is and whether or not it is delivered as intended to the targeted recipients" (Scheirer, 1994, quoted in Rossi, Lipsey, & Freeman, 2004, p. 171). Process evaluation typically tracks and documents an initiative's progress by quantifying what has been done; when, where, and how it was done; and who was reached. Thorough process evaluation documents actual implementation and compares it with planned implementation, but for marketers the primary purpose for doing so is to make improvements in the future.

■ ROLE OF PROCESS EVALUATION

Process evaluation should begin by capturing characteristics of the environment in which the program is implemented to provide context for the results. If the program provides services, process evaluation can involve assessing the extent to which the targeted population receives the intended services and their satisfaction with them. For promotional activities, process evaluation provides information on the number of opportunities to be exposed to the program messages and, ideally, characteristics of those who were exposed. For editorial coverage, it can also provide information on the extent to which messages appearing in the coverage were consistent with the communication strategy.

For multifaceted interventions, process evaluation is often piecemeal, because data are gathered separately—often using different techniques—for each component and often each tactic. Process evaluation works when it draws together the results of diverse program activities and provides an opportunity to examine overall performance systematically. It should tie together information on the implementation of different program components, providing managers with an overall picture of the effort and actionable recommendations for refinement.

■ PLANNING AND CONDUCTING PROCESS EVALUATION STUDIES

Planners should anticipate what process data will be needed and how they will be used before beginning a program. To be most useful, process evaluation must be built into an initiative's activities. It can be much more difficult and expensive to gather data retrospectively, and information collected after the fact is likely to be of little value in managing implementation.

Data from process evaluation can be used in many ways. Most commonly, they help organizers (1) make decisions about refining the initiative's products (including tangible goods and services), pricing strategies, promotions, channels of distribution, or activities; (2) document and justify how resources have been spent; (3) make a compelling case for continued or additional funding; and (4) provide information on what was actually implemented, so outcome evaluators can avoid a type III error, which is evaluating a program that was not adequately implemented and thus drawing incorrect conclusions about its effectiveness (Basch et al., 1985).

Making determinations about what process data are needed can be difficult, especially for new initiatives. The "backward research" approach developed by Andreasen (1985) can be helpful in identifying the questions process evaluation data will need to answer. Practitioners using this approach should

1. Determine what key decisions are to be made using the research results and who will make the decisions.
2. Determine what information will help management make the best decisions.
3. Prepare a prototype report and ask management if this is what will best help them make their decisions.
4. Determine the analysis necessary to fill in the report.
5. Determine what questions must be asked to provide the data required by the analysis.
6. Ascertain whether the needed questions have already been asked.
7. Design the sample.
8. Implement the research design.

9. Write the report.
10. Implement the results.

The key is to identify what decisions need to be made and justifications prepared and what data will be most helpful in making those decisions. A common pitfall is to collect information that is easy to collect rather than information that will help manage the initiative. Andreasen (1995, p. 128) noted the following:

> [S]ocial marketers may be tempted to keep track of how well they are doing by looking at the number of brochures distributed, the number of advertisements run, the number of people attending various events, or the extent of distribution of the products involved in the behavior. The difficulty with this approach is that the data may or may not bear any relationship to the program's objectives and goals. For example, large numbers of distributed but unread brochures accumulated by illiterate audience members should not be taken as a sign that the program is on target. Nor should television advertisements run at late-night hours with little or no audience.

Tracking the number of brochures distributed or the number of advertisements aired helps document the initiative, which is often necessary; however, it does not help manage implementation in any meaningful way (beyond ensuring that enough brochures are printed). To make sure process evaluation data serve as a management tool, planners should look at the initiative's measurable objectives and consider the best way to determine if these objectives are met. For example, if an objective is to frame the public debate through media coverage, planners can collect media coverage on the issue and analyze its content. If an objective is to persuade audience members to get more information through a hotline, the organization should keep track of the number of people who call and, possibly, identify how they heard about the hotline.

The nature and duration of the initiative will drive the type of process information needed and the frequency with which it will be needed. For example, if a referendum is on a ballot, a bill is coming up for a vote, or a regulatory agency is about to issue a rule, a campaign to impact the policy change will likely be of short duration (often 3–6 months and sometimes only a few weeks). Weekly reports and constant monitoring are likely necessary for this campaign. In contrast, initiatives to change individual behavior may be in place for years, assuming funding sources continue. Monthly or quarterly reports are more appropriate for this initiative.

Once evaluation objectives have been set and an overall approach has been determined, they should be outlined. The plan should list the proposed approach, study design, data collection instruments, analysis plan, timeline, budget, and staffing needs. Having this plan ensures that everyone involved with the activity is in agreement as to what information the evaluation will provide. It also facilitates management of the program by providing information on the timing and amount of upcoming resource needs.

■ COMMON PROCESS EVALUATION ACTIVITIES

Process evaluation can be simple or complex, largely depending on the simplicity or complexity of the intervention. The remainder of this chapter provides an overview of some common process evaluation methodologies and how they apply to various program components, particularly those related to tracking reactions to products or services and promotional campaigns. Many approaches discussed here can also be used as needs assessment tools when refinements to a program are being planned. For excellent discussions and illustrations of process evaluation applied to public health initiatives (some marketing-based and others not), including lessons learned and instruments from a broad array of interventions, see *Process Evaluation for Public Health Interventions and Research*, edited by Steckler and Linnan (2002).

Tracking Systems

Tracking systems can be paper logs or electronic databases. They can be used to collect information on attendance at events or trainings, delivery of tangible goods, distribution of materials, and utilization of services.

For materials or tangible goods, inventory tracking helps monitor stock, provides an opportunity to learn where materials are going, which ones are likely to be reaching the most people, and which ones are the most (and least) popular. A simple way to set up an inventory tracking system is to design a database or log in which the date, name, location, quantity of materials distributed, and number of participants for each event are recorded.

A similar system can be created to help programs track service utilization. Services could include training sessions, workshops, telephone hotlines, or health services. The information collected will vary depending on the service; however, planners frequently gather data regarding the number of people served, quantity of services used, peak usage days and times, and user feedback. These data can help organizations improve the services provided and help determine whether delivery is carried out as designed, whether it is reaching the intended target population, the extent to which it meets their needs, and whether the implementation is helping to achieve program objectives as planned. Delivery data can also be important in evaluating the value of a new product or service and whether it should continue to be offered.

It may be helpful to include information on the type of requestors (e.g., whether the requestor is an intermediary or an individual) and how they heard about the activity, service, or item. If requestors call to order the materials, planners can ask them how they heard about the material. If requestors complete an order form, a few pertinent questions can be included on the form, or order forms that are printed in other publications can be coded so that the publication can be identified. Planners can analyze the tracking system to gain insights into a number of aspects of program implementation. For example, the number of requests for information or utilizers of a service can be plotted by date and compared with the times when various program promotions occurred to help planners identify the more and less popular activities. This information can help planners shape their initiatives: Popular activities can be repeated, and less popular activities should be revised.

Client Satisfaction Surveys

Assessing client satisfaction with the tangible good(s), service(s), facilities, personnel, distribution channels, and pricing (if applicable) is an invaluable part of process evaluation. Approaches to measuring client satisfaction can be divided into three basic categories:

- Unsolicited client responses, such as suggestion or comment boxes. This approach is the least rigorous and, as Lamb and Crompton (1992) noted, is limited by its lack of generalizability (i.e., the views of those who comment may be very different from the views of those who do not) and inability to assess degree of satisfaction (i.e., services provide some minimal satisfaction and people may neither make an effort to complain nor be highly satisfied).

- Observation, by directly interacting with clients either informally or formally. Informal observation might involve a manager visiting a facility and talking to a few clients about their likes, dislikes, and suggestions for improving products or services. More formal observation can be conducted using qualitative research techniques, such as periodic focus groups or in-depth interviews with current and former clients.

- Surveys, ideally of both current and former clients. This approach has the advantage of being generalizable to the population served if probability sampling techniques are used and the questionnaire is constructed appropriately.

The last two approaches play an important role in developing a complete picture of client satisfaction. Quantitative methods measure the percentage of clients who use particular services and are satisfied or dissatisfied with particular aspects of the goods or services, the facilities in which they are delivered, and the personnel who delivered them. They are discussed in more detail in the subsequent section. Qualitative studies can shed light on the reasons underlying usage and satisfaction or dissatisfaction (Centers for Disease Control and Prevention, 1993). **Exhibit 11-1** presents some aspects of each that can be important.

Designing, implementing, and analyzing quantitative surveys is a complex endeavor. A good introduction to many of the issues involved with sampling, instrumentation, data collection, data processing, and analysis is provided in *The Survey Research Handbook* by Alreck and Settle (2004).

Andreasen (1995) and Lamb and Crompton (1992) recommended that organizations measure two dimensions of satisfaction: how important each aspect of a program is to the client and how satisfied the client is with it. First, respondents rate their satisfaction with various aspects of the program on a numeric scale and then rate each aspect's importance to them using a similar scale. Andreasen (1995) recommended using the resulting information to create a performance–importance matrix

---

Exhibit 11-1 Some Components of Client Satisfaction

Services
- Cost
- Waiting time after arrival (how long it takes to be seen)
- Waiting time to make an appointment

Facilities
- Transportation (distance, parking, convenience, access to public transportation)
- Waiting room (crowding, seating, comfort, entertainment)
- Exam/counseling rooms (comfort, temperature, privacy)
- Hours (convenience)
- Telephone experiences (amount of time on hold, number of times transferred)

Personnel
- Demeanor
- Knowledge
- Ability to answer questions
- Ability to explain issues clearly

Tangible Goods
- Cost
- Quality
- Packaging
- Value
- Availability

by plotting it on a two-dimensional graph. Knowing how important various aspects of a product or service are to clients can help managers make more informed decisions about changes to make. For example, if clients are relatively unsatisfied with the waiting room but it is not that important to them, changing it may have little or no effect on clinic usage. In contrast, if their satisfaction with clinic hours is moderate but the hours are most important to them, changing the hours may result in substantial changes in usage.

Depending on resources and the number of clients or participants, organizations may survey either all or a subset of participants. For some services, such as training sessions, a census approach may be relatively easy: Organizers can simply ask everyone to fill out an evaluation form. For others services, such as clinic services or hotline calls, a census would be tremendously burdensome, and sampling is necessary. If a probability sample is used, the results can be assumed to represent the population from which the sample was drawn. A sample is a probability sample if (1) all members of a population have a known (usually equal) chance of being selected and (2) participants are selected randomly. Alternatively, a convenience sample can be used; for example, every person using the service one specific day of the week or week of the month could be sampled. To minimize bias, the day or week should be rotated in case there are differences among people who use the service at different times. Convenience samples are more limited than probability samples but can be considerably easier to construct.

Planners can choose from a variety of methods by which to collect satisfaction data. The best data collection method depends on the program budget, audience characteristics, and type of service. Self-administered questionnaires can be confidential and work even in situations where identifying information, such as names, is not collected; however, they only work for relatively literate audiences. Alternatively, participants could be interviewed in person immediately after using the service, but they may not be willing to cooperate due to concerns about time or confidentiality. Telephone surveys are also useful with audiences with low literacy rates; however, clients may be unwilling to provide their phone numbers because that may jeopardize their feelings of confidentiality.

Media Monitoring

Promotional efforts through the mass media may include efforts to obtain editorial coverage, paid advertising, and/or public service announcements (PSAs). Below are some terms commonly used in conjunction with media coverage analysis.

Circulation and audience figures are used to estimate how many people may have seen each story. Circulation is the number of copies of a newspaper or magazine purchased, through either subscriptions or individual purchases. Because each copy of a newspaper or magazine may have multiple readers (i.e., magazines in a physician's office or in a household are generally read by more than one person), circulation does not equate to number of readers. Audience is sometimes used to describe the number of readers.

Audience size is used in conjunction with television and radio. It can refer to the number of viewers or listeners during an average quarter-hour or the cumulative (cume) number of viewers or listeners for the program or part of the day. (Obviously, cume figures are larger.) With television, audience size can be expressed in terms of the number of people or the number of households.

Taking all the stories on a topic and summing their circulation or audience size figures results in a number the industry terms *gross impressions*. Gross impressions provide an estimate of how many opportunities there were for messages to be seen. They do not account for frequency or the number of times a specific individual was reached. Most people are exposed to multiple magazines, radio stations, and television programs, and some newspapers or magazines may run more than one story on the same topic. In addition, not everyone reads every story in every issue, watches every program, or listens to every news item.

To determine the number of people who were "reached" (i.e., actually saw the message), planners must survey the population, which can be fraught with measurement difficulties. Gross impressions are quite useful; for example, if program objectives include generating a certain amount of media coverage, they allow progress to be measured against those objectives. And, perhaps most importantly, they can be used to estimate how much coverage particular tactics generated and track coverage over time. Both types of information help managers determine when tactics should be changed.

Because newspaper and magazine gross impressions are usually calculated from circulation figures, some practitioners multiply the final number by some amount (2.5 is common). Their rationale for doing so is that circulation figures do not account for pass-along readership (people who read the publication but do not buy it). Although this is true, not everyone reads every story, and the average number of readers per copy differs greatly from one publication to another. For example, 2006 estimates of readers of U.S. magazines per copy averaged 6.3 but ranged from 1.24 to 44.92 (Mediamark Research, Inc., 2006). Although multiplying circulation by a pass-along readership factor makes the number a lot more impressive, doing so is difficult to defend because it accounts for possible additional impressions without adjusting for people who did not read the stories. Those who want to calculate magazine audience size more exactly can refer to the studies conducted by market research firms such as Mediamark Research, Inc.

Another way in which to estimate the value of media coverage is to calculate how much comparable amounts of advertising would have cost.

These comparisons are known as advertising equivalencies, which have limitations to keep in mind, particularly if part of a program includes paid advertising:

- The dollar amount the vendor calculates is based on the total length of the story. Particularly in print media, program messages may have occupied a very small amount of the story. Consequently, a one-paragraph discussion of a topic in a two-page story is valued at what a two-page ad would cost.
- The price of advertising space is extremely variable and volatile, particularly in television and radio. The more unsold space there is as the deadline nears, the more the price drops. In advertising placement, location is everything. Different publications or programs cost different amounts; different locations within them also vary enormously in price. Using the standard advertising unit cost (or average) can grossly under- or overestimate the "worth" of various placements.

Tracking Editorial Coverage

Tracking and analyzing both the amount and the content of a topic's editorial coverage serves a number of purposes. Specifically, they help

- Calculate how many opportunities there were for people to be exposed to stories containing information about the topic of the initiative
- Identify which placement tactics are working best
- Identify what messages are appearing in the media, and what ones are not, to inform future efforts to frame the issue
- Monitor competing messages, to guide future efforts to frame the issue

Tracking news coverage of a public health initiative may require contracting with various vendors, sometimes different ones for each medium. Stories that appear in newspapers and magazines can be obtained through a major national clipping service; however, they do not include trade publications or academic journals. If planners wish to monitor these publications, they should do so by subscribing to those that are relevant.

Print media coverage can also be obtained using electronic services such as Nexis, Dialog, and ProQuest. These services often offer coverage of trade publications and academic journals (as well as some coverage of television and radio news programs). Their disadvantages are that they do not include all publications, do not provide information on circulation (or audience size for broadcast media), do not include comparable advertising costs, and generally do not capture any pictures or graphics that accompanied the story. Increasingly, media coverage can be monitored by looking at the websites of the individual media (for campaigns covering a relatively small geographic area) or by using a web search engine.

Some services also monitor some amount of network, cable, and major local television and radio coverage. Alternatively, such coverage can be obtained by contracting directly with vendors such as Video Monitoring Service. When monitoring television and radio coverage, organizations must recognize that the services' coverage of local radio is extremely limited and their television coverage does not include all markets. Television usage of information distributed by the initiative (e.g., video new releases, satellite media tours) can be tracked electronically if the material is encoded before it is distributed to stations.

Constructing the search terms or reading list is critically important to monitoring editorial coverage. The list needs to be as specific and concrete as possible, which is often quite difficult because it is not as simple as looking for mentions of a specific product or service. The reading list must be broad enough to capture stories of interest but narrow enough to exclude most of those that are irrelevant. As an example, if someone managing a cancer prevention and control initiative were to ask for all stories mentioning the word *cancer*, he or she would receive both obituaries and stories of interest.

As with a print clipping service, vendors tracking radio and television coverage work from a topic list and scan all programming to locate appropriate stories and return transcripts or air checks (copies of the segment on tape), accompanied by information on the station and market in which it aired and an estimate of the audience size reached. Additionally, for television materials such as video news releases, satellite media tours, and electronic press kits, tracking reports are often provided by the vendor distributing the material. Many vendors use Nielsen Media Research's SIGMA tracking service, which picks up the electronic code of the material each time it is aired. Reports usually indicate, for each time the video news release is used, the station, market, time, date, story length, and estimated cost if an ad of similar length was placed at that time. For an additional fee, air checks or transcripts can be obtained. Transcripts are inexpensive and useful for content analysis; air checks are expensive but useful for documenting implementation and showing others what the program has accomplished.

As an alternative to contracting with a vendor for monitoring, if program staff know when and where a relevant story appeared (whether on television, radio, or in print), the resources used by commercial advertisers can be used to determine how many people are likely to have been reached and an approximation of how much the placement would have cost if it had been paid advertising. Some of these resources are listed in **Table 11-1**.

Subscriptions to the services listed in Table 11-1 can be quite expensive, particularly if only local information is needed. If requests are reasonable, advertising agencies and public relations firms that already subscribe to these services may be willing to provide information or access to it on a pro bono basis to support the efforts of community organizations or other small nonprofits. In addition, some university libraries carry some

Table 11-1 Selected Sources of Media Information

Source	Information Available
Arbitron (http://www.arbitron.com)	Radio station audience size estimates and profiles
Mediamark Research, Inc. (http://www.gfkmri.com)	Magazine audience estimates and profiles
Nielsen Media Research (http://www.nielsenmedia.com)	Television audience size estimates and profiles; SIGMA tracking data
Standard Rate and Data Service (http://www.srds.com)	Newspaper and magazine profiles and ad pricing: television, radio, and outdoor profiles

of these resources. Alternatively, the information can be gathered by obtaining rate cards from individual stations and publications.

With editorial coverage, it is often desirable to go beyond the information provided by the tracking and clipping services. Because reporters generally use various sources to prepare their stories, it is necessary to analyze the content of coverage to determine the extent to which the coverage is on strategy (i.e., if it includes key messages and frames the issue as intended) and to identify any areas of confusion or negative coverage. The content analysis process involves reading each clip and coding it according to a previously developed message list, then examining the number of stories and estimated audience reach for each message. This analysis reveals what messages from program materials are being used, what ones are not, and how often conflicting messages appear, providing guidance for future media relations efforts. **Exhibit 11-2** presents an example of media analysis conducted to support the 5 A Day for Better Health program.

Tracking Advertising Placement
If an initiative relies on public service placement of its ads, tracking that placement is the only means of determining who may have been reached by a campaign; calculating gross impressions, reach, and frequency; and ascertaining what the placement would have cost had it been paid. For initiatives that pay for placement, tracking placement is far less critical; reach and frequency are normally estimated when developing the media plan that lays out where, when, and how often to run the ads. Even if these calculations were not made, they could easily be made using audience estimates supplied by each station or publication. Many commercial advertisers track placement of their own ads to verify they actually ran as requested, although many social change initiatives may not have resources to do so. Advertising tracking services can also be used to keep an eye on competitors' advertising spending and media schedules.

Exhibit 11-2 Analyzing Media Coverage: 5 A Day for Better Health Campaign

Background

The goal of the national 5 A Day for Better Health program, originally cosponsored by the National Cancer Institute (NCI) and the Produce for Better Health Foundation (PBH), is to encourage Americans to eat five or more servings of fruits and vegetables daily to decrease their risk of developing cancer. The program today is a complex web of activities conducted at the national, state, and local levels by government agencies, nonprofit organizations, and the private sector.

Both NCI and PBH have conducted media campaigns to disseminate messages encouraging increased consumption of fruits and vegetables. This case study draws from NCI's initial media analysis report (Eisner, Loughrey, & Davis, 1994) to illustrate how the process works. The report analyzes print media coverage appearing from July 1992 (when NCI's media campaign was launched) through October 1993.

The NCI used a number of tactics to generate media coverage of 5 A Day messages. Regular contact with the media was accomplished through the quarterly distribution of 5 A Day media newsletters to newspaper and magazine food editors. The newsletters contained story ideas, recipes, infographics, and camera-ready art. The materials were also available on an accompanying disk or could be downloaded through two computer services.

This regular contact was supplemented by a variety of special events and additional media contacts. The 5 A Day media campaign was launched in July 1992 with a press conference featuring U.S. Department of Health and Human Services Secretary Louis Sullivan, MD, and National Institutes of Health Director Bernadine Healy, MD; the launch was also supported by a video news release featuring press conference footage and Olympic swimmer Matt Biondi. In addition, media activities were conducted in conjunction with the launch of 5 A Day week in September 1993, radio and print public service announcements were produced and distributed periodically, and a magazine media tour was conducted. Beyond NCI's activities, PBH, produce manufacturers, and retail stores sponsored many additional media activities.

Method of Analysis

To assess the 5 A Day print media coverage, newspaper and magazine placements published from July 1992 through October 1993 were collected by a national clipping service. The clipping service attempted to clip all daily and weekly newspapers in the United States as well as nearly 7,000 consumer, trade, and professional magazines and newsletters. However, as expected with any clipping service, it is doubtful that all stories resulting from the campaign were obtained because no clipping service covers all publications in the United States and all services inevitably miss some placements. Nonetheless, the clipping service collected 7,625 stories published during the time period.

The first stage of the analysis involved estimating gross impressions by summarizing circulation figures and estimating worth by summarizing advertising dollar equivalencies. To evaluate the content of the coverage in a timely and cost-effective manner, a representative sample was drawn. Sampling was conducted by first grouping the clips by the distribution schedules

(continues)

Exhibit 11-2 Analyzing Media Coverage: 5 A Day for Better Health Campaign (continued)

---

of their publications—weekly, daily, or monthly. Clips from daily publications were grouped further by the day of the week on which they were published. Proportional samples were drawn based on the percentage of clips in each category (e.g., weekly, monthly, Monday, Tuesday, etc.). The sample included 1,103 clips.

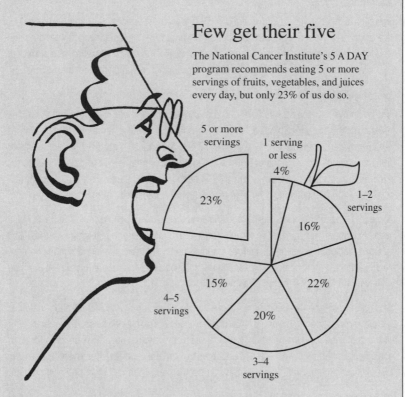

Few get their five

The National Cancer Institute's 5 A DAY program recommends eating 5 or more servings of fruits, vegetables, and juices every day, but only 23% of us do so.

5 or more servings — 23%

1 serving or less — 4%

1–2 servings — 16%

3–4 servings — 20%

4–5 servings — 15%

22%

Figure 11-1 Infograph from the 5 A Day Campaign
Source: Reprinted from Natlonial Cancer Institute.

The goal of the content analysis was to improve future media placement efforts by (1) assessing the extent to which media coverage contained NCI's key messages and (2) identifying tactics (in terms of type of information and delivery strategies) that were most successful. To that end, each story was read and coded using a message list that had been constructed with the following objectives:

- Determine the extent to which media coverage reflected NCI's key messages
- Identify what other story angles were covered

(continues)

Exhibit 11-2   Analyzing Media Coverage: 5 A Day for Better Health Campaign (continued)

- Assess what types of statistics and visuals were used most often
- Assess what sources of information (including spokespeople) were used most often

Some highlights of the analysis are presented below.

Quantity of Coverage

Circulation of the total 7,625 clips was 396,145,875; based on the size of the clips, the equivalent advertising value was estimated at $5,925,354. Coverage was highest the month the campaign was launched (889 clips with a corresponding circulation of more than 52 million) and the month 5 A Day week was launched (820 clips with a corresponding circulation of more than 40 million).

Content of Coverage

Content analysis of the stories revealed that the vast majority (89% of the 1,100 articles analyzed) contained one or more of NCI's key messages. However, some messages received far more coverage than others. For example, 77% of the articles reported that people should eat a minimum of five servings of fruits and vegetables per day—one of the key messages to increase knowledge. However, only 12% of the stories included another knowledge message—that five servings is a minimum, not a maximum, recommendation.

Messages designed to build skills by focusing on specific actions people could take to increase their consumption of fruits and vegetables received relatively limited coverage, with 28% of the stories including messages, such as a suggestion to add two servings each day or more specific actions people could take to add servings (such as having fruit or juice in the morning and having fruit and/or vegetables as a snack).

Messages focusing on the health benefits of eating five or more servings of fruits and vegetables each day received greater coverage: 41% of the placements mentioned a specific health benefit related to this level of consumption, with the association with reduced risk of some forms of cancer being mentioned most often (it appeared in 40% of the stories). Relatively few articles (5%) discussed the barriers to eating 5 A Day, such as seasonality, cost, or preparation time.

The analysis also examined the extent to which the coverage included other story angles of interest to NCI. Just over one-fourth (27%) of the articles discussed 5 A Day in conjunction with food (e.g., recipes, food preparation tips, a specific fruit or vegetable, or a Mediterranean diet). Details and background on the 5 A Day program were mentioned in 16% of the clips; about 5% mentioned an organization or group that had joined the 5 A Day program. About 8% of the articles discussed children and 5 A Day, usually in terms of the value of eating produce. Very few (2%) of the sampled articles mentioned a concern about pesticides used on fruits and vegetables.

Tactics Used

Nearly half (47%) of the sampled articles used materials and/or information that could be identified as coming from the NCI. About one-fourth (26%) used information from the July 1992 launch materials, 10% used information from the media newsletter, and 11% used information from NCI, but the precise source could not be identified. About one-fourth of the

(continues)

Exhibit 11-2 Analyzing Media Coverage: 5 A Day for Better Health Campaign (continued)

articles (26%) mentioned an NCI-provided statistic. Current fruit and vegetable consumption was the most frequent focus; 21% of all stories mentioned that Americans currently eat 3.5 servings of fruits and vegetables daily or that only 23% of American eat 5 or more daily servings. Thirteen percent of the sampled articles used visuals; 5 A Day infographs were used most often, followed by art from the newsletter and photographs.

Source: Data from E. Eisner, K. Loughrey, and K. Davis, 1994, *The National Cancer Institute's 5 A Day for Better Health Program: Analysis of Print Media Placements—July 1992 through October 1993.* Bethesda, MD: National Cancer Institute Office of Cancer Communications.

For initiatives relying on public service placement, tracking data also allow managers to

- Compare ads to determine which ones receive the most play
- Thank stations that are "heavy users" of materials and potentially explore the opportunity for station promotions around the issue
- Refine distribution lists based on who is and is not using program materials
- Discern whether there is a need for follow-up studies with nonusers to identify why they are not using the ads and determine if there is anything that can be done to increase their usage

PSAs that appear in magazines or newspapers can be obtained through clipping services. Regional and other specialized editions of magazines make it difficult to obtain all PSA placements (often a PSA will run in one edition that had unsold advertising space but not in all editions). If PSAs are being sent to professional publications, organizations may want to subscribe directly to the publications to ensure that PSA placement does not get overlooked.

In the United States, television PSAs can be tracked using SIGMA, Nielsen Media Research's electronic tracking service. To use SIGMA, the sponsoring organization contracts with a service provider that encodes the master tapes before duplication and release. This encoding uniquely identifies each PSA and is broadcast with the PSA, but it is not visible to the audience. Nielsen's computers identify this code each time a spot is aired. Airplay reports can be customized but typically include, for each airing of the spot, the station and market in which the spot aired (or network if it ran on a network), the date and time it aired, some basic audience composition information (including estimated audience size), and the approximate cost of the time if it had been purchased for commercial advertising. Because the price of television time is subject to extreme fluctuations, this last item is only a rough estimate. Radio PSA play in major markets can also be tracked electronically; however, doing so is extremely expensive, and many areas of the country are still missed.

Additional information of PSA placement can be obtained through a few different mechanisms:

- *Commercial verification reports*: Broadcast stations and print publications generally send these to commercial advertisers to verify that their ads ran as requested. Some stations and publications automatically sent these reports for PSAs; others will do so if asked. The reports typically list the name of the program airing when the PSA ran and the date and time it ran.

- *Follow-up phone calls with stations and publications*: Phoning public service directors to see if they plan to use a particular spot is labor intensive but can be quite useful, particularly if this technique is limited to priority gatekeepers or those for whom it will be difficult to collect other information, such as radio stations.

- *The resources listed in Table 11-1*: Local initiatives that know when and where their ads ran can consult these sources to estimate gross impressions, reach, and frequency.

- *Including phone numbers, websites, or addresses in PSAs*: If a PSA includes a hotline number, website, or address, information on who was reached and motivated enough to respond by requesting more information can be collected.

Monitoring Policy Changes

The way in which a policy change can be monitored depends on what type of change it is and who has the power to make it. For example, if a change is taking the form of a referendum, bond issue, or proposition that requires citizens to vote, tracking voter opinion can be critical, as is discussed later in this chapter. If private organizations are being asked to make the change, contact with their public affairs personnel or decision makers within the organizations may be the only way to monitor change. Many policy and funding decisions are made by governments at the local, state, or national level. This section provides some suggestions for monitoring these types of policy changes in the United States.

At the local level, attending city council meetings and maintaining contact with decision makers can be critical in tracking policy changes. Some activities, such as agendas for upcoming meetings and hearings, can also be monitored through contact with local government agencies or through the Internet. Search engines can help identify the websites of local governments, and the Library of Congress THOMAS site (http:// thomas.loc.gov) provides a number of gateways to local sites.

At the state level, it is increasingly possible to monitor the introduction and progress of bills through legislative websites. Most sites can be accessed from the state's main home page. Additionally, staff of the legislator sponsoring a bill (or legislators opposing it, as appropriate) can provide valuable information on the "behind the scenes" progress. States vary in how regulatory agencies operate, but many states have "government in the sunshine" laws that mandate access to some of the proceedings.

At the federal level, legislation can be monitored through the previously mentioned Library of Congress website (http://thomas.loc.gov). This site provides the complete text of bills as well as information on their status, sponsors, referrals to committees, and so forth. It also provides access to the *Congressional Record* (also available through the Government Printing Office in hard copy or on its website at http://www.gpo.gov) and to committee reports.

Once legislation is passed and signed into law, often an executive branch agency has to issue new regulations to implement the law. At this point, the *Federal Register* can be useful. It is also available in hard copy or on its website. When an agency is planning to issue a rule (regulation), it first publishes the proposed rule in the *Federal Register* and solicits comments; the notice stipulates where comments should be sent and the length of the comment period. The *Federal Register* also publishes final agency rules before their being added to the Code of Federal Regulations, as well as a variety of other notices from federal agencies, such as notices of hearings and investigations, committee meetings, agency decisions and rulings, and issuance or revocation of licenses.

■ TRACKING TARGET AUDIENCE AWARENESS AND REACTION

A primary focus of this chapter thus far has been on how to measure messages being sent out by a program but not how to measure the extent to which those messages are received. There are some practical methods of obtaining information about who was reached by building active response mechanisms into the dissemination effort itself, such as a telephone number or address to write to for more information. Quantitative tracking studies provide a means of monitoring reactions among the population as a whole.

Active Response Mechanisms

Both automated hotlines (those answered by a recording) and live-operator hotlines can provide a wealth of data. Analysis of call volume by date can be compared with other process data, such as dates of media coverage or community events, to craft a more detailed picture of which tactics are having the greatest impacts. If the hotline system is more sophisticated and captures area codes and prefixes or if callers leave their addresses, this information can be mapped and areas of high and low response can be identified. If live operators are available, a profile of who is asking for more information can be obtained by asking callers a few standard questions. For example, asking where callers learned about hotline numbers provides insights into what tactics are generating the greatest response. Learning basic demographics about callers enables program managers to assess the extent to which the caller's profile matches that of the priority population of interest and may provide insights into how to adjust communication or delivery strategies to focus them more effectively. If the population has been segmented using a stages of change approach, asking callers a few questions can determine their stages. Materials designed for people in a particular stage can then be sent, if they are available.

Websites also provide an opportunity for collecting data. In addition to analyzing how users navigate a site and which pages are visited more often, websites can include a pop-up customer satisfaction survey. Or, if the site provides individually tailored information (e.g., personal health assessments) such that people have to register to use the site, basic demographic and behavioral data (within ethical confines) can be collected during registration.

Including a coupon with print advertisements or on websites or a website or e-mail address on press releases, story ideas, and television and radio PSAs can provide additional opportunities to learn who is being motivated by the message. Although this approach does not provide information about the participants other than geographic location, it does provide some information on the number of people reached. Geographic information also can be useful, as discussed earlier regarding inventory tracking systems.

The coupon idea can be used creatively by public health initiatives that include partnerships with local businesses. For example, if local movie theater owners agree to include a slide about the program or a PSA or video clip in their premovie entertainment, viewers could be told on the slide (or video) that ticket stubs from the movie theater could be redeemed for a discount on a screening test or health service. Alternatively, the stubs could be redeemed with another partnering entity such as a local grocery store or restaurant for a discount on a specific healthier food purchase or at a pharmacy for a discount on a smoking cessation kit. Collecting and counting the ticket stubs provides information on how many people were reached and, more important, were motivated enough by the message to take action.

Quantitative Tracking Surveys

Quantitative tracking studies, such as public opinion polls, can be used to support implementation of social change initiatives that aim either to affect changes in individual behavior or policies or to promote public health as an institution. They provide a means of monitoring levels of knowledge, awareness, and self-reported behavior among the population.

For policy change initiatives, opinion polls provide an excellent way to determine whether the issue has obtained prominence on the public's agenda (Wallack & Dorfman, 1996) and monitor public reactions to various ways of framing the issue. The public opinion data can also be used to help persuade journalists to cover a particular aspect of an issue and to illustrate public support for (or opposition to) a change to policymakers. Most important, they can identify the need for fast action and can be used to rally additional financial support if needed.

An example of how public opinion tracking data were used quite successfully is the 1994 campaign against California's Proposition 188. Proposition 188 was a ballot initiative sponsored by Philip Morris that would have repealed all local antismoking ordinances as well as the state's law eliminating smoking in workplaces and replaced them with weak statewide smoking restrictions (Macdonald, Aguinaga, & Glantz, 1997). The anti-188 campaign coordinated grassroots advocacy, media advocacy, and paid advertising to deliver a common message. To monitor progress, the health coalition conducted periodic public opinion polls during the 3-month campaign. About 2 months before the vote, poll results showed that voters were about equally divided on the proposition. In response, the coalition produced television ads featuring former U.S. Surgeon General C. Everett Koop and paid to air them in major media markets the last week of the campaign, using contributions provided by the American Cancer Society and American Heart Association (Macdonald et al., 1997).

Initiatives focused on individual behavior change can use tracking data in two ways: to monitor progress and as a news hook to gain additional coverage. In some instances, they may want to incorporate tracking data that illustrates the population's progress in future media messages, thus providing social reinforcement for the change. In comparison with policy change initiatives, those focusing on individual behavior change are likely to conduct tracking studies less often. Many organizations conduct them once a year, often after their major media push and in time to feed into strategic planning for the coming year. Others have the resources to conduct them more often, perhaps as often as quarterly.

Initiatives that successfully use tracking studies often incorporate one or more of the following approaches into their study designs:

- Collect data periodically, not just at the end when outcomes are assessed. Periodic information is necessary to refine messages and improve delivery.
- Collect data immediately after major public events when awareness is likely to be highest and thus easier to detect.
- Include questions that ask where participants learned or heard about the program or its key messages, to help identify what tactics are working best.

Public opinion polls can be prohibitively expensive for small organizations but can be extremely cost-effective for larger initiatives. For example, in the United States, adding questions to a nationally projectable omnibus poll costs about $1,000 per question (less for close-ended questions, more for those with open-ended answers); tabulation of the question against demographic information collected as part of the study is included in the cost.

When public opinion polls are used to track the reach of an initiative's messages, it can be difficult to assess change over time because of the magnitude of difference needed to detect a statistical change. If the issue is very much on the public agenda, changes in awareness and opinion may be easy to track; however, if coverage has been relatively limited, it can be much more difficult to detect, either because such a small percentage of the population was exposed to the message or because the change was subtle. A change of one or two percentage points will be washed out in sampling error. The issues discussed in the client satisfaction section of this chapter are relevant to designing and conducting public opinion polls.

■ CONCLUSION

Adequately tracking and monitoring implementation is a fundamental aspect of the marketing approach. Process evaluation plays a critical role in ensuring that program components are constantly monitored and refined to improve their performance. Unfortunately, it is often overlooked or compromised in favor of outcome evluation. Appropriate process evaluation mechanisms can be built into every program tactic and provide important information on what was done; when, where, and how it was done; and who was reached.

References
Alreck, P.L., & Settle, R.B. (2004). *The survey research handbook* (3rd ed.). New York, NY: McGraw-Hill/Irwin.

Andreasen, A.R. (1985). "Backward" marketing research. *Harvard Business Review, 63*(3), 176–182.

Andreasen, A.R. (1995). *Marketing social change: Changing behavior to promote health, social development, and the environment.* San Francisco, CA: Jossey-Bass.

Basch, C.E., Sliepcevich, E.M., Gold, R.S., Duncan, D.F., & Kolbe, L.J. (1985). Avoiding type III errors in health education program evaluations: A case study. *Health Education Quarterly, 12*(3), 315–331.

Centers for Disease Control and Prevention. (1993). *Planning and evaluating HIV/AIDS prevention programs in state and local health departments: A companion to program announcement #300.* Atlanta, GA: Author.

Eisner, E., Loughrey, K., & Davis, K. (1994). *The National Cancer Institute's 5 A Day for Better Health Program: Analysis of print media placements—July 1992 through October 1993.* Bethesda, MD: National Cancer Institute Office of Cancer Communication.

Lamb, C.W., & Crompton, J.L. (1992). Analyzing marketing performance. In S.H. Fine (Ed.), *Marketing the public sector: Promoting the causes of public and nonprofit agencies* (pp. 173–184). New Brunswick, NJ: Transaction Publishers.

Macdonald H., Aguinaga, S., & Glantz, S.A. (1997). The defeat of Philip Morris' "California Uniform Tobacco Control Act." *American Journal of Public Health, 87,* 1989–1996.

Mediamark Research, Inc. (2006). Pocketpiece report results—Doublebase 2006. Retrieved October 6, 2006, from http://www.mriplus.com

Rossi, P.H., Lipsey, M.W., & Freeman, H.E. (2004). *Evaluation: A systematic approach* (7th ed.). Newbury Park, CA: Sage.

Steckler, A., & Linnan, L. (Eds.). (2002). *Process evaluation for public health interventions and research.* San Francisco, CA: Jossey-Bass.

Wallack, L., & Dorfman, L. (1996). Media advocacy: A strategy for advancing policy and promoting health. *Health Education Quarterly, 23,* 293–317.

CHAPTER

12

Outcome Evaluation

Outcome evaluation of social change initiatives can play a number of roles, depending on the nature of the effort being evaluated and the reason for the evaluation. This chapter introduces some of the ways in which outcome data are used to shape policy and to refine interventions, presents some of the key issues involved with evaluating such initiatives, describes some potentially useful evaluation designs in greater detail, and discusses the limitations of using randomized experiments to evaluate social change initiatives.

■ ROLE OF OUTCOME EVALUATION

Outcome evaluation is often conducted after a project is finished but may occur periodically throughout the life of a program. An outcome evaluation may be conducted for any number of reasons (**Exhibit 12-1**). At its most basic, outcome evaluation shows whether a project had the effects it was planned to have. Depending on its scope, it can serve as a management tool by helping to identify how objectives, target audiences, strategies, and implementation might be revised and improved. It may also identify any unintended consequences of a program, which is particularly important with policy changes.

In addition to serving a useful monitoring function, sometimes the results of outcome studies can be a powerful tool for future social change initiatives. A striking example is a study of the sales impact of local ordinances mandating smoke-free bars and restaurants (Glantz & Smith, 1994). The study compared restaurant sales in the 15 cities that first enacted such ordinances with sales in 15 matched cities without ordinances for the period from 1986 to 1993. It found no impact on revenues during the period after enactment of the ordinances. The tobacco industry tried to dismiss the study as "fatally flawed" and tried to sue Glantz's employer, the University of California, on charges of scientific fraud (Susser, 1997). The study was peer-reviewed twice, once before its original

Exhibit 12-1 Uses of Outcome Evaluation

- To assess the extent to which a project met its objectives
- To identify improvements or refinements in objectives, target audience, strategies, or implementation
- To assess reactions to a program
- To identify any unintended consequences
- To assess the cost efficiency of the program
- To provide evidence for future social change initiatives

publication and again in response to an unpublished critique cited by the National Smokers' Alliance; both times, all reviewers agreed the work was sound (Susser, 1997). Subsequent evaluations have substantiated the original study's conclusion that laws requiring smoke-free restaurants and bars do not have an adverse economic impact (Scollo et al., 2003).

Sometimes policy outcomes are tracked after the fact, when it appears that a new policy may have inadvertently created a new danger to the public's health. Airbag regulations in the United States are one example of unintended policy effects. As of October 1, 2001, there were 195 confirmed airbag-related deaths; of these, 119 were children (National Highway Traffic Safety Administration [NHSTA], 2001). After the deaths began occurring, NHTSA and other organizations responded with widespread efforts to educate the public about steps they could take to lessen the likelihood of airbag injury (e.g., never put a rear-facing child safety seat in the front seat; put children in the back seat when possible; if they or small adults are in the front seat, push the seat back as far as possible). Initially, NHTSA issued a rule allowing dealers and other car repair businesses to install manual on–off switches for airbags in vehicles owned by or used by people whose requests for switches are approved by NHTSA (NHTSA, 1997); later, NHTSA modified rules to require advanced airbags—multistage systems that inflate the bag fully, partially, or not at all depending on input from occupant-sensing devices that detect the presence or absence, relative weight, and seat belt status of a front-seat passenger (NHTSA, 2000).

■ CONSIDERATIONS WHEN PLANNING EVALUATIONS

Planning the evaluation in tandem with the initiative eliminates some potential problems and often results in a stronger intervention as well as a stronger evaluation. This section outlines some questions to consider when developing outcome evaluation plans. **Exhibit 12-2** illustrates some failures that can be avoided through proper consideration of these issues and careful program and evaluation planning. Although the exhibit was developed for communication interventions, the points apply equally well to marketing interventions.

Exhibit 12-2 Four Types of Failure Common to Communication Interventions

1. *STRATEGY failure:* Communication is really not the problem. People need better services, and messages are inadequate in themselves to effect change.

2. *EXECUTION failure:* Messages are badly needed, but they are poorly constructed, lack adequate exposure, and/or are addressed to the wrong audience.

3. *MEASUREMENT failure:* Communication was the right answer; it was well delivered but poorly evaluated. Either the instruments measured the wrong change or time was inadequate to permit the change to become detectable.

4. *EXPECTATION failure:* The problem is that real change occurred but did not meet the expectations of planners or funders. A success was declared to be a failure.

Source: Reprinted "From Prevention Vaccines to Community Care" (p. 332), by W. Smith. In *Public Health Communication: Evidence for Behavior Change* by R. Hornik (Ed.), 2002, Mahwah, NJ: Lawrence Erlbaum Associates. Copyright 2002 by Lawrence Erlbaum Associates. Reprinted with permission.

What Questions Should the Evaluation Answer?

Exhibit 12-1 alludes to some questions an evaluation can answer, such as To what extent did a program meet its objectives? What improvements or refinements can be made to improve the program? Will the public be generally receptive of or opposed to the intervention? Are there any unintended consequences resulting from the initiative that can be addressed? Is the initiative a good use of resources?

How Is the Intervention Expected to Work?

Planners should create a logic model or some other system to diagram the way in which a program will work. This model should include the program inputs (i.e., resources), activities, anticipated immediate outcomes, and anticipated long-term outcomes. Depending on the evaluation timeframe, planners may want to base their evaluation on the immediate outcomes, assuming these are proxy measures for the long-terms goals. For example, an intervention designed to improve cardiovascular health may have a long-term goal of decreased heart attack rates, which may be hard to measure because heart attacks may or may not occur for years. Instead, interventionists may look at cholesterol levels, blood pressure, or other more easily measured short-term outcomes to determine if they are having the desired effect.

Exhibit 12-3 provides a succinct description of a social change initiative from the viewpoint of a member of the target audience. As Hornik (1997b) said of this example, "this program is effective not because of a PSA [public service announcement] or a specific program in physician education. It is successful because the National High Blood Pressure Education Program

---

Exhibit 12-3   Social Change in Action

A person sees some public service announcements and a local television health reporter's feature telling her about the symptom-less disease of hypertension. She checks her blood pressure in a newly accessible shopping mall machine, and those results suggest a problem. She tells her spouse, who has also seen the ads and encourages her to have it checked. She goes to a physician, who confirms the presence of hypertension and encourages her to change her diet and then return for monitoring.

Meanwhile, the physician has become more sensitive to the issue because of a recent article in the *Journal of the American Medical Association*, some recommendations from a specialist society, and a conversation with a drug retailer as well as informal conversations with colleagues and exposure to television discussions of the issue. The patient talks with friends at work about her experience. They also increase their concern and go to have their own pressure checked. She returns for another check-up and her pressure is still elevated, although she has reduced her use of cooking salt. The physician decides to treat her with medication. The patient is ready to comply because all the sources around her—personal, professional, and mediated—are telling her that she should.

Source: Reprinted from "Public Health Education and Communication as Policy Instruments for Bringing About Changes in Behavior," (pp. 49–50) by R. Hornik. In *Social Marketing: Theoretical and Practical Perspectives,* 1997, Mahwah, NJ: Lawrence Erlbaum Associates, Inc. Copyright 1997 by Lawrence Erlbaum Associates, Inc. Reprinted with permission.

---

has changed the professional and public environment as a whole around the issue of hypertension" (p. 50).

Wallack and Dorfman (1996) provided an example of how a policy change initiative using a media advocacy strategy is expected to work. The expectation is that if the issue is appropriately framed in terms of access (to get journalists' attention) and content (telling the story from the policy perspective), it will get on the public agenda through media coverage. Once it is on the public agenda, it will mobilize groups or individuals who influence policymakers, and they, in turn, will put pressure on the decision makers, resulting in the policy being enacted or the change occurring. The airbag example mentioned above illustrates large parts of this process. The media started covering the airbag-caused deaths of infants and children, and NHTSA started getting pressure to allow the airbags to be turned off (car dealers and repair shops normally are not legally allowed to override safety equipment) pending a more permanent solution to the problem.

How Fast Is the Intervention Expected to Work?

Most population-based public health interventions targeting individual behaviors can expect small, gradual changes. However, there are some exceptions. Hornik (1997b) argued that "straightforward substitution of behaviors, when possible, may allow more rapid change than attempts to introduce new behaviors" (p. 55), citing as examples interventions to prevent Reye's syndrome (by using an aspirin substitute rather than aspirin) and sudden infant death syndrome (by putting babies to sleep on their backs rather than on their stomachs). He noted that both of these behaviors were very easy to change and that adopting the new behavior "sharply reduced the risk of a rare but devastating event" (p. 55). In both situations, adopting the new behavior was linked to a core human value: caring for children.

Interventions to bring about environmental changes can also be slow and gradual or fast-moving, depending on the type of change. Environmental improvements that require complex changes in multiple policies by multiple entities generally can expect slow, gradual changes. For example, efforts to improve end-of-life care in the United States can range from national and state changes (e.g., changes in federal regulations, state laws, health insurance provided by private insurers, medical school curricula, and continuing medical education programs) to a variety of local changes (e.g., increasing the availability of hospice care, changing hospital and long-term care policies, improving emergency medical services, and/or introducing or expanding services). Similarly, change may be slow and gradual, for example, environmental changes that may meet with substantial resistance such as trying to implement local smoke-free ordinances across a state.

What Outcomes Can Reasonably Be Expected?

Perhaps more than any other question, this one illustrates the need to develop evaluation plans in tandem with the plans for the initiative. The starting point for determining what outcomes are reasonable should be the initiative's objectives. As Rossi and Freeman (1993) and Kotler and Roberto (1989), among others, noted, objectives should operationalize a program's goals, thereby making them measurable. However, they also noted that program objectives often do not do this, rendering evaluation very difficult because the evaluators cannot tell what they ought to be measuring. Even if the goals are operationalized, the resulting objectives may be changes of unrealistically large magnitude.

Planners should consider three questions when thinking about effect sizes for social change initiatives:

1. What outcomes are reasonable to expect, given the structure of the intervention?
2. What magnitude of effect is needed to make a difference to public health?
3. What will be considered successful in this environment?

The first two questions give rise to all sorts of policy debates, but in the end, the answer to either may be an effect size far smaller than what most outcome evaluations designs can detect. The answer to the second question, in particular, can make outcome evaluation particularly challenging, because in some instances the magnitude of effect needed to make a difference to public health can be quite small. As Beresford and colleagues (1997) noted in discussing population-wide efforts to change eating habits, "the public health model, or population strategy, consists of shifting the entire distribution of a risk factor, including the mean, down. The diminution in risk for a given individual is typically small and may not even be clinically important. Nevertheless, because the entire distribution is affected, the impact on morbidity and mortality can be substantial" (p. 615). Citing Prentice and Sheppard (1990), they went on to note that "a 1% reduction in dietary calories from fat made population-wide could result in about 10,000 deaths saved in the United States in a year" (Beresford et al., 1997, p. 615). That 1% reduction would not be detectable at the community level using most available evaluation methodologies. Furthermore, if it were detected, it could not be said to be statistically significant because of sampling error.

The third question addresses how "success" is defined in the initiative's organizational environment. Organizers must recognize the amount of change that will be needed to be viewed as successful. Then, the organizers can attempt to structure the initiative so that it is of sufficient intensity and duration to achieve this level of success. Importantly, they must design an evaluation so the impact can be measured. As discussed above, sometimes a relatively small population-wide change—too small to capture in an evaluation—can have enormous public health consequences.

Demonstrating cause and effect can also be problematic. Other factors may influence outcomes, such as activities conducted by complementary or competing organizations. Evaluation may show an association between exposure to program components and increased awareness of, or engagement in, the appropriate health behavior, for example, but may not show definitively that the initiative caused the change.

Beyond looking to the initiative's objectives and likely definitions of success for direction, organizers must consider how, and how quickly, the intervention is expected to work against issues such as the expected duration and intensity of the intervention. It can take years to see the effects of initiatives targeting individual changes in prevention behaviors. For example, the large decreases in smoking rates and deaths due to cardiovascular disease are seen over a decade or more. Reviewing the results of other initiatives addressing the same or similar topics and using similar implementation strategies may provide some guidance.

The expected outcomes can influence evaluation plans in many ways. For example, if expectations are for small, gradual change, large sample sizes are required (and still may not attain the needed precision), and it would be wise to wait a sufficient amount of time before attempting to measure outcomes. In contrast, if large, rapid effects are anticipated, sample sizes can be smaller and outcomes can be measured more quickly.

How Will Outcomes Be Measured?

Outcome measures should be driven by the theoretical model used to develop the intervention and should be consistent with what the intervention was designed to accomplish. For example, if the intervention was designed to tell people how many servings of fruits and vegetables they should eat and to convince them to add two servings each day, the outcomes to be measured should be whether the number of people who know how many servings to eat is increasing and whether people are, in fact, adding two servings per day, not how many servings they are eating.

Beyond problems with measuring outcomes that do not reflect intervention objectives, sometimes outcome measures are not as sensitive to a range of possible changes as they might be. As just one example, consider parts of a commentary by Fishbein (1996, p. 1076) on a community intervention designed to increase the likelihood that young men would engage in safer sex:

> Kegeles [with Hays and Coates, 1996] evaluated their intervention by looking for a reduction in the proportion of men who engaged in any act of unprotected anal sex. The question that must be asked is whether this measure fully captures the effect of their intervention. Not reflected in this outcome measure would be a person who had reduced the number of unprotected acts of anal intercourse from 50 at baseline to 25 at follow-up or one who went from no condom use to 75% condom use, or who reduced the number of acts of anal sex or the number of partners, or who substituted masturbation or "outercourse" for intercourse. Did the outcome measures selected by the authors ask too much of their intervention? Was it fair to view a person who reduced unprotected sex acts from 100 to 0 as no more of a success than one who reduced such acts from 1 to none?

Other challenges arise related to the types of data that can be collected at reasonable cost. For example, for programs focusing on individual behavior changes, self-reported measures are often all that can be affordably obtained, and these are not always reliable. Sometimes people neither know aspects of their health status (e.g., blood pressure or blood cholesterol levels) nor know what they do (e.g., how many servings of grains they ate yesterday). At other times, social desirability influences their answer (i.e., they give what they believe the answer should be even if it is not what they do). Many researchers attempt to control for this third confounding variable by measuring social desirability traits as part of their studies.

What Was Actually Implemented?

As Orlandi (1986) observed, assessing effectiveness is difficult or impossible without knowing how the program was implemented. Without process evaluation to detail if and how the intervention was implemented, evaluators may make what Scanlon and colleagues (1977) termed a type III error: evaluating a program that has not been adequately implemented or is not measured as implemented (Basch et al., 1985). Before outcome evaluation is initiated, evaluators should review process evaluation data and determine whether any refinements need to be made to the study design or measures to adjust to a different implementation than was initially envisioned.

Reviewing process evaluation data before conducting an outcome evaluation is particularly important if the evaluators were not involved in program implementation. This may occur if an organization uses outside evaluators who are hired specifically for outcome evaluation. Even if the evaluators are on staff, for many large programs evaluation staff are totally separate from program staff, and they would have no reason to know whether a program had been implemented as planned or not. For multisite programs where collaborating organizations are responsible for much of the implementation, it may be difficult for program managers to truly know the degree to which particular program components have been implemented. Ongoing monitoring and process evaluation activities help ensure this problem does not occur.

■ CHOOSING AN EVALUATION STUDY DESIGN

Evaluation designs can be divided into three categories:

1. Experimental
2. Quasi-experimental
3. Other

Each category and each study design within each category has limitations and underlying assumptions that preclude using it in every setting.

Hornik (2002) outlined some broad principles about what makes evaluation designs stronger:

- The evaluation design needs to reflect the mechanism by which the program is likely to work—including how much exposure to messages will be achieved, who should be affected, how fast the effects should occur, and what their magnitude should be.
- Some study design elements are likely to buy better inferences, all else being equal. These include having many measures over time, incorporating treatment comparison groups if they exist, supplementing

evidence about outcomes with evidence that the program operated as intended, and having larger rather than smaller samples.

- Designs are specific to a context. A pre–post design may be good enough if evaluators can make a strong case that no competing activities could explain the change in behavior. Similarly, programs considered successful only if they produce large, rapid effects will tolerate a "lesser" design than programs that expect slow, gradual change.

The following sections present brief descriptions of each type of design and overviews of some of the issues to consider in using them. Those planning an evaluation would do well to consult standard evaluation texts, such as Rossi, Lipsey, and Freeman (2003); the classic works on experimental and quasi-experimental design (see, in particular, Campbell & Stanley, 1966; Cook & Campbell, 1979); and Hornik's *Public Health Communication: Evidence for Behavior Change* (2002), which discuss evaluation models and analyses appropriate for various types of programs.

Experimental Designs

A randomized experiment is the gold standard approach to outcome evaluation in which members of the population of interest are randomly assigned to one of two or more groups. One group, the control group, does not receive the program intervention. The other group(s) receive(s) the intervention (or variations of it, if there are multiple groups). Because participants are randomly assigned to the groups, one group should not differ in any significant way from the other group. Therefore, assuming that nothing differentially affected each group during the intervention time period, any observed differences in outcomes can be assumed to be the result of the intervention. Outcomes are assessed by comparing the treatment group(s) scores with those of the control group. Ideally, both groups are measured before and after the intervention.

Program managers often face tremendous pressure to use randomized experiments because they conclusively demonstrate whether the intervention succeeded and because they use a familiar methodology. Although randomized experiments are useful in a wide array of settings, using them to evaluate many public health interventions often fundamentally violates their assumptions.

Limitations of Experimental Designs When Evaluating Social Change

The premise that the intervention is the only thing that could cause a change in the treatment group because it is the only thing that is different between the treatment and control groups works very well when testing a vaccine in a laboratory—however, public health interventions are not vaccines (Smith, 1997, 2002). Using vaccines and clinical care as metaphors (**Figure 12-1**), Smith (2002) argued that the typical public health intervention is more like clinical care. The critical distinction between the two is that the vaccine model of disease prevention is largely characterized by a "develop and deliver" mentality, whereas the clinical care model is characterized by an assess, intervene, and adjust mentality.

There are three common problems with using randomized case-control trials to evaluate social change initiatives. One issue is that the randomized studies require stable, constant interventions that are not adjusted to changing conditions. However, social change efforts must be dynamic, responding to changes in the environment and the audience. Planners cannot reasonably expect that a program will be implemented in exactly the same way over time or at different locations at different times. If the program is used somewhere else, some adjustments have to be made to delivery mechanisms if nothing else.

The goal of evaluating a social change program should not be to determine if the program "worked" as initially envisioned or if it is stable enough to use somewhere else. It is not stable, and it is not intended to be. The goals should be to determine how much progress was made toward objectives and how that progress was made. When assessing social change efforts, evaluators must recognize the changes that were made along the way and document why those changes were made—what they were designed to fix or improve. This will give them a sense of the conditions under which combinations of goods and services, message appeals, delivery mechanisms, and so forth work best.

As Smith (1997) noted, one of the reasons some of the large community intervention trials may appear to fail is that the interventions are not altered to meet changing conditions. Discussing the 22-community, 4-year Community Intervention Trial for Smoking Cessation (COMMIT), he observed that "because it was a case control program, there were a lot of things that occurred during the four years that the interventionists could have changed because they found out they weren't working as well.

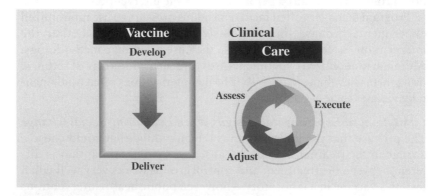

Figure 12-1 Two Metaphors for Intervention Development

Source: Reprinted from "From Prevention Vaccines to Community Care" (p. 329), by W. Smith. In *Public Health Communication: Evidence for Behavior Change* by R. Hornik (Ed.), 2002, Mahwah, NJ: Lawrence Erlbaum Associates. Copyright 2002 by Lawrence Erlbaum Associates. Reprinted with permission.

But they didn't change them because they were testing a 'vaccine' and the vaccine can't be changed in the middle of the test" (p. 12).

A second limitation to using a randomized trial is that community-based interventions generally lack a true control group. Although a group may not receive the program's intervention, it probably is receiving some intervention, in the form of secular trends if nothing else. Public health initiatives usually do not come into existence until there is a movement in society to make a particular change. Members of the control group may be exposed to these secular trends. "Science does not operate in a vacuum; the forces that operate to justify large, expensive community intervention studies also are operating among the general public to get them to accept the evidence and act on it even before scientific establishment does" (Feinlaub, 1996, p. 1697).

These secular trends can have a devastating impact on an evaluation's ability to measure program contributions accurately. As Rossi and colleagues (2003) noted in their classic evaluation text, "relatively long-term trends in the community, region or country, sometimes termed secular drift, may produce changes that enhance or mask the apparent effects of a program" (pp. 272–273). Secular trends combined with the need to keep an intervention "stable" may create a situation in which the control group has access to more state-of-art information and tools than the treatment group over the life of a multiyear program. A number of practitioners and evaluators have argued that secular trends may be why some very large community trials, where interventions take place in one set of communities and other communities are "matched" to those and treated as a control group, fail to show an effect.

Discussing COMMIT, Smith (1997) said, "a strong secular trend was affecting both intervention and control communities. Change occurred in both communities; everybody was getting better at decreasing smoking rates. The study showed that the intervention did not produce an effect any stronger than a very strong secular trend. Much of what was going on in the intervention group was going on in the control group as well" (p. 12). Another example comes from the Stanford Five-City Project, a large-scale, community-based intervention designed to test whether a comprehensive program of community organization and health education produced favorable changes in cardiovascular disease risk factors, morbidity, and mortality. Authors of one study concluded that "the net intervention efforts were modest. This is due, in part, to the strong secular trends in both health promotion and risk factors" (Winkleby et al., 1996, p. 1778).

Also discussing the effects of secular trends, Hornik (1997a) warned, "local activities build on a spine of national programs that work together. Don't evaluate, don't try to compare treatment and controls that are geographically defined unless there is really going to be a difference in exposure to messages. Don't accept trials as negative evidence until you look hard at the evidence for differences in exposure between the so-called treatment and control areas" (p. 59).

A third issue that limits the utility of randomized case-control trials is that the effect sizes required to demonstrate statistical change are often unrealistic. Most public health initiatives do not take place in a lab with 50 participants. They take place in communities and states. Sometimes they take place across the whole country. Unlike a lab, these settings offer little control over exactly who received the intervention and almost no control over exactly how much of it they receive. Yet evaluation standards demand statistically significant change before conclusions about the intervention's effect can be made. Fishbein (1996, p. 1075) noted as follows:

> Given the nature of our statistical tests and our tendency to use relatively small samples in experimentally controlled studies, this usually means that a public health intervention will be considered a success only if it produces an effect of at least medium size (e.g., a mean difference of at least half of a standard deviation, or about a 20%-to-30% change in a proportion), or, often, an even larger effect size (e.g., a mean difference of a full standard deviation, or a 50%-to-60% change in a proportion). One might ask whether such expectations are either realistic or warranted. That is, can we really expect a usually brief, relatively inexpensive public health intervention to produce medium or large effects? . . . Rightly or wrongly, we appear to be bound by the requirement to demonstrate statistical significance even though we seldom have the resources to evaluate our interventions with sample sizes necessary to detect a small effect.

To put these effect sizes in context, the Stanford Five-City Project described above, much more intensive than many population-based public health initiatives, estimated that the adults in the project's treatment communities would have been exposed to around 5 hours of education per year (Farquhar et al., 1990). Even a 20% change—the low end of the range just described—as a result of 5 hours of education over the course of a year may be unreasonable to expect. Most public health interventions deliver a much lower dose of exposure.

By comparison, commercial marketers, who also seek widespread population change, concluded that their "interventions" are a great success when market share increases 2% or 3%. Writing about this phenomenon, Fishbein (1996) remarked, "Thus, while a condom manufacturer would be more than happy if an advertising campaign increased the company's share of the market by 3% or 4%, a public health intervention that increased condom use by the same 3% or 4% probably would be considered a failure" (p. 1075).

Although there may be many reasons the standards in the two fields differ, two in particular probably play a part. First, expectations about appropriate effect sizes for social change were carried over from expectations about appropriate effect sizes for clinical studies; adjustments were not made for differences in intervention intensity. As Kristal (1997) noted, "the effect size for clinical interventions is large and hopefully fast. In a public health intervention, it's small, and at best, it's gradual" (p. 39). Second, evaluators of many public health initiatives are forced to rely on samples, which are a considerably less exact measure than sales data or many of the measures available in clinical studies. As Kraemer and Winkleby (1997) noted in a response to Fishbein's comments in the preceding paragraph, "if the same condom manufacturers lacked data from the entire population and needed to estimate the market share of the campaign, they might commission a survey research group to sample representative sites within the market area. If the survey research group concluded that the market share was somewhere between 2% and 6%, the condom manufacturers would be uncertain about the effect of the campaign and might be quite dissatisfied with the survey" (p. 1727).

Quasi-Experimental Designs

Studies in this category compare treatment and control groups; however, assignment to each group is not random (hence the designation *quasi-experimental*). As with true experiments, outcomes are most commonly assessed by comparing the groups' pre- and post-intervention scores. A major drawback to quasi-experimental designs is what has been termed "the fantasy of untreated control groups" (Durlak, 1995, p. 76). As discussed earlier in this chapter, social change initiatives are usually developed as a result of strong secular trends; it is unlikely that members of the control group are receiving no aspects of the intervention.

A variety of methods can be used to assign target audience members to treatment and control groups. One popular method of assignment with community interventions is selecting communities that match the communities where the intervention is put into place on key variables. This was the approach used in the COMMIT and Stanford Five-City Project community intervention trials mentioned earlier in this chapter.

An alternative approach that works for some types of interventions is to define different groups within a community. For example, schools could be divided into those that receive program materials and those that do not. For mass media components, some commercial advertising methodologies can be used to divide the overall population into two or more groups. For example, some cable systems can split households, transmitting one ad to half of the households and a different ad to the other half. Some magazines can split press runs in the same way, or they can insert an ad in one edition and not another.

Another technique is to create the control group when outcome data are analyzed, by comparing those who participated in the program (the treatment group) with those who did not (the control group). Because everyone in the community could have been exposed to program messages, even if they do not remember the exposure, there is no way to divide the groups; therefore, this approach rarely works for community interventions.

Quasi-experimental designs can be used for a number of reasons. They are often used to pilot test an intervention or to evaluate a demonstration project. A true pilot test normally takes place after traditional pretesting but before the planned full-scale implementation. Demonstration projects generally follow the complete program life cycle (e.g., planning, development, implementation, evaluation). The resulting evaluation data can help refine program components and, in some instances, help program planners gauge likely response to or demand for various program elements.

However, expectations of what a pilot test or demonstration project will provide should be carefully considered. Such tests can be expensive because materials and products have to be produced in final form and reproduced in small quantities, and the resources required to evaluate the results can far outweigh the costs of development and implementation. Additionally, expectations often are unrealistic because the pilot implementation is qualitatively or quantitatively different from what the future implementation will be. For example, demonstration sites often receive far more training and technical assistance than will be available to other sites when the program is implemented. Test sites may receive materials for free, whereas other sites have to pay for them. The small scale may allow proportionally more resources to be expended, increasing both the total number of people reached by the intervention and the frequency with which they are reached, leading to an overstatement of the likely effects.

Quasi-experimental designs are also used for comparison studies in which two or more implementation strategies are tested against each other. The implementations may differ along such dimensions as products or services offered, types of materials (e.g., different advertisements might be tested against each other), or mix of promotional activities (e.g., one implementation uses only mass media, another uses mass media plus community events, and a third uses only community events).

Other Designs

In situations where a randomized experimental design or quasi-experimental design is inappropriate or not feasible, sometimes an alternative design can be used that, although weaker than ideal, respects the way the program is expected to work and adequately considers alternative explanations for any observed outcomes (Hornik, 2002).

After-Only Design

Evaluators are often asked to evaluate an intervention that has been in place for some time and are limited to a "post-treatment" survey of the target audience. (This is one problem that occurs when evaluation is not planned in tandem with the program.) Although this is inherently the weakest of evaluation designs, Hornik (2002) offered some suggestions for how it can be useful. His suggestions assumed that the intervention was a promotional effort, although his logic could be extended to apply to other aspects of the marketing mix. Measuring recall of the messages, knowledge or beliefs those messages might have influenced, and self-reported behavior can allow evaluators to address the following types of questions:

- Does a reasonable amount of the audience report a substantial level of recall?
- Is there an association (in the expected direction) between recall and behavior?
- Is that association robust even when known predictors of the behavior and/or exposure to media are controlled statistically?
- Is there evidence that the intervention worked as expected? For example, if the intervention is presumed to "work" by changing a particular belief which in turn is expected to change behavior, is there evidence that exposure affected behavior through the targeted belief?

Pre–Post or Before–After Designs

As with experiments, these studies involve taking measures before and after an intervention; the difference is that there is no control group, so it can be difficult to make a compelling case that the intervention caused the change. Therefore, these designs are appropriate for interventions without competition from complementary efforts to address the issue. Measures are often collected by surveying representative samples of the target audience before and after an intervention, but other measures appropriate for the intervention can be used, such as sales data (e.g., to measure the impact of a smoke-free regulation on local businesses), number of callers to a crisis prevention hotline, number of children vaccinated, number of people in a cafeteria line including a fruit or vegetable on their tray, and so on.

Pre–post designs have a number of variations:

- Tracking studies involve taking one measure before the intervention and then multiple measures during and after the intervention. These studies can be used to assess various factors such as current practices, intent to engage in a new behavior, familiarity with an issue, and awareness of the initiative. Tracking studies typically involve independent cross-sectional surveys (in other words, interviewing a new sample of people at each point in time).

- Time-series analyses involve collecting many repeated measures of the same variables both before and after intervention and then comparing the measures to identify change. Sometimes this can be done using existing data sets; for example, to measure the impact of the U.S. National High Blood Pressure Education Program, trends in awareness, treatment, and control of hypertension were examined using National Health and Nutrition Examination Survey data, and stroke mortality rates were examined using data collected by the National Center for Health Statistics (Rocella, 2002). Time-series analysis can also use the preintervention measures to project what was expected to occur and then comparing this projection to the data from the postintervention time period (**Figure 12-2**).

- Panel or cohort studies involve measuring the same people multiple times. In some ways, this design is stronger than measuring outcomes with separate cross-sectional studies because it allows each person's pretest measure to serve as his or her own reflexive control. However, the sample's generalizability may be compromised over time as participants age, leave, or respond to repeated questions on the same subject (Siddiqui et al., 1996).

■ CONCLUSION

Outcome evaluations are necessary to measure the degree to which a program met its objectives. In addition, outcome evaluations can be used to identify unintended consequences, measure cost-effectiveness, and

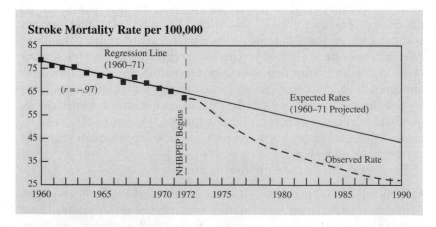

Figure 12-2 Age-Adjusted Stroke Mortality Rates: Expected Rates from a 1960–1971 Regression Line of Best Fit Projected to 1990, and Observed Rates from 1972 to 1990.

Source: From "Reduction of cardiovascular disease mortality," (p. 83), by E. Roccella. In *Public Health Communication: Evidence for Behavior Change,* by R. Hornik (Ed.), 2002, Mahwah, NJ: Lawrence Erlbaum Associates. Copyright 2002 by Lawrence Erlbaum Associates. Reprinted with permission.

guide future initiatives. This chapter has presented a number of factors planners should keep in mind when determining how the outcome of a social change initiative will be assessed. Foremost among them are the following:

- Choosing an evaluation design appropriate for the intervention in scope, in cost, and, most importantly, in its assumptions about how change will occur. The evaluation should be able to tolerate changes to the program design and implementation.
- Understanding the environment in which the initiative is taking place. Strong secular trends are often present and can mask the effects of an intervention.
- Ensuring that outcome expectations are driven by what is realistic for the intervention and evaluations are designed accordingly.
- Ensuring that the outcomes measured are those the intervention was trying to affect and that the range of possible progress toward those outcomes is adequately captured.

Evaluators may use one of several study designs to measure change. Experimental studies traditionally are more scientifically sound than other types of studies; however, they can be problematic for measuring social change. As Walsh and colleagues (1993) observed, "the very essence of social marketing is to adapt and change, whereas summative evaluation researchers need a program to stay the course" (p. 115). In other words, traditional outcome evaluation models expect a static, never-changing intervention, but social change initiatives using marketing principles are designed to be dynamic, constantly adjusting to changing environments and audience needs. Second, large effects may be needed to see statistically significant change, yet sometimes it is not reasonable to expect a large effect, and even a small one may have huge public health implications. Third, the outcome data can be difficult to interpret when strong secular trends are also at work. Other study design options include quasi-experimental, after-only, and pre–post designs. Evaluators and program managers need to work together to select a study design that is most appropriate for the intervention model and evaluation goals.

References

Basch, C.E., Sliepcevich, E.M., Gold, R.S., Duncan, D.F., & Kolbe, L.J. (1985). Avoiding type III errors in health education program evaluations: A case study. *Health Education Quarterly, 12*(3), 315–331.

Beresford, S.A.A., Curry, S.J., Kristal, A.R., Lazovich, D., Feng, Z., & Wagner, E.H. (1997). A dietary intervention in primary care practice: The eating patterns study. *American Journal of Public Health, 87,* 610–616.

Campbell, D.T., & Stanley, J.C. (1966). *Experimental and quasi-experimental designs for research*. Boston, MA: Houghton Mifflin.

Cook, T.D., & Campbell, D.T. (1979). *Quasi-experimentation design and analysis issues for field settings*. Skokie, IL: Rand McNally.

Durlak, J.A. (1995). *School-based prevention programs for children and adolescents*. Thousand Oaks, CA: Sage.

Farquhar, J.W., Fortmann, S.P., Flora, J.A., Taylor, C.B., Haskell, W.L., Williams, P.T., . . . Wood, P.D. (1990). Effects of community-wide education on cardiovascular disease risk factors. *Journal of the American Medical Association, 264*, 359–365.

Feinlaub, M. (1996). Editorial: New directions for community intervention studies. *American Journal of Public Health, 86*, 1696–1698.

Fishbein, M. (1996). Editorial: Great expectations, or do we ask too much from community-level interventions? *American Journal of Public Health, 86*, 1075–1076.

Glantz, S., & Smith, L.R.A. (1994). The effect of ordinances requiring smoke-free restaurants on restaurant sales. *American Journal of Public Health, 84*, 1081–1085.

Hornik, R. (1997a). Charting the course from lessons learned. In L. Doner (Ed.), *Charting the course for evaluation: How do we measure the success of nutrition education and promotion in food assistance programs? Summary of proceedings* (pp. 56–61). Alexandria, VA: USDA Food and Consumer Service.

Hornik, R. (1997b). Public health education and communication as policy instruments for bringing about changes in behavior. In M.E. Goldberg, M. Fishbein, & S.E. Middlestadt (Eds.), *Social marketing; Theoretical and practical perspectives* (pp. 45–58). Mahwah, NJ: Lawrence Erlbaum Associates.

Hornik, R.C. (Ed.). (2002). *Public health communication: Evidence for behavior change*. Mahwah, NJ: Lawrence Erlbaum Associates.

Kegeles, S.M., Hays, R.B., & Coates, T.J. (1996). The Mpowerment Project: A community-level HIV prevention intervention for young gay men. *American Journal of Public Health, 86*, 1129–1135.

Kotler, P., & Roberto, E.L. (1989). *Social marketing: Strategies for changing public behavior*. New York, NY: Free Press.

Kraemer, H.C., & Winkleby, M.A. (1997). Do we ask too much from community-level interventions or from intervention researchers? *American Journal of Public Health, 87*, 1727.

Kristal, A.R. (1997). Choosing appropriate dietary data collection methods to assess behavior changes. In L. Doner (Eds.), *Charting the course for evaluation: How do we measure the success of nutrition education and promotion in food assistance programs? Summary of proceedings* (pp. 39–41). Alexandria, VA: USDA Food and Consumer Service.

National Highway Traffic Safety Administration (NHTSA). (1997). Air bag on-off switches rule. 62 *Federal Register* 62406 (to be codified at 49 C.F.R. § 571 and 595).

National Highway Traffic Safety Administration (NHTSA). (2000). Advanced air bag safety standard. Retrieved October 6, 2006, from http://www.nhtsa.dot.gov/cars/testing/ncap/airbags/pages/FAQsAdvFrontABs.htm

National Highway Traffic Safety Administration (NHTSA). (2001). Counts for air bag related fatalities and seriously injured persons. Retrieved October 6, 2006, from http://www-nrd.nhtsa.dot.gov/pdf/nrd-30/NCSA/SCI/3Q_2001/ABFSISR.html

Orlandi, M.A. (1986). The diffusion and adoption of worksite health promotion innovations: An analysis of barriers. *Preventive Medicine, 15*, 522–536.

Prentice, R.L., & Sheppard, L. (1990). Dietary fat and cancer: Consistency of the epidemiologic data, and disease prevention that may follow from a practical reduction in fat consumption. *Cancer Causes Control, 15*, 522–536.

Rocella, E. (2002). Reduction of cardiovascular disease mortality. In R. Hornik (Ed.), *Public health communication: Evidence for behavior change* (pp. 73–84). Mahwah, NJ: Lawrence Erlbaum Associates.

Rossi, P.H., & Freeman, H.E. (1993). *Evaluation: A systematic approach* (5th ed.). Newbury Park, CA: Sage.

Rossi, P.H., Lipsey, M.W., & Freeman, H.E. (2003). *Evaluation: A systematic approach* (7th ed.). Newbury Park, CA: Sage.

Scanlon, J., Horst, P., Nay, J.N., Schmidt, R.E., & Waller, A.E. (1977). Evaluability assessment: Avoiding type III and IV errors. In G.R. Gilbert & P.J. Cronkin (Eds.), *Evaluation management: A sourcebook of readings* (pp. 264–284). Charlottesville, VA: U.S. Civil Service Commission.

Scollo, M., Lal, A., Hyland, A., & Glantz, S. (2003). Review of the quality of studies on the economic effects of smoke-free polices on the hospitality industry. *Tobacco Control, 12*, 13–20.

Siddiqui, O., Flay, B.R., & Hu, F.B. (1996). Factors affecting attrition in a longitudinal smoking prevention study. *Preventive Medicine, 25*, 554–560.

Smith, W. (1997). Confounding issues in evaluations of nutrition interventions. In L. Doner (Ed.), *Charting the course for evaluation: How do we measure the success of nutrition education and promotion in food assistance programs? Summary of proceedings* (pp. 11–13). Alexandria, VA: USDA Food and Consumer Service.

Smith, W. (2002). From prevention vaccines to community care. In R. Hornik (Ed.), *Public health communication: Evidence for behavior change* (pp. 327–356). Mahwah, NJ: Lawrence Erlbaum Associates.

Susser, M. (1997). Editorial: Goliath and some Davids in the tobacco wars. *American Journal of Public Health, 87*, 1593–1595.

Wallack, L., & Dorfman, L. (1996). Media advocacy: A strategy for advancing policy and promoting health. *Health Education Quarterly, 23*, 293–317.

Walsh, D.C., Rudd, R.E., Moeykens, B.A., & Maloney, T.W. (1993). Social marketing for public health. *Health Affairs, 12*(2), 105–119.

Winkleby, M.A., Taylor, C.B., Jatulis, D., & Fortmann, S.P. (1996). The long-term effects of a cardiovascular disease prevention trial: The Stanford Five-City Project. *American Journal of Public Health, 86*, 1773–1779.

Marketing Public Health: Case Studies

This section presents two case studies. The first case study examines the role social media play in suicide prevention, demonstrating how to use social media to engage audiences in social change. The second case study illustrates the strategic application of marketing principles to develop and implement a novel intervention to reform health behavior among rural women of reproductive age in Rwanda: a radio soap opera.

CHAPTER

13

Building a Movement with Social Media

Elana Premack Sandler,
LCSW, MPH

In September 2010, a 15-year-old named Billy Lucas died by suicide, one of thousands of young people who died by suicide that year. Yet it was his death that catalyzed a movement. Within 2 weeks of Lucas' death, columnist Dan Savage received a message on his blog, "Savage Love" (Savage, 2010): "I just read about a gay teenager in Indiana—Billy Lucas—who killed himself after being taunted by his classmates. Now his Facebook memorial page is being defaced by people posting homophobic comments. It's just heartbreaking and sickening. What the hell can we do?" (Savage, 2010, paragraph 9). Savage had been following the suicide deaths of other young people who were gay or assumed to be gay. He wrote, "I wish I could have talked to this kid for five minutes. I wish I could have told Billy that *it gets better*. I wish I could have told him that, however bad things were, however isolated and alone he was, *it gets better*" (Savage, 2010, paragraph 14).

Savage and his husband, Terry Miller, realized there *was* a way for them to tell kids it gets better: social media. Creating a channel on YouTube, Savage and Miller created and uploaded a video of them talking about their lives and the ways things had changed for them over time. With that simple action, a movement was launched that changed public discourse about lesbian, gay, bisexual, and transgender (LGBT) suicide, a topic that then refused to stay out of public consciousness.

In this chapter, we examine the "It Gets Better Project" (It Gets Better) as one of several initiatives that used social media to address youth suicide prevention. It Gets Better was not designed by public health practitioners but offers useful lessons, grounded in social and behavioral science theory, for professionals considering implementing social change campaigns or public health initiatives using social media. We also discuss other projects that applied social and behavioral science theories: "Take 5 to Save Lives" (Take 5), a campaign launched on World Suicide Prevention Day 2010, and the "Make It Better Project" (Make It Better), a community-organizing project initiated by the Gay-Straight Alliance Network that took the momentum generated by It Gets Better a step further.

■ SUICIDE PREVENTION

Suicide is the third leading cause of death among 15- to 24-year-olds and the second leading cause of death among 25- to 34-year-olds (Centers for Disease Control and Prevention, 2011). Among young Native Americans, suicide is the second leading cause of death; rates in this population are 1.8 times higher than the national average for that age group. Suicide attempts are higher among Hispanic and Black, non-Hispanic female high school students than among their White, non-Hispanic peers. Lesbian, gay, and bisexual youth exhibit more suicidal behavior, including suicidal ideation and suicide attempts, than other youth. Lesbian, gay, and bisexual youth have fewer protective factors, such as family support and safe schools, and more risk factors, including experiencing depression and engaging in substance abuse, than other youth. For youth who are part of any marginalized culture, discrimination is also a factor in suicide risk (Suicide Prevention Resource Center, 2008).

Suicide grew as a recognizable public health issue with the issuance of the National Strategy for Suicide Prevention by the U.S. Surgeon General in 2001. In 2010, a public–private partnership, the National Action Alliance for Suicide Prevention, was launched to continue to champion suicide prevention as a national priority, catalyze efforts to implement high-priority objectives of the National Strategy for Suicide Prevention, and cultivate resources to sustain progress in suicide prevention (National Action Alliance for Suicide Prevention, 2011). Suicide prevention public health activities are implemented at the local, community, state, tribal, and national levels by public and private agencies, tribal organizations, college and university campuses, and national organizations. Many of these activities are supported with public funds from the federal Substance Abuse and Mental Health Services Administration.

■ SOCIAL MEDIA

Social media are Internet-based services that "expand interactivity and collaborative content sharing" (Korda & Itani, 2011, p. 1). Included in the category are social networking sites, such as Facebook and MySpace;

blogs and microblogging platforms like Twitter; wikis, where content can be developed by multiple users simultaneously; and mobile messaging platforms that build on cell phone technology.

In the United States in 2000, just under 75% of teens ages 12 to 17 were using the Internet (Lenhart et al., 2010). By 2009, 93% were online. Among individuals ages 18 to 29, 93% were also online in 2009, compared with just under 75% in 2000. Among individuals ages 18 to 33 surveyed in 2010, 80% to 89% used the Internet to access social networking sites (Zickuhr, 2010). Adults across generations use social media less than the younger population, but 60% to 69% of adults ages 34 to 45 use social networking sites and 50% to 59% of adults ages 46 to 55 use these sites (Zickuhr, 2010).

A central idea in social media is "user-generated content." In Web 1.0, or the original Internet, information was delivered to audiences via websites. Websites were unidirectional means of communication (Solis, 2011). In Web 2.0, which includes social media, websites are the hosts for interactions, or conversations, between individuals or between organizations and individuals.

■ SOCIAL MEDIA AND SOCIAL CHANGE MOVEMENTS

Just as advocates for social change have used various forms of media to connect with and persuade their audiences, today's advocates have embraced social media for social change. The 2008 presidential election, for example, demonstrated that social media are essential to engaging a new generation of activists (Quily, 2008). During the campaign, Barack Obama dramatically outpaced John McCain in social media output, savvy, and presence. Obama connected with more than 2 million supporters on Facebook and more than 25,000 YouTube friends, in addition to enabling comments on MySpace to allow for interaction with constituents on that site (Quily, 2008). Social media allowed the Obama campaign to build a movement around a virtually unknown local politician competing to win against a well-known and seasoned political celebrity.

The Obama campaign recognized the importance of using social media to interact with the individuals whose decisions they wanted to influence. The goal of much public health work is to influence decision making by a target audience. Social media can be used in public health to reach an intended audience as well as to gain feedback from that audience to help in program or campaign development. Social media can be the foundation of a public health campaign or program or can be a tool used by a campaign or program.

Social media are living applications of several social and behavioral science theories, including diffusion of innovations (Rogers, 2003), stages of change theory (Prochaska & DiClemente, 1983), community-organizing theory (Staples, 2004), and social network theory (Milgram, 1967), each analyzed in this chapter. By nature and by design, social media are bottom-up conversations and dialogues, matching in philosophical approach with public health practice that seeks to empower and give voice to often-voiceless populations. Because of the vast reach of social media, as demonstrated through the example of Obama's 2 million supporters on Facebook, such media have tremendous power and offer an opportunity to drive action on an "unprecedented and exponential scale," (Livingston, 2010, paragraph 3).

It Gets Better

The dialogue between *New York Times* "Well" blogger Tara Parker-Pope and It Gets Better founder Savage in an interview encapsulates the intersection of user-generated content and social change movements (Parker-Pope, 2011):

> Parker-Pope: "It's so obvious to us now . . . we should have all thought of this ourselves." Savage: "I think it's clear from the response that if we hadn't thought of it, somebody was about to."

The message that "it gets better" was one Savage and Miller thought they could send by sharing the example of their lives (Parker-Pope, 2011). The new tools of social media opened a new door. In the past, conversations and connections between LGBT youth and LGBT adults drew accusations of recruiting and seduction into the gay lifestyle, or gay adults were accused of pedophilia. Now, sharing their message via new media was a subversive act, going above adults who usually connect with youth, such as parents, teachers, and clergy, to connect directly with youth (Parker-Pope, 2011).

It Gets Better quickly grew from Savage and Miller's initial YouTube video to a collection of more than 20,000 videos created and uploaded by Internet users all over the world, including U.S. President Barack Obama. The White House, Savage said, is in a position to make it better through implementing policies that lead to change (Parker-Pope, 2011). Recounting his coming-out process in the early 1980s, Savage remembered former President Ronald Reagan's silence about the AIDS epidemic. "To go from that to a president who only took three weeks to make an 'It Gets Better' video is itself evidence that it gets better, that it has gotten better" (Parker-Pope, 2011).

The theoretical underpinning of It Gets Better's success is the theory of diffusion of innovations, whereby an idea is spread through a social group by the members of that group, some of whom have more power, sway, or influence than others (Rogers, 2003). Savage and Miller wanted LGBT adults to share their stories first, which put LGBT adults in the category of target early adopters. Having LGBT adults share their stories of perseverance, diffusing the innovation of the It Gets Better video, was critical to the integrity of the campaign. If the stories told through the YouTube medium were inauthentic or too scripted, they would not be believable by LGBT youth.

The celebrities who followed as early-majority adopters (adopting the innovation after a period of time), late-majority adopters (adopting the innovation after the average member of society), and laggards (the last to follow) were important to the campaign's success but not as essential. President Obama may be seen as an early-majority adopter. Once It Gets Better tipped into the cultural mainstream, Obama became involved, and once Obama made an It Gets Better video, the practice became even more acceptable, with other public and political figures creating their own videos. The campaign continued to build as celebrity LGBT adults, including Fort Worth, Texas, City Councilman Joel Burns and television star Tim Gunn, recorded their It Gets Better videos within the first 2 months of the project.

The project intentionally used social media in selecting YouTube as the medium by which to promote the message. But the project gained a lot of social media capital through the dissemination of the YouTube videos via other social media channels, such as Facebook and Twitter. The example of It Gets Better shows that social media can be used as a platform for a campaign and a way to generate attention for a campaign.

Take 5 to Save Lives

Take 5 to Save Lives, a project of the National Council for Suicide Prevention (2011), used social media to encourage suicide prevention activism on World Suicide Prevention Day 2010. In 5 minutes, an Internet user could learn the warning signs for suicide prevention, join the suicide prevention movement by connecting with others online, spread the word by telling people about what they learned, learn how to support a friend who is struggling, or reach out for support from a mental health professional.

The term "slacktivism" was coined, meaning to do well without having to do much at all (Livingston, 2010). Because all actions involved in the Take 5 campaign could be done online, from the comfort of one's home, office, or school, it could be seen as a campaign created for slacktivists. But, as Livingston (2010) suggested, if digital activists are instead seen as individuals wanting to make a difference, they can be given credit, and a means, for making change.

By meeting individuals where they are already and matching the desired change or action with the audience's existing and familiar behavior patterns, the Take 5 campaign lets online activists spread campaign messages for organizers. The power of the campaign was the ease with which individuals could engage in achieving campaign goals. Although some of the goals of the campaign were focused on increasing knowledge or awareness, other goals were related to gaining skills and changing behavior. Extrapolating from the idea that "the ideal case here is when one's participation in digital activism doesn't subtract from—and instead enhances—one's eagerness to participate in real-life campaigns" (Morozov, 2009, paragraph 6), the ideal case for the Take 5 campaign is when digital activism and engagement leads to behavior change that contributes to suicide prevention. For some individuals, that change may have come from learning skills needed to help a friend. For others, reaching out to a mental health professional may have contributed to changing the course of their struggle with emotional distress.

The Take 5 campaign offers an example of how social media can allow audience members or individuals in a population to engage with behavior change at a variety of levels, perhaps leading to significant and meaningful behavior change. There is precedent in public health for viewing behavior change as a series of stages. In Prochaska and DiClemente's (1983) stages of change theory, individuals in the precontemplative stage are not thinking about changing their behavior, perhaps because they are unaware of the benefits of changing their behavior. In the contemplative stage, individuals are aware that behavior change may benefit them but have not yet committed to behavior change. In the preparation/decision-making stage, individuals intend to take action to change their behavior in the near future, although some of their recent actions may be inconsistent with the goal of behavior change. In the action stage, individuals modify their behavior, experiences, or environment. In the maintenance stage, individuals work to continue their behavior change over an extended period of time.

Focused on teaching nonprofit organizations how to better use social media, Beth Kanter (2010) defined a ladder of engagement for Twitter (**Figure 13-1**), which can be translated to other forms of social media as well. At the lowest degree of engagement, a user simply reads the information. At the next level of engagement, a user shares the information but does not offer any modification or opinion. At a medium level of engagement, the user shares the information or interacts with the source of information. At a high level of engagement, a user takes an action related to the source of information. Finally, at a very high level of engagement, a user takes an action and actively encourages others to do so.

Those moderating social media, or directing campaigns using social media, are responsible for stewarding people up the ladder of engagement (Livingston, 2010). Although some may view reading information as far from activism, the ladder of engagement helps illustrate how that initial action can lead to other, more engaged, actions. The ladder of engagement parallels stages of change theory and actually goes beyond stages of change

Degree	Action	Motivation
Very Low	Reads the tweet	Habit of reading Twitter
Low	Re-tweets without modifying the message	Has some passing interest in the Cause, feels they are doing something, may or may not know the original Twitter user
Medium	Re-tweets or @replies with a question about tweet or clicks through link	Trusts the Twitter user or Cause, has a personal or emotional connection to Cause, may have taken some action in the past or influenced by peer group
High	Makes a donation or takes some action	Has relationship with Twitter user or Cause online or offline, personal experience, reciprocity, or has taken action in the past
Very High	Makes a donation or takes action and actively encourages others to do so	Has a strong relationship w/Twitter user or Cause online/offline, personal experience, and was asked by the Cause

Beth Kanter: @kanter

Figure 13-1 The Twitter Ladder of Engagement

Source: Kanter, Beth. (2010, May 6). Twitter social good campaigns: Moving up the Ladder of Engagement. Beth's Blog: Nonprofits and Social Media. Retrieved from http://beth.typepad.com/beths_blog/2010/05/twitter-social-good-campaigns-moving-up-the-ladder-of-engagement.html

theory to diffusion of innovation theory and social network theory, spreading behavior change beyond the individual to peers and social networks.

Make It Better

To move beyond the hope that "It Gets Better," the Gay-Straight Alliance Network started the "Make It Better Project" in October 2010 as a response to the high-profile deaths that spurred the It Gets Better Project, according to Gay-Straight Alliance Network's Jill Marcellus. The goal was to give youth concrete steps to "make it better now, rather than wait for it to get better" (personal communication, 2011). According to project organizers, youth had been eager to learn what they can actively do on the ground to make change. The project moves youth up the ladder of engagement from initial connections to information to real-life activism.

The program model uses peers talking to peers via social media and in person. Youth write blog posts and interact on social media. The project trains youth through online activist camps, such as the Make It Better Summer, and youth then work in their schools and communities to make change. Thus, the "message of hope is coming from youth" who share the steps they have taken in their schools to advocate for improvements, according to Marcellus (personal communication, 2011). By using social media, feedback to the project is constant. Organizers are able to listen to their audience in real time; be responsive to questions, concerns, and issues; and actively build a community of youth activists.

Using a community-organizing approach (Staples, 2004), the Make It Better project is driven by youth concerns. Youth make decisions about what needs to change to make their lives better. Collective action, by organizing youth in groups, allows for change to be made through the power of numbers. The project uses social media as one part of the organizing strategy. Projects like Make It Better demonstrate that the initiative is not designed around the technology—social media—but that the technology is a tool for accomplishing the goals of the initiative. As outlined by Roberts-DeGennaro (in Staples, 2004), technology should not be a substitute for direct contact but a complement to face-to-face interactions. But, in the case of Make It Better, technology adds a dimension that can sometimes be difficult to achieve in organizing taking place solely in person. Taking place in a virtual space, online community organizing has the potential to shift or even reinvent power structures. The Internet is a great equalizer (Solis, 2011), particularly for youth, who often have more experience using social media than adult organizers (Roberts-DeGennaro in Staples, 2004).

Using online community organizing for public health can be another application of social media as both a platform and a process. Social media present a new way of implementing an old theoretical model. In some ways, social media allow for even greater empowerment than is possible in face-to-face organizing.

Tying Three Projects Together: Social Network Theory

The projects described above have a commonality that goes beyond their use of social media as a core part of strategy and implementation and their focus on changing behavior in a way that affects the ultimate outcomes of decreasing suicide risk and preventing suicide. A theoretical tie connects the projects as well. Stanley Milgram (1967) proposed that connections between individuals in a network provide a powerful way of transmitting information. Because social media are built on social networks, they use all connections, however strong or weak. When an individual user of social media puts out a piece of information to his or her network via a Facebook status update or a Twitter tweet, that information can then be sent to the network's networks. Via social media, information travels quickly and far, to people closely connected to those generating the original idea and to those only distally aware of those original idea generators.

Social media have taken the small world Milgram described more than 40 years ago to an entirely new level. People have always turned to their social networks to get information to aid them in decision making. Now, social networks can be reached at any time of day and across vast geographic boundaries. The significance of these dynamics for public health is just beginning to become clear. But one known element is that information—true and false—moves through social networks with incredible speed. Social media are used, and will continue to be used, to disseminate information, accurate or inaccurate. By engaging with social media and intersecting with people's social networks, public health practitioners have the opportunity to disseminate accurate information about the health issues on which they work. At the same time, dissemination is not the be-all and end-all. As is clear in the above examples, engagement is a key aspect of using social media in the practice of behavior change. If public health practitioners are not engaged in the conversation that is social media (Solis, 2009), the dissemination of information may be viewed as inauthentic.

■ IMPLICATIONS FOR PUBLIC HEALTH PRACTICE

The three projects described in this chapter offer many useful lessons for public health practitioners. Although the program developers, many of whom are outside the field of public health, may not have been aware they were using social and behavioral science theories in their programs, public health practitioners can intentionally use social and behavioral science theories to guide the development of their efforts to market public health. It is tempting to jump in to social media because of its incredible popularity. But, as can be seen in the above examples, projects that use social media and are grounded in sound theory are able to have great impact.

The first step for public health practitioners interested in using social media is to get to know the conversation taking place about the issue among the target audience. By monitoring conversations on social media, public health practitioners can grow in their understanding of what an audience is already thinking and saying, as well as what an audience wants to know, about a given health issue. Watching the conversation also allows practitioners to learn where the conversation is taking place (i.e., which media are being used) and who is driving and influencing the conversations. Understanding these elements of the conversation can inform how practitioners go on to use social media.

It may become clear, through observing the conversation, that it is the role of the practitioner to take part in the existing conversation rather than to create a new place or way for the conversation to take place. In addition, social media, despite their popularity, do not always fit with the audience or the goals of a given public health project. For example, a fall-prevention campaign aimed at caregivers of elderly individuals may not fit with any social media platform. Forcing social media into all public health projects is inauthentic; inauthenticity goes against the very values at the foundation of social media. The projects outlined above were successful in using social media because social media provided a good fit with the goals of the projects. Clarifying goals first and then determining whether and how social media can be used to achieve those can be accomplished by asking the following questions (Raymond, 2011):

1. What is the initiative trying to achieve?
2. What is the theory of change?
3. How is the decision maker influenced and when?
4. Who does the organization need to mobilize?
5. What means does the organization need to achieve this?
6. How will the organization know if the plan is working?
7. What will it cost to achieve this?

This strategic approach is appropriate especially because social media are constantly evolving. Public health practitioners should always be critically assessing how to use these media in practice.

Craig Lefebvre (2007) posed six questions for practitioners to ask that take into consideration the social networks that drive individual decision making:

1. How can linkages that already exist among people, organizations, and communities be enhanced to allow them to access, exchange, use, and leverage the knowledge and resources of the others?
2. How can the organization help develop, nurture, and sustain new types of linkages that bring together like-minded people, mission-focused organizations, and communities that share interests to address common problems and achieve positive health and social change?
3. How can the organization identify, encourage, and enable the many different types of indigenous helpers found in social networks so they can be more effective in promoting health?
4. What can the organization do to improve community engagement in monitoring, problem analysis, and problem solving; striving to health and social equity; and increasing social capital?
5. How can existing social networks of individuals, organizations, and communities be woven together to create new sources of power and inspiration to address health and social issues?
6. How does a networked view of the world disrupt the usual ways of thinking about and engaging the people, organizations, and communities with which the organization usually works? What insights can be gained from this perspective?

■ CONCLUSION

The three projects featured in this chapter were able to capitalize on the convergence of suicide prevention's appearance in the public eye and the ubiquity of social media at the public's fingertips. In many ways, the time is now for public health to engage in using social media thoughtfully. Public health practitioners are in a unique place to bring together social networks on social media for social and behavioral change. By being strategic and thinking critically, social media can be used to design and implement public health campaigns that have integrity through a strong theoretical base and positive engagement with the intended audience.

References
Centers for Disease Control and Prevention (2011). Web-based Injury Statistics Query and Reporting System (WISQARS). National Center for Injury Prevention and Control. Retrieved April 25, 2012, from www.cdc.gov/injury/wisqars/index.html

Kanter, B. (2010, May 6). Twitter social good campaigns: Moving up the ladder of engagement. Retrieved April 25, 2012, from http://beth.typepad.com/beths_blog/2010/05/twitter-social-good-campaigns-moving-up-the-ladder-of-engagement.html

Korda, H., & Itani, Z. (2011). Harnessing social media for health promotion and behavior change. *Health Promotion Practice*. DOI: 10.1177/1524839911405850 (epub ahead of print). Retrieved May 10, 2011, from http://hpp.sagepub.com/content/early/2011/05/10/1524839911405850

Lefebvre, C. (2007). The new technology: The consumer as participant rather than target audience. *Social Marketing Quarterly, 8*(3), 31–42.

Lenhart, A., Purcell, K., Smith, A., & Zickuhr, K. (2010). Social media and young adults. Pew Internet & American Life Project. Retrieved April 25, 2012, from http://www.pewinternet.org/Reports/2010/Social-Media-and-Young-Adults.aspx

Livingston, G. (2010, May 13). How to: Turn slacktivists into activists with social media. Retrieved April 25, 2012, from: http://mashable.com/2010/05/13/slacktivists-activists-social-media/

Milgram, S. (1967). The small world problem. *Psychology Today, 1*(1), 60–67.

Morozov E. (2009, May 19). The brave new world of slacktivism. Retrieved April 25, 2012, from http://neteffect.foreignpolicy.com/posts/2009/05/19/the_brave_new_world_of_slacktivism

National Action Alliance for Suicide Prevention. (2011). Retrieved April 25, 2012, from http://www.actionallianceforsuicideprevention.org

National Council on Suicide Prevention. (2011). Retrieved September 25, 2011, from http://www.ncsponline.org/takefive.html

Parker-Pope, T. (2011, July 5). Talking about the It Gets Better Project. Retrieved April 25, 2012, from http://well.blogs.nytimes.com/2011/07/05/talking-about-the-it-gets-better-project/

Prochaska, J.O., & DiClemente, C.C. (1983). Stages and processes of self-change of smoking: Toward an integrative model of change. *Journal of Consulting and Clinical Psychology, 51*(3), 390–395.

Quily, P. (2008, November 5). Barack Obama vs. John McCain social media and search engine scorecard. Retrieved April 25, 2012, from http://adultaddstrengths.com/2008/11/05/obama-vs-mccain-social-media/

Raymond, D. (2011, June). Getting beyond the slacktivism debate. *NTENChange: A Quarterly Journal for Nonprofit Leaders*, Issue 2, 31.

Roberts-DeGennaro, M. (2004). Using technology for grassroots organizing. In L. Staples (Ed.), *Roots to power* (pp. 270–281). Westport, CT: Praeger.

Rogers, D.M. (2003). *Diffusion of innovations* (5th ed.) New York, NY: Free Press.

Savage, D. (2010, September 23). Give 'em hope. Retrieved April 25, 2012, from http://www.thestranger.com/seattle/SavageLove?oid=4940874

Solis, B. (2009, March 30). The conversation prism v2.0. Retrieved April 25, 2012, from http://www.briansolis.com/2009/03/conversation-prism-v20/

Solis, B. (2011, May 10). The end of the destination web and the arrival of the information economy. Retrieved April 25, 2012, from http://www.briansolis.com/2011/05/the-end-of-the-destination-web-and-the-revival-of-the-information-economy/

Staples, L. (2004). *Roots to power: A manual for grassroots organizing* (2nd ed.) Westport, CT: Praeger.

Suicide Prevention Resource Center. (2008). *Suicide risk and prevention for lesbian, gay, bisexual, and transgender youth*. Newton, MA: Education Development Center, Inc.

Zickuhr, K. (2010). Generations 2010: What different generations do online. Pew Internet & American Life Project. Retrieved April 25, 2012, from http://www.pewinternet.org/Infographics/2010/Generations-2010-Summary.aspx

14

Urunana— Radio Health Communication: A Case Study from Rwanda

Narcisse Kalisa
Prudence Uwabakurikiza
Samuel Kyagambiddwa
Jeannette Wijnants
Stephen Collens

Health Unlimited, Rwanda

This chapter describes how basic marketing principles were used to develop an innovative radio health communications project in Rwanda— *Urunana*—which has contributed to changes in awareness and attitudes to reproductive health, sexuality, and relationships of women, men, and youth of Rwanda. It explains how a locally produced radio soap opera addresses culturally sensitive issues in an educational and entertaining manner, involving the target audience (rural women of reproductive age and youth) and a cross-section of stakeholders in its design and implementation. It also highlights the use of basic marketing principles used to research and understand the needs of impoverished, mainly rural listeners to inform the design and implementation of the *Urunana* radio program in a largely conservative and rural society. Although behavior change associated with mass media interventions remains difficult to measure, indirect and anecdotal evidence suggests that *Urunana's* "all-inclusive" approach has made substantial impact, not only on the target audience, but also on policymaking in sexual and reproductive health in Rwanda.

Rwanda is a small, landlocked country located in Central Africa with a total surface area of 26,338 sq. km. According to the national census conducted in 2002, the population of Rwanda was estimated at 8,128,553 inhabitants. About 90.2% of the population lives in rural areas, and women make up more than half of the population, with disproportionately high levels of widow-headed households (Ministry of Finance and Economic Planning, 2002b). The population growth rate is 2.8%. UNICEF's *State of the World's Children* report in 2005 indicates that 50% of its population is under the age of 18 and more than 30% of these children are orphans, due to the 1994 genocide and its aftermath and the high prevalence of HIV/AIDS.

Health status and overall socioeconomic status in Rwanda are poor. The under-five and infant mortality rates are 196 and 107 per 1,000, respectively (Ministry of Health, 2001). The maternal mortality rate rose from 500 per 100,000 in 1992 to an average of 1,071 per 100,000 in 1995–2000. In 2005, the Treatment and Research on HIV/AIDS Centre survey revealed that HIV/AIDS prevalence was 4%. The Rwanda Ministry of Health indicates that malaria remains the main cause of morbidity, accounting for 41% of all consultations in health facilities (Ministry of Health, 2004).

The Demographic and Health Survey carried out in 2000 showed that almost all women were aware of at least one family planning method. However, the use of family planning methods is hampered by the lack of availability and/or utilization of these methods and misconceptions regarding the side effects of modern family planning methods (Institute for Reproductive Health, 2004). Furthermore, the lack of open discussions around sexual and reproductive health issues remains another obstacle, which fosters unwanted pregnancies, the spread of HIV/AIDS, and other sexually transmitted diseases. In addition, talking openly about sexual and reproductive health has been considered taboo.

Regarding health services, before 1994, Rwanda had 34 hospitals and 188 health centers. During the war, many of these facilities were looted and the majority of their staff were killed or exiled. The loss of health professionals had serious consequences on the country's ability to attend to the population in dire need of moral and medical support.

During the immediate aftermath of the war, the country saw an influx of international NGOs (nongovernmental organizations) providing post-emergency services in various fields, but only a few seemed interested in long-term interventions to help rebuild the country.

This chapter is a case study of a successful health communication project in Rwanda: the "Well Women Media Project—Africa Great Lakes Region" (WWMP-AGLR). This public health intervention uses radio to provide primary health care information to the most vulnerable parts of the Rwandan population: rural women of reproductive age and young people. The chapter outlines the use of formative research in the development and implementation of the project, focusing on how it works with the target audience to formulate ideas and to make sure that the intervention appeals to the audience's core values. It also demonstrates how a brand was created for its main communication channel: the *Urunana* radio soap opera.

■ HEALTH UNLIMITED RWANDA: WELL WOMEN MEDIA PROJECT—AFRICA GREAT LAKES REGION

Founded in 1984, Health Unlimited, a British NGO, aims to "work with communities, service providers, policy makers and donors in difficult environments in Africa, Asia and Latin America to secure access to effective primary health care for marginalised people affected by conflict, instability or discrimination." Currently, Health Unlimited is established in 15 countries in sub-Saharan Africa, Asia, and Latin America. In 1997, Health Unlimited established its first project in Rwanda, the Well Women Media Project—Africa Great Lakes Region (WWMP-AGLR). The WWMP-AGLR has as its main purpose to "increase public awareness and discussion of women's sexual and reproductive health issues leading to positive changes in knowledge, belief, attitude, and behaviour in the target group." This continues to be a very challenging task in a society where most sexual and reproductive health issues are considered taboo, hence not addressed. Such sexual and reproductive health "taboos" include sexuality, condom use, and family planning. In Africa, sociocultural taboos such as these are often not adequately addressed, resulting in additional barriers to achieving positive changes in sexual and reproductive health knowledge, attitude, beliefs, and reported practices and to addressing sexual and reproductive health-related topics. Therefore, the WWMP was set up to raise awareness of these health problems by providing relevant and accurate information via radio and encouraging discussions on sexual and reproductive health issues.

Since February 1999, the WWMP has broadcast two radio programs: *Urunana* (meaning "hand in hand" in Kinyarwanda, the national language of Rwanda), a soap opera, and *Umuhoza* ("the consoler"), a radio magazine. The *Urunana* radio soap opera has been broadcast on the Great Lakes Service of the British Broadcasting Corporation (BBC) and on Radio Rwanda and the 15-minute stand-alone radio magazine is exclusively broadcast on Radio Rwanda. *Urunana* is broadcast on Tuesdays and Thursdays at 6:45 p.m. on BBC Great Lakes and an omnibus edition is broadcast on Sundays at 7:30 a.m. and 5:00 p.m.

Urunana combines humor and health messages. This method is called "edutainment," a blend of "education" and "entertainment." By using the edutainment strategy in *Urunana*, the audience is motivated to listen with full attention to storylines that include everyday village life, while addressing more sensitive issues that are often considered taboo, such as youth sexuality, condom use, and family planning. Since the beginning of the program on radio, *Urunana* has attracted many listeners; more than 74% of the Rwandan population regularly listens to the program (Health Unlimited Rwanda Well Women Media Project, 2005). Furthermore, feedback from the audience suggests that the *Urunana* serial drama also has a large audience in the entire Kinyarwanda-Kirundi speaking area of the Africa Great Lakes Region, including the whole of Burundi, the eastern part of the Democratic Republic of Congo, the western part of Tanzania, and the southern part of Uganda, where the program can be heard on BBC radio.

■ TARGET AUDIENCE

The main target group of the program is rural women of reproductive age and youth. The reason for choosing rural women of reproductive age and youth as the main target groups was the fact that they are the most vulnerable part of the population: They live in extreme poverty; desperately need sexual and reproductive health information to avoid unwanted pregnancies, HIV/AIDS, and other sexually transmitted diseases (STDs); and are in critical need of information on family planning methods.

After the genocide, there was a need to give this population information on their sexual and reproductive health in order to fight against HIV/AIDS, which was drastically devastating the country, to raise awareness on other prevailing diseases like malaria and tuberculosis, and to enhance awareness of the use of family planning methods, which were no longer valued. Only 7% of all women surveyed indicated that they used a family planning method, while this percentage was at 14% in 1992 (Institute for Reproductive Health, 2004). There was also a large need to lay strategies to adequately address youth sexuality and sex education and to curb the spread of HIV/AIDS and other sexually transmitted diseases among youth, who are the most vulnerable population.

It is worth noting that any project targeting women and youth must also involve those who are the main partners in behavior change. Therefore, the project targeted men as a secondary audience. This is why, for instance, while talking about family planning and the fight against HIV/AIDS, it is also very important to design messages targeting men; one must also stress the importance of their involvement and responsibilities. In order to help control the growth of the population, but also to improve maternal and child health, men need to be informed about the importance of family planning as well.

◼ USING RADIO TO COMMUNICATE HEALTH INFORMATION

In the specific context of Rwanda, producing a radio program with a large following for educational and entertainment purposes is quite a difficult task. During and leading up to the 1994 genocide, radio was effectively used to spread hate propaganda against part of its population. In the aftermath of the war and genocide, many Rwandans were suspicious of radio as a medium to pass on anything positive and educational. Yet Health Unlimited chose radio as a medium of communication in order to pass health messages to the target group, rural women of reproductive age and youth, as it has proven to be a powerful tool of communication that can be used effectively to change people's behavior, attitudes, beliefs, and practices (Adam & Harford, 1998; Crook, 1999).

In Rwanda, radio reaches a wider audience than any other medium. According to the national census (Ministry of Finance and Economic Planning, 2002a), only 61% of the population is literate. In this context, it is especially valuable to use radio to communicate health messages, knowing that other forms of communication, such as print media, are not appropriate for a primarily rural and illiterate population, and acknowledging that only 0.1% of the population owns a television set. The same census indicated that 41.7% of ordinary households own a radio set, but other research suggests that radio ownership differs very much from radio listenership, as people in rural areas come together to listen to their favorite radio programs, either at home, in the local bar, at the workplace, or on the bus (Health Unlimited Rwanda, 2005).

Another advantage of using radio is the fact that "Radio is based in oral tradition. Every culture has traditions of storytelling, and the fascination of listening to a good tale well told has never been lost. . . . A successful radio serial writer knows how to use this tradition to create an intriguing story that attracts and holds a listening audience" (DeFossard, 1997).

◼ THE USE OF FORMATIVE RESEARCH IN *URUNANA* PLANNING AND IMPLEMENTATION

This section focuses on how the WWMP uses formative research in the development and implementation of *Urunana*, its main output, and the way that knowledge gained from intensive study of the audience is used in designing the program.

Research has been at the heart of every stage of development and production of *Urunana*. This health communication project started in the specific post-genocide context of 1994, when the country was emerging from the terrible turmoil that had put ablaze not only its social and economic status, but also claimed up to one million lives. People were still haunted by the horror of four years earlier, and cases of trauma commonly occurred in villages around Rwanda. Scores of orphans and widows were still unattended to in terms of their shelter and basic health necessities. "The war and genocide affected men and women differently. It is estimated that more than 200,000 Rwandan women and girls were victims of some form of sexual violence. . . . Thus, many war widows and other single women survived to care for families alone, to take in orphans, and to assume duties traditionally carried out in patriarchal Rwanda by men" (USAID, 2000).

Furthermore, up to two million Rwandans who had fled the country as a result of war and genocide were being repatriated from neighboring countries, and among returnees, scores were suspected of having perpetrated the 1994 genocide. This massive influx of returnees heightened a climate of suspicion in communities and villages. The precarious situation meant that needs of the population had shifted from long-term development into ad hoc, tangible interventions to solve problems immediately at hand, such as the need for shelter, security, food, clothing, and so on.

With the peculiarities involved in post-genocide Rwanda, research was necessary in order to design and implement programs that were understandable, acceptable, relevant, attractive, and persuasive enough for the target audience to attend to and act on the information they receive.

Initial Needs Assessment

Before the actual start of any project, a media project needs to find answers to fundamental questions such as "Who is the program for?" (defining the target audience), "What are their needs and concerns?" and "How can we best address these concerns?" These questions serve as benchmarks throughout the project life and are an integral part of planning and implementing programs.

Before *Urunana* was created, initial research was carried out in 1998 and consisted of reviewing relevant literature on which the formulation of a hypothesis could be based. This consisted mainly of reviewing secondary source documents from government institutions, international NGOs, and United Nations agencies.

Initial KAPB Research

In 1998, the first research questionnaire into knowledge, attitudes, practices, and behavior (KAPB) was administered to a sample of 698 people comprised of 411 women (59%) and 287 men (41%). This sample was randomly drawn from rural areas of Rwanda, and interviewees were met in their homesteads during their typical daily activities (farms, markets, schools, etc.). After the analysis of the results, a list of lessons learned was compiled and recommendations were made. **Table 14-1** highlights major lessons learned, gaps, and strategies to answer the remaining questions after the initial needs assessment.

Qualitative research techniques, especially the focus group discussions and interviews with key informants, helped to shed light on gaps identified.

This involved going back into the communities and organizing separate discussions with young boys, young girls, and men and women. In the process of engaging project staff with the community, ideas on characters and setting of the soap opera were developed. Stories collected from the various focus group discussions were used to portray the real day-to-day life in a typical village of Rwanda. The name of the soap opera, *Urunana*, also was drawn from the aspirations expressed during various encounters with the audience.

Table 14-1 Summary of Formative Research

What we learned	What we need to find out	What we need to do
Age: only 9% of the sample are over 50 years old	What is the life expectancy in Rwanda?	Check the secondary source review
Religion: 77% of the sample are Catholics	Is the Catholic Church in Rwanda against modern contraceptive methods? This could affect the potential of birth spacing messages.	Talk to church leaders
Education: 42% of the sample cannot read or write	What are the factors that influence literacy?	Check during focus group discussions
Radio ownership: 32% of the female sample owns a radio versus 58% of men	How many people will be listening to the radio program?	Check with secondary sources or conduct a mini survey
Twice the number of men than women do not seek health information	What are the factors that influence this?	Focus group discussion
31% of the sample said that condom use protects people from HIV/AIDS; twice as many men as women knew this	Which age group knows this?	Re-check KAPB
Attitudes toward people living with HIV/AIDS vary from individual to individual	Why do people in the community feel afraid or want to discriminate against people living with HIV/AIDS?	Secondary sources, focus group discussion
Parents do not talk with their children about body changes and developments	Where do children get sexual and reproductive health information?	Focus group discussion, key informants

Source: Health Unlimited Rwanda Well Women Media Project, 1999.

Stakeholders' Meetings

After the write-up of all the research accounts, organizations in the social and health sectors were invited to participate in the first stakeholder meeting. This included a host of government institutions and national and international organizations whose actions may complement or impact the project interventions. The main objective was to present the projects and research findings and solicit the partners for their contributions in terms of information and message formulation. Subsequently, these meetings are held annually and participants are clustered according to their areas of interventions: sexual and reproductive health, health education, maternal and infant health, HIV/AIDS, people living with HIV/ADS, religious leaders, malaria, tuberculosis, and so on. Participants exchange information on the latest developments in their various fields of interest and suggest priority health messages. The value of the stakeholders' meetings is that partners promote and advocate for *Urunana* in their different field activities and to their own partners. The stakeholders' workshop also considers a draft project document of health messages prepared by the project staff based on both internal and external sources. The internal sources include data gathered during regular KAPB surveys, monthly audience surveillance visits, and issues from letters of listeners. External sources consist of research publications of other partners and national health policies and strategies. The final health messages document guides *Urunana* stories over the whole year.

Audience Surveillance

Each month, the head writer suggests an outline of stories and messages with possible options to the production team during a monthly script meeting. The latter choose and suggest other courses stories may take. But the final direction is decided by the audience during audience surveillance visits.

Since 2001, project staff, especially a team of writers and producers, have conducted monthly audience surveillance visits to various provinces of Rwanda. These visits aim at engaging with the communities in discussions on the past episodes that have been broadcast, including past storylines, acting, and the language. A cross-section of both listeners and non-listeners is gathered by a local volunteer in the open air, mostly under a tree. The project staff facilitates the discussions and a note-taker records the proceedings.

For gender-sensitive or culturally sensitive issues, participants are divided into groups, that is, youth (boys and girls separated) and women and men in their respective corners. In a patriarchal society like Rwanda, the presence of men in discussion could hamper the openness of women about issues that may be perceived as offensive to male self-esteem. Dividing the groups by gender helps prevent any possible inhibition or influence, especially of boys and men over girls and women, respectively. Homogeneity of groups increases a free flow of ideas in "normal words and emotions" about specific issues appropriate to a specific group. For instance, how would a woman talk about how her husband fails her in bed in the presence of a host of men, or how would a young girl feel talking about her first menstruation in front of boys? What about men cheating on their wives? The facilitators are gender matched to the groups.

Below is a sample of audience surveillance questions:

1. What do you make of last week's episodes? What did you like/dislike?
2. How do you think x, y, z (characters' names) will continue?
3. What do you think of x, y, z's (characters' names) behavior?
4. In x, y, z's (characters' names) place, what would you have done differently?
5. Are x, y, z's (characters' names) behaviors of common occurrence in this area? Give us examples.
6. After x and y have protected sex, what may trigger x to go for an HIV/AIDS test?
7. In which instances can y agree to have sex with x without a condom?
8. What does a dowry consist of in this area?
9. Who decides about the dowry?
10. What are the necessary preparations for receiving a dowry on the girl's family side?

The writers' team meticulously reviews the information gathered during the audience surveillance sessions and uses it to further develop plots and stories.

Involvement of the target audience in the production increases the ownership of the program as its contributions are truly valued and taken into account. The interaction with the audience allows the production team to stay abreast of current events in the target audience's private lives that lend themselves to a true-to-life product. Listeners identify with soap characters, follow their trials and tribulations, and emulate the heroism of their models. According to the social learning theory, involvement of listeners in characters' emotions, that is, their actions and personalities, has the potential to inspire listeners and lead to vicarious learning (Bandura, 1986).

The monthly audience surveillance is coupled with the KAPB survey **Table 14-2**. The same team visits villages other than those chosen for the audience surveillance sessions and administers a standard questionnaire to community members. Filled questionnaires are compiled and tabulated regularly to monitor the "barometer" of responsiveness of the audience in terms of program awareness and content.

Table 14-2 Formative Research Results

Preliminary results from the analysis of the Knowledge, Attitudes, Practices, and Behavior (KAPB) survey conducted between September 2002 and July 2005 show that:

1. Listeners to the *Urunana* radio drama largely find the health messages relevant (91%), practical (76%), and acceptable (94%), but rates of understanding (54%) are somewhat lower and can be improved;
2. Large proportions of listeners to the *Urunana* radio drama report that they engage in discussions of the sexual and reproductive health messages (55%–81%); and
3. Large proportions of listeners to the *Urunana* radio drama report that they advise others on the sexual reproductive health messages they have learned from the program (59%–81%).

Source: Health Unlimited Rwanda Well Women Media Project, September 2005.

The *Urunana* soap opera target audience is diverse in terms of social and demographic characteristics. Therefore, it proved hard to maintain a good balance between reaching women and reaching youth with specifically tailored health messages. In order to assess how youth might be more effectively reached, an action research study was conducted in 2002. About 200 questionnaires were administered, and six focus group discussions, three with boys and three with girls, were held. The outcome helped re-shape *Urunana*'s plots, providing ideas for storylines featuring young people and guidance in the use of appropriate language to better communicate the issues.

Rural Familiarization

Once a year, the team of writers engages for four days with the population in their daily activities and interactions and spends its days and nights with them in their homes. This activity helps the team to "live the life" of rural people in order to observe what people do and how they live rather than relying on what they say they do. The endeavor helps establish the general family interactions; that is, gender roles, health-related behaviors, and how things happen on a typical day. For example, who is involved in what at what time?

It would be otherwise difficult for an urban-based production team to imagine what happens in the villages where the target audience lives. Although team members may have been born in different rural places, having left their villages early for schools and having worked in cities has often influenced them. They may have lost touch with the village life of the target audience. These short opportunities to participate in village life strengthen still further the bond between the production team and the audience.

Behavior change communication strategies and interventions need to be "a two-way talk," rather than a patronizing top-down approach. Research informs the best ways to bolster the involvement of the target audience in the process of developing a product that has the potential to reflect their own needs. People respond positively to communications whose messages they can easily identify with and that portray them in a good light.

The Setting of Urunana

Everything happens in Nyarurembo, a typical rural village in Rwanda with schools, a church, banana plantations, a river and houses, and roads and streets in bad condition to reflect the reality in the Rwandan rural villages. This enables us to develop realistic and believable stories.

The name of Nyarurembo was randomly chosen—as far as we know there is no place in Rwanda called Nyarurembo—but it gives a picture of a typical rural village, and the target groups consider Nyarurembo as their own village. The language used in the program is the one used in the villages with proverbs and idioms appropriate to the rural population.

Priority health messages addressed in the program are related to the most prevalent diseases and health topics in rural areas. These include malaria, STDs, HIV/AIDS, tuberculosis, safe motherhood, and youth sexuality. Other, more social issues such as gender equality, domestic violence, and girls' education are also addressed. This is supported by the use of characters to reflect the reality on the ground in order to provide to the listeners the needed health information.

Urunana *Characters*

One of the most important aspects of a successful radio soap opera are convincing and credible characters. These characters reflect different attitudes in relation to the main theme of the soap and the population it is targeting. Listeners will follow characters they like in their daily endeavors in life, through their ups and downs. The *Urunana* soap opera has developed three types of characters with quite distinct behaviors and perceptions toward its educational messages.

Positive role model characters

These characters uphold and reflect values promoted in *Urunana*. They are role models in treatment seeking, in avoiding HIV/AIDS and other infections, and in advising their peers about bad attitudes that need to be changed.

The late Munyakazi and his wife Mariana are a good example of this kind of character. This couple is a reference for marital problem solving and communication over and above the basic primary health issues in the village. The couple played an important role in communication around HIV/AIDS and sexual and reproductive health issues. When Munyakazi found out that he was HIV positive, Mariana became the main character in the soap opera to address messages on stigma and discrimination against people living with AIDS. The story of having Munyakazi infected by HIV/AIDS was introduced in the soap to show that anyone can be infected. Even though Munyakazi was a role model in Nyarurembo, one day he cheated on his wife and got HIV.

This storyline made a big impact on the audience, who learned that you can get HIV even through one unprotected sexual encounter. Messages on stigma and discrimination were also introduced in this storyline, when Munyakazi developed AIDS and when Mariana took care of him until his death. During one community outreach session, a listener said. "I used to over-charge clients I suspected being HIV positive and sent them away, but after listening to *Urunana* programs on stigma, I abandoned the habit. I now take them as normal people" (a young barber in Gisenyi province).

This stigma against people living with AIDS was mostly due to the fact that these listeners did not have enough information on how HIV is transmitted. These role model characters are being used in *Urunana* as an instrument of behavior change in the target audience.

Another listener said, "The *Urunana* program came at the right time. It helps the young and old, literate and illiterate. It talks about our daily life. It makes us think about our future: being real people, giving our lives a direction and objective" (a student in secondary school). Following this impact made by the program on the target audience through realistic stories developed in the soap, there is a kind of confusion; there is a loss of a distinction between the actors and characters they are portraying. Josephine Mukamusoni, an actress playing Mariana, a health adviser in Nyarurembo, confided,

> being a role model in the soap opera has attracted many people who come to me for advice. Playing a health adviser in the soap made me an adviser in my village. I also personally receive letters and calls from people seeking advice from me. The latest letter was received from a Rwandese young girl living in Belgium.

Negative role model characters

These characters stand out to reject and act against positive values upheld in the soap. Characters in this group get penalized for their actions. Stefano, a man in his late 40s, proves to be the most mischievous in the village, an irresponsible guy who does not take care of his family and who beats his wife. At the insistence of his wife, Nyiramariza, recalling him to his responsibilities to provide for the family, Stefano bumps into another woman who "will give him peace of mind." It does not take long before the relationship ends in a pregnancy. Stefano denies his responsibility and fears Nyiramariza will turn against him if she happens to know. He contracts gonorrhea as a result of his infidelity.

Pressed hard by threats from his mistress to bring him to justice, Stefano eventually resolves to flee from the village. After meeting total failure in town, he returns to the village miserable, to face the consequences of his actions. First of all, he is not welcomed by his wife, for whom he failed in his promise to change. His wife accepts him back in the home but refuses to have sex with him. She recalls the health adviser's advice that "if you suspect that your partner has had other sexual partners, it is possible he/she has contracted HIV/STDs, suggest using condom all the time until you get tested, to prevent yourself from getting HIV/STDs."

Nyiramariza is sticking to this advice to protect herself from being infected.

The doubters

These characters are unsure which side to take, but as the plot develops, they realize they need to belong to the group that best serves their interests. They are easily "manipulated" by either side. They get rewarded or punished depending on the side or friends they choose.

Bushombe, *Urunana*'s funniest character, is one of the doubters. After long years of a childless relationship with his wife, going to witch doctors, and pushed by his fellow men, he decided "to try outside" to prove his "manhood." But after some time of an extra-marital relationship that also does not result in pregnancy, he has to accept that the infertility problem could possibly lie with him, and not his wife. Subsequently, the couple seeks medical consultation at the referral hospital in town, where Bushombe's hormone level is boosted, and finally the couple gives birth to a baby girl.

These three categories of characters are used to portray both negative and positive attitudes. The audience moves along with the characters, and they are encouraged to make decisions in relation to the messages addressed in the soap opera and the consequences their favorite characters experience after they fail to change their negative behaviors.

For instance, for the last two years, the program has addressed the issue of teenage pregnancies. Agnes, a young school girl in the story, was impregnated by her classmate, Semana. She is then shown to go through a variety of difficulties after the birth of her baby, including dropping out of school for one year, frustrations caused by her family, and loss of hope. By illustrating the negative impact of the teenagers' behavior, school girls and boys in Rwanda are encouraged to make the decision to avoid unplanned pregnancies and not have sex before marriage. In turn, parents have also been encouraged to allow their teenage daughters to return and complete school after giving birth.

Appealing to the Core Values of the Target Audience

For any project that is community based or dealing with sensitive issues to be successful, respecting the core values of the target audience or the community it works with is essential. Failure to take these into consideration during the designing or implementation of a program risks hitting a brick wall and failing to achieve the desired results.

The target audience will regard the program to be foreign or an intruder who has come to destroy their values and lose interest in it, leading to stiff rejection, when the core values of the target audience are not given due respect and attention.

The method that is used most often in *Urunana* to promote behavior change by appealing to compelling target audience core values is the information education communication principle of Persuade, Encourage, and Enable. Individuals' or communities' negative behavior is exposed, and consequences that can occur as a result of that particular behavior or practice are put into the spotlight. After the exposure of the negative behavior and possible consequences, the target audience is persuaded to take on the alternative behavior by showing the benefits of adopting it. Enabling the target audience to achieve the desired change follows persuasion. This is done by showing or providing means by which the audience can adopt the desired change.

In order to be successful, *Urunana* has taken the core values of the target audience into consideration, and this has most contributed to the production of realistic and believable programs, which have always reflected the knowledge, practices, beliefs, and attitudes of the target audience. Most of the target audience identify with situations and stories in the soap opera and the characters, as well as with some similar people in their communities. Appreciation of the program culturally has given *Urunana* a chance to successfully address several issues considered taboo in Rwandan culture. Much attention and respect was given to the language used and to the traditional practices of the Rwandan culture. This has been achieved by using an entire local production team that has strong knowledge and understanding of the culture.

Language

In Rwandan culture, the value attached to sexual and reproductive health is that it can only be talked about by adults, and only in their bedroom or other private places. Discussions between parents and children about sexual and reproductive health are almost nonexistent; children are left to get any information from peers who also have insufficient information about sexual and reproductive health (Ministry of Gender and Women, 2002).

One of the main challenges for the project was to bring what were considered "dark bedroom discussions" to radio airwaves and to highlight the importance of open discussions between parents and their children, and between peers, without offending the cultural values attached to sexual and reproductive health among the target audience.

Appropriate use of language has been fundamental throughout the production of *Urunana*. Words have been carefully selected and used in the drama. Very offensive words have been avoided and efforts made to find appropriate metaphors. In most cases, the production team has used humor to correct bad manners, *"ridendo castigare mores."* At the beginning, it was very hard to broadcast messages on condom use, but slowly listeners understood the importance of discussing ways of preventing unplanned pregnancies, sexually transmitted infections, and HIV/AIDS. Asked during a listenership survey whether they are offended by the messages, language, and topics addressed in *Urunana*, 86.6% of the listeners did not report being offended by the topics and the language used, with only 6.2% reporting being "offended" and 7.2% stating that they are "sometimes offended." These findings differ from earlier listeners' complaints reported in 2000, which revealed significantly more discomfort over the sexual and reproductive health messages broadcast in *Urunana*, even though the public health topics are similar.

It is often difficult to address certain issues because it could be considered going too deeply into private issues, which would conflict with the values of the target audience. However, *Urunana* builds up the stories, thus creating a need to talk about particular issues, as well as stirring anxiety in the audience, who want to know what is going to happen next to the character to get out of such a situation. With careful attention to balancing language, values, humor, and the objectives of the project, parents and children can now sit together to listen to the program, even as it addresses some very sensitive issues.

Settings of Actions

Settings in the *Urunana* soap opera have been carefully chosen in the development of stories to address health and other issues that affect the Rwandan society. Consideration is given to using places that are valued to be social gathering places for men and women or for children and young people. For instance, it would be unconvincing, if not insulting, to have men meet at a place that is traditionally a women's meeting place, such as the river bank, to fetch water and have them talk about issues affecting their homes, wives, or village. The *Urunana* production team instead chooses a more realistic and appropriate setting where men tend to meet, such as a bar, home, or somewhere sitting around sharing a drink and discussing issues.

This is not to say that *Urunana* does not promote breaking gender barriers. For instance, in *Urunana*, women also meet in the "Women Association activities" to share ideas regarding their health concerns, something which many "traditional men" have difficulty accepting. However, this is done carefully, and with attention to the perceived credibility of the program. For instance, traditionally in Rwandan culture men will not enter the kitchen or cook as cooking is usually a task for women. So, in most storylines, a scene will not be set in a kitchen with a man cooking as it would not be perceived as credible. However, when the message is one on gender equity and the producers want to encourage a culture in which men support women in all home activities and share responsibilities, they can introduce a man helping his wife to prepare food for the children. This way, the man's actions (i.e., doing a nontraditional man's task) are used to educate the audience on gender equity and sharing of responsibilities.

Traditional Practices

There are several traditional practices that are valued by the Rwandan society. As program makers, there is a need to respect these values so as to increase a feeling of ownership of the program and relevance to the target group. In Rwandan culture, for example, it is important that after a baby is born, friends and relatives visit to congratulate the parents on their newborn and also to perform a naming ceremony, which brings together many people. Traditional practices like this are promoted in the program. They help to create variety and bring about dynamics in the soap opera. Other unharmful and valued traditional practices referred to in the soap opera include traditional wedding ceremonies and burial ceremonies.

However, there are some other traditional practices that are harmful. These practices are addressed in the soap opera to discourage the target audience from practicing them. For example, there is a belief in Rwanda that if a man doesn't have sex with his wife eight days after giving birth, it will take very long for a woman to recover from delivery. The practice is referred to in Kinyarwanda as "*komora*." However, from a medical perspective, this practice does not help the woman recover from any painful side effects of the delivery; instead, it can cause infections and further complications for the mother. Another example is the belief of children having "false teeth" which should be extracted by a witch doctor, known as "*Ibyinyo*," when extracting the child's teeth is harmful, unnecessary, and risky when done by unqualified doctors. These and other common harmful traditional practices have been discouraged in the program without offending the culture. Different strategies have been put in place to address these traditional practices on air without offending listeners and the culture, such as mixing education and entertainment or using humor.

Creating a Brand for Urunana

Urunana, like any other product in the marketplace, needs to be well positioned in the minds of the audience in order to effectively achieve its objectives (Kapferer, 1992). The mammoth task of a mass communication intervention is to capture and maintain the audience's attention about the program in a competitive environment. The target audience must be convinced beforehand why they should listen to it, and listen regularly, and in which way this particular program is different from others.

The preliminary survey carried out before the actual launching of *Urunana* shows that drama ranked among the three most popular programs. In Rwanda, drama had always consisted of on–off traditional radio plays. Serial drama was still new. By its relentless nature, being long running with interweaving stories and with a stock of characters, a soap opera needs time to position itself correctly in the minds of listeners. But it is well-poised to do so.

In order to "hook" the audience, *Urunana* had to start with the most immediate thing: its name. *Urunana* in the vernacular Kinyarwanda means "hand in hand." In the Rwandan post-conflict and genocide, "hand-in-hand" seemed almost too enterprising when the project started. The Rwandan society was torn apart by the genocide, and suspicion was rife in the communities. The name suggested that people irrespective of their ethnic or family affiliation should come together to talk about the common health issues facing them. Yet this is exactly what the program has achieved: bringing people together and emphasizing their similarities, rather than their perceived differences.

The *Urunana* soap opera signature tune adds strength to the attributes the name embodies; "this is *Urunana*, which entrenches dialogue of those who share the walk. Let's come together, sit down on the grass to talk about issues." *Urunana* provides a forum where issues are discussed and solutions are mutually suggested. Internally, staff have gone a long way to understand that the program needs to be audience driven, that in order for *Urunana* to properly serve its target audience, there is a need to be close to them.

Providing accurate messages is one of the strengths of *Urunana* as a behavior change communication strategy in Rwanda. The accuracy stems from wide range consultations with all the stakeholders, and this increases ownership and credibility. In order to ensure this, *Urunana* also uses the services of an independent medical expert to cross-check the messages after scripts are developed and before the final stage in the production cycle studio production.

Respect of the culture of the wider audience in general and that of the target audience in particular is the best way for the program to rally acceptance of the listeners. Addressing culturally sensitive issues while trying to change people's behaviors proves to be very demanding. The biggest problem has been how to talk about sexual- and reproductive health–related issues to an audience composed of women, men, young boys and girls, and small children. The recent story about a young couple where a man had a problem of premature ejaculation caught the audience by surprise. In the Rwandan culture, like many other traditional cultures, talking about men's sexual problems equals attacking men's self-esteem. The language to talk about this does not come easily. After much pre-testing of various potential ways of talking about premature ejaculation, it was decided to describe the problem in one simple way: "to leave a cup of milk unfinished." Adults understood the plot and the message and never felt discomfort listening to the story in the presence of children.

The biggest promise of *Urunana* is to deliver a good balance between education and entertainment. The impact of *Urunana* educational messages has been expanded through the use of the soap opera in schools and youth centers. Questions about *Urunana* messages and stories have been used by the Rwandan National Examination Council for the primary and secondary school leavers. They are also used in youth centers as case studies and as discussion starters. In Rwanda, when *Urunana* is mentioned, names of humorous characters are immediately singled out. In order to produce a humor that will "titillate" the audience, the production team needs to know the audience inside out.

The pyramid in **Figure 14-1** shows the promises *Urunana* set out to deliver to the audience. On the top of the pyramid is *Urunana* beliefs and values: "Needs-based programs." If listeners perceive that the program talks about people like themselves, there is no doubt that they will become loyal to the program and develop trust in the messages and modeling of intended behaviors. This puts the target audience at the heart of production right from the conception. Sexual and reproductive

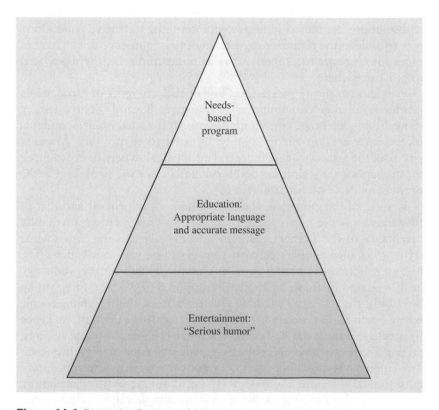

Figure 14-1 Distinctive Symbols of *Urunana*

health issues of youth as they are perceived differently from adults needed to be reflected upon in a particular way. The magic of soap opera does this in interweaving different plots at the same time. For example, the issue of Budensiana, whose father wants her to marry a wealthy man of the village against her will, runs concurrently with the story of the Shyaka couple going to the hospital in the city for their infertility problems. The relevance of the programmatic issues to the target audience stimulates listeners to sympathize with characters and emulate their good examples.

The middle level reflects benefits that *Urunana* confers to its listeners. Accurate messages in "non-scandalizing" language mean people will develop a listening habit. The long-running stories keep listeners interested to know the outcome of a situation their role models are struggling with: how they are getting punished for performing socially unaccepted behaviors and how they are rewarded for performing a socially desirable behavior. In the process, listeners will easily follow messages being passed along and learn from their models' experiences. The tribulations of the doubter Bushombe and his wife Kankwanzi in trying to have a child will linger in the memory of listeners. Messages are given naturally, through true-to-life experiences and in real time; for example, it takes nine months for a pregnant woman to give birth, so the drama stays in the real timeframe. The effect of stories like this one is in the recognition of the program and the fact that people associate easily with the characters and the messages they convey. For example, when one talks of "Nyiramariza," the image of a strong-willed, hardworking, and enterprising woman comes to mind, and how she resisted having unprotected sex with her wayward husband Stefano.

The third dimension of the *Urunana* symbol is entertainment. Humor is instrumental in keeping the audience tuned in, as most people under normal circumstances will not resist a good laugh and "the essential rhythm of human experience contains a balance of tension and humor. Humor is the survival mechanism of the tragic experience. It has been said that the emotional rhythm of the play dances on the listener's heart and mind: tension, humor, tension, humor, charm, and alarm" (Kotler, 2003). The popularity of comic characters has the potential to attract and maintain listeners for a long time. As listeners wait to be entertained by their cherished humorous characters, they simultaneously get educated.

Because of the great concern given to the values of the target audience, the program has achieved a high level of perceived relevance in the lives of the target audience. Of 965 persons surveyed between 2002 and 2005 about the relevance of *Urunana* messages, 91% confirmed that the messages were relevant to them (Health Unlimited Rwanda Well Women Media Project, 2005).

■ CONCLUSION

In Rwanda, *Urunana* is now the most popular radio program with up to 74% of the Rwandan population listening to the program (Health Unlimited Rwanda, 2005). More and more organizations seek partnership with *Urunana* for message insertion in the drama as it has a big outreach and listenership, particularly in rural areas of the country.

The involvement of the target population in designing and implementing the program and the combination of humor and education in addressing sensitive issues of sexual and reproductive health are the main ingredients that have led to the success of *Urunana*. It is upon this success that Health Unlimited is building a local independent organization that will have the name of the program: *Urunana* Development Communication.

The *Urunana* soap opera produced in Rwanda is proving that the combination of humor and education is an effective communication strategy to address culturally sensitive health and social issues considered to be taboo in rural areas.

The success of *Urunana* stems from a mix of communication and marketing principles linked to formative research to identify and understand the sexual and reproductive health behavior and core values of the target audience.

By using radio, which is accessible to the mainly illiterate target audience, *Urunana* listeners identify with stories and characters who serve as models to adopt promoted behaviors. The project continually promotes, in an integrated manner, key sexual and reproductive health issues, and also contributes to national and regional campaigns on public health.

■ ACKNOWLEDGMENTS

The authors wish to thank the following persons for their invaluable editorial support in the writing of this chapter (in alphabetical order): J. Gathogo, M. Mwangi, and A. Sharma.

This chapter was contributed by:

Health Unlimited Rwanda
P.O. Box 4720
Kigali, Rwanda
www.healthunlimited.org
UK Charity No. 290535

References

Adam, G., & Harford, N. (1998). *Health on air*. London, UK: Health Unlimited.

Bandura, A. (1986). *Social foundations of thought and action: A social cognitive theory*. Englewood Cliffs, NJ: Prentice Hall.

Crook, T. (1999). *Radio drama: Theory and practice*. Oxford, UK: Routledge.

DeFossard, E. (1997). *How to write a radio soap serial drama for social development: A script-writer's manual*. Baltimore, MD: The Johns Hopkins University School of Public Health, Center for Communication Programs, Population Communication Services.

Health Unlimited Rwanda. (2005). *Baseline survey report of the Urunana/ Umuhoza rural extension project: 2005–2008*. Kigali, Rwanda: Author.

Health Unlimited Rwanda Well Women Media Project. (1999). *Gaps analysis of KAPB research*. Kigali, Rwanda: Author.

Health Unlimited Rwanda Well Women Media Project. (2005). *Preliminary evaluation of the Urunana KAP monitoring data. Statement of major findings (September 2002–July 2005)*. Kigali, Rwanda: Author.

Institute for Reproductive Health. (2004). *Mid-term assessment of the Standard Days Method (SDM) introduction in Rwanda*. Washington, DC: Institute for Reproductive Health, Georgetown University.

Kapferer, J.N. (1992). *Strategic brand management: New approaches to creating and evaluating brand equity*. London, UK: Kogan Page.

Kotler, P. (2003). *Marketing management* (11th ed., international ed.). Englewood Cliffs, NJ: Prentice Hall.

Ministry of Finance and Economic Planning. (2002a). *Rwanda national census*. Kigali, Rwanda: Author.

Ministry of Finance and Economic Planning. (2002b). *Rwanda poverty reduction strategy paper (PRSP)*. Kigali, Rwanda: Author.

Ministry of Gender and Women in Development & United Nations Population Fund. (2002). *A study on beliefs, attitudes and socio-cultural practices related to gender in Rwanda*. Kigali, Rwanda: Author.

Ministry of Health. (2001). *Demographic and health survey*. Kigali, Rwanda: Author.

Ministry of Health. (2004). *Health sector strategic plan 2005–2009*. Kigali, Rwanda: Author.

United States Agency for International Development (USAID). (2000). *Aftermath: Women and women's organizations in postgenocide Rwanda* (USAID Evaluation Highlights No. 69, December 2000). Washington, DC: Author. Available at http://www.peacewomen.org/resources/Rwanda/usaid2.pdf.

APPENDIX

A
Suggested Readings

Andreasen, A.R. (1995). *Marketing social change: Changing behavior to promote health, social development, and the environment.* San Francisco, CA: Jossey-Bass.

Andreasen, A.R. (2006). *Social marketing in the 21st century.* Thousand Oaks, CA: Sage.

Andreasen, A.R., & Kotler, P. (2008). *Strategic marketing for non-profit organizations* (7th ed.). Upper Saddle River, NJ: Prentice Hall.

Backer, T.E., Rogers, E.M., & Sopory, P. (1992). *Designing health communication campaigns: What works.* Thousand Oaks, CA: Sage.

Bandura, A. (1986). *Social foundations of thought and action.* Englewood Cliffs, NJ: Prentice-Hall.

Bickel, W.K., & Vuchinich, R.E. (Eds.). (2000). *Reframing health behavior change with behavioral economics.* Mahwah, NJ: Lawrence Erlbaum Associates.

Chapman, S., & Lupton, D. (1994). *The fight for public health: Principles and practices of media advocacy.* London, UK: BMJ Publishing Group.

Cheng, H., Kotler, P., & Lee, N. (2009). *Social marketing for public health: Global trends and success stories.* Sudbury, MA: Jones & Bartlett Learning.

Gladwell, M. (2000). *The tipping point.* Boston, MA: Little, Brown.

Glanz, K., Rimer, B.K., & Lewis, F.M. (Eds.). (2002). *Health behavior and health education: Theory, research and practice* (3rd ed.). San Francisco, CA: Jossey-Bass.

Glanz, K., Rimer, B.K., & Viswanath, K. (Eds.). (2008). *Health behavior and health education: Theory, research, and practice* (4th ed.). San Francisco, CA: Jossey-Bass.

Goldberg, M.E., Fishbein, M., & Middlestadt, S.E. (1997). *Social marketing: Theoretical and practical perspectives.* Mahwah, NJ: Lawrence Erlbaum Associates.

Green, L.W., & Kreuter, M.W. (2005). *Health program planning: An educational and ecological approach* (4th ed.). New York, NY: McGraw-Hill.

Grier, S., & Bryant, C. (2005). Social marketing in public health. *Annual Review of Public Health, 26,* 319–339.

Hastings, G., & Saren, M. (2003). The critical contribution of social marketing. *Marketing Theory, 3*(3), 305–322.

Hornik, R.C. (Ed.). (2002). *Public health communication: Evidence for behavior change.* Mahwah, NJ: Lawrence Erlbaum Associates.

Kotler, P., & Andreasen, A.R. (2003). *Strategic marketing for non-profit organizations* (6th ed.). Upper Saddle River, NJ: Prentice-Hall.

Kotler, P., & Armstrong, G. (2011). *Principles of marketing* (14th ed.). Upper Saddle River, NJ: Prentice-Hall.

Kotler, P., & Lee, N. (2002). *Social marketing: Influencing behaviors for good* (3rd ed.). Thousand Oaks, CA: Sage.

Kotler, P., Roberto, E.L., & Lee, N. (2002). *Social marketing: Improving the quality of life* (2nd ed.). Thousand Oaks, CA: Sage.

Lee, N., & Kotler P. (2011). *Social marketing: Influencing behaviors for good* (4th ed.). Thousand Oaks, CA: Sage.

Lefebvre, R.C., & Flora, J.A. (1988). Social marketing and public health intervention. *Health Education Quarterly, 15*, 299–315.

Maibach, E., & Parrott, R.L. (Eds.). (1997). *Designing health messages: Approaches from communication theory and public health practice.* Thousand Oaks, CA: Sage.

Mark, M., & Pearson, C.S. (2001). *The hero and the outlaw: Building extraordinary brands through the power of archetypes.* New York, NY: McGraw-Hill.

McKenzie-Mohr, D. (2011). *Fostering sustainable behavior: An introduction to community-based social marketing* (3rd ed.). Gabriola Island, BC, Canada: New Society Publishers.

National Cancer Institute. (2002). *Making health communication programs work: A planner's guide* (NIH Pub. No. 02-5145). Bethesda, MD: Author.

Rogers, E.M. (1995). *Diffusion of innovations* (4th ed.). New York, NY: Free-Press.

Roman, K., & Maas, J. (2005). How to advertise (3rd ed.). New York, NY: St. Martin's Griffin.

Rossi, P.H., Lipsey, M.W., & Freeman, H.E. (2004). *Evaluation: A systematic approach* (7th ed.). Thousand Oaks, CA: Sage.

Rothschild, M.L. (1999). Carrots, sticks and promises: A conceptual framework for the behavior management of public health and social issues. *Journal of Marketing, 63*, 24–37.

Singhal A., Cody, M.J., Rogers, E.M., & Sabido, M. (Eds). (2004). *Entertainment-education and social change: History, research, and practice.* Mahwah, NJ: Lawrence Erlbaum Associates.

Steckler, A., & Linnan, L. (Eds.). (2002). *Process evaluation for public health interventions and research.* San Francisco, CA: Jossey-Bass.

Sutton, S.M., Balch, G.I., & Lefebvre, R.C. (1995). Strategic questions for consumer-based health communications. *Public Health Reports, 110*, 725–733.

Thielst, C.B. (2010). *Social media in healthcare.* Chicago, IL: Health Education Press.

Thomas, R.K. (2010). *Health communication.* New York, NY: Springer.

Wallack, L., & Dorfman, L. (1996). Media advocacy: A strategy for advancing policy and promoting health. *Health Education Quarterly, 23*, 293–317.

Wallack, L., Dorfman, L., Jernigan, D., & Themba, M. (1993). *Media advocacy and public health.* Newbury Park, CA: Sage.

B

Glossary of Terms

Audience segmentation: Dividing the population into groups with the goal of identifying groups whose members are similar to each other and distinct from other groups along dimensions that are meaningful in the context of the program.

Brand: A name, phrase, sign, symbol or design, or some combination of these that conveys meaning and value, typically by using our shared cultural code.

Coalition: A group of organizations that come together to address a common goal. Most often run by a committee composed of representatives from each (or many) coalition members.

Communication strategy: How the social change will be positioned in the audience's mind. It describes the target audience, the action they should take as a result of exposure to the communication, the key benefit they will receive in exchange, support for that benefit, the image of the action that the communication should convey, and how target audience members can be reached.

Core values: Deeply held principles, specific to the target audience, to which a communication should appeal. The stronger the core values to which a communication appeals, the stronger is its persuasive effect.

Creative brief: A one- to two-page summary of the communication strategy given to the creative team to use for guidance when developing materials.

Diffusion of innovations: Theory of the process by which an innovation (an idea, practice, or object that is perceived as new by an individual or other unit of adoption, such as an organization or community) is communicated through certain channels over time among the members of a social system.

Entertainment-education: Embedding social change messages in entertainment media (i.e., movies, television programs other than news, some radio programs, comic books). Also called edutainment.

Focus groups: A qualitative research technique that involves 1- to 2-hour structured discussions among 6 to 10 participants, led by a trained moderator working from a list of topic areas or questions. Appropriate for exploring and gaining insights into a target audience's behaviors, reactions, and motivations.

Formative evaluation: Studies conducted to assess reactions to proposed program components so they can be refined before they are finalized and implemented.

Framing memo: A document presenting an analysis of the ways an issue is framed by proponents and opponents. Its core is a matrix that summarizes, for each framing strategy, (1) the core position, or main argument; (2) the metaphor used (typically a familiar analogy); (3) catch phrases used to describe the argument; (4) symbols; (5) visual images evoked by the argument; (6) the implied source of the problem; and (7) the principle or core values appealed to.

Frequency: The number of times each target audience member is exposed to a particular message or material.

Gatekeeper: An individual or organization through whom a program's components or materials must pass to reach the target audience.

Goals: Translation(s) of a program's mission into specific behavioral outcomes. Distinct from objectives.

Gross impressions: An estimate of how many opportunities there were for messages delivered through the mass media to be seen or heard; calculated by summing the circulation and/or audience size associated with each publication of a story or advertisement. Not a measure of number of people reached.

Intermediary: An organization or individual that can or must be used to reach a target audience; part of a distribution channel.

Marketing: An organizational function and a set of processes for creating, communicating, and delivering value to customers and for managing customer relationships in ways that benefit the organization and its stakeholders.

Marketing mix: Product, price, place, and promotion; the variables that a marketer can change.

Media advocacy: Bringing about policy changes by using the media to put pressure on policymakers. This is accomplished by placing issues on the media agenda through media relations efforts and/or paid advertising or by seeing that issues already on the media agenda are framed from a policy perspective. The belief is that once issues are on the media agenda, they become part of the public agenda and force policymakers to act.

Message concepts: Statements that present key aspects of the communication strategy to members of the target audience.

Objectives: Quantification of goals; objectives describe the specific intermediate steps to be taken to make progress toward goals. For public health efforts, objectives are often changes in audience behavior over time; levels of participation in specific program activities; or measured changes in attitudes, beliefs, or skills associated with prevention practices, with the expectation that change in these factors will facilitate or reflect change in outcome behavior and, ultimately, morbidity and mortality. Distinct from goals.

Offering: The product (bundle of benefits) being offered to an audience.

Outcome evaluation: Research conducted to determine whether an intervention had the intended effects on behavior. Usually conducted after the intervention is finished, but can be conducted periodically during and after the intervention.

Place: Situations in which the target audience does or can perform the health behavior and outlets through which the target audience does or can obtain any tangible goods or services necessary for the health behavior.

Price: Cost to a target audience member, in money, time, effort, lifestyle, or psyche, of engaging in a behavior (or purchasing a product or using a service).

Primary research: Studies designed and conducted specifically to answer a current research question (as compared with secondary research).

Process evaluation: Studies conducted during and immediately after implementation to document what program components were delivered and to whom, how, when, and where they were delivered. This information can then be used to assess and refine components and delivery strategies.

Product: Bundle of benefits the target audience receives in exchange for taking the public health action. May or may not include a tangible good or service.

Promotion: Some combination of advertising, media relations, promotional events, personal selling, and/or entertainment to communicate with target audience members about a product, service, program, or behavior change.

Qualitative research: Provides insights into a target audience; addresses questions of why rather than how many. Results are not quantifiable and not projectable to the population from which participants were drawn.

Quantitative research: Provides measures of how many members of a population have particular knowledge or attitudes or engage in a particular behavior. If conducted with a probability sample and appropriately constructed questions, can be representative of and projectable to the population from which the sample was drawn.

Reach: Total number of people exposed to a message or material.

Secondary research: Studies that were originally conducted for some purpose other than the current research question(s) (as compared with primary research).

Social marketing: Application of commercial marketing principles to the analysis, planning, execution, and evaluation of programs designed to directly influence the voluntary behavior of individuals or the environments in which those behaviors occur to improve personal and societal welfare.

Social media: Forms of electronic communication through which users create online communities, share information, and increase engagement.

Strategy: Long-term (usually 3–5 years), broad approach(es) that an organization takes to achieving its objectives. Distinct from tactics.

Tactics: Short-term detailed steps used to implement a strategy. For example, a community event, a specific training module, and a specific public service advertising campaign are all tactics.

EPILOGUE

What Does the Future Hold?

If the public health field successfully embraces a marketing orientation, its future will be brighter. This is because there exists "a readily stimulated reservoir of appreciation for the services of public health, within the public in general and among elected officials in particular" (Kroger et al., 1997, p. 274). The existence of strong support for public health services makes marketing public health a great opportunity for the practitioner. The challenge is to define and frame the public health product to tap into this reservoir of support.

Public health practitioners at all levels of training, and public health training institutions, must embrace this marketing opportunity. Individual practitioners should take advantage of professional education programs to enhance their knowledge and skills in marketing, communication, and media advocacy and in new technologies and social media. Schools of public health should incorporate these disciplines into their research and training programs and should provide advanced training in these areas to experienced public health professionals. All public health institutions should seek collaborations with experts in these areas from the private sector or incorporate positions in these areas directly into their personnel infrastructure.

The federal government and, in particular, the Centers for Disease Control and Prevention should continue to play a lead role in placing an emphasis on marketing public health. The formative research conducted by the Centers for Disease Control and Prevention provides key strategic insights that will allow public health practitioners across the nation to understand target audiences for marketing public health as an institution. But nonprofit and private sector organizations should assist in these research efforts as well, and some level of formative research should be conducted by public health practitioners, even at the local level.

Will public health practitioners abandon the traditional selling orientation and bring a consumer orientation to their work? Will they embrace formative research and learn how to create, communicate, and deliver public health behaviors, programs, and policies in a way that satisfies the needs and wants of their target audiences, reinforces those audiences' core values, and develops a compelling positioning for public health, allowing strong relationships to be built with target audiences? Will they use new and innovative technologies to reach target audiences who increasingly rely on social media for information? Will public health institutions adequately provide for the professional training of new and continuing personnel in the areas of marketing, communication, and media advocacy?

As the public health practitioners of today and tomorrow, the future of public health is entirely in our hands. Capitalizing on our opportunity to shape this future will require three accomplishments. First, we must work to restore a unified vision of the mission of public health in society. Second, we must reassert our fundamental role as advocates for the achievement of this mission. Finally, we must turn to the people from whom our charge derives in the first place—the public—and learn how to create and deliver our programs and policies to meet their needs and wants. Successfully marketing public health requires that we put the public back in public health.

Reference

Kroger, F., McKenna, J.W., Shepherd, M., Howze, E.H., & Knight, D.S. (1997). Marketing public health: The CDC experience. In M.E. Goldberg, M. Fishbein, & S.E. Middlestadt (Eds.), *Social marketing: Theoretical and practical perspectives* (pp. 267–290). Mahwah, NJ: Lawrence Erlbaum Associates.

INDEX